VOICE AND VERSIFICATION IN TRANSLATING POEMS

VOICE AND VERSIFICATION IN TRANSLATING POEMS

James W. Underhill

University of Ottawa Press
2016

uOttawa

The University of Ottawa Press gratefully acknowledges the support extended to its publishing list by Canadian Heritage through the Canada Book Fund, by the Canada Council for the Arts, by the Federation for the Humanities and Social Sciences through the Awards to Scholarly Publications Program and by the University of Ottawa. We also thank the ERIAC Interdisciplinary Research Group, based at Rouen University, France, for additional funding.

Copy editing: Barbara Ibronyi
Proofreading: Gillian Watts
Typesetting: Counterpunch Inc.
Cover design: Édiscript enr. and Elizabeth Schwaiger
Cover image: *Einst dem Grau der Nacht enttaucht* by Paul Klee (detail), 1918.

Library and Archives Canada Cataloguing in Publication
Underhill, James W. (James William), author
    Voice and versification in translating poems / by James W. Underhill.

(Perspectives on translation)
Includes bibliographical references.
Issued in print and electronic formats.
ISBN 978-0-7766-2277-4 (paperback).–ISBN 978-0-7766-2278-1 (EPUB).–ISBN 978-0-7766-2279-8 (PDF).–ISBN 978-0-7766-2280-4 (MOBI)

    1. Poetry–Translating. 2. Versification. 3. Dickinson, Emily, 1830-1886–Translations–History and criticism. 4. Baudelaire, Charles, 1821-1867–Translations into English–History and criticism. I. Title. II. Series: Perspectives on translation

PN1059.T7U53 2016   418'.041   C2016-906268-6
                                          C2016-906269-4

For Derek Attridge, who has done more to explain how English poems move, and how they move us, than half of the recent century's specialists in rhythm and meter put together

Contents

Acknowledgements xi
Introduction 1
    The Difficult Task 10
    Hope for Poems 16

Part 1: Versification

Chapter 1: Form 25
    Formal Definitions of Poetry 27
    Recent Scholarship in Translation Theory 30
    Defining Form 39
    A Few Key Concepts 44

Chapter 2: Comparative Versification 49
    Different Cultures, Different Stages of
    Development 51
    A Brief History 54
    Opposing English and French 56
    Resisting a Reductive Model 58
    Terminology 60

Chapter 3: Meter and Language 65
    Rhythm and Emotion 65
    Stress Systems 68
    Syllable 73
    Stress 76
    Accent and Meter 86
    Metrical Manipulation of Accents 90
    Metrical Manipulation of Syllables 100
    Rhyme 105

Chapter 4: Beyond Metrics 125
    Acoustic Patterning 125
    Phrasing 130
    Repetition Proper 139
    The Orchestration of Rhythmic Elements 144

Part 2: Form and Meaning in Poetry Translation

Chapter 5: Theorizing the Translation of Poetry 149

Chapter 6: Translating the Sign or the Poem? 153
    Translating Form Blindly 155
    Translating a Poem with a Poem 158
    Translating Form Meaningfully 160

Chapter 7: Form and Translation 167
    Translating Stragegies: Forms of Reformulating 167
    Voices in Foreign Versification 172

Part 3: Case Studies

Chapter 8: Baudelaires 185
    Baudelaire Today 185
    Scott's Baudelaire 194
    Chronology 202
    Strategies 205
    The Whole Poem 233

Chapter 9: French and German Emily Dickinsons 243
    Introducing *une Emily Dickinson française* 243
    Gender and Personification 254
    Malroux: A Voice That Hears and Responds 257
    Voices after Malroux 260
    Delphy's Return to the Academy 263
    Malroux's Missed Rhythms 270
    What Liepe Hears 277
    The Untranslatable and the Untranslated 287

Chapter 10: A Final Word 291

Glossary 297
Bibliography 321

Acknowledgements

I would like to thank lecturers and students at Stendhal University, Grenoble, and the Université de Rouen for their feedback when I was putting this book together. Thanks are also due to friends and family. My teacher Mr. Watson at Hawick High School did much to open up poems to me, while Henri Meschonnic, the great Parisian translator-poet, helped convince me of the importance of poetics for understanding the act of translating.

I managed to convince a number of people to help me with the ideas contained in these pages. Back in the 1990s, when I was well underway with my rhythm project, friends, colleagues, and lecturers gave me considerable help in refining my ideas and offered liberal amounts of challenging criticism. Donald Wesling, Richard D. Cureton, and above all Derek Attridge were great sources of inspiration for me during my PhD research: my all-too-brief conversations and e-mail exchanges with them redoubled my enthusiasm and gave me greater insight. I'd very much like to thank Ian Tullock, Harbans Nagpal, Marko Pajević, Jean-Louis Cluse, Jacqueline Fontaine, Laure Gaudemard, Céline Reuilly, Kateřina Pavlitová, and Claire Simon-Boisson.

Henri Meschonnic, who directed my master's and PhD theses, from which this work on comparative versification is derived (Underhill 1999), is quoted sufficiently to make clear the debt I owe him. I have dedicated other books to him, and no doubt his voice will echo in the background of most of the books I write. The encouragement and support that came from Anne-Marie Ducreux in my first years in Paris were precious. Later on I was lucky enough to be given sustaining support by my wife, Laetitia.

Since then, colleagues and friends have continued to help me clarify problems of versification and translation. Many of them pulled apart some of my ideas, allowing me to put them back together to make my meaning clearer and my case stronger. Christine Raguet and Luise von Flotow, great translators and specialists in poetics, and the late linguist Michel Viel gave me excellent advice and solid criticism. I benefited from their goodwill at a time when it was not always obvious to others (or even to myself) that I needed praise and encouragement as well as criticism.

For stylistic help, my thanks go to Faye Troughton and, most of all, to Anne-Marie Pugh. The staff of the University of Ottawa Press certainly deserve great praise for their advice on improvements regarding the content, form, and scope of the project. Editors know more about readers and markets than authors, and readers therefore have editors to thank that academics do not unload more bloated, incoherent, and unreadable manuscripts upon them. Elizabeth Schwaiger's improvements and all-round efficiency in the editing stage helped ensure that we brought out a more polished finished product. I thank her most of all for elegantly solving the seemingly unsolvable problem of rendering Derek Attridge's binary scansion in print.

For allowing me to publish poems, extracts of poems, and extracts from other authors, I would like to thank the following publishing houses and Internet editors. Cambridge University Press gave permission for the publication of extracts from Derek Attridge's *The Rhythms of English Poetry* (1982). Penguin Books agreed to extensive quotations from *Baudelaire in English*, edited by Carol Clark and Robert Sykes (1997), and from *Baudelaire*, edited and translated by Francis Scarfe (1972). The editors of the wonderful website Charles Baudelaire's Fleurs du mal / Flowers of Evil (www.fleursdumal.org), which continues to compile both established and innovative translations of Baudelaire's poems, deserve thanks also. Gallimard must be thanked for enabling me to quote the original poems from Baudelaire's *Oeuvres complètes*, volume 1 (1975). Reclam Verlag deserves thanks for kindly allowing me to quote long passages from Gertrud Liepe's wonderful German translations of the poems in *Emily Dickinson: Gedichte* (1970).

Thanks go to Farrar, Straus and Giroux for kindly enabling me to publish an entire poem by Ted Hughes from *Collected Poems* (2003). And thanks go to Tony Kline for allowing me to publish his translation of Paul Éluard's "Amoureuse," an online version that I use as a model for rhythm and voice in free-verse translation. Thanks are also due to the editors for enabling me to reproduce Éluard's original from the Poetica website (www. poetica.fr). I would also like to thank the journals *Pathhead* and *Fras* for enabling me to quote translations of Baudelaire's poems by myself and by others that they have published. Finally, two online sites that offered crucial resources quoted in this work were the World Atlas of Language Structures Online (www.wals@info), which provides a vast and synthetic cross-lingual account of accentuation, and Project Gutenberg (www.gutenberg.org), for its inimitable range of multilingual texts. These resources will make it far simpler for readers to consult originals and compare their impressions with my own findings and arguments.

Introduction

Since Sophia Coppola's film *Lost in Translation* came out in 2003, the familiar phrase that gave the film its title has been used in common speech and in media headlines with a wide variety of meanings, referring to cultural misunderstandings and incomprehension between generations and between genders. In poetics the concept of loss in translation has a much more refined meaning, even if we do not always specify what is actually lost. For what is lost when a poem is translated? Is it the beauty of Hindi or Spanish that fails to penetrate the lexis of English? Is it the shape of French syntax that fails to reform when the poem is "re-form-ulated"? Is it the metrical tradition of one language that turns out to be incompatible with the linguistic norms of another language? Or is it those dominant styles that are currently asserting themselves in literary circles, and which are being endorsed and maintained by the established practices of publishers, that prevent us translating something that is essential in the original poem? Is the voice of the poet simply not to be heard in the translated text?

A human being speaks to other human beings by making use of the shared medium known to a linguistic community. In the same way, poets take their place in language at a given time, addressing others, even if they fail to perceive clearly whom their poems will eventually be addressing. Extracted from the poet's time, from his or her language and linguistic community, can the translated poem be expected to resound and resonate with the same urgency and vibrancy that the initial voice does? The voices of Shakespeare's characters, the voice of Goethe's Faust, the voices that emerge in the poems of Emily Dickinson, of Baudelaire, and of Neruda do reach out to the readers of English, German, French, and Spanish, uttering urgent words in captivating movements and disconcerting jolts. But can translations achieve the same expressive force? Surely Shakespeare deserves a Shakespeare and Goethe deserves a Goethe to translate their poems. But how many Shakespeares, Goethes, Dickinsons, Baudelaires, and Nerudas are there? Can we expect to find a similar voice in another language, a translator who is capable of giving voice to the poet who originally opened up one facet of reality and brought back to life, for his or her culture, an essential moment of meaning?

This book is not intended to be an easy answer to a difficult question. But neither do I intend to pay my respects to a long-standing negative theory of translation that has gained many adherents in recent decades and that has become something of an unanalyzed received idea: that is, translating poems is impossible. In Derrida's elegant prose this position boils down to affirming that "translating is a sublime and impossible task" (Derrida 2004: 423). Derrida was speaking as an observer rather than a practitioner or a poet, but poets themselves have often expressed doubts as to the fate of the translated poem. The great romantic poet Shelley, for example, argued that

> it were as wise to cast a violet into a crucible that you might discover the formal principle of its colour and odour, as to seek to transfuse from one language into another the creations of a poet. The plant must spring again from its seed or it will bear no flower. (2004: n.p.)

Ironically enough, this negative appraisal did not prevent Shelley from translating poems himself. He translated Homer from Greek, Virgil from Latin, Dante from Italian, Calderon from Spanish, and Goethe from German. This activity hardly supports his negative claim. The German scholar may point to losses in the transition of Goethe into English in the extensive fragments of Faust that Shelley translated, and the purist might regret Shelley's decision to drop the rhyme, but the easy flow with which Shelley's God and his

Mephistopheles speak in English blank verse, heightened by alliteration, would hardly make a good example for pessimism concerning the possibility of translating poems. The following lines come from the dialogue between Mephistopheles and the Lord at the beginning of the play, when they discuss their wager as to whether Faust will choose evil or good.

> *The Lord.* Well, well! it is permitted thee. Draw
> His spirit from its springs; as thou find'st power,
> Seize him and lead him on thy downward path;
> And stand ashamed when failure teaches thee
> That a good man, even in his darkest longings,
> Is well aware of the right way.
> *Mephistopheles.*   Well and good.
> I am not in much doubt about my bet,
> And if I lose, then 'tis Your turn to crow;
> Enjoy your triumph then with a full breast.
> Ay; dust shall he devour, and that with pleasure,
> Like my old paramour, the famous Snake.
>
> (Shelley 1917: 743)

Goethe also had doubts about translating poems. And this reservation proved equally curious, since he himself was not only a poet and a playwright, he was also (besides being a scientist and theatre director) a translator. In translating poetry, though, Goethe suggested we should drop not only the rhyme, as Shelley does, but also the rhythm:

> Ich ehre den Rhythmus wie den Reim, wodurch Poesie erst zur Poesie wird, aber das eigentlich tief und gründlich Wirksame, das wahrhaft Ausbildende und Fördernde ist dasjenige was vom Dichter übrigbleibt, wenn er in Prosa übersetzt wird. (I respect both rhythm and rhyme, by which Poetry becomes Poetry, but the thoroughly deep and effective, the truly shaping and demanding element in poetry is what remains of the poet when he is translated into prose). (Goethe 1973: 34, my translation)

Some poets remain equally skeptical about the success of poetry translation. Robert Frost even went as far as defining the essential nature of poetry as being that *je ne sais quoi* that defies translation. Indeed, he was defining poetry itself, not translation, when he suggested, "Poetry is what is lost in translation" (Untermeyer 1963: 16).

Derrida could hardly be said then to find himself in bad company when he voiced his own skepticism. Nonetheless, one argument tends to contradict the hypothesis that translating poems is impossible: the great importance of translation for our own language and the importance of translated poems for our literary tradition. Pound and Eliot are only two of the most prominent modern examples of writers who believed that the literary tradition could be rejuvenated and given the strength to dig its roots into reality by seeking sustenance in the poetries of other peoples and other ages. Translations of Greek, Latin, French, and German poets have never ceased to enrich the English poetic tradition throughout the centuries.

The objection that languages are barriers for poetic works, that they constitute walls between world views, hindering the communion of minds, only superficially supports the skepticism of Goethe, Shelley, Frost, and Derrida. And although the argument that metrical systems cannot be transposed holds true to some degree, this also ultimately proves misleading: because translation happens. It takes place every day. And that fact is the ongoing demonstration that translating poems *is* possible. It would be absurd to underestimate the task of translation or to refuse to recognize the constraints that lexis, syntax, meter, rhythm, and a whole host of other organizing principles impose upon the translators of poems, but the historical reality of the situation leads us to the inevitable conclusion that poetry is translatable. How else are we to understand that most literary traditions derive not only many of their poetic motifs but also their metrical systems from other languages? The French *décasyllable* grows out of the Italian *decasillabo* (decasyllable) verse line. So does the English iambic pentameter. In the same way the eight-syllable line passes from Czech and Polish into Russian verse in the seventeenth century, and in the eighteenth century Chaucer's English verse influences Lessing's German verse (see Gasparov 1996).

Metrical systems do not take flight and migrate as birds do. They pass from one language to another through adaptation of the existing tradition in the successful translation of poems. Voices make themselves heard in versifications that are partly imported, partly adapted. Long after the voices of individual poets are heard no more, the movements and organized patterns that those poets once helped to introduce continue to shape and embody poems in the source language. The English iambic pentameter and the French alexandrine outlived the translations that first helped them to take root in the poetic tradition of the languages that adopted them. The language that manages to integrate translations is revitalized by the foreign and the process of refashioning it.

How does this change happen? What takes place when poems are adapted and integrated into another linguistic and literary tradition? These are the questions with which this book is concerned. As with all poetry translation, considering these questions will involve playing with language creatively. But we shall be turning away from the playful poetics of Derrida, because his games turn out to be a poetics of the dead end, a negative poetics inspired by a negative hermeneutics. The negative dialectic consists in transposing a skepticism concerning the capacity of language to express ideas to the theorizing of translating poems. In solidarity with the great German linguist (and translator) Wilhelm von Humboldt, I stand against such negation. Language enables us to speak meaningfully to one another, just as meaningful speech sustains and perpetuates language as an instrument of expression. Poetry is not an exception and cannot be excluded from our conceptions of language, communication, and self-expression. Poets help remould our language as a shared medium of creative individual expression.

Poetry is concerned with reverie and dreams, but theory is not. If we are going to dream of the translation of poems, we must keep our feet on the ground. This book is concerned with neither the sublime nor the impossible, but quite simply with the difficult. If we are to move forward in thinking through the act of poems' breaking through from one language into another, we will have to proceed in a clear, concise, and pragmatic manner. There will be plenty of room for criticism, but if criticism leads only to reinforcing skepticism, it will ultimately be of no use. Condemning bad translations is facile; it's as easy as shooting fish in a barrel. The true test of criticism lies in providing a more finely tuned understanding of the task at hand. If criticism embraces this pragmatic vocation, then I trust that the reader (and the translators I cite) will forgive me if I permit myself to analyze what breaks down in order to see more clearly what can be built up.

In this endeavour it will be necessary to distinguish between four different dimensions of difficulty. The language system presents problems proper to itself when it comes to transposing a poem from one language to another. The metrical system, which takes root in the language but which is only one of various existing normative structures, also presents a challenge to translation. The orchestration of secondary organizing principles related to alliteration, repetition, and phrasing must not go unstudied—must not go unheard, so to speak. And finally the specific orchestration of the poem itself as an individual act of expression must also be listened to.

Translating Shakespeare does mean translating English, but Shakespeare's English is not the English heard in the underground in London, or on the radio in Glasgow. Shakespeare may use the pentameter in both the majority of his plays and the sonnets, but the use of enjambment and line endings is sensibly different in these works. Each poem orchestrates a meaningful movement that sets up expectancy and that provides surprise with free internal rhyming, repetition, and phrasing. This movement is obvious, patently palpable, to anyone listening to the poem. But sadly, and somewhat perversely, specialists in poetry and metrics, and increasingly linguists interested in studying poetry in order to try to understand what it shows about language, often forget to listen to poems. Interested in form and in rule-bound structures, they study poetry and forget the essential: that individual experience each successful poem promises to open up to us.

The task at hand will take us on a short tour of poetics in different languages and will focus primarily on the translation of poems from French to English and vice versa. We will need to make a series of fundamental distinctions pertaining to rhyme, rhythm, meter, and semantic and formal organization. In turn these distinctions will require the translation of—or the coining of—a fairly extensive set of definitions. These definitions are rigorously explained within the text, with the key terms listed in the glossary.

It would not be unfair to contend that good translators do not need theory, just as good poets do not need to learn the rules of metrics to write sonnets. Poets learn to write by reading and listening. In their own way they follow an apprenticeship that enables them to intuitively grasp and assimilate rules and cultivate their own aesthetic sensibility. Yet many translators feel the need to explain to themselves and to others what they are doing and why. And in their attempt to explain, ambiguous terms, tenuous arguments, and dubious guiding principles often obstruct understanding and discourage people from trying to understand what happens when poems are translated. Faced with bad theory, people may turn their backs on the process of theorization and rigorous reflection. The art form is no longer perceived as a craft to be mastered; it becomes an elusive magical activity that defies definition.

In my experience patience is not always rewarded when it comes to studying versification. After wading through treatises and articles on metrics and versification and listening to interminable discussions on the same themes in English, French, and Czech, I found that confusion is the most salient characteristic of much of the research, debate, and discussion. The problem is not simply that terms have different meanings in different languages. One term has various meanings in a single language, and an individual author will apply multiple related meanings to terms such as "rhythm," "rhyme," and "organization." "Form" proves to be one of the most elusive terms when it comes to attempting to understand what it means in the argument of an individual writer.

Translating terms from the idiolects of individual authors frequently leads to confusion and misunderstanding. After considering these questions for more than two decades now, I have come to the conclusion that a much greater danger lurks in wait for those who have a very real sensitivity to these questions and who share a desire to explain their poetic experiences. That danger is the so-called unfounded agreement. The French scholars who discuss Shakespeare agree that his rhythm is remarkable. Yet only after many years did I come to understand that where the first reader was fascinated with the undulating movement of the English language itself—so distinct from strong-syllable, weak-accented French—the second was in love with the iambic meter—so different from the alexandrine—and the third, often a specialist in English or a translator such as Jean-Michel Déprats, heard something specific to Shakespeare that he found nowhere else in English poetry. Putting some order into these impressions and approaches to rhythm and poetry is one of the primary aims of this book.

This book divides into three inseparable parts, each with a specific focus:

- Part 1 provides a comparative versification and a theory of voice.
- Part 2 invites readers to reflect upon translating poems.
- Part 3 provides two case studies, the first investigating the strategies adopted in translating Baudelaire into what can be termed "English Baudelaires" and the second considering the various strategies adopted in French and German to translate Emily Dickinson.

Part 1, the longest section, begins with an outline of the inherent difficulties in comparing metrical systems and versification in a more broadly defined manner. It focuses mainly on French and English and considers meter, rhyme, lines, and those essential organizing principles at work in both free verse and metrical verse (alliteration, phrasing, repetition, and so forth). Short extracts from translated poems are compared and contrasted in order to illustrate the ways that rhythmic elements and organizing principles can be transposed. Each element will be considered in a systematic order, but this methodical approach does not allow us to consider of poems and translations as wholes.

Readers more interested in poems than in theory might be tempted to skim over this first section lightly, so as to dive into the following sections on translating poems. While I understand this temptation, I would contend that as soon as translators seek to explicate what they are doing, both consciously and intuitively, they run the risk of falling into the difficulties that this first section helps eradicate from the poetics of translation: sloppy definitions and arguments based on spurious contentions about languages and versification systems.

In Part 2 the act of translating poetry is directly engaged, both theoretically and technically. I consider what is at stake in translating individual poems as meaningful acts formally unfolding. The question raised is whether the voices re-emerge in the versification of the translated poems or whether either meaning or form is privileged at the expense of the other and, more importantly, at the expense of the poem as an integral whole. I have taken the liberty of introducing a few of my own translations at this point, just as I have included them elsewhere as examples or counter-examples. At times I have chosen to retranslate extracts to highlight the difficulties at hand or to explain how another strategy would achieve something else. If I have chosen to do this, it is not to defend my skills as a translator. To present these translations as models would be so immodest as to be unlikely to convince anyone. Nonetheless, two reasons encouraged me to take this liberty. It seems only fair, after allowing myself to criticize the works of others, that I should offer up my own endeavours to public view and thereby expose myself to the same criticism that I undertake. The second reason relates to the conscious strategy involved in translating. Even though translating remains a creative act that, at its deepest level and by its very nature, defies self-analysis, I was aware of consciously attempting to resolve given problems when I was translating poems. The self-analysis recounted in the short commentaries that follow each of my own translations is intended to help clarify and theorize the difficulties translators confront when handling the orchestration of interacting rhythmic elements and their impact on the meaningful movement of poems.

Part 3 brings us back to the poem and the poet. The French poet chosen, Baudelaire, manifestly still speaks to English readers, judging from the vast array of English Baudelaires that continue to be born. The number and variety of Baudelaire translations available is essential for the task at hand in the case study. Emily Dickinson, the American poet selected for the second case study, likewise continues to inspire fresh translations, in French and in German. The various strategies translators adopt in translating the work of these poets enable us to explore different approaches to translating. They also allow us to critically reappraise the catalogues and oppositions used to distinguish between modes of translating and proclaimed objectives. This section asks whether a theory of voice and versification can help in conceptualizing and understanding what occurs and what is achieved when translating poems. This analysis moves beyond hermeneutics but also beyond formalism. In fact it should take us beyond the idea of poetry and back to the poem.

Translating poems is about meaning and what poems mean to us, but it is also about form: how meaning takes form and how the translated poem re-forms within our listening consciousness, our inner ear. If translated poems are to live on in the new tradition, then they must take us beyond meaning, beyond a sterile formalistic metrics of the rules of expectation, beyond the formal chimes of rhymes. If this seems like a tall order, it must be remembered that so many translated poems have succeeded in doing this. Voices resound in a new language in a reconfigured versification; they cannot be considered mechanical reconstructions in which some elusive hermeneutic core of meaning has been deposited or inserted. Voices take form in a second language, harness principles of organization, and resonate in what might be called an organic translation.

The organic translation cannot be reduced to translation of the meaning or the form. Neither does it enact a clumsy juxtaposition of the two, a semantico-formal adventure, as it were. Organic translations grow out of the meaningful shaping of rhythmic elements that enunciate and highlight the experience of poetic meaning.

The Difficult Task

If we are to make any progress in conceptualizing the process of translation, then we must turn from the negative tradition and look deeply into the act of translating with a pragmatic and optimistic eye. This examination does not mean falling into the opposite extreme of asserting that there are no problems, only solutions. Neither does it entail blindly believing that obstacles can and will be overcome. Ezra Pound, one of the great free translators of his time, researched the question of rhythm both rigorously and exhaustively. His ear was finely attuned to the balance of syllables and the echoes of alliteration and assonance. His idea that translation must replace a poem with a poem has gained wide acceptance in English poetics. But despite being a staunch defender of the importance of translation for the literary tradition, Pound came close to an anti-intellectual position when he affirmed that, in the end, good translations come down to something approaching divine miracles.

For my own part, I believe we will advance more surely with criticism. What is needed is neither skepticism nor faith. Theory will not provide us with tailor-made solutions for handling the supple architectonics of poems. Rigorous analysis of the interaction of rhythmic elements in the dynamic and meaningful workings of both the poem and the translation, however, should help us in our task, by allowing us to discern some of the main factors contributing to the success or failure of poems to make themselves heard in foreign languages. It is in this spirit that I offer as an example one of the less successful translations of Guy Jean Forgue. Arguably Forgue was the best of the first generation of French Emily Dickinson translators (following Messaien, in Dickinson 1956, and Bosquet, in Dickinson 1957), and his translation of a selection of her poems published in 1970 succeeded in securing a lasting place for Dickinson in the French literary tradition (Dickinson 1970b). Consider, for example, "Poem 254."

"Hope" is the thing with feathers— That perches in the soul— And sings a tune without the words— And never stops—at all—	L'espérance est la chose empennée Qui va percher dans l'âme Et chante le chant sans paroles, Toujours, sans s'arrêter.
And sweetest—in the Gale—is heard— And sore must be the storm— That could abash the little Bird That kept so many warm—	Elle est plus douce au fort de la tempête Et quelle violence il faudrait Pour décourager l'oiselet Qui a réchauffé tant de monde!
I've heard it in the chillest land— And on the strangest Sea— Yet, never, in Extremity, It asked a crumb—of Me.	Je l'ai entendu aux plus froids pays, Sur les mers les plus étrangères— Mais jamais, dans ces extrémités, Il ne m'a demandé une miette.

(Dickinson 1970a: 62–63)

Skeptics, siding with Goethe, Shelley, Frost, and Derrida, might consider this as evidence of the impossibility of translation. Translating a poem is of course a tremendously difficult experiment, and it would be pointless and presumptuous to denigrate Forgue's attempt. Perhaps certain French readers will react favourably to his rendering of Dickinson, and French-speaking students will certainly benefit from it if they are looking for a ladder to help them climb towards a better understanding of Dickinson's poem. For my part, however, Dickinson's poem speaks to me and the translation does not. Is this a mere value judgement? I would argue that it is not. If this is more than a personal appraisal, if this can be explained in technical, formal, aesthetic, and semantic terms, we will have made some progress in explaining what happens when poems are translated. Doing so may equip us better, as translators, for the task of translating. It may enable us to render living, breathing metamorphoses rather than corpses that come into the target language "dead on arrival."

What exactly breaks down in the translation process? Perhaps the first thing that strikes the ear is that Forgue has dropped the rhyme and chosen not to offer a metrical rendering of the poem. Goethe would find nothing to criticize in that. Would we? What is missing in the translation? Is it the pleasant chimes of rhymes? Is it the reassuring undulating accentuation of metrical beating? These questions bring up a more fundamental question, one that is vital for the metamorphosis of poems: is there an inherent value in form itself? As the following chapters will illustrate, the French poet Paul Valéry (1871–1945) and the great German translator-thinker Walter Benjamin (1892–1940) believed there was. Both posited that the essence of poetry is essentially formal. Their defence of form was part of a celebration of poetry. But can poetry be boiled down to form? Defining poetry in terms of form leads to the inconvenient conclusion that nursery rhymes are poetry and that doggerel is more poetic than free verse. Obviously Valéry and Benjamin had no intention of defending limericks, nursery rhymes, or what the Scots call rat rhyme. Unfortunately the logic of their argument leads unwittingly to a defence of meaningless and lowbrow verse in the name of an abstract aesthetics of form itself. Surely the importance of form and the function of form lie elsewhere.

If the meter and the rhyme work in the poem by Dickinson, then they work by paying their way. If they are to be held essential then it must be because they form part of the dynamic expressive process by which the poem formulates its meaning. Is this the case? Actually, in this poem the coupling of words (soul/all) forms only a half-rhyme. Dickinson's other rhymes, however, highlight significant elements of the poem's meaning and forge meaningful links between the words (storm/warm, Sea/Eternity/Me). This is equally true of the alliterative foregrounding. Alliteration and rhyme cannot be reduced to merely formal elements, stylistic flourishes intended to embellish the meaning. Alliteration links words, as in the phrases "sore must be the storm" and "abash a Bird." If form foregrounds, then it foregrounds meaning. Form makes the poem more meaningful; the poem hits harder than prose.

In the same way the movement of the poem moves us. To some degree this effect is true of any metrical verse. Meter exercises a pull on us (an explanation of the charm of nonsense verse, doggerel, and comic verse). In this poem Dickinson is using her favourite verse form, the iambic tetrameter quatrain, which manifests itself in lines of four metrical beats in which the last beat is not always realized but is often replaced by a pause (called an "implied offbeat" in Attridge 1982: 174). In the opening stanza of Dickinson's poem, only the third line has four beats, though the first two and the final lines are clearly tetrameters followed by implied offbeats.

Metrics and scansion will be taken up in the chapters in Part 1. For the present moment it will be sufficient to emphasize three points regarding Dickinson's use of meter. First, the poem presents itself as an organized whole. Second, phrases are divided regularly into lines whose ends, whether rhymed or not, are used to highlight significant elements of the poem's meaning. Third, there is what may seem like an almost pathological use of dashes (thirteen in twelve lines) that expressively disrupts both the syntax and the meter. This is a distinctive feature of Dickinson's poetry (see Wylder 1971).

Translating the meaning of a poem of such a subtle and at times hermetic poet as Dickinson presents relatively little problem to Forgue. He shows a gift for exploiting the semantic resources of the French language in translating "little bird" as "oiselet." In contrast to Slavic languages and to Italian, the range of diminutives in English is poor. French is somewhat richer than English, and Forgue makes use of that richness here to avoid a clumsy word-for-word rendering (*petit oiseau*). Neither does he prove indifferent to rhythm. Forgue may have decided not to subject his translation to the constraints of a *forme fixe*—a conventional metrical and rhymed structure in French verse—but the lines of his translation reveal a tendency to flirt with metrical lines. Many of them form *vers pairs*, that is, lines of an even rather than an odd number of syllables, as here in a sequence of 6-8-6: "Qui va percher dans l'âme [6] / Et chante le chant sans paroles [8] / Toujours, sans s'arrêter [6]." Note that the eight syllables in the second line result from classical pronunciation of the mute *e* at the end of *chante*. This is a fairly common technique adopted by contemporary French poetry translators. The intended effect is that of a translated poem that gravitates towards tradition; it sets off the poem against arbitrary prose rhythms by freely introducing a fluid series of lines in which the regularity of the tradition is echoed. Was it to preserve the flow of the lines that Forgue decided to drop the dashes? Only one out of thirteen has been preserved, which is somewhat surprising, since Forgue often preserves these dashes where his predecessors chose to cut down on them dramatically.

What is traditionally termed euphony (alliteration and assonance) is rare in his translation, though Forgue does introduce one free internal rhyme, "Sur les mers les plus étrangères," which renders "And on the strangest sea." Forgue's line is a beautiful one, lyrically inviting. It might well remind readers of Baudelaire's evocation of the exotic sea, "La musique souvent me prend comme une mer / Vers ma pâle étoile" (Baudelaire 1975: 106). Indeed, it would be tempting to praise Forgue for such a line, but does it help to reproduce the mood and meaning of Dickinson's poem? Dickinson's "chillest lands" and "strangest seas" are far from enticing. They are the cold, hopeless landscapes and seascapes where despair invades us, environments in which the only thing that can sing warmth into our hearts is that pitiful bird within us, hope. Forgue and Dickinson both pull us towards poetry, but poetry of very different natures. The fact that this rhyme is the sole one in the translated poem foregrounds the aesthetic departure all the more poignantly.

Similarly, the disappearance of the dashes in Forgue's version seems to suggest an aesthetics of poetry very different from that to which Dickinson adheres. Forgue is certainly rhythmically interesting. For him poetry can be free. Writing in 1970, after three generations of free verse, Forgue might well have believed that poetry *must* be free in order to be poetry, so fully had free verse vanquished meter. Contemporary French poetry has espoused freedom as an aesthetic prerequisite. But if he seems indifferent to metrical constraints, Forgue is manifestly not indifferent to rhythm. He seems to believe that poetry should flow: flow in and out of regularity. T. S. Eliot advocated something very similar when he argued that "the ghost of some simple meter should lurk behind the arras in even the 'freest' of verse; to advance menacingly as we doze, and withdraw as we rouse" (Eliot 1953: 90).

This position raises another question, however. Does Dickinson's poem "flow"? Should this elegy to the pathos of hope—the small bird within us that refuses to abandon us even in the direst of circumstances—move peacefully and naturally? Should it assume the movement of a *berceuse* (lullaby) that rocks us gently back towards peace and serenity? Certainly meter has the power to do this, and Dickinson's poem is metrical. Nonetheless, the dashes tend to disrupt the reassuring effect of meter. What we have here is something quite characteristic of Dickinson's verse: a fairly acute tension between speech rhythm and meter. While the meter imposes order, coherence, and harmony, the speech rhythms drag against it. The result is the highlighting of words within the lines. The most poignant effect is the act of separating hope from the hoper in the last line: of hope, we are told, "never, in Extremity, / It asked a crumb—of Me." The loneliness of that last "Me," left hanging at the end of the line and foregrounded by the triple rhyme (Sea/Extremity/Me), seems to all but deny the power of hope. At the very least it undermines hope's capacity to comfort the person it sings within.

Forgue does not adopt the meter, so an expressive tension between syntax and meter becomes impossible. It is perhaps understandable, therefore, to remove the dashes; to preserve half of what provokes tension is not necessarily better than preserving nothing at all. In any event, the stylistic and aesthetic preconceptions of what poetry is intervene here in the process by which Forgue apprehends and interprets the poem, appropriating and translating it. The ultimate and essential question is, do we hear Dickinson's poem or Forgue's poetry?

At this point it becomes crucial to apprehend what the act of translation involves. We do not translate a language, we do not translate poetry; we translate a poem. As long as we remain close to the poem, we will remain close to a voice that emerges in its versification. Meter helps make sense. Rhymes underline meaning. Alliteration forges links between words and lends those words a greater, more penetrating force. But as translators it is difficult to distance ourselves from the rhythms and movements at work within our conception of poetry. Our individual sensibilities are such that we have a predilection to use meters and sound patterning in a certain way, and this tendency betrays the underlying assumptions of our own conceptions of poetry and reveals a great deal about the nature of our own sensitivity to poetic language. As translators, once we allow our own aesthetics of poetry to intervene, we easily fall victim to allowing formal elements to take the translation in a direction separate from the original. If this direction coincides with reformulation of the poem's meaning, then the result may work. If not, we can find ourselves on the path to a very different kind of poem.

As we shall see in the Baudelaire case study, many of the translators appropriate Baudelaire's poems and give a living, breathing form to the translated poems. Robert Lowell's Baudelaire translations (in Baudelaire 1997), it might be argued, take leave of the originals, but the poems he produces nonetheless hold together as what might be termed "coherent transgressions," following the logic of their own tangents. Often, however, disassembling the poem and putting it back together again involves sticking together random impulses that are shaped by conflicting desires. Like an unsuccessful salad vinaigrette, the translated poem simply does not come together. The individual lines and stanzas, the expressive potential of the sound patterning, and the rhythms, however expressive they might be, begin to express things contrary to the meaningful movement and organization of the original poem.

Hope for Poems

It is certainly not my intention to debunk or reject Forgue's attempt. The case study on the French interpretations of Emily Dickinson's poems reasserts Forgue as a formidable translator. Nor is it my intention to feed skepticism about the potential to translate poems. Strategies that produce unsatisfying results can be of interest to a work of this kind only if they help us to refine our understanding of the difficult task at hand. Criticism should cultivate sensibility of the complexity of the task. If it helps achieve this goal, then it should be perceived as indirectly optimistic, not perversely pedantic.

Lest Forgue's translation and the accompanying critique put a damper on the reader's spirits, examples of a few successful translations may be a good idea at the outset. Failures and translations that break down, or fail to find an ear in the target language, make good material for analysis, but readers who are asked to pore over many pages of comparative versification should not be begrudged some nourishment to sustain them in this endeavour.

Examples are surprisingly easy to find. Opening, almost at random, Gérard Gâcon's French translations of the sonnets of Philip Sidney, Shakespeare's contemporary, I stumble upon verses carved with craftsmanship equal to those of the original. So smooth and so efficient is the translation in bodying forth the message of the poem that for a moment I find myself asking what is the poem's original language. A few examples of Gâcon's translations of Sidney should suffice to make the point. Here is the first stanza of Sidney's "Sonnet 20."

Fly, fly, my friends, I have my death wound; fly,	Fuyez, amis, fuyez! A mort on m'a blessé!
See there that boy, that murthering boy I say,	Voyez là cet enfant, ce petit assassin: C'est un voleur dans d'obscurs halliers embusqué
Who like a theefe, hid in the darke bush doth ly,	Guettant de son sanguinaire plomb le larcin.
Till bloudie bullet get him wrongfull pray.	(Sidney 1994: 34–35)

The urgency of the original is made equally manifest in the translation, even though the third incitation to "fly" is dropped by Gâcon. The translation runs energetically but smoothly in alexandrines of both a classical kind (divided 6:6) and in the more original romantic form (8:4). The rhyme is preserved. And *blessé/embusqué* has the merit of harnessing words of poignancy for the poem, even though it does not qualify as a full rhyme because, as we shall see later, French rhyming tends to be more demanding on the whole. It does contribute to making meaningful links with sound patterning, nonetheless. What do we find in the original? "Fly"/"ly" is a functional rhyme that supports the narrative, but "say"/"pray" is weak, while Gâcon's *assassin/larcin* (assassin/robbery) hits home hard with a meaningful coupling that foregrounds the central idea that life has been stolen by a prankster kid.

Is this simply a lucky find? On browsing the translations more fully, this does not seem to be the case. Gâcon proves equally masterful in the opening stanza of Sidney's "Sonnet 31."

With how sad steps, O Moone, thou climb'st the skies,	Quel sombre pas, ô Lune, pour gravir les cieux!
How silently, and with how wanne a face,	Quel étonnant silence, et quel blafard visage!
What, may it be that even in heav'nly place	Se pourrait-il donc qu'en ces célestes parages
That busie archer his sharpe arrows tries?	L'archer pour lancer ses traits soit aussi fougueux?
	(1994: 40–41)

Sidney's moon climbs sadly into the skies. But the archer who energetically bends his bow in the translation is linked in contrast to the moon's sullen pace. This makes the rhyme *cieux/fougueux* (heavens/ardent) a dynamic coupling. In order to maintain a functional structure in translating fixed-form verse, Gâcon, for his part, reproduces not only the rhyme but also the *abba* rhyming scheme of the original. This entails reproducing the final rhymed couplet, so characteristic of the Elizabethan sonnet, that resolves the poem. Would the following French lines look out of place in an anthology of classical French verse?

Those Lovers scorne whom that Love doth possesse?	Ces Amoureux qu'Amour détient en servitude ?
Do they call Virtue there ungratefulnesse?	Nomment-elles Vertu leur fière ingratitude ?

("Sonnet 31," Sidney 1994: 40–41)

These verses may sound antiquated to the modern ear, and indeed Gâcon does strive to reproduce an archaic syntax and diction. But this form is more than mere artifice; it is more the style and the rhetoric of the poetry of the time that make the form of Sidney's poetry both distinctive and effective.

Gâcon's Sidney goes some way towards demonstrating that the difficulties of metrical verse translation can be overcome. But how does verse of a more modern, freer kind translate? The question proves fraught with difficulties. It might seem reasonable to translate non-metrical verse into prose. Many contemporary translators opt for this supposed solution, cutting the lines of their translations into the same slices as the ones they find in the original, irrespective of other rhythmic effects of phrasing and free patterning. This choice often proves a misguided and disappointing strategy, however, because free verse remains poetry—highly stylized and formally organized. Such poetry works thanks to the way its meaning is formulated and bodied forth. Is the poetry of Ted Hughes arbitrary? Are we indifferent to the rhythms of William Carlos Williams, Ezra Pound, and Walt Whitman?

For Pound, Whitman was the last poet whom a teacher should dare to introduce in the classroom, so difficult is it to explicate what holds Whitman's verse together. His verse launches itself forth with great gusto, flowing in a highly stylized form of patterning peculiar to itself. The energy of Whitman's breath was so powerful that it made his verse a poetry for the whole American people. Opening Whitman at random allows us to enter into that movement and organization that is quintessentially his.

> I have heard what the talkers were talking ... the talk of the beginning and the end,
> But I do not talk of the beginning or the end.
>
> There was never any more inception than there is now.

> Nor any more youth or age than there is now:
> And will never be any more perfection than there is now.
> Nor any more heaven or hell than there is now.
>
> Urge and urge and urge.
> Always the procreant urge of the world.
>
> ("Song of Myself," Whitman 1959: 26)

What do Whitman's French translators make of this movement? Eric Athénot offers the following version:

> J'ai entendu parler les discoureurs … le discours du
>   commencement et de la fin,
> Moi, je ne parle ni du commencement ni de la fin.
>
> Jamais il n'y eu plus de commencement qu'à présent,
> Ni qu'à présent plus de jeunesse ou de vieillesse;
> Et jamais il n'y aura plus de perfection qu'à présent,
> Ni qu'à présent plus de ciel et d'enfer.
>
> Toujours le même élan,
> Toujours l'élan procréateur du monde.
>
> (Whitman 2008: 53)

The movement of both the French translation and the English original are a far cry from what is often ambiguously called prose rhythm. This is poetry, not everyday spoken language. The lines are highly patterned in terms of phrasing and parallelism. The same phrases are taken up again and again like waves rolling over one another. Words and phrases are repeated, and the free verse strophes give shape to ideas that are formulated in coherent self-contained blocks, stylistically distinct from one another.

How does this translate? To my ear, Athénot's translation, though successful overall, suffers from a few minor stylistic tics. At times Athénot seems to find Whitman's repetitions tiresome. It is doubtless for this reason that he refuses "talkers . . . talking," preferring "parler les discoureurs." He tries to knit together Whitman's overlapping syntax with a tighter, more grammatical synthetic organization, preferring to introduce *ni/ni* (neither/nor), where Whitman is happy with "or" ("I do not talk of the beginning or of the end"). Athénot anticipates repetition. Whitman, more fully anchored in the present moment, lets repetition come washing over him. Most of all, this urgent presence is made to pulsate in the undulating strong-weak-strong-weak-strong accentual patterning of "Urge and urge and urge." Urgency was never more balanced, never so inescapable. Athénot's attempt proves weaker: "Toujours le même élan." Neither word repetition nor accentuation play any role in enacting the idea.

It is important not to overstate the case and focus pedantically on details at the expense of the whole. Athénot's translation works, notwithstanding what I have called his stylistic tics, and he does prove very sensitive to the problem of formal coherence when he sets up a repetitive link that binds together this two-lined free strophe into one organized whole: "Toujours le même élan, / Toujours l'élan procréateur du monde."

Jacques Darras offers a more balanced, Whitmanesque translation than Athénot of the same passage (to my ear at least):

> Je sais, j'ai entendu les belles paroles des beaux parleurs qui
>   parlent de la fin et du commencement,
> Or moi, de la fin ou du commencement jamais je n'en parle.
>
> De meilleur commencement qu'à la minute même où je parle
>   je n'en connais pas d'autre,
> Ni d'occasion plus juste de jeunesse ou d'âge,
> Ni d'exemple plus vrai de perfection absolue,
> Ni de temps plus réel de paradis ou d'enfer.
>
> Pression, incessante pression,
> Inlassable pression procréatrice d'univers.
>
>   (Whitman 1989)

Darras does not link up the two-line strophe in the same manner but he consolidates the parallelism in the middle strophe. He does not seek to edit out Whitman's repetitions or to organize his syntax. While he cannot maintain the urgent undulating accentuation of the original, Darras opts for a syntax that cuts the lines of the final strophe into parcels of meaning that can be strongly stressed. Moreover, the alliteration (**pr**ession/**pr**océatrice) helps bind together and consolidate this patterned movement: "**Pr**ession, incessant **pr**ession, / Inlassable **pr**ession **pr**océatrice d'univers."

These significant elements of formal patterning allow a translation to resound more or less strongly with the voice of the original poem. They therefore invite critical appraisal. Even so, we should not allow details to perturb our overall impression of the translated poem. Whatever their specific merits, the overpowering impression these two translations give is one of free but meaningfully patterned poetry. The lines of both Athénot and Darras bear no relation to patternless prose, ideas thrown together in unorganized and uninteresting chunks.

The following sections turn from criticism to theory in order to analyze more fully the conceptual and the technical questions that arise in the act of translating poems. The linguistic and stylistic investigation will discuss the transposition of rhythmic elements, meter, and rhythm. To some extent, this examination will force us to leave to one side the poetics of poems. Readers more at home with linguistic norms and stylistic structures should find this approach reassuring, but many translators and literary scholars may well find it frustrating. For many good reasons formalist investigations arouse suspicion. Often they are felt to be irrelevant in explicating the nature of poems and translations or in cultivating a sensitive understanding of them.

Theory, however, is crucial for the present work, since we should be able to rise above individual poems and posit some greater overarching principles related to the nature of the French and English languages, the natures of their diverse and changing metrical traditions, and the way those traditions have been superseded by language-specific forms of free verse. Such an investigation involves theorizing the nature of linguistic resources and of metrical structures and the interaction between them. If theory can help with these questions, then it will have paid a great service to translators, who are all too commonly heard expressing the idea that theory is useless and that all real translation is simply intuitive.

Intuition certainly constitutes that prerequisite without which no translation is possible. Intuition is the capacity to seize the text as a whole and perceive the way its parts work together as a system. Intuition enables us to resolve questions semiconsciously. These questions, however, can be brought into consciousness and rigorously interrogated. Henri Meschonnic had this principle in mind when he argued that we must move beyond practice and theory and beyond the sterile opposition between the two. Meschonnic advocated that we begin thinking through what we are doing and begin doing what we think we should be doing. He encapsulated that principle in this pithy formula "penser sa pratique: et pratiquer sa pensée" (Think through your practice, and put into practice what you think; my translation).

His strategy explains the very different natures of the three sections in this book: the theoretical one on comparative versification, the one on translating form and meaning, and finally the case studies. They form three distinct manners of investigating facets of the same question: how do we translate the poem? We treat a poem first as linguistic material within a literary tradition. Then we treat it as the inextricable whole that must be dismantled into formal and semantic elements, which must be reassembled to form a coherent whole in the translation. Finally we return to the poem speaking to us. At this last stage, theory will be left in the background, encroaching only when it becomes pertinent to highlight specific moments in which metrical patterning or semantically charged sound patterning is important.

This strategy should serve to help devise a pragmatic interpretation of translation without demanding too much from theory. Theory should allow us to define our task and analyze the elements involved in the act of translating. Criticism should allow us to verify to what extent our attempts to translate poems have been successful, or to what extent the translator's theory of language and his or her unconscious aesthetics or poetics are coming between readers and the poem. Nonetheless, intuition alone will allow us to apprehend the poem as a whole and to encounter the translation as a poem. Theory and criticism will discipline our capacities of appraisal and may well even hone our skills and sensibility, but poems and translations can be apprehended intuitively only as wholes. Ultimately neither theory nor criticism will be of any service if they do not bring us back to poems and translations and the way we apprehend them.

PART 1

VERSIFICATION

CHAPTER 1

Form

Forgue's Dickinson, Darras's Whitman, and Gâcon's Sidney have demonstrated the complexities of translating verse without making the difficult seem like the impossible. Considering where a talented translator such as Forgue stumbles should serve to alert us to the pitfalls awaiting the translator. As we saw in the translations of Dickinson, Sidney, and Whitman, questions that first appeared to be formal turned out to have a bearing on the poem's mode of expression.

We might already have guessed that a mere prose translation of a poem's meaning would be less than satisfactory. For the moment, however, it remains unclear what we mean by a prose translation—dropping the form, presumably. But this puts form on the side of conventional structures, meter, and rhyming schemes. And what about the parallelism, the repetition, and the sound patterning of Whitman's verse? Is this not form also? The manifest complexity of the formal organization of the meaning of a poem—both free and metrical—means we must face up to the necessity of redefining form.

My work has been heavily influenced by the great poet-translator Henri Meschonnic, who believed that what counts is neither the meaning nor the form, but rather the signifying process of the poem, that is to say the binding together of meaning into shapes and forms that endow the poem with greater resonance. For Meschonnic, formal echoes are always meaningful links. "Do or die" and "look before you leap" are merely conventional proverbial examples of the capacity of speech to bind together key features into meaningful moments of heightened attention. Form foregrounds meaning.

Dickinson's lines are given greater force and resonance when she links suffering with the storm in the line "sore must be the storm" (Dickinson 1970b: 62–63). And Forgue's line would have been less moving if he had chosen to opt for "moins connues" instead of "plus étrangères" (in "les mers les plus étrangères") for the loss of that free internal rhyme that heightens our attention to the elusive nature of the seas that he evokes (63). The tug of the sea's tide is what tugs at the heart in the following line from Baudelaire, but it is the alliterative link between *mer* and *musique* that renders so poignant the line "La musique souvent me prend comme une mer / Vers ma pâle étoile [...] ." Compare the following two improvised translations of this line and the importance of formal organization should be clear:

> Music often takes me like a sea
> towards my pale star [...]

> Music rises up inside me like a rising tide
> Tugging me towards my palest star [...] .[1]

Sound resounds within the mind, enabling us to assimilate the full force of meaningfully orchestrated moments of formal foregrounding. Meschonnic would not consider these mere formal embellishments of the meaning. They are part of what he calls a *sémantique sérielle*, which I translate as "meaningful movement." This forms part of Meschonnic's conception of rhythm as the organization of a poem by the lyrical subject. This concept of rhythm moves beyond stress and syllable count. Meschonnic considers alliteration, assonance, and rhyme, but he also takes into account all forms of repetition and patterning. Most importantly, he refuses to view these as purely formal elements. He rejects the division of the poem into form and content and he refuses to accept the theory of the sign (signifier/signified) as a working paradigm for poetics.

Indeed, Meschonnic believes that part of poetry's richness lies in the fact that it demonstrates the inefficiency of the theory of the sign for interpreting what language is and what language does. A theory of linguistics incapable of perceiving the importance and the specificity of poetry, a theory deaf to what poems do, remains an incomplete theory of language from Meschonnic's perspective. Listening to language also means listening to poems.

In his theoretical writings Meschonnic advocates listening to the poem—to the subtlety, the complexity, but also to the power of formal organization—just as Pound argued in his essays that we should listen to the poem. Once we return to the poem, the power of poetry makes itself perfectly plain, perfectly audible. A whole series of theoretical obstacles prevent us, however, from grasping the true nature and role of form in poetry. And curiously, it is often the specialists—those who prove to be the most sensitive to poetry—who provide the most misleading arguments when it comes to defining form. The most common misconceptions of form result from a failure to listen to the poem as a meaningful moment of heightened attention to movement and organization. Four trends in contemporary thought tend to obscure the problem at hand when defining form and its importance for poetry and poetics. First, formal definitions of poetry tend to obscure the formal organization in individual poems. Second, recent scholarship in translation theory has tended to ignore or marginalize attention to form. Third, traditional theories of metrics are on the whole reductive and misleading, being based on fundamental misrepresentations of order and organization. Finally, recent linguistic theories of meter, while making great progress on individual questions, have tended to leave behind poetics and aesthetics, apart from noteworthy exceptions that will be considered in later chapters. As a consequence, these linguistic theories have inevitably had little impact on mainstream poetics and translation theory.

Formal Definitions of Poetry

If you ask someone, even a teacher or specialist of literature, what makes translating poems difficult, they will no doubt reply that it is meter and rhyme that pose the greatest problem. This is a curious reply, however. Mainstream poetry has been taken over by free verse, which no longer accepts formal structural constraints—a state of affairs that has lasted for more than a century. Moreover, on deeper reflection it becomes clear that rhyme and meter have never been considered the essential criteria by which poetry must be measured.

Indeed, lines that observe the rules of versification but either lack inspiration or fail to aspire to lofty or elevated ideals are not usually considered to be poetry at all, but rather verse. For this reason we speak of comic verse but not comic poetry, and political verse but not political poetry. It is a cruel irony that the preoccupation with metrics has become known as versification, a term that has been used (in both French and English) disparagingly for bad verse or doggerel. Versification, in the evaluative use of the term, is hollow verse that lacks inspiration. It obeys the formal requisites but fails to move or uplift us.

Having considered the complexity of translating Dickinson's poem, it will be obvious that reducing form to meter and rhyme is a mistake. As long as we consider poetry rather than poems, we will find ourselves inclined to leave behind the essential dynamics of the meaningful movement and organization of the individual poem; instead we will find ourselves trying to analyze the poem by reflecting within the conceptual limits of general truths concerning the structural organization of poetry in general. We may still perceive something specific in the individual poetic event, but it will have become subordinate to the general truths applicable to poetry as a whole. We may still intuit something of the meaningful movement, but we will try to speak of that meaningful movement in terms of form and content.

This endeavour may prove provisionally justified. Certainly specialists of metrics such as Derek Attridge, Benoît de Cornulier, and M. L. Gasparov do make progress in providing conclusions that prove valid for poetry as a whole. But Attridge knows only too well that metrics must be used in the service of understanding poems. The converse strategy is a mere perversion, an inverted academic reflex. It makes little sense to use poems simply as examples of poetry. The general rule is of use only inasmuch as it permits clearer perception of the poignancy of a personal encounter with the rhythmic movement of the individual voice of a given poem. To fail to see the poem as the ultimate target of all metrics is a serious mistake.

Curiously, poets themselves, translators, and specialists in aesthetics and poetics often provide no better conception of form. Translation is invariably considered as passing on the meaning of an utterance or a text from one language to another. But where does this leave poetry? Can poetry be reduced to meaning? Surely not.

The hermeneutics of translation, which champions interpretation of the text, leads us into two culs-de-sac in the poetics of poetry translation. Those working with traditional theories of translation are often eager to please the defenders of poetry by paying homage to form. They admit the exceptional nature of poetry but they marginalize it by making it an exception; poetry does not fit into their theory of language and translation. This gesture is intended as one of respect, but in practice it comes down to little more than disposing of poetry as a conceptual problem.

Moreover, it little profits the poem to reduce it to its form, and such a reduction is the inevitable result of such reasoning. Since, according to the logic of this argument, the poetic is essentially formal, the meaning of the poem is regarded as secondary—all but irrelevant. Attributing a privileged status to form de-forms our impression of the poem and our impression of its voice, since only its expressive mode is taken into account. As I have mentioned, this criticism is not directed solely at traditional theories of translation, such as those applied in France, Britain, and the United States. It also applies to a great many translators who have tried to make explicit the implicit theory that directs their own modes and strategies of translating.

Walter Benjamin is often quoted by translators and theoreticians alike, yet Benjamin's formulation from 1923 proves perplexing:

> Was 'sagt' denn eine Dichtung? Was teilt sie mit? Sehr wenig dem, der sie versteht. Ihr Wesentliches ist nicht Mitteilung, nicht Aussage. Dennoch könnte diejenige Übersetzung welche vermitteln will, nichts vermitteln als die Mitteilung— also Unwesentliches. (Benjamin 1963: 156)

> For what does a literary work "say"? What does it communicate? It "tells" very little to those who understand it. Its essential quality is not statement or the imparting of information. Yet any translation which intends to perform a transmitting function cannot transmit anything but information—hence, something inessential. (Benjamin 1992: 70)

To compensate for the traditional marginalization of form, Benjamin swings to the other extreme by marginalizing the meaning of the poem. Translating the sense, for Benjamin (who, unlike Meschonnic, remains within the conceptual limits of the linguistic sign), thus comes to mean translating the "inessential" (*Unwesentliches*). Benjamin wished to do justice to the poem, but in so doing he paid homage at the shrine of a theory that makes poetry ultimately incomprehensible: the sign that carves the poem into form and content.

Refusing to reduce poetry to meaning is a valid gesture, but Benjamin fails to do justice to the poem as a strikingly meaningful process of signifying, a foregrounded act of meaningful expression. He deprives poetry of its meaning. This is similar to Oscar Wilde's claim in the preface to *The Picture of Dorian Gray* that all art is ultimately "useless." Refusing the cult of utility championed at the end of the nineteenth century and in the middle of the Industrial Revolution, Wilde was refusing to evaluate culture in terms of the alien criteria of industry, efficiency, and profitability. His statement was meant as a jibe at philistinism as much as a defence of art. He was denouncing the uncultured and their insensitivity to the higher claims of poetics and aesthetics.

But where Wilde was renowned for his sense of humour, Benjamin has been taken all too seriously in his native Germany, in France, and throughout the English-speaking world. Benjamin is often quoted as a defender of poetry. Perhaps it would be fairer to consider Benjamin's translations as a defence of poetry, but in his critical writings, his failure to escape the schismatic logic of the linguistic sign, which carves all into form and content, makes him a poor champion for a radical aesthetics of poetry translation. What good can come of thinking that the meaning of a poem is superfluous? Poems with form but without meaning would be as meaningless, as frivolous, and as useless as ribbons without hair to tie them in.

Recent Scholarship in Translation Theory

The number of publications in the field of translation theory has exploded in recent decades, producing various schools of *traductologie* in France and in the United States. The Routledge *Translation Studies Reader* (Venuti 2004) pays tribute to the wide diversity of research that has focused on the act of translating. This development is to be welcomed. Writers as different as Pound and Lawrence Venuti have insisted on the marginal place that translation has been allotted in the history of ideas and in the literary tradition, and if their work comes as some remedy to this state of affairs, then they are to be thanked.

Nevertheless, poetics has undeniably suffered somewhat in the wake of this renewed interest in translation. Traditionally translation studies attributed a central position to poetry translation, no doubt partly because a concern for classical authors tended to dominate the field. For many years translation was not considered to be part of linguistics but rather part of philology. In 1987, when Penguin Books wanted to pay tribute to the work of the great translator Betty Radice, it published a selection titled *The Translator's Art: Essays in Honour of Betty Radice,* edited by William Radice and Barbara Reynolds, a work in which meter in both theatre and verse was central to the themes of the various essays. Art and craft were the central questions. Work of this kind perpetuated a tradition in which poetry and poetics were central. Meanwhile in poetics, C. B. McCully showed a similar concern for such themes when he published his selection of essays by poets whom he had invited to consider the relationship between meaning and art, in his *The Poet's Voice and Craft* (1994), a volume containing contributions from Fleur Adcock, Donald Davie, and C. H. Sisson.

Donald Wesling and Derek Attridge are only two examples of established voices defending readings of poetry that highlight the importance of the role of form in making meaning. Nevertheless, in literary studies and in translation theory, these were to become marginal voices in a wave of criticism and theory that was investigating new territories.

Throughout the 1990s Lori Chamberlain (2004), Gayatri Chakravorty Spivak (2004), Rosemary Arrojo (1994), and Luise von Flotow (1997) all made serious contributions to thought on gender and translation. This work is unquestionably revolutionary. For Spivak, "The task of the feminist translator is to consider language as a clue to the workings of gendered agency" (2009: 201). Spivak argues that "the writer is written by her language." But this turns out to be further complicated by the fact that writers from different cultures and writers of the past are "written" differently. This means that feminist translators must, in Spivak's opinion, reposition themselves in relation to gender, history, language, and translation.

In her highly influential essay from 1998, "Gender and the Metaphorics of Translation," Lori Chamberlain makes a radical break with the tradition that advocates "fidelity" in translation, arguing that "the translator must usurp the author's role" (2004: 307). In something that approaches a feminist version of Freud's idea of the fantasy of patricide, the feminist translator must break with the father, with the "authority" of the author, and with the gendered enslavement of the text translation, which Chamberlain presents in a male/female paradigm. The debate that ensued led to a vast array of diverse and conflicting creative responses to translating that Luise von Flotow chronicles in her excellent *Translation and Gender: Translating in the "Era of Feminism"* (1997). Central to such responses was the program to engage in "interventionist feminist translation." This practice advocates that translators correct the source text if the so-called facts or ideas it contains appear to be unfounded or indefensible, by transforming the original text in order to bring it in line with "feminist 'truths'" (von Flotow 1997: 24).

Spivak saw all too clearly the way in which founding religious texts contributed to maintaining gender roles and patriarchy. Perhaps because feminists are both open-minded and radical, they were at the outset slow to criticize other cultures and somewhat reluctant to consider the way in which religions in non-Western cultures contribute to maintaining gender inequality. The realization of the importance of religion for socialization and gender construction led to a great wave of retranslations of the Bible (which von Flotow treats, 1997: 52–57) and, to a lesser extent, feminist revisions of the Koran (Hassen 2011). As von Flotow points out, this practice of feminist revision of the Bible has continued throughout the past ten years as part of wide-ranging feminist projects in the university and the publishing industry (2011: 1–3). This response is true on both sides of the Atlantic; Pascale Sardin edited a collection of essays on feminist positions and gendered translation for the translation journal *Palimpsestes* (published by the Nouvelle Sorbonne in Paris) in 2009. These and many other projects tend to give credence to the idea that feminist work on translation has had a strong international influence on the humanities in general, as von Flotow argues (2011: 2).

One obvious example is the way in which feminist revisions and interventionist practices have influenced the translation strategies adopted by adherents of gay and lesbian studies and queer studies in particular. Keith Harvey's "Translating Camp Talk: Gay Identities and Cultural Transfer" (2004) is representative of a wave of literature that was to follow in the first decade of the twenty-first century. Somewhat predictably, Harvey argues that homosexual language—"queer-talk" or "camp," as Harvey prefers to refer to it—has long been attested. He prefers to focus on literature since the 1940s, though a case could be made for camp in the work of Oscar Wilde, for example. Harvey goes on to quote dialogue from Tony Kushner's *Angels in America* (1992), focusing on erections and blow jobs. Like feminist critiques of standard language and accepted moral and aesthetic norms, Harvey convincingly argues that "Language games such as these may be characteristic of a type of critical semiotic awareness that is especially heightened by gay people, resulting from a long exclusion from mainstream signifying practices" (1998: 301).

The argument is plausible: all outsiders tend to perceive more acutely the norms that others unwittingly live by, since they have often been ostracized or punished for not submitting to them. Similarly, Jews, historically excluded from various fields of Christian society, recognized the inherent racism of exclusive practices that the dominant majority culture perceived as normal and natural. The objects of oppression perceive the logic of the discourse and the dynamics of the power structures used to keep them in "their place." In this case both feminist critiques of translation strategies and queer critiques might be said to renew debate on cultural exchange and expose the power play between introduction of the foreign and resistance to that introduction from dominant parties in the domestic market.

Antoine Berman, Venuti, and Meschonnic have all made contributions to the political dimensions of questions of a poetic or aesthetic nature. An ethics of translation has emerged in their works and a series of recent publications has consolidated this trend over the past decade. A certain confusion has been generated, however, by politicized approaches to translation that have often reduced positions to buzzwords and slogans; "ethnocentricsm," "domestication," and "foreignizing" are the most obvious examples. The popularity Venuti has won over the past ten years makes it necessary to reappraise exactly what has been taken from and celebrated in his work.

The reception of Venuti's work has, in my experience, led to a curious state of affairs. Like many successful scholars, Venuti suffers from the inevitable consequence that his work is quoted more than it is read. Over the past decade it has become fashionable to use his terms "domesticating" and "foreignizing" to describe translation practices. Admittedly these are terms that Venuti uses frequently, but since his work is adamantly ideological, such expressions have often been adopted more as slogans than as translation principles or theoretical tools for discriminating between different practices.

Consequently, I maintain that it is therefore necessary to distinguish among three approaches:

1. Venuti's own theoretical approach (which has been outlined and critically appraised in Underhill 2006a and Folkart 2007).
2. The first—and healthier—of two Venuti effects: his critique of ethnocentric practices, which has been given wide publicity. Barbara Folkart and other translators will welcome this examination. Cultures tend to perpetuate stereotypes, for example, the French as intellectuals, the Germans as philosophers, the Russians as people with soul. These clichés are ingrained in our cultures, and publishing houses subjected to market constraints inevitably play along by consolidating them in the texts they choose to translate into any language culture. In exposing this strategy Venuti does a great service.
3. The second—and less positive—Venuti effect: drawing attention to the translation as a translation. The desire to do so is not necessarily negative and might be welcomed, but the disruptive poetics Venuti espouses in the name of alterity and difference leads to extolling all forms of transgression, inevitably making it difficult for the text to function as a text. We often lose track of the meaning of the poem in the translations Venuti celebrates. What are we to conclude? That meaning is secondary. Venuti suggests that his approach is "frankly polemical" (1995: ix), and his followers see foreignizing translation as a radical opposition to conventional writing and translating practices. But upon examination of the models proposed, it often turns out that Venuti is celebrating practices that are far from radical but rather well-established ones sanctioned by modernist and postmodernist poetics.[2]

Folkart proves highly critical of Venuti's positions, practices, and rhetoric, but this should not distract us from the point the two authors converge on: the critique of transparency. Like Venuti, Folkart argues that "there is no such thing as 'plain' or 'non-interventionist' translation, from which the translator could be totally absent" (2007: 121). In the light of radical feminist translation, this critique is important because it underscores the fact that ideology and individuality are at work at all levels of poetics and aesthetics. Translators cannot be self-effacing; they manifest themselves in all of the choices—linguistic, aesthetic, and ethical—that they make in the process of rendering the foreign accessible.

This strong idea did not, however, come to Folkart from Venuti. Though Venuti's main work was published in 1995, twelve years before her own, Folkart owes this idea to Antoine Berman. Quoting Berman, Folkart reminds readers that it is absurd to ask of the translation that it appear as "pure" writing (*"pure" écriture*), which is itself, in Berman's opinion, a mere myth (Berman 1984: 249, quoted in Folkart 2007: 308).

To do him justice, however, it was Venuti who greatly contributed to making Berman's work known to the English-speaking world, by including an extract of Berman's 1985 work in his *Translation Studies Reader* (Berman 2004) that he himself translated. Though Folkart finds fault with the style and linguistic rendering of the translation (and I find myself forced to concur with her appraisal), Venuti succeeded in introducing and clarifying Berman's ideas for people unable to read French. Berman lists the different strategies by which the translator intervenes in the process of transforming the text; he highlights "deforming strategies," which Venuti faithfully renders as

1. rationalization
2. clarification
3. expansion
4. ennoblement and popularization
5. qualitative impoverishment
6. quantitative impoverishment
7. the destruction of rhythms
8. the destruction of underlying networks of signification
9. the destruction of linguistic patternings
10. the destruction of vernacular networks or their exoticization
11. the destruction of expressions and idioms
12. the effacement of the superimposition of languages.

(Berman 2004: 280)

What Berman was concerned with in the 1980s was a series of linguistic, ethical, political, and poetical questions. Rhythms and patterning were held together with ethical questions of identity. The problem with the ideological turn that translation studies took in the 1980s in English-speaking nations was that a concern for the craft and art of translation came to seem somewhat anachronistic. In the midst of this renewed interest in translation studies, the aesthetic dimension—so manifest in Berman's list—was pushed to the sidelines. This becomes very clear in the way that Venuti utilizes Berman and in the way Venuti himself has been used. Venuti invariably highlights the question of alterity and ethnocentrism in his celebration of Berman's work; he pays little attention to rhythm and patterning in it.

This is somewhat perplexing and paradoxical. After all, Venuti himself pays great attention to metrics in his critique of flowing, fluid, transparent texts (Venuti 1995). But in fifteen years of attending conferences on translation studies, I have yet to come across anyone who makes reference to rhythm and metrics in relation to Venuti's work. What Venuti took from Berman and what contemporary translation studies pay heed to in Venuti's own work appear to be restricted by an ideologically motivated selective reading.

It is clear that Berman is speaking from a different time and a different milieu with very different aesthetic and poetic concerns. Barbara Folkart, in her *Second Finding: A Poetics of Translation*, therefore finds herself swimming against the tide and forced to write what she calls a "cantankerous book," an "irritated" retort to an increasingly politicized field of thought that is putting ideological concerns before textual analysis of aesthetic questions (2007: xv–xvii). To her credit, Folkart is still listening to the poetic within the political, and it is for this reason that she proves a sensitive reader of Meschonnic and Berman, who both consider the historicity of poetic creations. Berman, however, has increasingly been quoted by those who defend more the political and ethical concerns that he voiced, especially his defence of *alterité*. His poetics have often been left by the wayside in France and in English-speaking countries.

How are we to proceed? Clearly, any work on translating poetry has to return to poetics and consider the way rhythm shapes the contours of the individual poetic voice. Venuti, for his part, throughout his main work, *The Translator's Invisibility* (1995), paid great attention to form, to metrics, and to the question of fluid movement and harmony. To a great extent his argument that translations pose as originals depends on the idea that a fluid translation is a "fluent" one, one that presents the translated poem as a poem that could have been written in the target language. Venuti interprets this as an attempt to efface the act of translating and the alterity of the foreign language, along with the work's original author.

Indirectly voicing Meschonnic's ideas (1972, 1978), assimilated through his reading of Berman, who was Meschonnic's student, Venuti argues that this constitutes an act of ethnocentrism. Berman owed his critique of ethnocentrism to Meschonnic, his PhD supervisor. He learned from Meschonnic his perspicacious approach to the way we can uncover the covert translation strategies implicit in aesthetic and poetic choices. Meschonnic had, after all, published widely on such questions throughout the 1970s and was himself a translator of the Bible from Hebrew (2001a, 2002, 2003).

This forces us to reappraise Berman's list of deforming strategies in order to ascertain what is new in his creative synthesis. Expansion, clarification, and the destruction of idioms and expressions are well-established linguistic processes, familiar to translators and to translation theorists (e.g., Vinay and Darbelnet 1977). Ultimately it has to be admitted that Berman owed his more radical concepts to Meschonnic, among which we should stress, first, the destruction of rhythms; second, the destruction of underlying networks of signification; and finally, the destruction of linguistic patternings.[3]

Meschonnic grounded his critique of these strategies within a coherent and far-reaching theory of language, translation, and poetics. Berman's choice of speaking of destruction here deforms Meschonnic's thought, because it implies that the translation effaces or destroys the original. The original goes on living and new translations will follow. Meschonnic was concerned not with replacing the original but with responding to it. Neither was he impressed by arguments that certain texts are untranslatable; in reaction to this he distinguished between the "untranslatable" and the "untranslated," which he defined as what has yet to be discovered and introduced to the foreign language. Neither did Meschonnic see literature or translation as doing violence to language. Language is, Meschonnic believed, reanimated by novels, plays, and poems. And great translations—what he called "translation texts"—contribute to this ongoing process of reinvigorating language. Refusing a formalistic reduction of rhythm to meter, Meschonnic argued that it is the configuration of meaning that must be carried forward in the translation; it is the act of signifying, the functioning of the poem, that has to be re-enacted in the translation.

Venuti took up some of Meschonnic's ideas, filtered and assimilated through his reading of Berman, but as he adopted them, Venuti was thinking within and responding to a very different context. His concepts of the language, tradition, and the canon were very different from those of Meschonnic, who saw writers as engaged in a never-ending re-personalization (what he called *subjectivation*) of language and culture. For Venuti, literature is by nature rebellious. And this leads him to think of all forms of norms and conventions in terms of authority that must be contested. Consequently Venuti gets entangled in tortuous arguments in defence of a postmodernist poetics of translation. But what does this amount to when we come to the conclusion of arguments and contemplate the examples he provides? We appear to be faced with a defence of obscurity: a curious inversion of the translator's vocation as the guide through foreign territory.

Making the reading process a problematic, almost painful process is, Venuti argues, a meaningful and redeeming act. It forces the reader to reflect on the difficulties of communicating in language and the importance of self-critical texts that pose the question of the limits of representation.[4] The point that should be stressed is that Venuti's work responded to a political climate and was inevitably received as a political statement. This reveals a great deal about the way translation studies have been transformed over the past few decades. Moreover, Venuti is quoted as a defender of translation. His work is considered a contribution to the ethics of engaged translation. His consideration of rhyme and meter is, to my knowledge at least, rarely mentioned. This omission is worrying, since his ideas about rhyme and meter transpire to be crucial for understanding Venuti's argument in favour of unbalanced lines that resist coherence. Those ideas help explain his taste for making traditional poems read as modernist or postmodernist verse in English. Only in the light of his discussion of the mechanics of versification can we hope to understand Venuti's tribute to Zukovsky's obscure translations of Catullus (Venuti 1995: 214–24).

Paradoxically, Venuti himself has consolidated the present trend in translation studies away from poetics, leading it further into ethics with his choice of texts for the Routledge anthology, a work that allows gender studies and political concerns to crowd out art, craft, and poetics. This tendency does not bode well for the present work. Like Folkart, in focusing on the poetics of translation, I am swimming against the tide. The theory of translation has moved on. And, to a large extent, it has left poetics behind.

Defining Form

The present book is conceived as neither a "polemical" one, as Venuti proudly claims his work to be, nor a "cantankerous" one, as Folkart firmly asserts her own resistance to the present wave of ideological work to be. This book on translating poems must be essentially pragmatic. For, after all, why should pragmatics and poetics be opposed? *Poesis* means "making" for the Greeks. And this is something that the name for poets in Scots, *makkars*, reminds us of. But turning from politics to poetics is not the easy way out. As we return to practice, we find ourselves embroiled in questions of aesthetic and poetic orders that were always highly problematic. In contrast to many of the transient debates animating translation studies, the questions of poetics will continue to haunt translators in coming generations, for the simple reason that understanding the movement of poems that move us requires sensitivity, intuition, lucidity in analysis, and rigorous conceptual definitions. It requires an attention to what makes poetry exceptional as a form of expression. For poetry is exceptional as a linguistic form of expression, and poems are revealing in that they demonstrate something essential about the nature and organization of languages, in terms of the way they handle syllables, accents, phrasing, and sound patterning. The case I am making is this: a return to such questions is not a retreat into formalism. It constitutes facing up to the matter that enables meaning to take form and engender emotion, reaction, and forceful thought.

Our tour of rhythmic elements will take us from free verse into metrical verse. Form will be central to our preoccupations. Meter does present specific problems, and it will therefore be treated in some detail in the following chapters. One of the essential problems of meter in translating the poem is that it has come to be considered the form of the poem. What we understand by form, and how we treat it, changes from age to age. Classical philology was inevitably preoccupied with how we should transpose the long and short syllables of Latin metrics. Transposition of syllable-count meters from French into the undulating weak-strong movements of accentual syllabic meters in English was considered the primary difficulty to be resolved by translators of French. This was a limited, metrics-centered version of form. Even rhyme tended to be downplayed in this conception of translation. Rhyme is, of course, essential, both structurally speaking and in terms of the meaningful arguments that rhyme contributes to making individual poems. But rhyme is only one of many formal elements that serve to shape the movement and the organization of the poem.

Meter and rhyme tend to be rule-bound constraints, and for this reason traditional poetics has stressed their importance more than what I shall call "free patterning"—salient forms of emerging organization (repetition, parallelism, alliteration, and so forth) that foreground the act of expression—without establishing norms that allow us to anticipate the development of the poem's movement. Again and again, authors, critics, and linguists have tended to privilege one or another version of form by highlighting a single element. Free-verse advocates often fell into the same error, as did linguists who sought to explain its formal efficiency—even the great Russian linguist and philologist Roman Jakobson (1896–1982) in his essay titled "The Dominant" (1981: 751–56).[5] Ultimately, however, the success of the poem and the success of the translation can never be reduced to one single organizing principle. Different principles emerge and assert themselves in what Jan Mukařovský calls the foregrounding of the poem (*aktualisace* in Czech; 1964).

One obvious example of free patterning would be repetition proper. Shakespeare's "Sonnet 66" (1988: 35), which begins "Tired with all these, for restful death I cry," continues from line four to line ten to list the objects that inspire the lyrical narrator's lassitude. The fatigue of the voice is made palpable by the relentless repetition in each of these lines of the same first word, "And." The phrasing contributes to the effect of the list by reproducing like movements. In a more modern example, Ted Hughes begins ten of the nineteen lines of his poem "Examination at the Womb-door" with the word "Who" (2003: 218), setting up a question-and-answer dialogic rhythm. The answer is invariably the same: "Death." This comes as the crushing reply, the final word, in all but the ultimate line of the poem.

These forms of free patterning are plain enough and should not necessarily pose any particular problem to the translator. There are, however, series of mistakes that are often made. Translators can be so preoccupied with form as meter and rhyme that they fail to give such effects the status they obviously demand when we listen to them in individual poems. Thinking "poetry" and not "the poem," the translator frequently transposes the traditional structures, while ignoring the particular patterning of individual poems. Translators of free verse often pay more attention to free patterning because they intuitively search for an organizing principle that holds the poem together where rhyme and meter are no longer employed. Jakobson tends to proceed in a similar manner in his analysis of poems. This method is, however, misguided. True, Hughes's poem does tend to erect a counter-structure with repetition. Shakespeare's sonnet, on the other hand, makes equal use of repetition and parallelism. This should clarify two points: various free and codified principles are simultaneously and interactively at work in many poems, and free patterning is just as much at work in traditional structured verse as it is in so-called free verse.

Form should therefore be understood as a more complex type of semi-structured organization, and this form of organization is patently manifest when we listen to the poem. It is easier to intuit form than to explain it. It is more difficult to grasp in its interactive complexity, once we begin to analyze it. The essential point is that each rhythmic element, each pattern or part of the structure, works within the dynamic organization of the whole. And that whole is a meaningful whole. This understanding explodes the meaning/form opposition, and all the clumsy conceptual attempts to resolve their unity that stem from starting from that opposition. Form always embodies meaning. If repetition is invoked, then it serves a purpose: insisting on lassitude in Shakespeare's poem and hammering home the inevitable end, death, in Hughes's poem. Repetition invariably shapes the movement, organization, and repetition of phrasing, and often alliteration or assonance shapes the phrase that is repeated.

These observations are often made clear in the choice of words and phrases used as refrains. In his lyrical celebration of his childhood on the Caribbean island of Guadeloupe, Saint-John Perse speaks of the lush sensuality of an oozing nature that is in a constant state of fecundity—the mangroves' heavy scent, the acrid taste of the sea, the slow pace of legs moving through the grasses, and the fusion of limbs melting together when bathing in the green waters of the forest pools. It is this primal pre-Christian world that Perse celebrates when he exclaims again and again his refrain, "Ô! j'ai lieu de louer."

This refrain comes three times in a short three-stanza section ("VI. Pour fêter une enfance," Perse 1960: 36–37).

Perse perfects an early form of French free verse that consists in privileging lines that are balanced in a way reminiscent of regular verse. Verse lines of six, eight, ten, and twelve syllables, but also three and nine, are interspersed and alternated freely within what might be termed prose strophes. Regularity and the reassuring echo of the tradition never seem to be far away, but the verse preserves a free patterning that is both innovative and dynamic and that allows certain moments of heightened expressivity to be foregrounded.

In Perse's refrain the alliterative link between "lieu" and "louer" and the fact that the verse line is a hexameter (six-syllable line)—reminiscent of the most traditional division of the principal French verse line, the alexandrine (6:6)—greatly contribute to assuring the effect of balance and harmony that the poet seeks to celebrate in this hymn to nature. How should the translator proceed? "Ah, I have reason to praise" would make a poor substitute for this lyrical refrain, though the meaning is preserved, and nothing in the structure of the original requires us to obey any metrical constraints. But it hardly seems appropriate to reproduce the meaning and focus on freedom and the absence of traditional metrical requirements in this case. Are we to conclude that translating poems is impossible, and that the magic of Perse's lines defies translation? In Meschonnic's terms this would be confusing the untranslated with the untranslatable. By paying attention to the role of repetition and the dynamic interaction of the foregrounded refrain with the movement of the verse as a whole, we can suggest something more convincing, for example, "Oh, let me lift up my voice in praise." The tetrametrical (four-beat) line remains fairly free, but the double alliterative link makes it function much more efficiently as a refrain intended to celebrate nature. This refrain can give a hint of patterning to the free poem, holding it together as a harmonious, free, unfolding form.

Free verse is often represented as a revolt, a rebellion, a form of transgression. Indeed it was repeatedly celebrated as such by its protagonists. Nonetheless, the great free-verse improvisers Pound and Eliot were not seeking to escape from form; they were looking for an alternative form of organization. They wanted to invert and reinterpret structures and bring their own creative will to bear in engendering new, re-personalized patterns of organization. Though they were later celebrated for their experiments, and though Eliot was celebrated for cacophony, dissonance, and rupture, both Eliot's and Pound's critical writings make it plain that they were in fact searching for a new form of order. Jakobson was following exactly the same logic when he wrote his article "The Dominant" (1981: 751–56). As a linguist, he was trying to explain why free verse is not free, just as the poet Eliot affirmed "there is no freedom in art" (1953: 87), maintaining that "there is only good verse, bad verse, and chaos" (91). Pound, Eliot, and Jakobson were trying to find an alternative, a substitute for traditional structure. The rule-bound system organizing the stanza was supposed to be replaced by a single organizing principle, equally efficient but totally different in nature.

Despite Eliot's great sensitivity as a poet, and despite the vast erudition of Jakobson,[6] both were mistaken in striving to reduce the complex dynamics of the poem to a single organizing principle. As we have seen in the introduction, in Shakespeare's sonnet and Dickinson's poem (see "The Difficult Task," page 10), various organizing principles coincide, interact, and compete in foregrounded moments of expression. At times repetition will become far more salient than meter. Hughes's poem is so tightly bound together in a dialogic movement that meter becomes superfluous. It might, therefore, be argued that meter becomes secondary in Shakespeare's sonnet, in which repetition and parallelism take over as organizing principles. These, rather than the alternating undulation of weak and strong syllables, hammer home the monotony of disenchantment. And it is the soft alliteration that lifts Perse's voice in praise, giving a balance to the free patterning of his verse.

In the following chapters I will try to give meter its proper place as one of the great structuring forces of traditional verse. This attempt will require reappraisal of traditional foot metrics, which has long proven to be unworkable. It will involve considering carefully the status of meter in translation in the work of the great Czech theoretician Jiří Levý and alternative approaches to rhythm and meter in the works of Meschonnic and Cornulier in France and Attridge, Wesling, and Richard D. Cureton in English. All of these authors, in their own ways, provide pragmatic solutions to real problems in metrics. Nonetheless, the contribution each makes to bringing us back to the poem will differ in many respects. If we allow ourselves to reduce form to rhythm and rhythm to meter, we have already become deaf to the poem. We no longer hear the way it strikes us and moves us, opening up our sensitivity to peaks and troughs of feeling.

If we separate form and content, we will find ourselves translating poems into ideas and translating form into frilly decorations fit for the Christmas tree.

Form is neither the "echo to the sense," as Alexander Pope puts it (2005: pt. 2, l. 363), nor the shell that holds the kernel of truth. It is neither a barrier nor an embellishment. Form constitutes the dynamic emerging of the formulated idea. A voice emerges in its versification, and in the translated poem the versification must serve to permit this second coming. If form is reduced to meter and separated from meaning, we lose track of the very force of language that Aristotle had in mind when he wrote his *Rhetoric* (1954). It is not a question of downgrading meter but of remembering that stressing something means giving greater accentuation to certain phonemes among others, highlighting aspects of meaning within the organized movement of the work as a whole. Meter is a powerful tool, but if it is not made to be "meaning-full" in poems and in the translation of poems, then it becomes meaningless—superfluous, pointless.

A Few Key Concepts

My approach requires a fairly extensive overhaul of some of the traditional concepts used in poetics. The transposition of foreign concepts and their translation into English also deserve some explanation. In the present work, "voice" will be used in a similar manner to the way in which Meschonnic used the term *rythme* from the time he wrote his *Critique du rythme* (1982) onwards. Voice represents the lyrical subject of the poem, the "I" that creates it but that is also created in and by the poem. This "I" is neither Shakespeare nor Hughes, neither Baudelaire nor Perse. Individual poets do of course exist, but the voice of the poem comes into existence and is sustained solely by virtue of the poem. A poet may have many voices that develop, change, and oscillate between radically different manners of expression and open up vastly different realms of experience. The voices of e. e. cummings, the French-Canadian poet Rina Lasnier, and the English-Canadian poet Malca Liovitz are distinctive, but the voices of Robert Burns, Ted Hughes, and Carol Anne Duffy are multiple. Many poets adopt stances in their poems. They look at questions from new angles, and this engenders a healthy, provisional form of schizophrenia: the self fractures into multiple voices to investigate the various facets of existence. Poets such as Eliot and Pound make pastiche and adopting poetic voices a part of the young poet's apprenticeship.

The lyrical "I" is a deeply personal and specific "I," one that may change from poem to poem as Pound or Eliot adopt different masks, different personae. We can define the voice of the poem, but that definition must remain supple and, ultimately, multiple. The voice remains

1. The voice of a language
2. The voice of an era
3. The voice of a literary movement or context of influence
4. The voice of a poet
5. The voice of the particular poem.

Each of these dimensions will help shape the voice. English shapes Shakespeare's voice, as does Elizabethan verse and the verse of his contemporaries, Marlowe's most of all. Shakespeare's other voices may be echoed in any one poem. Yet each poem marks out its own space, its own peculiarity that must be heard. Sensitive translators are intuitively aware of these various facets and shaping forces; they will sometimes employ techniques characteristic of a given poet even when translating poems that do not make use of them, if they help redouble the poem's expressive force.

"Versification" will be used in the present work in a way that distinguishes it from traditional usages. It will not, of course, be used as a term of abuse, a synonym for doggerel. But neither will it be restricted to meter and rhyme. Versification will be used in a much wider frame of reference to designate the dynamic interaction of all formal elements, thereby covering both structural constraints and free patterning. Versification will cover meter and rhyme (which invariably introduce rule-bound constraints), but also free internal rhyming and heightened accentual syllabic phrasing of the kind commonly found in the verse of Perse and Hughes. It will also include sound patterning (alliteration, assonance, and consonance), as well as repetition and, just as importantly, syntactic patterning (the repetition and the parallelism of organized phrasing). This organization of phrasing may be considered at a local level or at a general level. Phrasing can contribute to organizing the whole or simply to giving heightened importance to a certain part of the poem, a meaningful moment of attention.

Form will thus cover structure—the codified traditional organizing principles governing the poem as a whole—and two forms of free patterning: overall patterning and local patterning. The phrasing of "Who ... ? Death" in Hughes's poem can be considered a kind of alternative meter, an unshakable, unbreakable, inescapable syntax-shaping force that patterns the whole poem. Only breaking out of this patterning allows the poem to come to a close. Often, however, repetition, alliteration, and phrasing will be used simply to foreground a particular moment in the poem's movement. Though both forms of patterning are free, overall patterning sets itself up and means to stay, whereas local patterning comes and goes, leaving space for other dynamic interactions to take their place in the limelight.

It is my conviction that people know how to read poems and translators very often know how to translate them. This work involves great sensitivity to the complex interaction of various forces that focus our attention and play upon our feelings. Much of the work we do in reading and translating poems is intuitive rather than conceptual. The poem impresses us: it leaves its impression upon us. Our apprehension of the poem is by nature impressionistic. We seize the whole (or are seized by it); we are not moved by the nuts and bolts of the poem's formal composition, which analysis dismantles.

It may indeed seem laborious to dismember the poem and to dissect individual elements. For this reason I will move swiftly in my analysis of translations in the case studies, refusing to spend multiple pages explaining what should be clearly audible when a stanza is read aloud. Yet the essential complexity and subtlety of versification must not be denied; it should be underlined at crucial moments when the translation achieves a like or alternative organization that works. Relying solely on an intuitive response to versification and the voices it engenders would be taking a step backwards into complacency and obscurity, a refusal of rational explanations.

I believe much of the frustration with theory stems from the misplaced importance accorded to certain elements, and theory's incapacity to conceive of the poem as a meaningful whole. Hermeneutics strives to extract the meaning by pillaging the poem. Metrics reduces individuality to generality: it reduces the poem to poetry and the voice to tradition. If we are to succeed in avoiding such reductive and counterproductive approaches, we must bear in mind that all explanations, definitions, and abstractions should ultimately help us return to poems and listen to them. Meaning resounds within form and tradition echoes within individual voices, not rules and structures. Our visit to metrics is an important one, but we will be visiting metrics only in order to return to the poem.

Notes

1. I offer these two improvisations merely to illustrate the point. For the same reason I at times take the liberty of rewriting the lines of translators in order to stress how their solutions are more successful than they might have been.
2. Folkart's critique of Venuti's position (2007) is more acidic than my own (2006a), perhaps because of her greater exposure to the jingoistic celebration of his stances. While perceiving the problems that preoccupy Venuti—the "ethnocentric violence, forcible replacement, violent rewriting of the foreign text" (Venuti, quoted in Folkart 2007: 306)—Folkart prefers to speak of "dumbing-down and levelling-off to lack of artistic ownership" or "ineptitude" (306) and is concerned with "the poem and the act of poeming," in her opinion the least of his interests. Folkart makes five fundamental criticisms of his approach: "foreignizing" caters to the celebration of an exotic otherness "that enthralls the gawking, culturally uninformed tourist" (310); Venuti makes linguistic blunders in Italian and fails to appreciate the style of French; only a very sensitive linguist can perceive the difference between the language system (*idiome* is the word she uses) and the speech act (*énoncé*), in Meschonnic's terms distinguishing between the language system and the discourse specific to an individual author; the translation fails to preserve or re-enact what is specific to its mode of signifying if we stumble over linguistic differences in French that surprise and delight us; and Venuti adheres to postmodernist aesthetics with its celebration of intertextuality, and "intertexts travel poorly in both space and time—they can get lost in crossing borders and generations" (2007: 84).
3. Ideas concerning rhythms and patterning as forms of semantic signifying processes are discussed and refined by Meschonnic in his *Poétique du traduire* (1999), but the basic concepts of his approach to language and poetics are clearly being used in his earlier works (1972, 1978), and many of his key concepts relating to rhythm are elaborated in great detail in his monumental *Critique du rythme* (1982).
4. I have considered this question in my critical appraisal of Venuti's work (Underhill 2006a).
5. Jakobson considered that "the dominant may be defined as the focusing component of a work of art: it rules, determines, and transforms the

remaining components. It is the dominant that guarantees the integrity of the structure" (1981: 751). This argument shows that Jakobson was framing the dominant within his own structuralist poetics. He did, however, stress that the concept of the dominant was introduced by the Russian formalists (751), who, it should be remembered, focused more on poetics than the structuralists who came after them, and who focused primarily on the specific nature of literariness or poeticity within the framework of the language system.

6. Jakobson was a linguist who not only read poetry in many languages but also wrote about poems in seven different languages, as demonstrated in his *Selected Writings* (1977–82).

CHAPTER 2

Comparative Versification

If the poem is expressive, then it owes that expressivity in part to the means furnished by the language system: English, French, German, Czech, Hindi, Finnish, and so on. The linguistic matter must be forged into a meaningful movement and an organized whole by any given poet. The organized patterning of syllables and of accentuation, intonation, syntax, and the very cadence with which the voice moves all differ from language to language. Being forced to discard the movement of one language and to adopt a foreign movement does, therefore, inevitably threaten to undermine the expressive potential of the poem. Losing the accentual undulation of English, which has been harnessed and crafted into a vast array of personalized styles, can indeed prove disastrous for the translation.

If we consider, for example, the way Shakespeare tailors the cloth of the English language to make audible very distinct voices, the formal linguistic constraints of the language may seem a truly daunting stumbling block for the translator. Try reading aloud the following lines from Shakespeare's *A Midsummer Night's Dream*.

OBERON. By some illusion see thou bring her here.
        I'll charm his eyes against she do appear;

> PUCK.   I go, I go—look how I go,
>   Swifter than arrow from the Tartar's bow.
>
>   (3.2, 1987: 588)

The stately tone of Oberon, King of the Fairies, makes itself manifest in balanced pentameters. Puck, the impish troublemaker who delights in causing chaos and confusion, answers his master, on the other hand, in an entirely different tone, with a free ballad-style tetrametrical verse. The varied number of syllables in the lines and above all the interjection of multiple unstressed syllables between the beats give Puck's line a highly expressive urgency, perfectly attuned to its meaning, as Puck sets off to do the bidding of his master: tricking Titania, Queen of the Fairies, into falling in love with Bottom, complete with an ass's head.

Let us suppose that it is impossible to translate balanced pentameters and free-moving tetrametrical ballad-style verse from one language to another. What does this signify? The pessimist, who allows the detail to obscure the whole, who examines the texture of the bark of the tree but fails to hear the sound of the breeze in the woods, will conclude that expression must be sacrificed at the altar of translation: that meaning can pass from one language to another, but not form, not poetry.

An insidious logic is at work here. And if we are to defend translation and make a contribution to it as an art, then we must identify the individual steps that lead us to the conclusion that poetry defies translation. Pessimism invites us on this tour.

1. We divide form and content.
2. We reduce form to meter.
3. We identify structural differences in language and conclude that transposing meters is impossible.
4. Having reduced form to meter, we find ourselves forced to conclude that form cannot be transposed.
5. We fall back onto the strategy of a prose translation—the transposition of meaning—having concluded that translating poetry is impossible.

The logic seems watertight to the pessimist, but this is a conclusion that the present book sets out to unmask as complacent prejudice. In the following chapters and, most of all, in the long case studies on translating Charles Baudelaire and Emily Dickinson, we will have ample opportunity to consider the way form and expression in one language are transposed to another. Ultimately there is a more fundamental error involved in the logic at work in the pessimist's reasoning. This argument reposes on the idea that expression is irrevocably rooted in linguistic form, and that languages that do not share the same linguistic form cannot express the same things. This conclusion is surely a great absurdity. Would anyone truly suggest that Czech, French, German, or Hindi lacks the capacity to express emotion? In French, Corneille, for example, finds no problem making his characters express a poised and stately tone in well-balanced alexandrines. His characters can express urgency and excitement just as they can express despair and despondency. If languages were not expressive, they would not work as shared mediums of communication that are cherished and maintained by their linguistic communities.

It is, of course, speech and not language that is expressive. Every language enables expression, and each poetic tradition develops its craft by carving the specific linguistic means at its disposal into meaningful movement. Our task is double:

1. We need to compare and contrast the differing textures of the wood we are working with, in each language, in order to understand how poets such as Shakespeare and Corneille carve it into expressive forms.
2. We need to investigate strategies the translator can adopt in order to enact the same expressive moment using different means.

Different Cultures, Different Stages of Development

Versification as a science—namely the categorization of verse forms and analysis of the rhythms of individual poets—has evolved to varying degrees in different language cultures. Alex Preminger's enormous *Princeton Encyclopedia of Poetry and Poetics*, re-edited with T. V. F. Brogan in 1993, contains extensive coverage of theoretical and aesthetic debates related to verse form and poetic experimentation in various languages at various periods in history. It does not, to my knowledge, have any equivalent in French, German, or Czech. Henri

Morier's *Dictionnaire de poétique et de rhétorique*, published in 1961, marks a high point in French versification. The great sensitivity, vast knowledge, and penetrating insight of the Swiss scholar Morier into technical questions related to accentuation, organization, harmony, and expressive rupture remain unmatched in France today, and subsequent dictionaries of poetics and rhetoric—always shorter—are for the most part intended as summaries or updates of his work. At any rate, nothing in French has since been published to replace his monumental 1,320-page volume. No work in English mirrors the ease with which Morier takes on questions that are inextricably technical, semantic, and aesthetic in nature. Henri Meschonnic's *Critique du rythme*, published in 1982, remains the reference work for disentangling tortuous arguments intended to bolster sloppy systems and ill-defined terms, especially in enthusiastic but ultimately incoherent celebrations of rhythm.

Meschonnic stands alone when it comes to uncovering the metaphysical, philosophical, and ideological premises on which the aesthetic judgments and poetic questions are advanced and discussed. What politics and aesthetics are at work in the celebration of order and tradition? How rebellious are free-verse poets? And how can we distinguish between those who simply go along with the flow of movements, adopting emerging trends and practices? How does Saint-John Perse launch himself into the future while seeking to remain anchored in the past in terms of form and rhythm, in terms of tradition and innovation, at the level of the movement of his poems? These are poetic questions, metaphysical questions, but they remain questions of rhythm for Meschonnic. Various traditions, from the maligned outsider championed by admirers of *les poètes maudits* to dropout beatnik haikus and the prose poems of Jack Kerouac, posit the poet as standing outside society. But ultimately there is no escape from society into aesthetics. For Meschonnic, rhythm is not a neutral space in which to seek refuge from political problems. How our speech and our poems move reflects something about our presence in this world and about our relationship with others—and with tradition, with systems of order, and with the ideal of individual creativity.

Like Aristotle in the *Poetics* and the *Rhetoric* (1954), Meschonnic himself defines meter as a part of rhythm, a rhythm among rhythms.[1] But despite isolated attempts to distinguish clearly between them (see, for example, Astésano 2001; Guaïtella 1996; Lévy 1926), *mètre* and *rythme* are invariably confused in French or else they are used in various contradictory ways. Moreover, the reliance on foreign sources does not help to clarify things in French. Corine Astésano (2001: 30), for example, relies on Elizabeth Couper-Kuhlen's English definition of meter in her *English Speech Rhythm: Form and Function in Everyday Verbal Interaction* (1993). But this reliance inevitably entails a discussion of isochronous meter, and that in turn proves misguided. For although Astésano seems to differ when it comes to the agreement between Guaïtella and Couper-Kuhlen that such rhythms belong more to poetry, the isochronous principle turns out to be only a virtual player in English verse. And certainly no specialists of poetry would argue that reading French verse to a metronome might prove possible or in any way enhance its expressivity.

One great service Meschonnic does for poetics is to strip away the artifice of unfocused musing in literary criticism and sloppy metaphorical thinking. As he points out, much of the obscurity in discussions of rhythm arises from trying to hide the fact that the writers do not know what they are talking about. To this end a whole panoply of Greco-Latin terms comes to the rescue, lending a veneer of sophistication that amounts to no more than obfuscation. Complex explications of variation and inversion in foot metrics invariably turn out to be totally incoherent. Foot metrics does not work, as all specialists on meter agree. Inventions such as "wrenched stress" and "hovering stress" and attempts to explain metrical inversions are only fingers stuck in the cracks of a dam waiting to burst. Meschonnic cuts through the technical explanations of how the verse line works, in order to demonstrate that it is not the verse line that determines the poem but rather the poem that determines the structure of the verse line. We read the alexandrine and the pentameter as such because we find them in a poem, and we anticipate a given metricality that can be realized within the line, which would not be realized were the same stress contour to be found elsewhere.

Meschonnic refuses to allow himself to be penned in by metrical analysis that neglects the meaning and reduces the form to the meter. He reminds us of something that we instinctively apprehend in the poem and intuitively grasp: that expressivity does not repose upon metrics, that it is the meter that emerges out of expression. Phrasing comes first. This is something that American authors Richard D. Cureton, in his *Rhythmic Phrasing in English Verse* (1992), and Donald Wesling, in his *Scissors of Meter: Grammetrics and Reading*

(1996), have explored more fully than their French counterparts. Derek Attridge, who has brought about a revolution in metrical analysis, felt forced to adapt the system that he introduced in 1982, in *The Rhythms of English Poetry*, in his 1995 *Poetic Rhythm: An Introduction*, in order to give greater scope to phrasing of the kind Cureton and Wesling were exploring.

Attridge and Wesling now concur with Cureton's postulate that it is phrasing that shapes meter rather than meter that shapes phrasing, an idea that has yet to penetrate French metrics, though this tenet clearly underlies Meschonnic's *Critique du rythme* (1982). In recent decades French metrics has seen something of a transformation, or at least a series of challenges. In contrast to the dominant paradigm upheld by Maurice Grammont (1989) and Jan Mazaleyrat (1990), Benoît de Cornulier (1980) and Meschonnic (1982), in very different ways, insist much more on the importance of accentuation, which concentrates on syllable count and which has invariably been marginalized in traditional French metrics. These two writers would give very different accounts of the importance of the expressive potential of accentual patterning. Nevertheless, both Cornulier and Meschonnic have introduced scansions to account for accentuation, and both would agree that accents must be considered either as metrical constraints, essential at certain points in the verse line for upholding the meter, or as secondary forms of stylistic patterning.

A Brief History

In French- and English-speaking nations, comparative versification—the science to which this work on the translation of poetry constitutes a contribution—remains in its infancy. On the other hand, the linguists of Slavic languages have made much more progress in this field. Nothing, to my knowledge, compares to the astute understanding of verse patterning and the problems of transposing rhythm in the work of Jiří Levý, whose *Umění překladu* (The Art of Translation), published in 1963, remains one of the founding pillars of the much-admired Prague School of translation. If French thinkers have been able to investigate certain aesthetic and technical problems in verse translation, it is thanks to the French translation of the work of Russian scholar Efim Etkind by Wladimir Troubetzkoy, *Un art en crise* (1982).

Roman Jakobson, working closely with Jan Mukařovský during the 1930s in the Prague School of Linguistics, made a great contribution to comparative versification in the various articles he wrote on prosody in a wide range of languages. There was one crucial difference, however. The poetics of Mukařovský and Levý was very much a poetics. Jakobson, on the other hand, remained a philologist-linguist. The Prague School focused on aesthetic and poetic questions of expression. The text was always central to the preoccupations of Mukařovský and Levý, and the poem as an expressive unit was always the beginning and the end of their analysis. Mukařovský was not so much interested in extracting universal or general findings from texts as he was concerned with how those texts worked individually and specifically. What was interesting for him was the way in which the individual style of either a poet or an era compared with others, and what made individual poems powerful.

Jakobson, for his part, was busy introducing a much more formalistic version of structuralism to the West, one that was to be challenged and finally abandoned (all too ironically) at the very time when Mukařovský's aesthetics and his idea of aesthetic foregrounding finally began to make some small waves in Anglo and French poetics in the 1970s (Fontaine 1974). Levý, however, seemed likely to remain a Czech for the Czechs, a seemingly unexportable "product." A German translation appeared in 1969,[2] though I have never seen it quoted; in English scholarship, aside from a couple of articles, none of Levý's ideas on translation have managed to penetrate debates on the poetics of translation. For this reason it came as a great surprise to me that John Benjamins decided to bring out an English translation of Levý's challenging work in 2011. The potential influence of such a translation remains unforeseeable at the present time.

To his great credit, Levý mastered many languages, but what is even more impressive is that he mastered the established traditions of versification in those languages. He was, furthermore, able to compare them in a rational, unbiased, scientific manner, a rigorous and objective approach that did not prevent him from remaining deeply intuitive in his understanding of the expressive potential of rhythmic effects to make an impact on the reader. As we shall see later on, Levý's conception of rhyme was much more refined and, ultimately, much more pragmatic than the reductive formal definition of traditional versification in French and English.[3]

Opposing English and French

This historical overview is all very well as an academic account, but what does the great Levý have to say about rhythm? I find myself in the perplexing position of being forced to criticize someone who deserves much greater praise than he has ever received. Nonetheless I am constrained to part company with Levý on the question of rhythm, because in following the traditional metrics of French and English, he opposes these two metrical systems. In conflating rhythm and meter, Levý takes a false step, one shared with the majority of specialists. It would be absurd to chastise him for not resolving in Czech the difficulties that the specialists of each language themselves found almost impossible to overcome in their own traditions.

Nonetheless, the working model Levý leaves us with puts meter first and phrasing second, contrary to the justified intuition of Cureton, Wesling, and Attridge. Levý reduces rhythm to meter and accounts for rhythm in the terms provided by French and Anglo metrics. This approach has the great disadvantage of downplaying the similarities and dissimilarities found in these two languages that are closely related, and it also leads Levý to misrepresent the similarities in rhythm that can be observed in languages that are far removed from one another. Levý introduces a schema that is based solely on accent and syllable and that classifies and orders languages according to the status that their versification systems accord to accentual and syllabic organization. We are left with a rather curious system of ordering that brings about a rapprochement between English and Russian, and where Polish and Spanish find themselves closely related neighbours. The following is the schema Levý proposed.

Accentual-Syllabic	**Syllabic**
English	Polish
Russian	Spanish
German	Italian
Bulgarian	French
Serbian	
Czech	
	(1963: 281)

This schema was based on findings taken from K. L. Pike's theory of intonation, which suggests that English tends towards isochrony: the roughly equal alternation of stress and off-stress (1945). Pike's work is highly debatable, though there is no question that the undulating nature of English is clearly perceived by speakers of other languages and must be mastered by students of English.[4] Nor is there any question that English song and, to a lesser extent, English verse move towards this principle of regular alternation, or at least are perceived to be doing so.

Levý also introduced a quadripartite theory of verse structure:

1. Temporal verse, or metrical verse based on long and short syllables. In Levý's opinion, this system governed classical Greek and Latin verse but is no longer in operation in modern languages (1963: 242–49).
2. Tonic verse, often called strong-stress rhythm, such as English metrical verse governed exclusively by the number of accented syllables. The number of unstressed syllables in such verse is varied and, to an extent, arbitrary. Levý agreed with English specialists in considering Anglo-Saxon Old English poetry as offering a classic example of such verse (255–58).
3. Syllabo-accentual verse, governed principally by the accentual structure but supported by the number of syllables intervening between stresses. Levý considered all modern English verse to be of this kind (259–64).
4. Syllabic verse, governed by the number of syllables in the line. Levý believed that accents do not play a crucial role in such verse. French, he believed, offers the most obvious examples (249–55).

In opposing French and English, Levý put his finger on something that English-speakers and French-speakers intuitively react to when they hear each other's language. Curiously, people often remark on the musical character of the foreign language, but in my experience, when English-speakers exclaim, "French is like a song!" they are referring to intonation and the movement of the phrase—the very phrase that will form the basis of the metrical unit. When French-speakers exclaim, "*L'anglais est chantant!*" in my experience they are referring to an accentual undulation that reminds them of rock 'n' roll, a form of song rhythm that foregrounds the binary strong-weak movement implicit in English accentuation.

Impressions are important, and valid, as rhythmic experiences; Levý's schema is not, therefore, to be cast aside lightly. The opposition between syllable organization and accentuation is not without a certain experiential power. Nonetheless, as will become clear, it remains a highly problematic reductive reading of versification. We cannot hope to move forward in resolving translation problems until we have unravelled some of the complexities that such an opposition embroils us in or effaces.

Resisting a Reductive Model

On a more superficial level, this schema must be amended to account for certain verse forms with which Levý was not familiar. French is capable of generating isochronous temporal verse—French nursery rhymes (*comptines*) work in this way. Take, for example,

/ / / /
Une poule sur un mur

/ / / /
Qui picote du pain dur.

Such verse depends on what Attridge (1982, 1995) would call "promotion"—elevation of an unstressed syllable into a metrical accent that enables us to preserve the undulation of the meter (a phenomenon we shall consider in more detail in the chapter on metrical manipulation of accentuation). This process of stress elevation is what is at stake here, with the stress on the prepositions *sur* and *du* in the above example. More striking examples can be found in contemporary French rap. Take, for example, the song "Bye Bye":

/ /
Tu es la seule qui m'aille.

/ /
Je te l'dis sans faille.

/ /
Reste cool bébé,

/ /
Sinon je t'dirais "bye bye."

(Ménélik 1999)[5]

In such chanted but unsung verse, rappers not only "promote" syllables, they "demote" them too. That is to say, they weaken the stress and length usually accorded to syllables in spoken language. Such syllables are not deprived of stress, but their stress is downplayed, reduced in order to force whole series of syllables into the dynamically charged offbeat. Just as Shakespeare's Puck, the prankster, fits three unstressed syllables between his accents ("Faster than the arrow from the Tartar's bow"; Shakespeare 1987: 3.2, 588), the rapper in the above example elides one syllable (*te* to *t'*) and fits another three syllables ("Sinon je t'dirais") into the offbeat position.

English rap offers an infinitely vaster array of such examples. Indeed, French rap, chanted primarily by black youths and youths of North African origin, seeks its inspiration in models of rap generated by Afro-Americans and Jamaicans. The accentuation of such English is highly marked, and it is these rappers' form of incantation that has captured the imagination of the children of immigrants looking for a voice to express themselves in contemporary France. Seen as outsiders, they have searched outside France for inspiration, and it is English—and American English "hood" or ghetto rhythms, with a markedly undulating form—that they have imported into French musical diction. Nothing in the era of Johnny Hallyday and the French recuperation of rock 'n' roll in the 1960s could have allowed us to envisage such a transformation of the way in which French can be chanted. Indeed, this borrowing shows the flexibility of the language. It also demonstrates the danger of reducing the structure of a language to its system of versification. Though the French alexandrine and the English iambic pentameter both reveal something about their respective languages, neither is natural to the language to which it belongs. Both are highly stylized forms of speech that take up residence within the language as part of its cultural tradition. And a resident form can be "evicted." For many speakers of French and English, the rules governing the meters of their metrical poetry—formerly assimilated intuitively by readers—have now become largely incomprehensible.[6] To many people those rules have come to seem ridiculous and laughable, and even to many students of literature they appear absurdly contrived.

A much more fundamental misconception that Levý's model leads us into is the idea that French verse can be reduced to syllable count without reference to accentuation. As we shall see, accentuation is fundamental for defining metrical units in French, as is rhyme.

Levý is on the side of tradition, but tradition is mistaken when it fails to distinguish between two entirely different forms of accentuation. All language is subject to what Attridge calls "stress contour." The stress contour is both formal and semantic. Words are accorded stress in terms of their semantic value. On the whole, verbs are more important than nouns in English, while nouns are more important than adjectives and adjectives more important than prepositions. The organization of the sentence and the juxtapositions of these parts of speech will shade this general principle, but it remains true that significant words are highlighted in terms of pitch, intensity, and length. A word will not be deprived of stress in a poem, nor can an insignificant syllable become a strong focal point within the meter, if it is promoted. But weak syllables can be promoted and strong syllables can be demoted in order to preserve the perceived undulation of a structural constraint that has clearly asserted itself within a given stanza in English metrical verse. The essential question remains to distinguish between metrical stress—called "beat" by Attridge and "ictus" by Levý and others—on the one hand, and the stressed syllables of everyday speech on the other. Classical metrics has always conflated these two forms of accentuation that prove linked in poetry but, nonetheless, remain entirely distinct in both form and function.

Even more fundamental is the misconception that arises with the reduction of form to meter. True, this is no more than a provisional strategy, adopted by Levý to allow him to gain a vantage point and look down on a vast array of poetic traditions in various languages. In tracing the influence of metrical traditions among Indo-European languages, M. L. Gasparov (1996) adopts the same technique. But this option inevitably distorts our perception of what is happening in the movement and the organization of stanzas and poems. In short, Levý's erudite and rich research takes us on a great journey, and his analysis of individual translations proves penetrating and perspicacious. But much of his perspicacity he owes to his sensibility of poetry rather than to his conceptual paradigms.

Terminology

To move forward we will need to employ a series of crucial definitions and make a series of distinctions. This approach will entail adopting the following principles: syllabic verse must be abandoned as a non-functional paradigm; the role of the accent in French verse must be ascertained; and a distinction between beat and offbeat on the one hand and stressed and unstressed syllables on the other must be preserved. The former belong to metrical organization and the latter belong to speech; both can be at work in expressive verse.

In order to speak about the movement and the organization of poems and translations more lucidly, I suggest we adopt the following definitions.

METER The term "meter" shall be reserved for speaking about the codified, rule-bound constraints of verse, as used in sonnets written in either French alexandrines or English iambic pentameters.

METRICAL CONTRACT The phrase "metrical contract" refers to the agreement set up between the poem and the reader, who interprets it by intuitively responding to a given organization and by anticipating the continuity of that organization. This contract involves the complicity of the reader, who must respond to phrases in which the stress contour does not coincide with the meter (more often the rule than the exception) but can be realized by reading it in such a way as to allow the right number of metrical accents (beats) or syllables to be perceived.

METRICAL COMPETENCE A term Attridge owes to generative metrics, "metrical competence" refers to the capacity of the reader to realize the potential of the poem to fit clearly defined constraints put into play by the opening lines of the poem. Metrical competence is on the wane. Since free verse became the norm rather than the exception, many readers have difficulty responding to metrical constraints. This challenge partly explains why many people today find declamation to be ridiculous and absurd.

MOVEMENT In the present work, "movement" refers to free organization of syntax and phrasing, untouched by the constraints of meter or the expressive impact of foregrounded free patterning.

CADENCE The term "cadence" refers to the free undulation of strong and weak syllables that is highlighted or foregrounded in much free verse but which defies traditional scansion and neither engages readers in a metrical contract nor depends on their capacity for metrical competence. A cadence is a heightened form of undulation that often emerges at times in free verse, only to disappear. Ezra Pound and William Carlos Williams frequently allow a cadence to emerge in their verse, and cadence is the constant of Whitman's verse, which defies all attempts to fit it into metrical scansion.

RHYTHM   In the present work, the use of the word "rhythm" will be restricted to the resolution of both line and syntactic movement. We can speak of the rhythm of free verse, thereby designating the way phrases are shaped and organized, cut up and held together by lines. But it is in the study of the interaction of meter and line that rhythm becomes a key concept, because it introduces the idea of tension. For this reason I often choose to speak of the movement of free verse.

These distinctions and definitions should allow us to untangle a series of misconceptions and confusions in studying what is actually going on in the writing and the translation of poems. They should provide a more solid basis for discussion and a sounder set of tools for our task. They should allow us to return to the essential question that rightfully preoccupied both Levý and traditional metrics: how do the accent and the syllable contribute to the shaping of rule-bound metrical verse?

Notes

1. This position had already been taken up in French by Lévy (1926).
2. Levý's key work was published in German in 1969, only a few years after being published in Prague. Given that the work focused on Czech verse and questions of translating into and from Czech, there seemed very little hope of its being translated into English. This state of affairs was turned around with Patrick Corness's English translation, *The Art of Translation* (Levý 2011).
3. I discuss Levý's contribution to a structuralism that failed to make it into Western poetics (Underhill 2010b). This article can be found online at https://www.academia.edu/323896/Jakobsons_Dominant_Hyperliteracies_and_Structures_of_History.
4. To my knowledge only Delattre (1966) appears to question the idea that English shows a greater propensity for undulating rhythms than French. Delattre finds that the difference in length between accented and unaccented syllables is more marked in French than in English; see also Astésano 2001: 33. This observation may turn out to be true, though it is obviously the coupling of accentual length and intensity

that makes the undulation of English speech distinctive. Pierre R. Léon (1996: 107–08) takes a more standard view, defining French accentuation in terms of length (*durée*), intensity (*intensité*), and pitch (*hauteur*). Léon contends that intensity is often not marked sufficiently to enable us to distinguish between accented and unaccented syllables in French, and that such a distinction relies primarily on the length of the syllable; accented syllables, he suggests, can be two or three times as long as unaccented syllables. Léon's discussion is interesting in that it goes on to consider the specific ways in which individuals stress syllables. He also tackles the gender question, affirming that research seems to indicate that in French men stress the length of accents more than women do (1996: 108–09).

5. One website gives the lyrics without contractions ("Tu es la seule qui m'aille, je te le dis sans faille, reste cool bébé, sinon je te dirais 'bye bye'"). I have respected the actual pronunciation as the lines are chanted in the song. See the video at https://www.youtube.com/watch?v=wHOS586xoo&feature=youtube.

6. This is certainly true of iambic pentameter, which requires a familiarity with the poetic tradition. The four-beat ballad meter continues to be assimilated by English-speakers whilst still in the cradle, with the chanting of nursery rhymes.

CHAPTER 3

Meter and Language

Rhythm and Emotion

From the point of view of the poet and the poetry lover, the unforgivable error of specialists of metrics and versification has always been that they offer only a formal understanding of sound. As all poets and readers know, poems are meaningful. The poetry in poems can never be reduced to form, pure or otherwise. Even nonsense poems such as Lewis Carroll's "Jabberwocky," in *Through the Looking-Glass, and What Alice Found There*, are humorous largely because they remind us of meaningful words. In language there is no escape from meaning, even in negating it. Humpty-Dumpty kindly explains that "slithy" means both "lithe and slimy" in Carroll's poem, but readers will already have guessed as much intuitively. And for all the genius of Carroll, this kind of verse is common to other poets writing in English and in other languages. German *Unsinnspoesie*[1] (nonsense verse) and French equivalents are likewise considered highly evocative.

In poems, rhythm is the movement of meaning. It should hardly come as any surprise, then, if the movement of meaning is moving—if it elicits an emotional reaction. We are moved by movement, particularly when the meaning of the words is heightened so that the force with which they strike us is redoubled. Incantation, spell casting, childish rhymes, and insults all draw their dramatic strength from this inherent force in language. Indeed, rhythmic speech is a superlative form of speech act. From the chanting of shamans to the Christian grace said before breaking bread, rhythm acts upon the world, even if it does so merely by acting upon our shared apprehension of the world and the rituals we enact within it by venerating objects and procedures of symbolic import.

Poetry merely harnesses this emotive potential in language, the expressive charge of organized movement in speech. The modern American poet Louis Zukovsky quotes the poet-translator Ezra Pound, who argued that "Emotion is an organizer of forms" (Pound 1970: 114). In his 1918 book *Pavannes and Divisions,* Pound formulated a credo, stating: "I believe in 'absolute rhythm,' a rhythm, that is, in poetry which corresponds exactly to the emotion or shade of emotion to be expressed. A man's rhythm must be interpretative, it will be, therefore, in the end, his own, uncounterfeiting, uncounterfeitable" (1970: 83).

The poet's vocation, Pound argued, is to investigate reality and to body forth emotion. This was a double investigation, into both the poet's experience of the world and his own examination of the process of internalizing and expressing that experience. Rhythm was part of this process; it could not be reduced to rules and schools. Learning metrics was only the first in a series of steps towards engendering a meaningful motion in poems, a rhythm that would solicit an emotional reaction in the reader or listener. In his 1910 book *The Spirit of Romance,* Pound had already argued that rhythm is an essential dimension of the act of poetic creation, for rhythm was individual, not conventional; as he put it, "Rhythm is the hardest quality of a man's style to counterfeit" (1970: 39). Pound, of all people, was in a good position to appreciate that fact. Hadn't he been an ardent advocate of the idea that each poet should follow a poetic apprenticeship in striving to master his craft, by studying the masters of rhythm, expression, and diction? T. S. Eliot, arguably the most famous English-speaking poet of the twentieth century, followed Pound's advice and explored other voices in striving to find his own. In his dedication of *The Waste Land* in 1922, Eliot calls Pound, who edited the work in manuscript, *"il miglior fabbro"* (the better artisan; Eliot 1969: 59).

In a letter to Iris Barry written in 1916, Pound argued, "Your first job is to get the tools for your work" (1970: 61). Not only were reading and assimilating, studying and imitating rhythm and style a means of cultivating one's personal talents as a poet, this work was part of Pound's practical philosophy for regenerating modern poetry in English. When he published his contribution "A Few Don'ts by an Imagiste" in *Poetry* magazine in 1913, Pound already had a fairly clear idea about what the beginner must come to terms with. As Pound defines his task,

> Let the candidate fill his mind with the finest cadences he can discover, preferably in a foreign language so that the meaning of the words may be less likely to divert his attention from the movement.... Let the neophyte know assonance and alliteration, rhyme immediate and delayed, simple and polyphonic, as a musician would expect to know harmony and counterpoint and all the minutiae of his craft. (1970: 43)

Pound had some rather curious ideas about the movement of verse, and the logic of his arguments was often tortuous. He said, for example, that poets should abandon the metronome and "compose in the sequence of the musical phrase" (quoted by F. S. Flint in the same magazine, in the article "Imagisme"; Pound 1970: 41). This recommendation is perturbing, to say the least, when we consider that musicians, not poets, learn their craft by using the metronome. Nonetheless, Pound's sensitivity is unquestionable and the earnestness of his project cannot be doubted. The influence he had—and continues to have—moreover, seems to indicate that his ear was highly attuned to something fundamental in language and of great importance for the success of poems as acts of expression. Unsurprisingly, Pound's ideas on translation and poetic craft have continued to this day to inspire specialists of poetics from Henri Meschonnic (1982) to Derek Attridge (1982) and translation specialists such as Lawrence Venuti (1995) and Barbara Folkart (2007).

Poets also often pay homage to the finesse of Pound's understanding of a well-balanced line. This is because Pound understood—both conceptually and intuitively—four things. He understood the way syllables and accents work together; he was aware of the way individual poets express themselves in moulding the constraints of their language and their poetic forms to their own special expressive needs; he perceived the importance of the interaction of syllables and accents with other rhythmic elements such as rhyme, repetition, and alliteration; and finally, he grasped the inextricable nature of form and meaning, which can never be divided, either in the creative experience of writing or in apprehending the poem as a reader or listener. These conclusions amount to one very simple but fundamental working principle: having served his own apprenticeship and having gained what he could from theory, Pound listened to the poem.

Stress Systems

I have already emphasized the importance of the poem as an integral whole and the interaction of rhythmic elements as part of the entire experience of the poem. Nonetheless, in order to understand the interaction of rhythmic elements, each one must be analyzed individually. If we are to understand something about the linguistic constraints exerted on syllables and accents, we must provisionally step back from the poem and ask ourselves what the essential nature of the syllable is and what the accent does. For this comparative examination, intended as a contribution to translation studies, the question is whether or not there are essential differences between syllables and accents in the English and French languages. We must therefore provisionally engage in formal analysis before returning to individual poems in the case studies.

Recent scholarship in comparative linguistics has made remarkable progress since the times of K. L. Pike and Jiři Levý. *The World Atlas of Language Structures Online* (WALS) provides a vast array of analytical and synthetic data on linguistic difference when it comes to the syllable, to the accent, and to rhythm as a whole.[2] The richness of such research is unquestionable, and WALS constitutes a research tool that surpasses by far the dreams of scholars working a couple of generations ago. Nonetheless we would be well advised to proceed warily in adopting and applying the findings of comparative linguistics, for a series of inherent problems haunts comparative projects. Three precautions should be observed in order to avoid unnecessary confusion. First, comparative research is by nature wide-reaching, but the further we open our arms, the less we manage to seize each language in its specificity. Much contemporary research is carried out by linguists who have not mastered the languages studied; they write up their findings for linguists and students who have no firsthand knowledge of those languages, let alone the poetic traditions of those languages. This is work of a much wider scope but inevitably much more superficial than that of linguists and philologists such as Wilhelm von Humboldt (1767–1835) and Levý. This kind of work cannot provide the same level of finesse that is found in the impressions and insights of translators who offer us their own accounts as they explain how they overcame problems of transposing rhythm and expressive speech.

Second, caution is equally required in using the terminology of contemporary linguists. Interested in stress and rhythmic grouping, these scholars tend to derive many of their key concepts from traditional metrics—that is to say foot metrics, a school of analysis that has been widely criticized and largely discredited. Although such linguists meaningfully redefine terms such as "foot" and "rhythm," we must be careful with affirmations that certain languages appear to have no rhythm or no stress. Definitions of stress and rhythm in terms of syllable length and intensity are subject to so much debate and redefinition that confusion easily arises. Perfectly legitimate and reasonable conclusions can thus appear incomprehensible if the exact context in which such statements are made is not carefully recorded. At other times such conclusions will be rightly considered false once a different concept of stress and rhythm is brought to bear on the discussion.

Third, the information technology revolution and the use of recording equipment throughout the twentieth century have made it possible to ascertain with much greater certitude the actual weight and length of stresses and the true nature of repetition and metrical beating. This change is to be welcomed. Nonetheless, stress and rhythm remain perceived realities—impressions—and to neglect the impact of these impressions on readers and listeners would be a mistake. Only readers who are native speakers are truly linguistically competent when it comes to estimating the degree to which formal configurations are highlighted in poetry and the degree to which one poet stands out from another by meaningfully harnessing rhythmic organization in poems.

In spite of these potential misunderstandings, WALS is a fascinating source of rich and varied, and also highly organized, findings related to stress and syllable structure. It is mainly chapters 15 through 17, by Rob Goedemans and Harry van der Hulst, that are of interest here (2013a–c). Goedemans and van der Hulst provide maps to illustrate the complexity of their findings, and their definitions have the virtue of being both clear and comprehensible (2013a, 2013b).

They also manage the difficult task of avoiding oversimplification in making a coherent and meaningful synthesis of their revealing findings. Of five hundred languages, they find that more than half of them (261) do not appear to be weight-sensitive, or at least the nature of their relationship to weight and stress remains obscure or undocumented. As they put it, "In about half of the sample languages, syllable weight plays no role for word stress" (2013c). Languages, such as French, in which the long vowel provides the basis for heavy stress were clearly in the minority (65 of the 500 languages studied; 2013c: sec. 2).

Judging from their world language map (2013c: feature 16A), there is no immediately obvious logic organizing trends that assert themselves in the distribution of languages in which similarities in stress and syllable weight and length can be found. South Africa, South America, and Australia all offer examples of languages with no apparent or known weight factor. But the same can also be said of Asia and other parts of the world. Nevertheless, Goedemans and van der Hulst do offer the following conclusions with regard to geographical distribution:

i. We notice a number of broad generalizations:
ii. We find no lexical stress in South America and Australia.
iii. Quantitative weight is found in all areas and families.
iv. We find a relative high frequency of prominence systems in Austronesian languages (where the contrast is between reduced vowel and full vowel).³
v. In Europe, the north shows more quantitative weight, while the south shows more prominence.

(2013c: sec. 3)

WALS allows us to take into account subtleties in stress that are difficult for English-speakers to get their heads (or rather their mouths) around. In my own experience, a native speaker of English will inevitably assume that length and stress will coincide, but this is not the case in all languages. Czech, for example, distinguishes systematically between stress and syllable length. The first syllable of words is always accented (except when proceeded by a preposition, in which case the stress is transferred to it). But the *čárka*—the length accent—will often force speakers to lengthen an unstressed syllable. In words in which the two coincide, such as *úterý* (Tuesday), the English-speaker will experience no particular problem, rhythmically speaking. The fact that the final syllable is long does not disturb English-speakers, who slip easily into the strong-weak-strong rhythm that mirrors the requirements of their own rhythmic competence. On the other hand, words that require a long second syllable while maintaining the obligatory first-syllable stress require much greater flexibility for English-speakers, who instinctively reject this form of distinction. Words such as *otázka* (question) are particularly irksome for English students of Czech. The English-speaker's rhythmic competence instinctively induces him or her to opt for a weak-strong-weak stress pattern, but the first-syllable stress rule of Czech prevents this. While the second syllable must be lengthened, the word accent falls clearly and decisively on the first syllable. The difficulty English-speakers experience in trying to come to terms with this stress distinction often gives rise to much laughter, for example, when English girls address their lovers using the male-gendered term of endearment *miláčku*, which can be translated as "honey." A term of endearment must be pronounced with tenderness but firmness, and the English-speaker's hesitation and stumbling over stress can appear both ridiculous and unconvincing to Czech-speakers.

This anecdote should remind us of the importance of distinguishing between primary and secondary stress. Goedemans and van der Hulst's research proves particularly interesting when considering the relationship between primary and secondary stress in languages, because highlighted accentuation invariably manipulates syllables (as we shall see in subsequent chapters). They argue:

> Assuming that the phonemes that make up words are organized into syllables, modern linguistic theory claims that **rhythm** is a manifestation of the fact that syllables are further grouped into constituents called **feet**, which are usually binary groupings of syllables. Standard Metrical Theory takes the grouping of syllables into feet as fundamental for the assignment of bounded primary stress. StressTyp is based on a separation of the treatment of **primary** and **secondary stress**. (2013b: sec. 1; emphasis in original)

As they argue in their discussion of "bounded systems" (2013a: sec. 2.1), weight-sensitive primary stress locations can take four different forms (at each edge of the word). "Rhythm types," in their opinion, "fall into just two categories, due to the fact that a rhythmic foot cannot contain two heavy syllables (because every heavy syllable constitutes a rhythmic beat)" (2013b: sec. 1). As a consequence, they argue that this difference may make it necessary to describe primary and secondary stress patterns separately (2013b: sec. 1).

At this stage, however, we are importing terms from metrics into linguistics, and it is far from clear whether the natural rhythm of the language and the manipulated and highlighted meter of an individual poem follow the same pattern. Nor is it clear whether we are speaking about the same kind of rhythm at all. Dividing phrasing into units may prove useful, but it significantly deforms our perception of continuity and organization in rhythm, and we should be wary of analysis that downplays continuity at the expense of highlighting the repetition of individual units. Goedemans and van der Hulst's findings are fascinating when it comes to considering the relationship between primary and secondary stress,[4] but we will have to return to languages we speak in order to verify whether such findings prove useful in explicating what is going on in speech and what is being transformed in the writing and reading of poems.

Before returning to French and English, it is nonetheless worth situating languages within the framework assembled by Goedemans and van der Hulst. Czech is one of the majority of languages that prefer first-syllable stress (the trochaic form). Goedemans and van der Hulst provide a breakdown and observe: "The prototypical rhythm pattern stresses every odd syllable from the left in languages with initial main stress, and every even syllable from the right in languages with penultimate main stress" (2013b: sec. 2.1). Trochaic rhythm dominates in Europe and South America and is crushingly dominant in Australia. This seems straightforward enough, but what are we to make of their conclusion "languages that have main stress but no rhythm abound" (2013b: sec. 2.5)? In their own opinion it remains "an open question whether the 'no rhythm' languages do have a foot type grouping but lack a clear phonetic manifestation of this grouping; in some cases such 'silent' grouping can be detected because it conditions other aspects of the phonology of a language" (sec. 2.5). In both French and English, as we shall see, the definition of rhythm and its analysis are always questions open to discussion.

Syllable

This venture into comparative linguistics should have one advantage. It should have prepared us for the fact that comparing syllables and accents in French and English proves to be considerably more complex than might initially have been expected. We all believe we know what a syllable is. Few English-speakers would have any difficulty determining the number of syllables in the words "today" or "tomorrow," and most speakers intuitively perceive "hire" to be monosyllabic while "higher" is perceived as disyllabic. In French, *bonjour* is clearly disyllabic and *au revoir* is trisyllabic. But in everyday speech an *e* is often added to the *r* in (*bonjour-e*) by the specialists of welcome etiquette: secretaries, switchboard operators, and shop assistants. On the other hand, it is commonplace to glide over the *e* in *au r(e)voir,* thereby reducing the expression to a disyllabic one, while *bonjour-e* becomes trisyllabic.

What happens in English? Most of us are not aware most of the time. It is hard to perceive, since the unstressed syllable is so frequently reduced to an ə, as in "elephant" (el-ə-phant). The natural tendency to reduce unaccented vowels in English in such words and phrases as "forgive" (fər-give), "oblivion" (ə-bli-vi-ən), and "I suppose so" (often pronounced sə-ppose so) can make it difficult to tell whether a syllable is being pronounced or not. Furthermore, dropping the subject of a sentence in dialogue in English is common, only going to prove that the necessity of systematically using pronouns is a cultural and grammatical norm rather than a semantic requirement. Slavic languages such as Czech, Polish, and Russian get by without pronouns most of the time, and so can English, as long as the speaker and his interlocutor are clearly identified in the conversation.

In truth the number of syllables pronounced and heard is often highly difficult to determine in everyday speech in English. Compare "dunno" to the equivalent expression in French, *sais-pas.* In everyday speech in French, speakers clearly drop the pronoun *je* and neglect to use the complement of the negation *ne* in *ne pas.* The four syllables are truncated into two clearly pronounced syllables. *Sais-pas* is emphatic and phonetically well defined. In the English example, "dunno," it is far more difficult to ascertain the syllable change. Does the "I" in "I don't know" actually disappear or is it reduced to a lightly pronounced ə?

This difference in the treatment of syllables is explained by the fact that the *structure phonématique* of the syllable is determined by a group of rules that vary from language to language (Dubois et al. 1994: 459). The syllable is a phoneme grouped around the vowel, but the vowel can be preceded or followed by a consonant (or both or neither). We can therefore distinguish between four forms of syllable: V, CV, VC, and CVC (V stands for vowel and C for consonant). True, certain languages seem to dispense with vowels, but this is only partially true. For English-speakers, "Bulgaria" is clearly quadrisyllabic, but for Bulgarians the first syllable in English is a clumsy rendering of the hard accent that separates the *B* and the *l* (B'lgaria, България).

Whether a vowel is heard or not in Czech is also difficult for English-speakers to determine. Czech is famous among linguists for a four-word sentence without vowels: *Strč prst skrz krk*, meaning "Stick your finger through your throat." This playful phrase demonstrates that Czech makes use of a liquid *r* that is perceived by the English-speaker's ear as a softened version of rə.

The definition that David Crystal (1997: 438) offers for the syllable concurs with the one provided in French by Jean Dubois and his coauthors (1994). While French linguists understand the syllable as "the fundamental structure that forms the basis of all groupings of phonemes in the spoken chain" (regroupement de phonèmes dans la chaîne parlée; Dubois et al. 1994: 459, my translation), Crystal understands the syllable to be "an element of speech that acts as a unit of rhythm" (438). Kirsten Malmkjær (1991), like Dubois and his colleagues, stresses that the constitution of the syllable varies from language to language. In addition, languages differ phonologically in terms of the kinds of syllable structure they permit. Every known language contains CV syllables—composed of a consonant followed by a vowel—but languages such as English and German permit a high degree of consonant clustering at the beginnings and ends of syllables, whereas Fijian and Hawaiian do not (Malmkjær 1991: 274).

French resembles Fijian and Hawaiian in this respect. Though there may be more than one consonant at the beginning of the syllable, the syllable form that dominates French is the CV one. The French-speaker will intuitively divide up *Je suis désolé* (I'm sorry) into five monosyllables—*Je suis dé-so-lé*—all of which follow the CV form, since the final *s* of *suis* is mute. This in itself contributes to consolidating the character of the French syllable. In fact the most fundamental difference between the syllable in French and English is accentual in nature. While the tonic accent of English words is strong, the structure of the French syllable is itself much more stable. Ironically, it is the strength of the accented syllable in English that helps dampen the unstressed syllable. In French, to a greater or lesser extent, all syllables are stressed, but weakly stressed. Phonetic analysis will prove easily enough that the length, intensity, and stress of each syllable in French words vary widely, but nonetheless each syllable preserves its integrity. If, for example, an *e* is cut in standard French, as in *sam(e)di* (Saturday), or preserved in southern French, as in *samedi*, the French-speaker's ear—and, indeed, the English-speaker's ear—will experience no difficulty in perceiving the exact number of syllables pronounced. As Henri Morier points out (1961: 146–49), the mute *e* (*e caduc*) is weakened to the point of disappearing in spoken French, though in the case of pronouns and personal pronouns, the muting of the *e* remains an option, as in *J(e) te dis la vérité* (I'm telling you the truth).

There is a historical dimension to this story of the solidity and stability of the French syllable. Until the sixteenth century, French, like English, had diphthongs and double vowels. "Time," "road," and "space" all contain diphthongs in modern English, and French had similar forms. But over the years these double vowels disappeared as the single vowel asserted itself. There are, therefore, three reasons why the French syllable became the central focus of poets and versification systems: the lack of the reduced vowel ə, the systematic tendency to privilege the CV form, and the absence of diphthongs.

These three traits made the syllable a stable element upon which French meters could rely. As we shall see, the meter can manipulate the syllable count. Contemporary French allows a certain leeway in the number of syllables pronounced, and the meter can encourage us to separate vowels or truncate them in order to preserve the syllable count. Whether we consider French verse as syllabic or accentual syllabic, it remains certain that the syllable count is crucial to perceiving regularity in French verse. However important the accent turns out to be, it is upon the syllable that the principles of order and harmony are based in French metrics. This focus has never been the case in English. Attempts in English to develop purely syllabic verse, such as those made by John Donne, invariably appear irregular to the modern ear. We do not perceive the repetition of series of syllable counts as soon as the underlying undulating accentual structure is removed.

Stress

Once we understand that word accent is less pronounced in French than in English, we will have grasped something fundamental in the difference between the movement of English and French speech. Furthermore, when we perceive the tendency to stress certain syllables at the expense of others in English, we will understand a distinguishing characteristic of that language. French tends to consolidate the status of the syllable; the syllable resists reduction and prefers to be truncated rather than downplayed. French is therefore perceived more as a repetitive movement of clearly discernible syllables, whereas English undulates in a rising and falling motion.

Paradoxically, both French-speakers and English-speakers experience the language of their counterparts as musical and often remark upon its singsong quality. In my experience, however, the same terms are used to express quite different impressions. English-speakers are remarking on the intonation of French that rises and falls in an animated, vivacious fashion. Of course, American soap operas have accustomed us to almost hysterical intonation patterns—quite unlike those to be found in most American dialects—but most English-speakers feel their intonation to be rather flat and unremarkable compared to that of French. On the other hand, French-speakers appear to be referring to accentuation when they notice the songlike rhythm of English, the strong-weak-strong-weak accentuation promoted so well on the international scene by rock 'n' roll on MTV.

Clarifying the difference between accents and syllables in French is far from straightforward; a schematic opposition between French and English based on phonetics will not suffice to clarify how the voice of the poem emerges in its versification. Stress patterning is complex because it involves linguistic constraints, specific styles, and social as well as personal patterning. The teacher does not use the same accentuation as the student, nor the doctor as the patient. And all of us are many people—a man must play the husband, the father, the colleague, and the friend. In everyday life each of us moves from role to role, adopting different stances, and each stance entails distinctively different intonational and accentual patternings as we move from relationship to relationship.

Accentuation does not stand outside politics either: it has a class dimension. The so-called upper classes speak to those they perceive as inferior with an accentuation that reveals both their complacent sense of superiority and the nervous self-consciousness of those unsure as to whether that supposed superiority will be recognized and acknowledged. These distinctions are legitimate sociolinguistic concerns, and they should not be dismissed. But we must stand back from such questions for the moment in order to form an overall picture of accentuation. What are the fundamental linguistic constraints of accentuation, and how do they compare in French and English?

The accent is something of a sore spot in French poetics. The French poetic tradition has been going strong since the late Middle Ages and shows no signs of dying out, despite regular outcries from the Académie française and public lamentation in the French press about the forces threatening the purity and clarity of the language and its literature. French poetry needs no defenders. Strangely, however, for more than two hundred years an almost unbroken tradition chants an undercurrent in French verse: the melody of misgiving. A great many French poets, translators, and specialists in versification lament the weakness of the French accent. Maurice Grammont and Henri Morier make frequent reference to Latin meters with their long and short syllables (e.g., 1989; 1961). And when Morier waxes poetical about the poetry of rhythm and the rhythm of poetry, he often falls back upon German poetry, with its meters based on strong stress. In 1763 Olivet complained about the weakness of French accentuation, "Comment voulez-vous donc qu'un étranger scande des vers qui n'ont aucun poids certain, aucune régularité?" (How do you expect a foreigner to scan lines of verse that have no weight, no regularity?; quoted in Gouvard 1996: 228). And L. Bonaparte joined Olivet in his lamentation in 1819:

> La versification française manque de rythme; les syllabes que nous appelons accentuées sont disposés à caprices sans aucune raison, de sorte que celles d'un hémistiche ou d'un vers s'opposent quelquefois diamétralement à celles du vers suivant, et ainsi les accents sont variés et sans ordre. (French versification lacks rhythm; the syllables that we call accented are arranged arbitrarily without reason, so that the accented syllables in one half of the line sometimes oppose diametrically those of the next line: thus the accents are varied and without any order; quoted in Gouvard: 239, my translation.)

This theme would be taken up once more by Charles Bally. A sad song lies behind the theme: If poetry is poetry, it is because of its rhythm. Poetry without rhythm would be prose. The logical conclusion of this reasoning is, as we shall see, absurd but inescapable. If there is no rhythm in French poetry, then there is no poetry in French. French as a language is inapt for poetic creation. This is an argument so much at odds with the reality of things that no English-speaker would think of uttering it. But to a more rationalist mindset, unhampered by the pragmatics of the reality of a living and moving poetic tradition, the argument found many ears, and adherents were far from rare. Just as French teenagers often scorn the use of French in pop songs today,[5] lovers of French poetry are often uncomfortable with the weakness of French word accent and feel a sense of awe on hearing Shakespeare or Goethe when actors declaim their metrical verse.

This was the attitude that Meschonnic was struggling against when he wrote his *Critique du rythme* (1982). His monumental contribution to poetics, aesthetics, and the philosophy and politics of rhythm in this and other works is hard to summarize, to say the least (see also Meschonnic 1985, 1990, 1995b, 1999, 2001, 2007b). Meschonnic sees poetic creation as the height of linguistic creativity and speech as a living organ of thinking (to use Humboldt's turn of phrase) that enables human beings to define and create themselves. Like Pound, Meschonnic sees rhythm as an expression of individuality, and individuality is not transposed into language from the outside. Speech is essentially intersubjective: language is shaped by the personalities of speakers and writers. This conclusion makes speech and literary creation the locus of becoming. Just as thinking takes place in language, the poet creates himself in the poem.

As a poet himself, Meschonnic was hardly likely to accept the absurd reasoning that led French poets to doubt the capacity of the language to sustain its tradition. Relying on Émile Benveniste's reappraisal of Plato's definition of rhythm as strong-weak-strong-weak undulation (1966: 327–35) associated with the verb "to flow" (*couler* in French; 1966: 327), Meschonnic went on to develop a whole new theory of *rythme*.[6] This redefinition of rhythm will inevitably prove difficult to grasp for the English-speaker. I would argue that what Meschonnic has in mind when he speaks of *rythme* bears more resemblance to "configuration" and "patterning" in English than what is commonly referred to as rhythm. Like French, English has tended to borrow the Platonic meaning attributed to the term, and English-speakers may well resist a definition of rhythm that runs counter to this dominant tradition.

A further difficulty arises in the semantic role of rhythm in Meschonnic's thought. Because rhythm is meaningful in his thinking, I have preferred to use the term "voice" to designate the orchestrated patterning of syllables and sounds in meaningful configurations. Meschonnic's contribution to poetics and versification is immense, and few scholars have his erudition or master as many languages as he does. Like Roman Jakobson, Levý, and M. L. Gasparov, Meschonnic waltzes into half a dozen languages and reappraises the validity of the so-called rules of versification used to attempt to explain regularity and stylistic innovation. Meschonnic, unlike Levý, was also perfectly well versed in the shortcomings of traditional English foot metrics.

Nonetheless, Meschonnic's refusal to join those who lamented the weakness of the French accent should be put in perspective. Although it often gives rise to obscure, unfounded arguments, intuition is rarely totally misguided. Olivet, Bonaparte, Bally, Grammont, and Morier were reacting to something very real when they listened to the difference between French and English accentuation. If rhythm is reduced to meter and meter is reduced to strong-stress rhythms or syllable-stress rhythms, then French must of course be found to be lacking. French cannot sustain these forms of meters without imposing very strong constraints on the movement of everyday speech, as French rappers do. Stress-based rhythms may be popular and they may sound cool to French ears, but they do not sound natural. To most French-speakers, they still do not sound French.

Disentangling these arguments proves difficult, and things are not helped by the fact that in neither English nor French has a clear distinction been made between rhythm and meter. Even in the works of the most prominent scholars in the field in English (Attridge 1982, 1995, 1996; Cureton 1992, 1996; Wesling 1996) the terms tend to be conflated. And French scholars tend to fall into the same trap (Grammont 1989; Mazaleyrat 1990; Morier 1961). This omission leads less discerning critics such as Jan Mazaleyrat to celebrate rhythm as some kind of compensation for the lack of stress-based meters (1990: 11–14, 15–19, and 28–30).

Not until Meschonnic and Benoît de Cornulier began to clarify things (in very different ways) did the true importance of accentuation in French verse assert itself. In his *Théorie du vers* (1980: 279–88), Cornulier puts things very simply. The only accent that is of metrical significance is the terminal accent at the end of the hemistich. In the following line from Victor Hugo's "À un poëte aveugle," the only two accents of metrical importance are those that fall at the close of the first hemistich on "ombre" and, at the close of the line, on the final syllable of "clarté":

>   /   /
> L'aveugle voit dans l'ombre un monde de clarté.
>
> (Hugo 1967: 521)

What happens to the mute *e* (*e caduc*)? As we shall see, metrical rules govern syllabic pronunciation when reading French verse. The mute *e* is pronounced and counted if it occurs within the hemistich. If it occurs at the caesura or at the end of the line, however, it is truncated. In this way "aveugle" becomes trisyllabic and "monde" becomes disyllabic, but "ombre," falling at the caesura, is pronounced as a monosyllable. Poetic diction maintains the meter. Regularity is preserved through metrical manipulation of the line both internally and at its end. This observation entails two very important distinctions. First, the metrical unit of French verse is not the equivalent of the metrical unit of English verse. Second, the verse line of French verse is not the equivalent of its English counterpart. While the metrical unit in French hinges on the phrase, which may vary from four to six syllables, the metrical unit of English hinges on the clitic group—the accented syllable and its attendant unaccented syllables, prior to it and following it.

In French the longest uninterrupted verse line—the longest *vers simple* (simple verse)—is the octosyllabic line. Cornulier argues that the ear cannot discern a longer series of syllables (1980: 16–35, 90, 258–62). Whether he is right remains to be seen, but the metrical tradition would seem to agree, for no longer lines can be found undivided in conventional French verse. Alexandrines usually break up 6:6, as in the following example: "Elle était déchaussée, / elle était décoiffée" (Her shoes were off, her hair undone; "Aurore: XXI," Hugo 1967: 521). Decasyllables invariably break up 4:6, as in Ronsard's line "Ainsi je sçay, / que Poëte je suis" ("La lyre," quoted in Morier 1961: 344). As Morier points out, in the most ancient French poetry, dating back to the twelfth century, decasyllables using what is called the *césure a majori,* which breaks the line 6:4, can be found (345). Voltaire made use of this form of decasyllable in the eighteenth century, and in late nineteenth-century verse it made a comeback with Verlaine, who used 4:6 and 6:4 forms together, as in the following lines:

> Pour une bonne fois, / séparons-nous, [6:4]
> Très chers messieurs / et si belles madames. [4:6]
>
> (quoted in Morier 1961: 344)[7]

What does this mean for accentual configurations within the hemistich? They are free. Free, that is, from the metrical point of view. Order and harmony will be sustained so long as the syllable count is preserved, consolidated by the end of the verse line or hemistich coinciding with the end of the phrase and the phrase-terminal accent, as in the preceding example. Of course, as Meschonnic emphasizes, all accentuation is meaningful, and poets excel at juxtaposing and contrasting different accentual events. This was the point Pound had in mind when he insisted on the power of poems to trace emotions. This is what he meant when he spoke of how difficult it is for poets to try to capture and imitate another poet's rhythm. Nonetheless, meter is not about style or personalized movement. Meter is a simple framework, an expressive space. Rhythm must animate it and make it dynamically eventful if the poem is to attract and sustain our interest. In this respect poems may open with verse lines that are rather flat and draw little attention to themselves, while the following ones build up into a dynamic climax full of movement. Syntax and the accentual patterning internal to the verse can either confirm or tug against the pounding regularity of meter. In the following example, the three final lines of the strophe (and the poem) return to metrical syntax in appeasement after a charged opening line that does not, however, contradict the metrical structure and that respects the 6:6 division perfectly.

> Chante! Milton chantait: chante! Homère a chanté.
> Le poëte des sens perce la triste brume;
> L'aveugle voit dans l'ombre un monde de clarté.
> Quand l'œil du corps s'éteint, l'œil de l'esprit s'allume.
>
> (Hugo 1967: 521)

Accents of different natures and functions are at work here. Certain accents are harnessed by the meter in order to maintain the structure. Others form part of the varied and dynamic free play of rhythm.

The difference between the movement of French and English verse is consolidated by two further factors. The first is related to the place of the accent within the phrase itself. The second is related to the way we perceive the movement of speech in consecutive phrases. The main accent of the sentence may occur at any place in English. In French, on the contrary, the main accent of the phrase invariably falls upon the final syllable. If we compare the two following phrases we can see this clearly:

> /
> Cette année
>
> /
> Cette année-là

Or, to take a more dramatic example:

> /
> Parce que je t'aime!
> (Because I love you!)
>
> /
> Parce que je ne t'aime pas!
> (Because I don't love you!)

In French there tend to be no post-tonic syllables (*syllabes post-toniques*).[8] As syllables are added to the phrase, the phrasal accent is displaced to the final syllable. Unlike English accentuation, French stress is not primarily word-dependent. For this reason exclamations are often arranged differently in the two languages, syntactically speaking. An English-speaker has no trouble hammering home his love of tea by redoubling the stress on "love," as in the following phrase:

> /
> I just love tea!

French-speakers expressing the same sentiment will tend to opt for apposition—division of the phrase into two parts. They can thus hammer home with the same vigour their love of tea by emphasizing the phrase-final stress of each part of the sentence.

       /   /
Le thé, je l'adore!

The word-stress on *adore* would be weakened if it were not placed at the end of the phrase.

How does the fact that French allows for no post-tonic syllables affect the way we perceive one phrase flowing into another? Fundamentally. This impact can be heard clearly if we compare the following phrase and its French translation:

The movement / of English / rises / and falls.
Le mouvement / de l'anglais / monte / et descend.

The division of these sentences into segments gives an entirely artificial representation of the actual movement of the phrase itself, but it should suffice for our purposes to show the way that the two languages move. English flows freely into various unfolding forms. The accent of the clitic phrase can be situated at the beginning, at the end, or in the middle. Similarly, the main syntactic accent can be found at any place within the phrase. The main focus of the French clitic phrase is the end, and the last syllable of the sentence is invariably the main focus of the sentence. For the same reason the end of the hemistich and the end of the verse form the logical focal points of French stress patterning in metrical verse.

The lack of strong word-stress in French induces French-speakers to manipulate their syntax in order to ensure that the end is always highlighted in verse, and that a major stress is always found at the end of the phrase. This point should not be laboured, and the diversity of the movement of French should not be underestimated. There is great variety in French syntax, but the various forms in use are subject to this rule. If we want to translate "I'll never trust you again!" with heavy emphasis on the "you," then *toi* must be manoeuvred to the end of the phrase or the phrase must be broken up:

Je ne ferais jamais plus confiance à toi!
or
À toi, je ne ferais jamais plus confiance!

Is English more expressive, more poetic, than French? The very question is absurd.[9] All languages enable their speakers to express themselves. Indeed, a language that does not have the potential for poetic expressivity, in the widest sense of the word, is hard to imagine. It would certainly be laughable to presume that French poets did not have the expressive means to do their job. In this sense Meschonnic's critique of the formalist prejudice involved in celebrating strong-weak rhythms is welcome, and a revision of the Platonic conception of poetic rhythm reduced to undulation should open up new horizons. Free verse and free-verse theory would seem to make such a critique unavoidable.

From the comparative perspective, the question is simpler. French poets make use of their language and their language provides them with a means of setting up patterns of regularity using syllable count and terminal accents. English makes use of the undulation proper to all strong-stressed Germanic languages. Syllables count in English verse, but they count only in relation to accents, as the offbeats between beats.

It is, nevertheless, worth highlighting the importance of accentuation in French in order to dispel the prejudice that Meschonnic and Cornulier were working against. Morier, whose ear for the movement of verse is unequalled among contemporary specialists in versification, fell prey to a certain nostalgia for Germanic meters. Perhaps the fact that he was Swiss did not help. In a country in which German dominates, the presence of stress-based rhythms must have encroached on the literary circles in Geneva in which he moved. Morier's taste for metrical beating is obvious in the German examples he gives, in his celebration of rhythm in poetry, and in his analysis of tempo in the reading of poems. But he certainly did not allow his taste for accentuation to pervert his perception of the movement of French verse. Morier proved highly sensitive to the diversity of French accentuation, distinguishing between five types of accent in French and giving examples (1961: 19–42).

1. *Accent horizontal (accent de longueur)* (the horizontal accent, length accent):

    /
    Papa! (Morier 1961: 20)

2. *Accent vertical* (the vertical accent), which could be divided into an affective one:

         /
   C'est fantastique! (28)

   and an intellectual one:

             /   /
   Il ne s'agit pas d'induction, mais de déduction. (31)

3. *Accent vertical mixte* (the mixed vertical accent):

     /   /   /
   Le Père, le Fils et le Saint-Esprit (35)

4. *Accent diagonal* (the diagonal accent):

                       /
   Les korrigoans venus menus, hop! (36)

5. *Accent oxytonique polymorphe* (the polymorphous oxytonic accent):

       /
   C'est Vénus toute entière à sa proie attachée. (38)

Like many of the Greco-Latin inventions of versification systems throughout Europe, these terms are not exactly user-friendly, but the accents themselves are very real, palpably expressive. What is of course remarkable is that these accents are expressive in speech in general. What does this signify? It reveals something fundamental that should be simple but which theory and formalist paradigms have tended to obscure: that it is language that is expressive—speech, not stress. Language attracts attention to itself when something meaningful is said and when the meaning is highlighted in a meaningful manner. At all levels, from the word to the phrase, from the syllable to the strophe, accentuation functions by highlighting powerful speech. It is speech that provides the means and the force for a meaningful poetic moment. Only when we have reduced rhythm to meter and meter to syllables and accents, chopped up, do we forget where the rudimentary force of poetic speech originates.

Accent and Meter

It should now be clear why we must understand the relationship between the meter and accents: not all accents are metrical. Are all accents rhythmical? For Meschonnic and Cornulier, yes, and Grammont and Mazaleyrat would concur. But where the latter two confuse and conflate metrical and rhythmic accents, it important to distinguish, as Meschonnic and Cornulier do, between conventional metrical requirements—accentual structures that emerge and impose themselves—and free line-internal rhythmic patterning. Metrical accentuation leads us to anticipate the repetition of conventional forms. Indeed, when we perceive a metrical structure asserting itself, the French poem induces us to maintain that structure by pronouncing and counting syllables such as the mute *e* (*e caduc*) within the line and truncating those syllables at strategic positions at the ends of hemistichs and lines to maintain the syllable count.

Structures require conformity. Rules are set up to be obeyed or transgressed, not to be ignored and disregarded. Traditional French meters require conformity at the end of each line or hemistich, but within the scope of the structure, French accentual patterning is rich and varied. Free-verse apologists tended to set up a straw man when they criticized conformity. Pound and Eliot and other innovators did not take such a line. They admired tradition but sought to revitalize it by breaking out of the harness of established forms and structures. The iambic pentameter and the French alexandrine had become such established forms that it was difficult to imagine English and French without such meters. The conventional had come to seem natural. Even in experiments it kept creeping back.

Nonetheless, however difficult it transpired for free-verse poets to break free of meter, it is important to stress the inherent freedom within meter. Meter is no prison. Meter is a game within which the rules open up free space for play. Three players are involved in the realization of metrical structure: First there is the meter itself, a clearly discerned rule-bound, established structure that sets up a basic repeating schema, be it based on syllable count, stresses, or a mixture of the two. Second, the syntax, varied and changing, can opt to fully and firmly realize line endings and stanza endings by coming to a full stop, or light pauses can be used at the ends of lines to leave precarious endings or send us moving onwards with the tug of the as-yet-unfinished phrase. All great poets know how to use syntax to pull against the meter and how to use the meter to underscore the finality of a phrase. This sensitivity must, however, be discerned by the third player: the reader, who may choose to stress the phrasing or the meter or may oscillate between the two in his or her emotional response to the meaning of the poem.

The reader, the meter, and the syntax are thus involved in a complex tug-of-war between sense and sensibility in which meaning, movement, and emotion work together. This combination was something that the great poeticians, such as Morier, Meschonnic, Jan Mukařovský, Attridge, and Donald Wesling, implicitly understood. But it has often been forgotten by specialists in metrics and linguists—even the greatest of them, such as Roman Jakobson.

Ultimately it all comes down to the question that Pound used to ask: do we listen to the poem? If so, we remain within the dynamic interacting forces of meaningful expression. The poem will bring us back to meaning and movement, to sense and emotion. The study of metrics, on the other hand, tends to encourage us to think of poems in terms of poetry and movement in terms of structure; it invites us to think in terms of form, not meaning. The answer is simple: stress is always meaningful, from the child's cry *Papa!* in Morier's accent example in the previous section (page 84) to the profoundly expressive monotony of despair expressed by Shakespeare's Macbeth in these famous lines:

> Tomorrow, and tomorrow, and tomorrow
> Creeps in this petty pace from day to day
> To the last syllable of recorded time.
>
> (*Macbeth* 5.5., Shakespeare 1987: 1332)

It will be necessary to return to poems to fully understand how accents assert themselves, how phrasing consolidates syllable count, and how rhythm dramatically and dynamically both realizes and tugs against the overarching framework meter. We must return to see whether our theorizing advances us in practice—this is the test of all theory. For the present, this discussion of poetic form, which has by necessity divorced us from the close analysis of poems, has the merit of advancing the comparison of versification systems. It enables us to make six fundamental distinctions between French and English verse that should help clarify the nature and the role of meter.

1. Meter is not an abstract schema that imposes itself on poems but is part of the organic movement of the poem itself. The meter is indivisible from the language in which the poem is written. In English the syllable is weak and the accent is strong. For this reason English versification harnesses accentuation, reinforcing strategically placed accents and subordinating accented and unaccented syllables to the meter. In French the syllable is strong and clearly defined. Consequently the meter harnesses the syllable and downplays the rhythmic interaction of accentuation within the metrical unit, using stress as a means of redoubling closure at the end of the metrical unit.

2. Meter is dumb; poetry does not speak. Even poems themselves are voiceless until they are apprehended and interpreted. The reader must intuitively realize the meter. In traditional English verse this involves discerning and preserving the metrical beating. In traditional French verse this involves highlighting stress at the strategic points at the end of the metrical unit, the hemistich, or the verse line.

3. Just as English metrics focuses the reader's attention on stress and French metrics focuses attention on syllable count, the metrical units in the two forms of versification are very different. The metrical unit of English verse is based on the clitic group: the main stress and attendant unstressed syllables. The metrical unit in French verse is based on the phrase. In this sense the ten-syllable pentameter usually has five metrical units in English, while the twelve-syllable alexandrine usually has only two.

4. The difference in the nature and the size of these two metrical units exerts different constraints on the two systems of versification. In French the caesura and the line ending become metrical prerequisites. If either is downplayed or effaced, it becomes difficult to perceive the principle of regularity that the meter serves to assert and maintain. In English verse, on the contrary, there is no metrical requirement that the caesura be preserved. It is the relentless flow and repetition of accentuation that asserts itself in the

example from Macbeth's "Tomorrow" soliloquy quoted above. Where are we to mark the caesura? And, in truth, do we need one? The meter pounds on, beat after beat, whether strategic pauses intervene or not. In this sense pausing belongs to the expressive realization of speech and poetic rhythm, not to the metrical requirements of English verse. In a similar way, though to a lesser extent, the line end in English verse is less significant than its French equivalent. The meter will flow on in English whether the line is clearly marked or not. Run-on lines in English verse are commonplace; they are understandably rather rare in traditional French verse.

5. The status of the line ending makes rhyme in French versification more important than in English versification. Rhyme, stress, and syntax combine to define the metrical unit, the line, in simple verse, and the second of the two metrical units in complex meters such as the alexandrine and the decasyllable. Unrhymed metrical verse in French is extremely rare, while in English blank verse is commonplace. The crucial role that rhyme plays in French metrics goes some way to explaining why Shakespeare's characters speak in unrhymed verse for the most part, while those of Corneille, Racine, and Molière speak in rhymed verse.

6. Meter sets up a principle of regularity. In the French and English systems of versification, however, we are dealing with distinct forms of regularity. The principle of regularity that English verse gravitates towards is isochrony, the regular beating of accentual repetition. In French a similar force induces us to pronounce each syllable clearly in order to preserve the syllable count; this principle is known as *isosyllabisme*. André Spire suggested that *isosyllabisme* is misleading as a notion. As he put it, "Les syllabes d'un alexandrin toutes différentes de durée, d'intensité, de timbre ne sont identiques que de nom" (The syllables of the alexandrine, each one different in terms of duration, intensity, and timbre, are identical in terms of their name alone; Meschonnic 1982: 401). As a reading of any English sonnet will prove, the isochronous principle is no less mythical. Beats in poems

rarely conform to the metronome that Pound mentioned. But in music and poetry it is often the impression that proves more powerful than the reality.[10] The essential point is that regularity *is* perceived in English metrical verse. A heightened regularity must be perceived and maintained by the reader in both French and English verse. In French this regularity must gravitate towards a principle based on phrases, defined in terms of syllable count.

Metrical Manipulation of Accents

To understand the metrical manipulation of stressed and unstressed syllables it is necessary to understand how the forces of meter make it possible to "promote" and "demote" syllables—that is to say, how it consolidates weak syllables in order to make them work as beats and weakens strong syllables in order to make them work as the ebb of the meter in the offbeat position. It was Derek Attridge (1982) who coined these crucial terms to explain these fundamental processes that had long remained unexplained, and that were, in fact, obscured by clumsy attempts to integrate metrical manipulation into traditional foot metrics. Indeed, Attridge's system integrates these phenomena elegantly into a coherent and fairly simple system of versification that is based on his own binary scansion.

Attridge was not the first literary scholar to distinguish between metrical beating and accentuation in poetry, but he was the first poetician to insist on the necessity of a binary scansion that distinguishes between stress contour, the accentuation of syntactic phrasing, and metrical beating. As a lover of poems,[11] Attridge remains at all times close to Morier, Meschonnic, Mukařovský, and Levý in his appreciation of the interaction of meaning and poetic form. His book *The Rhythms of English Poetry* (1982) caused a minor revolution in metrics throughout the English-speaking world (see Cureton 1992; Wesling 1996). As well, it had some impact in Germany (Küper 1988) and found an echo in France to a lesser extent (Underhill 2009b, 2009d).

However, in a recent exchange of emails, Derek Attridge expressed his disappointment that in the classroom the situation has changed little since the beginning of the twentieth century when it comes to discussing poems, rhythm, and metrics. A hundred years of free-verse experimentation has taken the emphasis off regularity, and the lack of familiarity with regular verse seems to have dampened sensitivity to metrics in students and readers (and perhaps among teachers and translators too). But free verse is not to blame. The dry formalism of metrics and versification themselves has put both teachers and students off the subject. Poems speak to us, but treatises on versification often seem very far removed from the moving experience of the poem. At any rate, many people seem unable to find anything of significance in work on versification when it comes to explaining the way language moves us by its movement.

Attridge's work, like that of Wesling and Richard D. Cureton in the anglophone world and that of Levý and Meschonnic in their countries, has often been scantily read. As a consequence, the lessons such work has to teach about metrics and versification have rarely been understood or retained in analysis. This situation is sad, because as both Meschonnic and Attridge know all too well, traditional metrics is no more than a dead end: foot scansion can explain nothing about metrical regularity and how it is maintained. Promotion and demotion, Attridge's innovative solutions, are necessary elements when it comes to explaining the coherence of meter, the way it asserts itself, the way it is coloured by personal rhythms, and the way it can be undermined or abandoned by free verse or competing meters.

The first point that must be underlined is that the stress contour does not have to conform to the meter. To say that an iambic pentameter is a line with five accents is misleading. As Marina Tarlinskaja suggests (1976), the pentameter often has four accents. But, more importantly, it may have either four or six, or three or seven. Meanwhile, a five-stress line is often a tetrameter, a four-beat line. As Tarlinskaja's study clearly demonstrates, accents and metrical beats fail to coincide more often than not. Consider the first line of Shakespeare's first sonnet:

/ / / /
From fairest creatures we desire increase,

("Sonnet 1," 1988: 3)

Despite its four accents, this line is perceived (and invariably read) as a perfectly regular five-beat line. Other lines draw further from the five-stress metrical schema:

\ \ /
So is it not with me as with that Muse

("Sonnet 21," 1988: 13)

In this line, only "Muse" is clearly stressed, with "not," "me," and perhaps "that" each carrying a lighter secondary stress (which I indicate here as \) in the natural undulating movement of English. Once again, however, this line is perceived as a perfectly regular pentameter. It is partly because we do not tend to read poetry as we pronounce everyday speech. The expectations we have of the sonnet, as a regular poem comprising fourteen pentametric lines, encourage us to seek out regularity where it can be found. This entails manipulating the stressing of normal speech. Traditional foot metrics sought various means of explaining this process and invented a whole series of terms (such as "wrenched accent" and "hovering accent"; Cuddon 1991: 1045). Such terms and explanations were never integrated into a coherent explanation of the rules of regularity. The very concepts were, moreover, revealed to be totally useless when it came to explaining why one three-stress line appeared regular while another was perceived as wholly irregular. Worse still, traditional theories found it impossible to explain why many five-stress lines could not function as pentameters and why four-stress lines failed to work as tetrameters.[12]

Unfortunately we must enter into the chaos of traditional foot metrics, with its obfuscation and its pedantic taxonomy, if we are to appreciate the elegance and efficiency of Attridge's system. It would certainly be unfair to hold a literary dictionary editor such as Cuddon responsible for this state of affairs. However, using an entry from his well-informed and widely read *Dictionary of Literary Terms and Literary Theory* (1991) should give a fairly standard example of the way traditional foot scansion tries to account for metrical manipulation and the way, as Attridge sadly pointed out, students continue to be trained in reading and analyzing poems.

Cuddon tries to explain the way meter manipulates stress by focusing on four lines from Alexander Pope, a poet who, it should be remembered, was strict in his adherence to meter and who furthermore favoured clearly defined, syntactically reinforced line endings. As the reader should instinctively perceive, the lines present no apparent problem from a metrical point of view—these are four regular iambic pentameters. (Only the sentiment expressed might seem objectionable to today's readers.)

> Nothing so true as what you once let fall,
> Most women have no characters at all.
> Matter too soft a lasting mark to bear,
> And best distinguish'd by black, brown or fair.
>
> (Cuddon 1991: 1020–21)

This appears simple enough, but when traditional metrics is brought to bear, confusion opens up. Cuddon finds no particular difficulty in accounting for the first and third lines as iambic pentameters (rightly considering the first-foot inversion in both lines to be a perfectly traditional stylistic effect). He scans these lines as follows:

> / x   x / x / x / x /
> Nothing / so true / as what / you once / let fall,
> / x   x / x / x   / x /
> Matter / too soft / a last / ing mark / to bear,

The other two lines, however, cause havoc with his system of interpretation. Because, like most traditional analysts, Cuddon lacks a coherent distinction between stress contour and metrical beating—between beat and accent—his explanation quickly becomes tortuous and incomprehensible. The line "Most women have no characters at all" he scans as follows:

> /   /   x x x / x x   x /
> Most wo / men have no / characters / at all.

Cuddon explains this as a sequence involving a spondee followed by a tribrach (which is rare, he reminds us), then a dactyl followed by an iamb. He makes no attempt to explain how these four feet make up a five-beat line. He offers two alternative readings (which the reader is spared here), but neither explains how the line is perceived as a regularly alternating series of stresses and unstressed syllables. The fourth line he scans as follows:

> x /   x / x   x /   / x /
> And best / distinguish'd / by black, / brown or fair.

This, Cuddon informs us, constitutes iamb/bachius/iamb/cretic (or amphimacer). Once more he offers an alternative reading but no explanation of the perceived regularity of the verse. How do they work as regular lines? "Pope has such a sensitive ear for the delicate nuances of words that he often eludes scansion," Cuddon suggests (1021). Once we have understood the clarity and efficiency of Attridge's alternative system, it should be clear that it is Cuddon and foot-metrics analysts who are eluding the issue, not Pope who is eluding the meter. Hiding behind technical terms, foot scansion proves wholly incapable of explaining anything.

Attridge, on the other hand, distinguishes between three levels of stress: stressed (+s), unstressed (−s), and stressable (s). These make up the stress contour—the way the phrase would be read were it not to be found in a metrical poem. Beats (B) and offbeats (o) are invariably realized, but implied offbeats do exist. These are moments, pauses between words—often signalled by a comma in the syntax—moments at which the pause functions as a weak point between juxtaposed accents. Equipped with this crucial distinction, Attridge's scansion proves perfectly adequate for explaining the perceived regularity of Pope's lines:

```
+s −s  s  +s −s    +s   s   +s  +s  +s
Nothing so true as what you once let fall,
 B   o   B  o    B    o B      o  B

+s  +s −s    −s    s   +s −s −s  −s +s
Most women have no characters at all.
 o   B    o    B   o  B  o B   o  B

+s −s s  +s  −s +s −s   +s   −s   +s
Matter too soft a lasting mark to bear,
 B   o  B   o  B   o   B    o   B

−s +s  −s +s  −s  −s +s   +s    −s +s
And best distinguish'd by black, brown or fair.
 o  B   o  B    o   B  (o) B   o   B
```

Does the metrical beating appear regular? Yes. Does it pervert the stress contour? Only if we understand stress contour to mean that beating acts upon word stress. It would be more accurate to speak of shading. The metrical beating will appear to deform word stress only if we presume that some mechanical metrical force is being imposed on the poem. This is certainly the caricatured representation of meter that many specialists of metrics endorse. Bombastic declamation would be perceived in the same way, but this is hardly what Attridge is suggesting. He does not offer the beating of syllables as the end result of a process of metrical manipulation of stress. He demonstrates that two unresolved forces are at work shaping the line, ensuring suppleness and variety, without which mechanical metrical beating would soon become unbearable. The above scansion shows the way in which "once" and "fall" are reinforced as accents while "let" is demoted in the phrase "once let fall," and the way "too" is weakened to allow "soft" to be redoubled energetically as the focal point of the accentuation. It would be possible to read "by black, brown or fair" with a promoted beat on "by" and a demoted stressed syllable on "black," but the above reading appears more natural: the comma between "black" and "brown" invites us to pause between the two stresses. In this way the undulation remains unperturbed.

The intricacies involved in promotion and demotion should not be underestimated. When is it possible to demote a stressed syllable and when is it possible to promote an unstressed syllable? Attridge explains this in some detail (1982: 164–72), just as he explains the rules governing the introduction of implied offbeats (172–75). The general principles of these mechanisms can, however, be grasped fairly quickly.

Attridge defines the "promotion rule" as follows: "An unstressed syllable may realize a beat when it occurs between two unstressed syllables" (165). He offers this line of verse: "Balanced on her wings of light." Attridge explains that because three unstressed syllables follow the initial stress on "Balanced," a provisional stress asserts itself on the central syllable. The weakness of "-lanced" and "her" invite the rhythm to promote "on."

Does this make for a strong stress? No. Indeed, promoted beats are often experienced as less salient than demoted stresses. The meter does not obscure the meaning of the poem, and the beat can neither eradicate word stress nor deny the significance of the word in question. But the stress is diminished, and a light pull on the stress contour will reshape the movement in order to prevent us from getting the impression that the line has strayed too far from acceptable metricality. English and other strong-stress languages favour the alternation between strong and weak syllables, so this metrical convention that is intuitively imposed by poetry readers is, to some extent, only realizing one of the essential properties of the language. Children learn rules of demotion and promotion in nursery rhymes, and they go on to apply those rules when they invent their own rhyming chants.

Just as three weak syllables can realize a beat on the internal syllable, demotion involves manipulation of the central stress of three consecutive stresses. Attridge defines the "demotion rule" as follows: "A stressed syllable may realize an offbeat when it occurs between two stressed syllables, or after a line-boundary and before a stressed syllable" (1982: 169). He offers these two examples: "Then out bespoke the brown, brown bride" and "Full fathom five thy father lies" (169). In the first, the series of three stresses—"brown, brown bride"—allows the internal stress to be downplayed to the profit of the two external stresses. In this way the undulation is preserved. In the second, the beginning of the line acts as a minor pause and the first stress is demoted to the profit of the second, which once again enables the line to move from weak to strong, thereby continuing the beating of the poem. "Full" remains full—full of sense—the alliteration itself highlights this fact. But the meter allows the syllable to be subtly demoted to maintain the regularity of the verse.

Where did foot metrics fall down? In attempting to impose one form of accentuation on another, by reducing stress contour to meter or meter to stress contour. To conflate the two is disastrous. Attridge's system provides a more subtle and ultimately more reliable model because it remains closer to the reader's and the listener's experiences of the poem. Two forces are set in motion: meaning and meter must combine, and there are no strict rules for determining which one will prevail in the interactive tension set up when the two come together. Various sensitive readings of the above lines are possible, but to deny the existence of meter or meaning would be to lose much of the interest of these lines. Attridge is concerned with interpreting the underlying forces at work, but only the reader can interpret the poem itself, and each interpretation says much about our intuitive understanding of poetry and how we feel about rules and tradition.

As we saw in the example of contemporary French rap, chanted verse in French can gravitate towards isochrony. But traditional French *comptines* invariably observe strict syllable counts, far stricter than in "Humpty Dumpty" and "Little Miss Muffet." Implied offbeats and offbeats made of multiple syllables are unheard of in French *comptines*, though they are common in French songs and indeed in contemporary French rap. What does this mean for comparative versification? On the whole, Attridge's system of metrical analysis would gain little from being applied to French verse; its metrical requirements are entirely different from those of English verse.

But what about the verse of other strong-stressed languages and their systems of versification? The German specialist of metrics Christoph Küper, in his *Sprache und Metrum: Semiotik und Linguistik des Verses* (1988), is, like Attridge, heavily indebted to the generative metrics tradition, and Küper takes on board Jakobson's Slavic metrics, which influenced that tradition. Küper is concerned with the abstract metrical schema and the way it imposes itself on the lines of verse (1988: 102–34). He is interested in metricality (*Metrikalität*, 156–67), metrical ambiguity (167), and metrical complexity (176). These are important questions because, as Attridge's scansion proves time and time again, complexity does not necessarily result in tension. Often the stress contour will stray widely from the metrical requirements without contradicting them. At other times, on the other hand, it will suffice to stick together two stresses to provoke a rupture. Indeed, this effect can be used to slow down the line to provide a sense of closure in the final words of a poem. Küper shares many of Attridge's concerns; he does not, however, adopt Attridge's binary scansion (though he edited the two articles on versification published in *Poetics Today* with the exchange between Attridge and Cureton, following publication of Cureton's *Rhythmic Phrasing in English Verse* in 1992; Attridge 1996; Cureton 1996).

Can Attridge's scansion be transposed to German, then? My own research and discussions with German colleagues lead me to believe so. Take the opening lines from Joseph von Eichendorff's "Auf meines Kindes Tod," written after the death of one of his children:

> Von fern die Uhren schlagen,
> Es ist schon tiefe Nacht,
> Die Lampe brennt so düster,
> Dein Bettlein ist gemacht.
> (von Eichendorff 2015: n.p.)

I would translate Eichendorff's lines as:

> Far away the church bells toll,
> Deep in the middle of the night.
> Your cot's bedclothes are neatly made
> Under a small lamp's meagre light.

I have responded to Eichendorff's moving lines by trying to reproduce the same steady pace of solace. What I hear in his words is the struggle to deal with bereavement through a slow, rhythmic rocking. Cradling his grief, the lyrical subject tries to face up to the grim, inescapable fate of loss. But how do German-speakers respond to Eichendorff's lines? While my German colleagues all perceived the regularity of these lines, they all experienced some difficulty with explaining to me as an English-speaker the nature of that metricality. Several of them were perplexed and found it difficult to say where the accents should go. Most fell back on the stress contour, but that did not help matters, because they could not explain how that stress contour did not contradict metrical requirements. Indeed, "Es ist schon tiefe Nacht" appeared to several colleagues to scan x x / / x /, which is of course highly irregular. The poem was written in iambic trimeters, the same colleagues informed me.

How are we to proceed? If we apply a binary scansion to these verses rather than striving to reduce stress contour to meter or vice versa, things look a lot simpler.

```
     –s  +s  –s   +  –s      +s –s
Von fern die Uhren schlagen,
  o  B   o   B   o    B  o

     –s –s  +s +s –s    +s
Es ist schon tiefe Nacht,
  o  B   o   B  o  B

     –s  +s –s  +s     –s  +s –s
Die Lampe brennt so düster,
  o  B   o   B      o  B  o

      s  +s –s   –s  –s +s
Dein Bettlein ist gemacht.
  o  B   o   B   o   B
```

In neither the second nor the fourth line is there any semantic reason for stressing the word "ist." But the promotion rule seems to apply. A metrical reading that lightly promotes this central syllable in a series of three unstressed syllables appeared to my German colleagues to be wholly acceptable, and I have since had a chance to hear recorded versions of Eichendorff's poem in which the word is indeed clearly promoted.

Küper, in the approach to metrics he put forward in *Sprache und Metrum*, meets me halfway in these conclusions. Like Attridge, he was influenced by the generative metrics of Morris Halle and Samuel Jay Keyser, notably in recognizing the necessity of distinguishing between "the abstract patterns and the correspondence rules which enable a given string of words to be viewed as an instance of a particular abstract pattern" (Halle and Keyser, quoted in Küper 1988: 152, my translation). But, like Jens Ihwe, Küper considers the way that generative metrics treats complexity and ambiguity to be "totally naïve" (*völlig naiv*; Ihwe, quoted in Küper 1988: 176, my translation).

The main objection to generative metrics is that it fails to introduce a concept of diction. It thus oscillates frenetically and unconvincingly between the abstract meter and the concrete discourse without recognizing the way that diction and (in its most extreme form) declamation transform stress contour. It is not a question of simply recognizing that a metrical position can go unrealized so long as certain accentual rules are not infringed. Any staging or recording of Shakespeare's plays or sonnets clearly demonstrates that promoted beats *do* act upon the reading of the line. In all the recordings I have been able to consult (Shakespeare 2005b), in the first line of Shakespeare's first sonnet—"From fairest creatures we desire increase"—the word "we" carries a light accent, though there is no relevant semantic reason for according this syllable any particular salience.

Küper does introduce a binary scansion following the Halle and Keyser distinction between meter and stress contour. Thus he demonstrates that metrical accent and word stress coincide in lines such as the opening of Goethe's "Erlkönig":

/ / / /
Wer reitet so spät durch Nacht und Wind?
x X x x X x X x X

(Who comes riding so late through the night and the wind?)

(1988: 130)

But Küper's system does not seem to integrate promotion and demotion. Consequently he classifies as ambiguous lines in which the stress contour does not coincide with the meter. He gives the following line from Goethe's *Faust* as such an example:

> Und ihrem Fall dumpf hohl der Hügel donnert,
>
> (1988: 170)

Küper recognizes that the meter continues undulating weak-strong throughout the verse:

> Und ihrem Fall dumpf hohl der Hügel donnert,
> X   X   X   X   X

But without the promotion and demotion rules that Attridge provides, this beating seems at odds with the stress contour because of the three consecutive stresses on "Fall dumpf hohl." This line actually proves to be a prime example, since promotion here is followed directly by demotion. The three-stress rule, in which the central stress can be demoted, and the three-unstressed-syllables rule, in which the central syllable can be promoted, seem to be clearly demonstrated in this example. The first three syllables are unstressed: "Und ihrem"; the following three syllables are stressed: "Fall dumpf hohl." And yet the undulating movement of the line goes on unperturbed, seeming to prove conclusively that meter interacts with stress contour in regular German verse in much the same way it does in English verse.

It would be a mistake to underestimate the difference between stress and accentuation in English and German. But when metrical requirements turn out to be the same, often metrical solutions will coincide. For this reason I am led to believe that much of Attridge's system may be transposable to German and to other Germanic languages. How much remains to be seen. Only further research by native speakers highly conversant with poetry and poetics will tell. French, on the other hand, is an entirely different case. French forces us to come to grips with other forms of metrical manipulation. Tackling French metrics requires a much greater effort for the English-speaker whose metrical competence proves wholly unadjusted to reworking speech rhythms. The syllable will inevitably be the main thing that is at stake in such manipulation.

Metrical Manipulation of Syllables

Meter manipulates syllables. All manipulation of word stress and sentence stress involves handling syllables differently than they would otherwise be treated. Promotion and demotion do not magically make syllables appear or disappear, but they do involve shading and highlighting them. French metrical verse does not promote and demote syllables as English metrical verse does. It manipulates syllables, however, and it does this primarily through two processes: synaeresis and diaeresis.

Synaeresis (*synérèse* in French; see Morier 1961: 1175–76) comes from the Greek, meaning "seizing together," as Cuddon rightly asserts (1991: 943), and it "occurs when two normally separate vowels are combined into one syllable. For example 'seeest' becomes 'seest'" (943). Contraction and elision are alternative terms for synaeresis but are not exactly synonyms, since the synaeresis in Cuddon's example from Middle English obviously refers to the way syllables are read in theatrical and poetical works. "T'is" and "t'other" would be other obvious examples, though dialects often show that such procedures are still common in everyday speech and not necessarily a stylized manipulation of discourse.

Diaeresis receives only a short entry in Alex Preminger and T. V. F. Brogan's excellent *New Princeton Encylopedia of Poetry and Poetics* (1993). The work defines diaeresis as the "pronunciation of successive vowels as separate sounds and not as a diphthong, e.g. Chloë, cooperate" (1993: 288). The greater part of the short discussion of diaeresis is devoted to classical texts. Cuddon (1991: 237) provides only a two-line entry and one example, "noël." Attridge has no entry for diaeresis in his index, though he devotes several entries in *The Rhythms of English Poetry* to the opposite procedure, elision (see especially 1982: 163–64, 239–48). What would this seem to indicate? Certainly not negligence on the part of our specialists. Diaeresis tends to be rare in English, and the examples put forward suggest that when it does take place, it often affects words borrowed from foreign languages.

Synaeresis, on the other hand, appears to be widespread throughout English metrical verse. *The New Princeton Encylopedia* quotes the opening line of Milton's *Paradise Lost*: "In 'Of Man's First Disobedience, and the Fruit,' the 'ie' in 'Disobedience' changes to what is called a 'y-glide,' reducing the word from five syllables to four" (Preminger and Brogan 1993: 1259). The entry goes on to explain that to some degree synaeresis "is simply a normal linguistic process carried on in ordinary speech all the time, of which the poet simply takes advantage for writing verse with a regulated syllable count" (1259), quoting words such as "heaven," which may be pronounced as either disyllabic or monosyllabic. The *Princeton* entry for elision is somewhat longer, but though the authors stress that elision is important for metrics, "many prosodists over the centuries have failed to grasp that the reductive processes at work here are normal linguistic ones, not 'poetical devices' peculiar to metrical verse" (325).

Certainly the examples Attridge provides for elision suggest that synaeresis is common to the English language in general: "And never a spray of yew"; "Strew on her roses, roses"; and "She bathed it in smiles of glee" (1982: 163–64). In these phrases, "never" can easily be reduced practically to a monosyllable; "on her" tends towards the monosyllabic in a rapid reading, because of the reduction of the two vowels of these unstressed syllables; and the same can be said of "it in" in the third example.

Elision occurs when our speech picks up speed; we glide over unstressed syllables until ultimately they disappear. "I'm," "you're," "he's," and "wouldn't" are simply more conventionally recognized forms of a procedure that provides us with "would've," "t'you," and "gizza" (give us a). In elision, poets are not so much bending the rules as using them to their advantage. The entry for elision in the *New Princeton Encyclopedia* reminds us that poets exploit this essential linguistic tendency abundantly (Preminger and Brogan 1993: 325). And Attridge stresses that elision must be taken into account in handling offbeats. Indeed, he stipulates in his "offbeat rule": "One (or two) unstressed syllables may realise an offbeat in duple verse" (1982: 162). What he is arguing is that in strictly syllabo-accentual verse in which the alternation is monosyllabic (iambic or trochaic), two unstressed syllables will be found to be acceptable if they can be fully or partially elided. Elision—that is to say, synaeresis—depends upon speed in both everyday language and in metrical poetry, but in metrical poetry it is the pulse of the meter that encourages us to emphasize the accents and glide over the unstressed syllables. It is probably best to bear in mind a tripartite distinction here: "it's" is a linguistic convention and "t'is" is a poetic convention, while synaeresis in "on her" and "it in" remains a possibility. How we perceive the degree to which syllables are elided depends in part on the degree to which they become established in the written language.

How does this compare to French, in both the spoken language and in poetry? *Synérèse* is commonplace in the French language. We have already considered examples such as *J(e) te l(e) dis!* But even the word "poet" in French, *poète*, was considered acceptable as a monosyllable at the end of the nineteenth century, something that appears absurd to French-speakers today (Morier 1961: 1175). Certain words are considered acceptable as monosyllables in French, though they would normally be disyllabic, for example, *lion*. *Centurion*, Morier tells us (1176), can be pronounced as a three- or a four-syllable word. It is synaeresis that imposes itself in the following example from Morier:

> Centurions, répondez! Il import à César
> De compter ses amis—, et cela sans retard.
> (Answer me, centurions! Caesar must know who his friends are without delay.)
>
> (1175, my translation)

Synaeresis is common, therefore, to both the French and English languages, and it is exploited by poets in order to preserve syllable count in French verse, just as it facilitates the undulating rhythm of English verse. A result of rapid reading or rapid speech, it is harnessed by poets at strategic moments to maintain metricality. But while English verse has little use for the opposite process, diaeresis, this phenomenon turns out to be fundamental to French metrics. As Morier writes, "La poésie préfère la diérèse dans une foule de cas où la prose, dans son discours rapide, choisit la synérèse" (Poetry prefers diaeresis in a great number of cases, while prose in rapid speech opts for synaeresis; 1961: 1175).

Like the English forms of synaeresis—"t'is," for example—French forms of diaeresis often appear unnatural and affected to the ears of French-speakers today. This was already the case in Morier's day, when he wrote his *Dictionnaire* in 1961 (370). Rather than being unnatural, the forms diaeresis takes are often archaic. Poets sometimes preserve previously existing forms or hearken back to former modes of expression. This explains why modern readers often have a hard time understanding the syllable count of verse from past centuries. As Morier points out, before Corneille (1606–84) *trier*—today clearly disyllabic—was a monosyllable. *Meurtrier* and *vitrier* were disyllabic.[13] Diaeresis, however, increasingly asserted itself in French, and over time *meurtrier* and *vitrier* were pronounced as trisyllabic words, while *duel* was transformed from a monosyllable to a disyllable.

A few examples should suffice to make the point that French poetry makes ample use of diaeresis, unlike English poetry. It is commonplace in classical French poems and plays. In "Sonnet sur la mort du roi Louis XIII," Corneille has us pronounce "ambition" as a four-syllable word: *L'ambi*-TI-ON, *l'orgueil, l'audace, l'avarice* (Corneille 1862). The syllable count 6:6 is thereby preserved. In twentieth-century verse, Paul Valéry, who resisted the free-verse movement, would seem to have us pronounce "patience" as a trisyllabic word in the following line, where it would in everyday speech be disyllabic: "Patience, patience" ("Palme," Dupriez 1984: 157).

Bernard Dupriez offers us another curious example from the highly esteemed comic writer Raymond Queneau, known for his stylistic experiments in prose. Queneau's example is interesting for two reasons: first, it couples synaeresis with diaeresis, and second, the example he provides of diaeresis is the very opposite of those classical examples that appear affected and pretentious to French-speakers today. It shows the use of the open vowel usually associated with a vulgar, unpolished diction. In his example, the verb *voir* (to see) becomes a disyllable: "J'demande à vôhar, interrompit Satrunin" ("Le Chiendent," Dupriez 1984: 157). This example is interesting for our comparative study because it reminds us that expressive pronunciation often elongates vowels and diphthongs to the point of separating syllables. "Yeah" can be pronounced "ye-ah," and both the vowels of "no way" can be drawn out emphatically. These are strategies similar to word repetition: "No, no, you don't!" or "Yeah, yeah, of course you can!"

What conclusions can be drawn for comparative versification?

1. Synaeresis is common to the French and English languages.
2. While English verse makes ample use of synaeresis in order to maintain the meter, French verse invariably makes use of diaeresis, which is less common than synaeresis in the French language but is frequently found in traditional French verse. Indeed, without diaeresis, the syllable count of many classical French lines would break down.
3. While French verse is concerned with preserving the syllable count, English verse is more concerned about maintaining the metrical beating. Syllables count in English

verse, but only in relation to the undulating movement of the meter. For this reason it is not always clear if a series of two syllables has been completely reduced to a monosyllable. Elision is by nature a vague process, but it is precisely this vagueness that makes it useful for the meter. It is a question of further weakening the lull of the offbeat.

4. Diaeresis is rare in English, though, as in French, the number of syllables accorded to words can vary.
5. Synaeresis and diaeresis inevitably assert themselves more clearly in French than in English, for the simple reason that the syllable itself is more clearly defined as a phonological unit. Syllables are weak in English, while accents are strong. Since syllables are more clearly defined in French, their disappearance or their elongation into disyllables is perceived more palpably in both everyday speech and metrical verse.

Rhyme

Invariably rhyme comes at the end of a line of verse, though it can intervene at the opening of the line or in the middle of the line if there is a caesura. In free verse we find what I term "free internal rhyming." Such rhyming is designed to surprise us and draw attention to the coupling of words. In traditional metrical verse, however, rhyme serves a structural function: it consolidates the verse line and sets up anticipation. We recognize rhyming schemes and expect rhymes. For this reason the verse of Emily Dickinson, which dabbles in half-rhymes, often upsets readers who expect a rhyme at a given place and have indeed been led to expect it by the poem itself.

Thus far it would seem that rhyme performs the same function in both French and English versification. But this is not quite the case. As we have already seen, the line end in French verse is of strategic importance. This is true in English verse, of course, up to a certain extent; strategic words can be foregrounded at the end of the line, and the rhyme clearly contributes to their foregrounding. Enjambment can introduce tension. In "New Year Letter," for example, W. H. Auden draws attention to the end—the word and the idea—by strategically placing it at the end of the line:

> [...] may the end
> I bring to the grave's dead-line be
> More worthy of your sympathy [...]
>
> (quoted in Attridge 1982: 136)

Such run-on lines are common in French free verse and metrical verse. The very fact that enjambment is borrowed from French should make us wary of binary oppositions when comparing French and English verse. The verse line is of strategic importance for French metrics, and rhyme consolidates the line end. Given this, several phenomena become easier to explain, such as the absence of a strong blank-verse tradition in French and the frequency of run-on lines in English blank verse from Milton to Wordsworth. The line end can be undermined or effaced in English; the reader can follow the speech rhythms of the stress contour, rushing on without pause over the line end, without this perturbing the undulating movement of the meter. This is because the metrical unit is based on the clitic phrase—the stress and its attendant unstressed syllables before and after the stress. This metrical unit is sufficiently strong, sufficiently coherent, to resist the weakening of the line as a separate entity. Indeed, it makes little difference if the stanzas of Robert Burns's poem and song "John Highlandman" are written and read as eight-beat couplets rather than four-beat quatrains; their metrical character will remain unperturbed by the change. Try reading this Border ballad as eight-beat lines:

> We rangèd a' from Tweed to Spey, an' liv'd like lords an' ladies gay,
> For a lalland face he fear'd none, my gallant, braw John Highlandman.

In fact, the piece was written in the more conventional four-beat form:

> We rangèd a' from Tweed to Spey,
> An' liv'd like lords an' ladies gay,
> For a lalland face he fear'd none,
> My gallant, braw John Highlandman.
>
> (Burns 1981: 38)

In these lines, "none" rhymes with "Highlandman," following Burns's lowland Ayrshire pronunciation. But ballads often rhyme *xaya*, a fact that tends to underscore the underlying couplet movement of the ballad quatrain.

It might be argued that classical French verse, which prefers the complex verse lines of the alexandrine and the decasyllable, might also be divided up into two lines: 6:6 and 4:6. Certainly the importance of the caesura in French would support such an argument. Whatever the case may be, the fact remains that rhyme stabilizes the French meter, and without it, syllable count becomes difficult to discern. In other terms, while syllable count supports the metricality of stress-based undulation in English verse, rhyme supports the metricality of the syllable count of French phrasing, at the level of both the simple verse line and the *hémistiche* in complex verse lines.

This examination clarifies the function of rhyme. But how should we define the nature of the rhyme? This is a difficult question to answer and one that traditional versification has made confusing. The fact that the English definition of rhyme is derived from French is clear in the persistence of French terms. In English, *rime riche* refers to repetition of a vowel with the same consonants used both before and after it: "well"/"well," "stare"/"stair," "plate"/"contemplate." *Rimes croisées* refer to the alternation of masculine (stressed) and feminine (unstressed) final syllables in the rhymes (for example, in a quatrain that rhymes "stop"/"water"/"hop"/"daughter"). *Rimes embrassées* have alternate of masculine and feminine rhymes in which the feminine ones are encircled by the masculine ones in an *abba* rhyming scheme (for example, "row"/"falling"/"calling"/"throw"). *Rimes mêlées* have an arbitrary, unstructured interaction of masculine and feminine rhymes.

It would seem therefore that the English owe much to the French when it comes to rhyming. Although this might be true in the sense that one language often learns from another and introduces new forms of verse via translation, it remains very much the case that rhyme has neither the same function nor the same form in English and French verse. This becomes clear when one considers that English verse makes use of a rhyme that would by rights be excluded from the French taxonomy of rhyming. "Go"/"know" and "see"/"tree" are rhymes in English, but *eau/sceau* is not in French, and it would be unthinkable to rhyme *je* and *te* in French: the first might pass for assonance—the repetition of a vowel sound—but the latter would be excluded, since neither of the pronouns carries sufficient tonic word stress. Besides, vowel repetition is commonplace in French, far more common than in English. This difference can be explained by the fact that the number of vowels in English is far greater than in French. The International Phonetic Alphabet offers a list of twenty English vowels, compared to twelve French vowels.[14]

Quite simply, French words rhyme more often because there are fewer vowels. The absence of diphthongs and triphthongs in French contributes to this state of affairs. Rhyming in French is, consequently, easier than in English. To avoid the charge that I am seeking to defend English translators by exaggerating the difficulties they face, some examples must be given. The *Dictionnaire des rimes orales et écrites* (Warnant 1992: 403–04) proposes 120 rhymes for *amour*. The silent *s* in *discours,* for example, the silent *t* in *recourt,* the *d* in *sourd,* the *g* in *bourg,* and the *e* in *courre* contribute to making rhyming words with *amour* easier than with its English counterpart, "love." In contrast, *The Penguin Rhyming Dictionary* (Ferguson 1985) offers only eleven rhymes for "love." This is a minor tragedy for English romantic poetry; it limits the scope for thinking about love in rhymed verse and for stressing this key concept. The rhymes for "love" in English are quickly exhausted. We know most of them by heart—"dove," "glove," "above"—and even the masters of English poetry such as Shakespeare cannot overleap these constraints. We find all three used in *Romeo and Juliet,* for example. An imaginative poet might find some way of rhyming "shove" and "love," but who can imagine anyone but a satirist rhyming it with "guv"?

As Levý rightly points out (1963: 281–307), in what are known as the synthetic languages, which privilege the use of grammatical suffixes (languages subject to declination, such as Latin), the number of rhymes is massively multiplied. German, Italian, and most of all Slavic languages such as Russian and Czech show a great propensity for rhyming, because the same suffixes attached to different words facilitate rhymes. In Italian, *amore* can be rhymed with a whole host of words in the form of *amo, amavi,* or *amerete*. With "loves" we simply find ourselves falling back on "doves" and "gloves," for "above" is difficult to envisage in the plural. The Czech word for love, *láska,* on the other hand, can rely on its suffixes to provide literally thousands of rhymes. This richness opens up verse to whole new horizons of forceful thought. What is English to do?

English poets opted for a looser definition of rhyme. This in itself is justified, because what is important in rhyme is not the essential phonemic structure but the fact that rhymed verse highlights regularity. In terms of spoken English, assonance rhyming (show/blow, three/key) is far rarer than in spoken French, given the diversity of English vowels. This fact should be taken into account when comparing versification in French and English and when considering the adoption of French terminology for rhyming in English.[15]

Four consequences of the poverty of English rhyming can be noted for this comparative versification:

1. Rhyming schemes in English are often more basic than their French equivalents, with *xaya* rhyming schemes being common.
2. Blank verse sidesteps the problem of rhyming.
3. Rhyming is often more basic in formal terms. Assonance is acceptable and reinforced because of the weight of the tonic accent that French assonance cannot rely upon. In English, *rime leonine* is rare and *rime riche* (repetition of the two consonants before and after the vowel) is not particularly common. In French it accounts for 55 percent of the rhymes used by Joachim Du Bellay and 58.3 percent of rhymes used by Valéry, according to Pierre Giraud (quoted in Levý 1963: 296).
4. Because of the tortuous nature of rhyming, poets are often forced to marry disparate words—strange bedfellows. For this reason, the more rhyming becomes complex, formally speaking, the more the verse that has recourse to it tends to fall into comic verse.

Following on the last point, this anonymous poem from a celebrated collection of comic verse, *Verse and Worse*, selected by Arnold Silcock, clearly illustrates the comic potential of complex, contrived rhyming:

Manners
There was a young lady of Tottenham,
Who'd no manners, or else she'd forgotten 'em;
    At tea at the vicar's
    She tore off her knickers,
Because, she explained, she felt 'ot in 'em.

(1958: 189–90)

Comic verse has the virtue of making riches out of poverty. The more contrived the rhyme, the greater the comic effect. Rhymes such as the ones above disrupt conventional usage. Transgression at the moral and linguistic levels coincides. It is not done to rhyme "knickers" with "vicar's." In a comic poem this lapse in etiquette is successful. But on the whole the danger of rhymed verse in English is that it can fall into monotonous patterns of predictable rapprochement between words. Form can impoverish content if it becomes a constraint that the poet masters only mechanically. This is a danger in any language, and more particularly in given poetic movements and traditions. In French *amour* is often coupled with *toujours*, while *pleurs* (crying, tears) is often coupled with *douleur* (grief, pain). In English, however, the poverty of the language's rhyming potential means that this danger is particularly pronounced, and this should make us question whether the formal definition of rhyme is sufficient.

It may seem surprising that so much English poetry is rhymed. Yet the *New Princeton Encyclopedia states* that 60 percent of English sonnets opt for the demanding *abba abba* rhyming scheme in the octave—the first two strophes or first eight lines (Preminger and Brogan 1993: 1168). This number may point to a great virtuosity among English poets, but that is not necessarily the case. Indeed, it is not hard to rhyme in English, but it is hard to avoid banal rhymes. And this conclusion leads us back to meaning, back to the poem.

The question for this comparative versification, and for the translation of poems, is the functional value of rhymes to the poem as a working whole. Meschonnic was pitiless in his criticism of translators who subject themselves to the constraints of rhyme scheme without paying sufficient attention to the meaning of the words rhymed or managing to avoid banal rhymes. His critique of the translation of three Shakespearean sonnets by various translators makes this plain (Meschonnic 1999: 258–307). What is the point, he seems to ask, in translating poetry into something that already exists in French? Shakespeare must not be churned out as warmed-up Lamartine, with predictable rhymes and phrasing. This was Meschonnic taking a stand against the French formalist tradition in versification and translation.

Levý's approach to translation and versification was far more innovative and advanced than that of his French and English counterparts, in that it had already integrated the semantic function of rhyme. This idea formed part of his tripartite definition of rhyme.

According to Levý, rhyme serves three functions: meaning (*vyznam*), rhythm (*rytm*), and euphony (*euphonie*). In reverse order, rhyme constitutes a sonorous linking element; it serves to define the end of a metrically defined phrase; and it brings words together, often enacting a creative contrast (Levý 1963: 281–82).

English versification and metrics invariably forget the meaning of rhyme and its significance for the aesthetic argument of the poem. Rhyme is invariably seen in formal, structural terms. Ironically, because it was seen as a prop of conventional metrical verse, it was disparaged or abandoned by free-verse poets, among them T. S. Eliot (who paradoxically, and ambivalently, often rhymed his poems nonetheless).

Following Levý and Meschonnic, it seems like a good idea to put the record straight on this point, especially since translators must ask themselves whether it is worth preserving the structural function of rhyme, given the linguistic constraints. Can we justify rhyming as a practice if it induces translators to produce hackneyed, worn-out, or contrived rhymes? Ultimately in verse translation the question must remain: does the rhyme help the translated poem to work as a meaningful act of speech in movement? Before I differentiate between four forms of rhyming, it is first essential to distinguish the three functions of rhyme.

Three Functions

THE FORMAL FUNCTION Though patently obvious, the formal function of rhyme should not be neglected. Any fixed form constitutes a structure with culturally established constraints. We already expect fourteen lines in a sonnet and a fairly established number of possible variations in the rhyming scheme. If these rhyming constraints are respected, then we are reassured. The formal function sets up expectations and reassures the reader with these expectations. As has already been stressed, rhyme serves to highlight certain strategic moments in the structure of the verse: line end, stanza end, and the end of the poem. What I term "free internal rhyming" exists in both free and metrical verse, and it tends to function differently from conventional rhyme. Shakespeare often introduces playful rhymes within the line itself, and in free verse, free internal rhyming is commonplace. But it tends to do the opposite of reassuring us—it startles us. Free verse establishes no structure and therefore does not set up rule-bound expectations.

THE INSISTENCE FUNCTION Rhyme foregrounds the rhymed word in the discourse of the poem. For this reason Wesling maintained that the argument of a poem can often be surmised by simply scanning the rhymed words at the ends of the lines (1996). Take the first four lines of Shakespeare's "Sonnet 108":

> O, never say that I was false of heart,
> Though absence seemed my flame to qualify.
> As easy from myself might I depart
> As from my soul, which in thy breast doth lie.
>
> (1988: 57)

Shakespeare's rhymes insist on the basic message of the sonnet, concerning the unfaithful lover who has departed but returns, true of heart, to the soul of his love, that shrine and habitat that is closer to him than he himself. But Shakespeare also manages to manoeuvre the lines in order to stress that this argument might be "qualified." He undercuts his line of argument and strategically insists on "lie" with its double meaning: "repose" or "rest" and "bear false witness." This example is a particularly subtle and playful one, but it demonstrates the paradoxical truth about rhyming. Rhyme quite simply highlights meaning, but the effects of that highlighting are often far from simple.

THE SURPRISE FUNCTION Rhyme serves to bring about creative contrasts. The clash between words can be both meaningful and memorable. Philip Larkin, with his palate for the prosaic, liked to rhyme "gutter" with "butter," but he was capable of fusing the prosaic with the lyrical in subtle combinations such as "loaves" and "groves" ("Essential Beauty," 1988: 144). Thomas Hardy could rhyme "born" and "scorn" ("In the Restaurant," 1995: 99). With a relentless but overpowering pessimism, he could also rhyme "rain" with "vain" or "pain" (162), and "bedside lamp" rhymes with "dark and damp" (194). In Hardy's lyrical universe even the most affirmative of words, "ensure," is almost immediately undermined when it rhymes with "obscure" (162). There is a certain continuity to the meaningful fabric or sonorous texture of the arguments that Hardy is building in his rhyming. Yet each doleful argument is delicious and delightful, because Hardy's world-weary cynicism shows the spark of true creativity by inverting and reversing the expected and worn-out rhyming patterns established in the poetry of his time. Charles Baudelaire shows a similar genius when, rather than celebrate the exoticism of Africa, he rhymes "Afrique" with "phtisique" (consumptive) and "brouillard" (mist) with "hagard" (haggard) in the poem "Le cygne":

> Je pense à la négresse, amaigrie et phtisique,
>   Piétinant dans la boue et cherchant, l'œil hagard,
>   Les cocotiers absents de la superbe Afrique
>   Derrière la muraille immense du brouillard;
>
> (1975: 87)

Rhyming and the Poet's Cosmos

To a great extent, rhymes engender what might be termed the poetic cosmos of the poet. Poets not only present the world as they see it: they order and organize it, and to a large extent that order is intuitive and sonorous. Sound helps the poet shape the world and give it meaning, whether that world be full of understanding and harmony or despair and misgiving.

Each great poet's cosmos erupts in the world, forcing us to reappraise the nature of our world and our modes of apprehending it. Do poets rebel against the world and against language, then? It would be fairer to say that they distinguish themselves from tried and tested means of expression. Rebellion is a metaphor that tends to reduce language to a static, lifeless set of constraints. Speech is instead constantly reanimating language, and literature forms part of language. Language itself is creative and is constantly being recreated, sustained, and reshaped. Without opposing poets to language and making them rebels against norms and traditions, it makes sense to consider the way each poetic cosmos engenders itself and the way the meaning of the individual cosmos is brought into being. How is it formulated? What formal elements are brought into play? How does rhyme structure organize the poems of a given poet? How do poets shake us out of the routines of everyday speech and disrupt and circumvent our usual patterns of thought?

Poets take their stand within their mother tongue. The cosmos of the poet revolves within the universe of the poet's language culture. And that language culture can be very foreign to the reader's world view. French remains to a large extent a Catholic language. This is clear in expressions such as *C'est pas très catholique, tout ça!* in which "catholic" means right-minded, fair, or trustworthy. French poets often break away from conventions and religion, but poets such as Baudelaire remained very much anchored in religious imagery, and even their rebellion against religion takes form in ironic and inverted uses of church imagery. Rhyme joins this continuity when conventions are transgressed. Baudelaire rebels against his Catholic faith but he cannot escape it. He rhymes "célèbres" with "ténèbres" (famous/darkness), "toi" with "Foi" (you/Faith), and "vastes" with "chastes" (vast/chaste) in "Les yeux de Berthe" (1972: 9).

When Francis Scarfe translates "Foi" as "trust" instead of "Faith," what is he doing? He is either showing insensitivity to Baudelaire's inherently Catholic world view or he is demonstrating his desire to adapt it to a more modern atheistic outlook, one more palatable to his readers. At the same time Scarfe's prose translation leaves behind the semantic power of sound patterning. It would be unfair to put Scarfe on trial for this. His prose translations do not pretend to replace a poem with a poem, and they have proved useful for two generations of students. Besides, Scarfe's translations are often much more subtle than this single example suggests. In the following example, though once more he drops the rhyme in his prose translation, Scarfe handles the meaning much more skilfully when he translates "Que pourrais-je répondre à cette âme pieuse / Voyant tomber des pleurs de sa paupière creuse?" as "What could I answer that pious soul, as I saw the tears fall from her hollow lids?" (Baudelaire 1972: 11). Still, what makes Baudelaire's couplet so poignant is his sacrilegious emptying of holiness into hollowness: the pious is swallowed up in the abyss of Baudelaire's poetic cosmos. A rhyme such as "pieuse"/"creuse" digs a grave for piety. Far from being a formal prop, a mere structural constraint, rhyme proves to be inseparable from the poet's style and persona.

If we begin a semantics of rhyme, we are forced to admit that the meaning of rhyme is specific to the poet, the tradition, and the language in which he or she writes. Moving from nation to nation, often the same language will change, and so will the poetic tradition. Inevitably habits and traditions, trends and modes of rhyming change with it. In many ways the Québécois poetry tradition is a continuation of the French one. In the seventeenth and eighteenth centuries Corneille and Molière were being performed in Québec. Nineteenth-century poets such as Louis Fréchette (1839–1908) took Hugo as their model, and poets like Pamphile Lemay sought inspiration in the intimate poems of the Parnassians. An echo of the *poète maudit* is clearly to be heard in the lines of Émile Nelligan (1879–1941): "C'est le règne du rire amer et de la rage / De se savoir poète et l'objet de mépris" (Cotnam 1992: 58), which might be translated as "It is the reign of bitter laughter and rage / to know yourself a poet and the object of contempt." Such lines would seem to indicate that Nelligan saw himself as a soulmate of Verlaine and Rimbaud, and critics such as Jean Royer celebrate him as such, somewhat naively portraying him as a victim of his own anti-conformist genius ("l'incarnation du poète maudit, victime de son anti-conformisme absolu"; Royer 1989: 35).

All artistic traditions seek inspiration in other cultures, and often their roots reach deep into the source culture. But it would be absurd to see Québécois poetry as warmed-up French leftovers. The specific nature of Québécois poetry is disconcertingly obvious to the English-speaker's ear. And the translator of Québécois is confronted with three modes of contextualization. The translator must discern the quintessential nature of the individual poet's cosmos, the way the configuration of that cosmos is encapsulated within the French tongue, and the way the Québécois world view situates itself and defines its landscape and contours within the French-speaker's language culture, in the widest sense of the word.

The continuity of the Catholic tradition in rhyming is much more manifest in Québécois poetry up to the modern period than it is in contemporary French verse. Octave Crémazie (1827–79) rhymes "Seuls et silencieux" with "remonter aux cieux" (alone and silent/ go up to heaven; Cotnam 1992: 15). William Chapman (1850–1917) takes us into a celebration of the Promised Land of the French colonials with rhymes such as "civilise" and "Terre promise" (civilize/ Promised Land; Cotnam 1992: 31). With rhymes such as "la forêt infinie" and "cette langue bénie" (the endless forest/this blessed language; 30), Chapman harnesses the vastness so particular to the Canadian conception of space, and the forest, so symbolic for the Canadian celebration of creation. Such rhymes contribute, in their own small way, to remodelling the landscape of the French language itself.

The French language would civilize the world, according to the nineteenth-century linguistic and cultural ideology exported from Paris and proclaimed by the Revolution. The Québécois poets took this ideology on board, but they made it theirs and enrooted it in their earth and their culture. This ideal chimes within their rhymes. In his rhapsodic celebration of his language and his culture and its divine right, Chapman doesn't hesitate to rhyme—somewhat clumsily—"louer Jéhova" with "la messagère immortelle qui va" (celebrate Jehovah/the immortal messenger that goes; all examples from Chapman's "Notre Langue," Cotnam 1992: 30–31).

Albert Lozeau (1878–1924) echoes Baudelaire by rhyming "moi" and "foi" ("Intimité," Cotnam 1992: 49)—but not quite. Lozeau returns to piety and veneration, the celebration of love. Baudelaire's cutting irony is absent, and so is his playfully perverse inversion of Catholic sacredness. There is a playfulness and originality in Lozeau's rhyming, but it is the inversion of inversion. Lozeau "un-perverts" the rhymes of his times: he cleans them up. He takes up the *poète maudit* rhyme "ivresse"/"tendresse" (drunkenness/tenderness) but converts it into "sereine et chaste ivresse"/"la fidèle tendresse" (serene and chaste drunkenness/faithful tenderness; "Intimité," Cotnam 1992: 49). Similarly, when Nelligan uses the same rhyme, "ivre"/"vivre," in "La romance du vin" (Cotnam 1992: 59), he is not declaring the necessity of transportation and transcendence through drugs and drunkenness, as Baudelaire and Rimbaud were. Indeed, Nelligan makes a point of saying that he is not drunk, though he is "madly happy" (follement gai), and insists that he is "finally happy to live" (enfin heureux de vivre). It would be facile and flippant to mock such rhymes with modernist cynicism or postmodernist irony. But that would probably reveal more about our own limits and our aesthetic and ethical ethnocentrism. Humour, sensibility, structures of feeling, and world views change over time and from place to place. Piety means something for the Québécois poets. It is not simply hollow dogma; it has a palpable resonance. And these Canadian poets are pious right down to their rhymes.

Powerful breaks with Catholicism, its imagery, and its rhetoric will come in Québécois verse. Among the contemporary poets, Pierre Trottier (born 1925) rewrites creation in reverse, giving back all that is, all that exists, to the void, until light and divine breath are consigned to nonexistence. But the Catholic imagination is still at work in the shaping of the imagery of Trottier's post-religious lines.

Even without rhymes, the Catholic tradition resonates in the line ends: "wine," "bread," "Father," "his Will be done," the Apostles, and Noah and his flood are all found highlighted at the ends of the lines in Trottier's "Le temps corrigé" (Cotnam 1992: 1978). Negation appears to reaffirm, albeit ironically, existing conventions and modes of feeling. Even when rhyming is abandoned, the tradition's echo can be heard shaping consciousness as the poet reshapes that shared consciousness.

What are we to conclude? Rhyming and the use of line ends are linguistic, cultural, and personal. The translator is not obliged to convert to or promote Catholicism, but he or she must take it into account as a structuring element at work in the way meaning is bodied forth and formulated in Québécois poems.

Evaluating Rhyme

In discussing the meaning of rhyme and the way it functions in the poem and within the poet's cosmos, we have moved beyond a reductive formalist definition of rhyme. But we still have to consider an evaluative definition of rhyme. The importance of this will become obvious if we consider the aptness of rendering Baudelaire's rhymes with rhymes devoid of any special meaning (go/slow or how/now, for instance). How much would such rhymes weaken the effect that Baudelaire procures in French? In order of merit, it is worth considering the following four definitions to see how we can guard against clumsy translation practices that are passed off as humble adherence to the structural constraints of the original poem.

MEANINGFUL RHYME   The meaningful rhyme realizes the full potential of rhyming. As in the examples in the previous section, it highlights words significant for the argument of the poem and enacts meaningful fusions, clashes, and contrasts. The force of the poem is inseparable from the logic of this intuitive process of weaving meanings together. Rhyme reinforces. Rhyme surprises. It would, however, be a mistake to suppose that great poets always employ great rhymes.

FORMAL RHYME   The formal rhyme serves no purpose in terms of the meaning of the poem but simply fulfills the structural requirements of the poem. Yeats has recourse to formal rhyme when he rhymes "where" and "despair." It is worth quoting the lines because they themselves are not meaningless but rather beautiful.

Nonetheless, it should be self-evident that the quality of the verse does not derive from any great ingenuity in rhyming:

> Labour is blossoming or dancing where
> The body is not bruised to pleasure soul,
> Nor beauty born out of its own despair.
> ("Among School Children"; Yeats 1997: 222)

HACKNEYED RHYME The hackneyed rhyme occurs when pairs of words are overused and become conventional and boring. Worse than prose, which is arbitrary, the rhymes are predictable. Rather than embellishing the poem, they tarnish it. Rather than animating it, they deaden the sensitivity of the reader. In the worst examples it seems that the poet has let convention complete the poem in his stead. Surprisingly, hackneyed rhyme is often found in beautiful verse, but once more it is not the rhyme that contributes to the interest in the lines. Baudelaire, for example, is not above rhyming *douleur/ pleurs* ("Moesta et Errabunda," 1975: 63), *sœur/douceur* ("L'invitation au voyage," 53), and *ombre/sombre* ("Le possédé," 37), all of which lack inspiration though they function perfectly well, formally speaking. In the same way, Shakespeare in his sonnets rhymes "thee"/"me" ("Sonnet 31," 1988: 18) and "light"/"sight" ("Sonnet 7," 6). What are we to conclude? Nobody is perfect, and even the greatest of geniuses cannot be expected to be inspired in all levels of their writing at the same time. At times parallelism, metaphor, or alliteration might take over in the foreground of the poem while rhyming takes a back seat and simply carries on performing its structural requirements. Hackneyed rhyme does not, therefore, necessarily draw attention to itself; it simply reassures the reader by satisfying the structural expectations set up by the rhyming scheme.

CLUMSY RHYME The clumsy rhyme draws attention to itself because of its contrived and forced character. It is the hallmark of young apprentice poets and bad translators unwilling to free themselves from the requirements of convention but unable to master them sufficiently to fly with their own wings. Clumsy rhyme does not simply heat up leftover rhymes, as hackneyed rhyming does. After all, *pleurs/douleurs* and "love"/"dove" at least make sense. Clumsy rhyme, on the other hand, makes no sense; it highlights nonsense and pointlessly foregrounds arbitrary words. Curiously, even great poets sometimes fall into this kind of rhyming, which belongs more to doggerel. Though his admirers and postmodern critics might suggest he does so for satirical reasons, T. S. Eliot introduces a clumsy rhyme when he combines "and" with "hand" in the following lines:

> When lovely woman stoops to folly and
> Paces around her room again, alone,
> She smooths her hair with automatic hand,
> And puts a record on the gramophone.

(*The Waste Land*, Eliot 1969a: 69)

Luckily Eliot at least managed to put the more significant word last: "hand"/"and" would have been a considerably more maladroit ending. As we have already seen, comic verse revels in contrived and absurd rapprochements between words. In such verse "pelican" can be rhymed with "belly can" and "hell he can," just as "Miss Flora's" can rhyme with "adorers." Predictably, limericks manage, by a multitude of paths, to bring us back to smutty and sordid meanings. Penetration is usually the point of such rhyming. Moving from the sublime to the coarsely ridiculous is all part of the fun, and the predictability of the content is offset by the inspiration and ingenuity of the strategies by which such refined vulgarity is accomplished.

This concludes our short tour of rhyming—what it does, what it says, and what is literally said between the lines—when the voice reverberates with the semantic links set up between line ends. We must still deal with both conventional and innovative sound patterning.

Notes

1. Nonsense poetry in German, known (among other things) as *Unsinnspoesie*, is still going strong; see Peter, Rühm, and Walser 1995. The following lines by Walser are fairly representative:

   ### iii. Professoren-Liedchen
   Büchlein, Büchlein an der Wand
   wer ist der Klügste im ganzen Land?
   Der Doktor Doll, der Daktor Dall
   der Diktor Dill [...]

   (1995, n.p.)

The first two lines might be translated as "Little book, little book on the wall / who is the cleverest of them all?" The following two lines defy translation, with the slip from "Doktor" to "Daktor" and then "Diktor" playfully evoking "poet" (*Dichter*) and "thinker" by reminding readers of the past tense of the verb "to think," in something approaching "the thunker" in German.

2. The *World Atlas of Language Structures Online* database (WALS; http://wals.info) was first published in book form in 2005. The third edition appeared in 2013 and is updated on an ongoing basis by a team of fifty-five authors.

3. Goedemans and van der Hulst state that "prominence systems form somewhat of a mixed collection." According to them there are several non-quantitative salient syllabic properties that can form the basis of heavy/light distinctions. One of the most common is the opposition between full and reduced vowels. As an example of such languages they suggest Chuvash, a Turkic language spoken in Russia (2013c: sec. 2.5).

4. Goedemans and van der Hulst propose interesting findings on the mismatches between primary and secondary stress in weight-sensitive languages (2013b: table 2).

5. The disaffection of French youths for their own language as a means of expression in songs is a feeling that has been subject to diverse influences over the past few decades. Those who opposed MTV in France back in the 1990s and supported *la chanson française* were walking a fine line between protectionism and cultural reappropriation. In resisting American culture, pop music, and films, one of the strategies adopted was copying the products of American culture while imposing and promoting the French language. Consequently a rather curious, if not absurd, trend arose in which ageing French rockers such as Johnny Hallyday (in their own time ardent adherents of American culture) enthusiastically promoted versions of rhythm-and-blues songs that adapted French to rhythms and melodies patently appropriated from English counterparts. This new kind of French music was something very different from *la chanson française* made popular by Edith Piaf and Yves Montand and disseminated throughout the world. In Eastern European languages, for example, the Poles and Czechs adapted their own intonations, melodies, and accentuations to French patterns in that art form. As is invariably the case in creative domains, diverse contradictory reactions arose to this new form of French song. There was a Celtic backlash: the emergence of a rustic French folk-grunge, with bands from Rennes representing a kind of French essentialism in which French was essentially *gaulois* (like Astérix). There was state-supported and media-financed promotion of the appropriation of Frenchified rhythm and blues, which went hand in hand with French interpretation of English songs in English. At the same time a rejection of French as a means of

expression in songwriting emerged. This sentiment arose from the fact that French had become associated with variety songs promoted by TV music programs and "rising star" competitions. A question commonly discussed in chat-group forums was "Pensez-vous qu'on peut chanter du rock prog en français sans que ça fasse variètoche?" (Do you think you can sing progressive rock in French without it sounding like variety crap?; http://myspace.com/aelendir). These various reactions and counter-reactions show no signs of grinding to a halt. They are, rather, consolidating into established trends, with fans and factions supporting and rejecting one another. They are also evolving rhythmically speaking. A few decades ago, attempts by French artists to sing in English were unconvincing and rhythmically incompetent in the strict sense of the term. Charles Aznavour, a French variety singer, parodied this state of affairs when he sang, "You are for me, for me, for me, *formidable*." But contemporary artists such as Lily and the Prick can no longer be distinguished from their counterparts on the other side of the Atlantic when it comes to accent, accentuation, rhythm, and phrasing.

6. Neither Benveniste nor Meschonnic is particularly interested in reading Plato for Plato. They are interested primarily in the effect Plato had on the Western conception of meter. There is, however, an insightful and awe-inspiring critique of rhythm in Plato's work, especially in *The Republic* (1968). Rhythm and poetry are essential for Plato because poems move men, and Homer, the poet of the Greeks, was very much the teacher of the Greeks and the guardian of traditional knowledge. In questioning the effect that music and poetry have upon the body, the mind, and the soul, rhythm becomes an aesthetic, moral, political, and even military question for Plato.

7. Morier points out that Hugo, Brizeux, and Sully Prudhomme introduced the *césure médiane* (5:5) in their verse in the nineteenth century (1961: 346), though he notes that since Latin and Irish verse also used this kind of decasyllable, it may in fact be older than the more dominant forms (345). At any rate it is not found in Renaissance verse, and Voltaire mocks the *césure médiane* in the chapter on the hemistich in his *Dictionnaire philosophique* (quoted in Morier 1961: 345). Verlaine, however, does not hesitate to use the *césure médiane* repeatedly in his verse. The following lines come from a series of such verse lines:

> Quand Marco dansait / sa jupe moirée [5:5]
> Allait et venait / comme une marée, [5:5]
> (As Marco danced, her shimmering skirt
> rose and fell like the tide)
>
> ("Marco," quoted in Morier 1961: 346)

8. One obvious exception to the supposed rule that French does not allow post-tonic syllables is those words of Latin origin that have retained their original stress in modern French. Often such words have been truncated: *mari* (husband), for example, is derived from the Latin word *maritus*, in which the accent falls upon the first syllable. That such word stress is foreign to the nature of French accentuation will become obvious if we compare the stress of *mari* to that of *mariage* (wedding) or *marié* (bridegroom). Only in *mari* is the first syllable stressed, while in the latter two the stress falls on the final syllable, *-age* (with the final *e* being mute) and *-é* respectively, in accord with the norms of French pronunciation. *Mariage* and *marié* have been produced by French; *mari* still retains the marks of its importation into French. An older, more refined but still current synonym for *mari* in modern French is *époux*, which entered the French language in the mid-eleventh century. Interestingly, this word was derived from the Latin word *sponsus* but was assimilated into the French stress system: the word lost its suffix and gained a prefix, thereby assuring that the stress falls upon the final syllable.

9. I maintain that preferring the poetic potential of one language over another merely displays one's taste, experience, and personal limits in looking for something in a foreign system of versification that one has learned to respond to intuitively in one's mother tongue or adopted second language. No comparative versification can start from such a premise or move towards such a conclusion. Each system can be judged as potentially expressive only within the scope of the mother tongue of any linguistic community. Nevertheless I am forced to concede that among the most sensitive and well-read polyglots with whom I have discussed such questions, it is not uncommon that English is praised for the variety and flexibility of its accentual patterning. Speakers often criticize their own mother tongue, stressing its lack of variety. This tendency is perhaps no more than a celebration of the exotic when the mother tongue is compared to foreign languages. French seems more melodious to the English ear, for example. It is also true that metrical systems at times contravene norms proper to the language in order to establish poetic norms. Czech, for example, is naturally trochaic in form, with words beginning strong-weak. But in order to avoid monotony, the dominant metrical form inverts this order, and traditional Czech verse has adopted iambic meters.

10. Albeit to a lesser extent, the idea of regularity in music is also approximative—more of an impression than a reality. If musicians could keep the beat, metronomes would be superfluous. Drummers are often chastised for not keeping the beat.

11. Despite being influenced by linguistics, and especially by generative metrics, Attridge distinguishes himself by always thinking of the poem first and the meter within it, rather than trying to extract linguistic data from meter. The latter tendency is all too clear in the work of Morris Halle and Samuel Keyser, Paul Kiparsky, and other linguists who work in generative metrics. For such scholars the poem is not the focus, but rather a means of theorizing something general about language and the historical changes languages undergo.
12. There exists a great variety of terms used to refer to the processes of promotion and demotion in treatises on versification: "hovering stress," "hovering accent," "level stress," "variable syllable," "wrenched stress," "syllaba anceps." The very diversity of the terms points to the fact that these are ad hoc, improvised names used to refer to something only vaguely understood.
13. The seventeenth century exalted concision in both vowels and consonants. At the time, the *l* at the end of *avril* was silent. As a result, the plural form, *avrils* (Aprils), rhymed with *fils* (son; Morier 1961: 369).
14. For English, see the International Phonetic Alphabet at "The Sounds of English and the International Phonetic Alphabet," Antimoon: How to Learn English Effectively (www.antimoon.com/how/pronounc-sound-sipa.htm). For French, see the International Phonetic Alphabet at "French IPA Symbols – Vowels" (http://french.about.com/library/pronunciation/bl-ipa-vowels.htm).
15. Defined in formal terms alone, the French terms prove useful enough:

    1. *Rime pauvre ou faible:* a vocalic rhyme, for example, *joué/cassé*. This is assonance, common in French free verse but rare in traditional metrical verse in French.
    2. *Rime suffisante:* rhyme's version of work-to-rule, assuring the bare minimum for acceptable rhyming in French. The vowel rhymes and so does the consonant before or after the vowel, as in *roc/bloc* or *main/carmin*.
    3. *Rime riche:* the rhyming of the vowel and two consonants before or after the vowel, as in *tordu/perdu*.
    4. *Rime leonine:* a disyllabic rhyme with vowels and consonants coinciding, as in *de voir/devoir*.

CHAPTER 4

Beyond Metrics

Acoustic Patterning

"'Tis not enough no harshness gives offence, / The sound must seem an Echo of the sense," argued Alexander Pope in his *Essay on Criticism* (Pope 2005: pt. 2, lines 364–65). The elegance of Pope's phrasing is such that the phrase was to echo through the generations to become a fixed part of stylistic dogma. But what did Pope mean? Is form to be considered an afterthought of meaning—a support, a crutch? Does poetry owe its expressive force to its vocalic and consonant echoing, to assonance, rhyme, and alliteration? Does sound echo sense, as Pope puts it? Maurice Grammont certainly seemed to believe it did; he devoted sixteen pages of his short *Petit traité de versification française,* published in 1906, to the question (1989: 122–38). Henri Morier devoted eighteen pages to it in his *Dictionnaire* (1961: 1286–304). The *New Princeton Encyclopedia of Poetry and Poetics* (Preminger and Brogan 1993) contains sizeable entries for sound, sound colour, sound effects in poetry, sound symbolism, and iconicity.

Morier was convinced that certain vowels correspond to the expression of "feelings of affliction" and things related to "shadows, evil, sin and pain." He found a profound but explicit repulsive evil in the sounds of words such as *honte* (shame), *basse* (base), and *monstre* (monster). And he found pain and affliction in *gémissement* (groan), *chagrin* (sorrow), and *désespoir* (despair; 1961: 1291). Poetry is powerful, and we do feel the tug of sounds and the emotion invested in sounds when someone reads a poem well. Despite the seductive power of poetry, however, arguments such as Morier's and Pope's soon break down. It will suffice to take one of Morier's examples. He argues that it is the sounds in Victor Hugo's lines that make them moving:

> Vos veuves aux fronts blancs, lasses de vous attendre,
> Parlent encor de vous en remuant la cendre
> De leur foyer et de leur cœur!
>
> ("Oceano nox," from *Les Rayons et les ombres*,
> quoted in Morier 1961: 1291)

We only need to compare the use of these sounds with any commonplace utterance to demonstrate the absurdity of the sound-as-echo-of-sense argument. Indeed, we find the same sounds (*ou*, *ah*, and *é*) that Morier believes engender despair in the simple, everyday phrase *Ah, vous attendez le métro?* (Ah, so you're waiting for the metro?). We might choose to introduce surprise or irritation into this phrase, just as we can read the lines from Hugo in an expressive manner that lengthens and emphasizes certain key words and thereby reinforces the links established by sound repetition, but it is meaning and not form that is the inspiration for such expressive readings. Meaning motivates the interpretation. What exactly is happening, then? Sound does not echo meaning; it both invites and enables us to heighten the expressive force of the words.

This point will seem difficult to grasp only if we uphold the form/meaning opposition. We mistakenly try to find in the form the origin and the power of meaning that have been foregrounded by an emphatic reading and get entangled in the various stages of interpretation. We mix up the materials of language with the meaning and, in turn, we mix up both with the reader's interpretation of the verse and the listener's response to that reading. Pope and Morier both propose explanations, but by separating sound and sense and then magically enacting their rapprochements, they do nothing more than make the waters muddier than before. As Nietzsche knew, admirers of such explanations are never hard to find, because we like to assume there is profundity in the puddles we look into, as long as we cannot see the bottom. Things are paradoxically more complex but ultimately simpler. To ascribe to poetry a secondary signifying process is to confuse language and diction.

The poet engenders and the reader apprehends—both intuitively—the latent capacity of poems to foreground meaning, not to echo it. We can lengthen the *é* in *désespoir* just as we can lengthen the second vowel in "despair"; the effect is expressive, but neither of these sounds begs such an interpretation. Try reading out loud *décompte syllabique* or "stair"—the meaning does not invite an expressive reading and would indeed make one absurd. The iconic or onomatopoeic function in language does exist, but it is marginal. Sometimes the liquid *l* in "flow" is said to flow (as in the phrase "the slow river flows"), but though we can lengthen the internal rhyming syllable here and stress the *l*, we will do neither in "Go get the flour, Joe!" The *l* flows in "flow" but not in "flour"—or "flower," for that matter.

Sound is not onomatopoeic in poetry. Another myth that should be dispelled before the translator sets about reconstituting the poem's sound and sense is the idea that sonorities engender harmony. The rhyming scheme does, of course, play a reassuring role as a structure that sets up anticipation and fulfills expectations, but it is often argued that sound patterning creates beauty or harmony in verse. The beautiful celebrations of harmony are so widespread and commonplace, in poetry from Shelley to Dylan Thomas, that it is pointless to quote an example here. But once more it is important to stress that the meaning of the poem harnesses largely arbitrary sounds to activate them in meaningful constellations and configurations. A counter-example will suffice to stress that what is expressive does not necessarily engender harmony or reassure the reader. Thus Milton's repetition of *m* procures an ironic satirical effect in the phrase "**m**oping **m**elancholy / And **m**oon-struck **m**adness" (*Paradise Lost*, Book 11, lines 485–86; Milton 2008: 592). The repetition is inescapable: four *m*'s.

We should, however, be wary of assuming that the number of repetitions alone contributes to highlighting words. In each language certain sounds recur; consequently those sounds will not necessarily draw attention to themselves. After all, how many readers noticed that the previous sentence had three z phonemes in it? Foregrounding sound depends not on the number of repetitions but upon two things: the number of repetitions compared with the frequency with which those sounds are usually used, and the positions of the sound in the words. Though common enough, *m* as a phoneme is less frequent in English than z. Placing it at the beginning of each stressed word in the line redoubles the force of repetition as a highlighted effect. These two factors—relative rarity and word position—contribute to distinguishing Milton's line from what might be called, for want of a better term, ordinary speech.

It is of course important to distinguish between letters and phonemes. The letter *s* can be pronounced *s*, as in "sun" or "miss"; *z*, as in "those"; or as the phoneme ʃ, as in "she" or "crash." The game Scrabble, nonetheless, provides a rough idea of the repetition of most sounds in the language. The fact that more points are awarded for using *p* or *f* than *t* indicates something about the frequency with which these phonemes occur in everyday spoken English.

One important distinction that should be made between French and English is that in expressive diction French-speakers will often hammer home what is called the *accent d'attaque*, which falls upon the consonant rather than the vowel. Thus, in expressions of repulsion, the French will stress the *d* in *dégoutant* where the English will tend to redouble the accent on the stressed syllable. Compare:

$$\text{C'est } \overset{/}{\mathbf{d}}\text{égoutant} \qquad \text{That's } \overset{/}{\text{disgusting!}}$$

In fact it is perfectly possible to hammer home the *d* in English at the same time as the vowel is emphasized. The essential distinction between the two languages should not be obscured, however: the vowel and the stress dominate in expressive reading in English. Differentiating between the linguistic character of each language and their expressive resources is crucial. This is the basis of comparative versification. But there is something more essential at stake here: the expressive potential of each language. Once again it is essential not to confuse the linguistic means at hand in any language and the expressive force with which those means can be manipulated by poets and people in everyday life. French and English do not provide the same linguistic means. Nor do speakers and poets handle and shape those linguistic resources in the same way. Expressivity in speech and poetry reveals nothing about the relative richness or poverty of the linguistic resources of any given language. Rather, it shows something about the capacity of people and poets to harness the expressive potential proper to their language.

The example "disgust" demonstrates once more, only too clearly, that expression proves equally possible in both French and English.

Romantics, nostalgic about the seemingly magical power of Pope's sound/sense argument, might be inclined to see an inherent expressive meaning in the *d* and will point to the fact that the two languages demonstrate this by attributing the same sound to words of the same meaning. This is the false science of backward reasoning. Etymology can make us associate *d* with negation, but there is nothing inherently disgusting about the sound *d*. If there were, "La**d**y **D**iana was **d**elightful" would be something of a grotesque sonorous parody, whereas it only serves to parody the sound-is-the-echo-of-sense argument.

What is at stake in our voice and versification project? The question in sound patterning is to establish whether sound patterns are an arbitrary result of the limited number of sounds used in any one language, examples of highlighted formal embellishment, or meaningful links forged between foregrounded words of import to the poem. As examples of these three possibilities, we might compare the following phrases:

Colin's not **c**oming to the **c**lub tonight.

Mistress of **m**any tongues; **m**erchant of chalcedony
("Canto LI," Pound 1986: 251.)

Beauty is **b**arren oft; **b**est hus**b**ands say
("Elegie 2: The Anagram," line 35, Donne 1990: 73)

Ironically, but logically enough, the fewer the sound effects, the more they will take on salience in the poem as a whole. For this reason a certain prejudice has taken root. It is often argued that free verse uses sound patterning in order to compensate for lack of rhyme. This claim turns out to be only partially true. It is misleading because traditional metrical verse makes great use of line-internal sound patterning; assonance and alliteration are of course commonplace, and at times metrical verse exploits free internal rhyming. The idea that such sound patterning belongs more to free verse arose only because, once rhyming was taken away, readers paid greater attention to these free forms of sound patterning. Translators, therefore, have to remain attentive to what forms of sound patterning emerge in free verse that make it different from prose, and they should not allow a focus on meter and rhyme to obscure other—palpably powerful—acoustic patterning in conventional metrical verse.

For poetics in general, and for translators of poetry in particular, this reappraisal of sound patterning should encourage us to move beyond the iconic myth that sound engenders or echoes sense, and to ask a series of new questions:

1. How often are sounds echoed in the poem and in the language in general?
2. Where are the sounds found: at the beginning, the end, or in the middle of the word?
3. What is the immediate context of sounds?
4. Do the sound configurations highlight meaningful links like the rhymes in Hardy's poems (pain/rain/vain), or Donne's opposition of "beauty" and "barrenness" or Milton's satire of "moping melancholy" in the examples just quoted? Are they simply sonorous embellishments, stylistic flourishes devoid of semantic interest, or do they form part of an uninteresting and inevitable repetition of sounds, like the *t* in the word "repetition" itself?

Because free verse is forced to rely more heavily on its sound configurations than traditional metrical verse (even though it may not have greater recourse to this secondary form of free sonorous patterning), considering the role that sound patterning plays within the poem at the level of the part and the whole is important. The questions then become

1. Does sound patterning introduce and maintain a rule-bound structure, as the rhyme scheme does?
2. Is the poem as a whole, free or otherwise, characterized by a constant but free form of sound patterning?
3. Does sound patterning form part of a sporadic process used to highlight certain sections of the poem?

We will return to these questions in the case studies in Part 3.

Phrasing

It would be absurd to claim that metrics ignores phrasing. The number of words used across languages to refer to the ways poets cut up lines and highlight line ends testifies to the metrical interest in phrasing and the way poems tend to draw attention to openings, climaxes, and closure in the sentence. Line breaks are strategic for highlighting the meaning and drawing attention to meaningful pauses in the flow of ideas. Physical spacing forces us to intuitively perceive what is being said. For this reason it is interesting in translating to re-enact strategic semantic breaks where possible. The following example from Charles Baudelaire's "Les plaintes d'un Icare" illustrates this point, for the space itself is highlighted by the line breaks:

> En vain j'ai voulu de l'espace
> Trouver la fin et le milieu;
>
> (1975: 143)

To preserve the meaningful spatial pauses that highlight space itself and the middle (*le milieu*), I would suggest translating these lines as follows:

> In vain, I wished for space,
> To find the edge and the in-between.

Free verse makes ample use of line ends to expressively highlight movement, as in the following example from Saint-John Perse's first poem in his collection *Éloges*:

> [...]
>   et orné de sueurs, vers l'odeur de la viande
>   il descend
>   comme une femme qui traîne: ses toiles, tout son linge et ses cheveux défaits.
>
> (1960: 42)

I would suggest the following translation:

> And, jewelled, in sweat, towards the smell
>   of the meat he descends.
>   Down the staircase he comes
>   like a woman who trails
>   all her linen
>   her clothes
>   and her loose-hanging hair.

The visual image of the stairway is enacted in my translation. This is functional rather than decorative, in that it encourages the reader to pause a little longer at the beginning of each line. What I am responding to, and what I am trying to capture, is the slow, regular movement of descent that is highlighted by both the syntactic breaks and the line ends in the original poem.

Of course translators generally respond intuitively to such movements and expressive pausing. Yet if poets, translators, and specialists in versification often prove sensitive to phrasing, and the way it is broken up expressively to highlight meaningful moments and disturb the standardized use of punctuation, they do so somewhat in spite of theory rather than thanks to it. If they listen to the way poetry "re-punctuates" prose, it is more because their experience with poems has cultivated in them a certain sensibility, rather than because theory has trained them and explained the importance of phrasing. Theory tends to remain caught up in meter and sees phrasing as secondary.

It is no exaggeration, therefore, to claim that a minor revolution was required in English versification before scholars understood that it is the phrasing of poems that makes them meaningful, not the meter or the lack of it. Until recently, specialists of metrics and versification perversely continued to consider phrasing only in terms of its interaction with meter. And most specialists persist in this perversity. They put phrasing into the lines rather than seeing the lines as an additional structure or shaping of phrasing itself.

This misunderstanding is understandable to some extent. Meter is such a powerful structuring force that formalist readings of poetry encourage the assumption that expressive phrasing derives from the meter rather than the sentence. My counter-examples from everyday speech in this book are partly intended as a shock strategy to put the focus on expressivity within the context of discourse, rather than to see discourse in terms of stylistic effects emerging from versified language. Everyday speech has ample means to highlight words through accentuation, lengthening syllables, meaningful pauses, and repetition. In this sense poetry must always be considered as merely a refined form of speech. Meter and line ends, caesuras and stanzas, openings and closures must be seen as refined, reorganized forms of fundamental and omnipresent syntactic possibilities.

Three voices in contemporary English versification have stressed the importance of phrasing and worked to reinstate the sentence as the unit of meaningful organization upon which more formalized patterning is imposed or, rather, out of which the poem's movement grows and develops. Of the three—Richard D. Cureton, Donald Wesling, and Derek Attridge—Cureton certainly deserves first place for his erudite and thought-provoking *Rhythmic Phrasing in English Verse* (1992). Attridge was greatly influenced by Cureton's approach to phrasing and considerably modified his own approach to rhythm in response to it, as is shown in his later work *Poetic Rhythm: An Introduction* (1995: 21–24, 182–209). True, Attridge perceives a formalist bent to Cureton's approach, and he suggests that Cureton is to some extent the inheritor of Jakobson.[1] But the claim that Cureton falls into formalism is only partly justified. His approach to rhythm focuses on grouping, and grouping is always cognitive for Cureton. As he puts it,

> In this theory I assume that rhythmic structures are cognitive representations of the flow of energy in the stream of our experience. The essential feature represented in these structures is *relative prominence*, and the major vehicle for this structuring is the well-formed *hierarchy*. (Cureton 1992: 121; emphasis in original)

"Structure," "prominence," and "hierarchy": these are the key terms of Cureton's approach. Readers respond to the poem because they have the "rhythmic competence" to respond to "internal and external events" in the poem (120). Cureton was taking the study of phrasing far beyond traditional metrics. He was assuming that rhythmic competence is fundamental to understanding the shaping and organization of syntax in general, and for this reason he had no qualms about taking on free verse and the movement of the King James Bible, which has often been celebrated for its rhythm but defies traditional metrical analysis (224–32).

Cureton provocatively argues against reducing rhythm to meter: "Linguistic rhythms seem to involve all aspects of discourse organization that presently escape rigorous linguistic description," among which he lists paralinguistic gesture, sound orchestration, and intonational forms and meanings, as well as syntactic and semantic organization in discourse (1992: 69). This critique is to some extent inspired by his reading of Henri Meschonnic. And indeed, Cureton is one of the few English-speaking specialists in versification who was capable of making a clear and creative response to

Meschonnic's provocative *Critique du rythme* (1982). What Cureton takes from Meschonnic is the idea that "*rhythm* in language is nothing less than the full 'figured sense' of a discourse.... It is the organization of the speaking subject as discourse, in and by discourse" (Cureton 1992: 69; emphasis in original). He draws his own conclusion: "Like the speaking subject, rhythm is not a homogeneous totalization; it is fragmentary, diverse" (69).

This idea is of crucial importance for Cureton's concept of rhythmic phrasing, which shaped his study of verse. His essential idea is summed up in the conclusion to his chapter titled "Implications":

> While meter is an important part of many verse rhythms, phrasal forms are the most universal, expressively powerful and theoretically central components of all verse rhythms, especially the rhythms of art verse, in which meter is often relatively flat and therefore perceptually weak. In most cases it is the phrasal rhythm of the poem that defines its unique rhythmic shape and therefore serves as the dominant vehicle of prosodic expression. ... Therefore a theory of verse rhythm that takes meter as central and generative of other structures implicitly dismisses all of the global rhythmic organization in these texts as rhythmically peripheral, or, worse yet, arythmical. (1992: 431)

Cureton was heavily influenced by Wesling's "grammetrics," and though Wesling's *The Scissors of Meter* (1996), in which he formulates his grammetrics theory of verse, was not published until after Cureton's *Rhythmic Phrasing* in 1996, Cureton had, like myself, read it in manuscript form and had taken on board its central thesis. That thesis posits that we should not observe the syntax within the meter but rather consider syntax and meter as the two blades of a pair of scissors coming together. Wesling points out the absurdity of comparing minor pauses with full stops at the ends of arguments. The poet can poise delicate pauses at the end of a stanza or introduce major syntactic closure within a line. Both of these procedures will be ignored, however, if we pay attention to syntax only when it fails to coincide with meter—and this is precisely what traditional metrics encourages us to do. Pauses and movement in rhythm are a question of grading and shading; the degree to which a pause or a group coincides with the requirements of meter and the line is what interests Wesling.

This is not the place to go into detail about Wesling's analysis of poems, but his analyses of Shakespeare (1996: 87–99) and Emily Dickinson (126–27) are revealing. In Shakespeare's "Sonnet 129," Wesling convincingly argues, for instance, that the "cognitive intensity" and "suppressed fury" derive to a great extent from the "incoherence and unexpectedness of the syntax" (93). Indeed, the fourteen lines of Shakespeare's sonnet form one single sentence. This is a poem about lust, in which the sonnet's single sentence insistently overleaps all of its quatrain divisions.

In Dickinson's "The Soul selects her own Society," Wesling's grammetrics reveals an entirely different rhythm, in which "the symmetries and the breaking of symmetries, the exaggeration of stoppage and scissoring, makes the style of the poem" (Wesling 1996: 127). What would traditional metrics conclude in the cases of these two radically different styles? Simply that both poems fulfill the structural requirements of metrical verse. Does this not efface the essential specificity of each individual voice? Certainly metrical analysis tells us very little about the specificities of movement of the voice in Shakespeare's and Dickinson's poems if we do not look into and beyond the structure. Wesling is arguing for something entirely different: awareness of the way in which the poem focuses attention through the scissoring of phrasing and lines.[2]

What is important to retain in the approaches of Meschonnic, Cureton, Wesling, and Attridge is that these sensitive readers did not lose touch with something that specialists had forgotten. Structuralists and linguistics in general had made meter into something formal. As Cureton puts it, "Like the Slavic metrists, most generativists assume that meter/rhythm is essentially linguistic or algebraic rather than psychological" (1992: 37). Formalism had taken over debates on rhythm in the 1970s and 1980s. Meschonnic, Wesling, Attridge, and Cureton all remind us to return to the poem, to its meaning and its movement. For Cureton the poem is a cognitive experience. For Meschonnic it is an invention of the linguistic subject, a process of individuation. For Wesling and Attridge the specific timbre of the voice that emerges in the poem has an emotional quality that is inseparable from the motion of the poem itself—from the way it opens, closes, and foregrounds strategic moments.

Perhaps it is now time to return to poems and listen to them. The best way of insisting on the differences between the rhythms of different poems is to juxtapose two uses of the same meter. This experiment can then be followed by juxtaposing two free-verse poems in order to show the degree to which freedom differs from poet to poet. The first two examples are fairly representative of their poets, though metrically speaking they are identical iambic pentameters. Pope's sentence breaks with the line end, and a caesura can easily be maintained in both of the lines without disturbing the phrasing:

> The same ambition can destroy or save,
> And makes a patriot as it makes a knave.

("Essay on Man II," 1963: 144)

Now compare this balanced pentameter with the irrepressibly free iambic pentameter of Milton's phrasing in the opening of Book Four of *Paradise Lost*. (The reader must forgive me for not including the full length of the sentence, as quoting thirty-one lines would inevitably be considered labouring the point.)

> O for that warning voice, which he who saw
> The Apocalypse heard cry in heaven aloud,
> Then when the dragon, put to second rout,
> Came furious down to be revenged on men,
> *Woe to the inhabitants of the earth! that now,*
> While time was, our first-parents had been warned
> The coming of their secret foe, and scaped,
> Haply so scaped his mortal snare; for now
> Satan, now first inflamed with rage, came down,
> The tempter ere the accuser of mankind,
> To wreak on innocent frail man his loss
> Of that first battle, and his flight to hell:

(2008: 421)

I stop at the first point where meter and syntactic coincide with a colon. True, Milton uses colons as contemporary journalists use full stops, but in both contemporary journalism and Milton's poems, the phrasing invariably runs on into the next grouping; if anything, Milton's syntax is more reliable in this respect than contemporary uses of punctuation. Milton's phrasing powers on, unstoppable, into Heaven and Hell, chaos and passion. Meanwhile, Pope, like Byron, succinctly resumes his witty and insightful dictions. The style of their delivery is inseparable from the way they neatly encapsulate their ideas. Balance and concision are strategies used by Pope to ensure that his insights work upon readers, either offering them well-turned wisdom or inviting them into thought-provoking and even awe-inspiring contemplation. Cognitive, meaningful, emotional, and, above all, emotive syntax moves us by seizing our attention and dragging us along with its movement. This is what rhythm does. Meter serves its purpose, establishing a recognizable structure, setting up expectations, and satisfying them. But this is only the basement level of rhythm theory. Meschonnic and Cureton, Attridge and Wesling are already several floors above and aiming far beyond this rudimentary level of perceiving movement and organization in the poem.

The tension between meter and phrasing is lost in free verse, of course, but the line end remains. Consequently the essential rhythmic force, so particular to each poet, still makes itself felt. The free-verse lines of Carol Anne Duffy and Medbh McGuckian, for instance, interact with line ends in very different ways. As we can see in the following lines from Duffy, the phrasal groupings themselves are short, and they tend to coincide with line endings with only delicate enjambments, though sentences do come to an end within the line itself:

> What I have learnt I have learnt from the air,
> from infinite varieties of light. Muted colours
> alter gradually as clouds stir shape till purple rain
> or violet thunderstorm shudders in the corner of my eye.
>
> ("Poem in Oils," 1985: 47)

McGuckian's phrasing has a much freer quality, with lines of more varied length and less predictable endings:

> I never loved you more
> than when I let you sleep another hour,
> as if you intended to make such a gate of time
> your home.
>
> ("Minus 18 Street," 1997: 42)

Poets know that readers intuitively respond to phrasing, line ends, juxtapositions, parallelism, and abrupt endings. Only when we allow pedantic science, with its formalist formulas, to impose paradigms and procedures on perception do we fail to hear the poem. Meschonnic, Cureton, Wesling, and Attridge offer very different paradigms, ones that sensitive readers such as Morier, Alex Preminger, and T. V. F. Brogan did not have, but which did not prevent them from listening to poems. The latter scholars were wading through a swampland of sloppy definitions but they never lost sight of the way the poem works upon us, the way the voice of the poem makes itself heard. This is a struggle, and Meschonnic, Attridge, Cureton, and Wesling help us struggle on by moving beyond sterile, outdated, and misleading formalist and structuralist paradigms. Their concepts, which seize the poem without divorcing form and content, help us analyze meaning, cognition, and emotion in the motion of the unfolding phrase.

The comparisons of phrasing in the poems above, however insufficient, give some idea of the challenge. The translations considered in the case studies of Baudelaire and Dickinson will provide ample opportunity to reconsider phrasing, but for the moment, the examples above serve to underscore the interest in formulating the following questions for a comparative versification and poetics of translation. The questions themselves are simple enough, but they should direct attention to crucial issues related to the success of the poem and the translation.

1. How long are the sentences?
2. How complex is the phrasing?
3. Do the phrases allow overall patterns to emerge (parallelism) or do they contrast widely in shape and form?
4. Does the phrasing respect line ends?
5. Where phrasing respects line ends, how do line-internal groupings and syntactic breaks generate a counter-dynamics?
6. To what extent do major and minor syntactic breaks coincide with
    a. line endings?
    b. stanza endings?
    c. the closure of the poem?

These same questions apply equally to both French and English verse, not too surprisingly. It is important, nevertheless, to stress the point, because it demonstrates that—beyond the inescapable truth that French and English metrics differ greatly in the ways they are constructed and in their relationship with the line end—they share one fundamental quality: the way meters interact with phrasing is broadly similar in the two languages. In their poems, Meschonnic and André de Bouchet favour short phrases and short lines. Hugo's sentences are varied; with the versatility of the virtuoso, in his syntax he can adopt both the balanced concision of Pope and the momentous surging fury of Milton. Baudelaire's phrasing rarely does either, and if anything it resembles more the phrasing of Duffy than either Pope's or Milton's. Corneille's phrasing is wonderfully varied, and actors in his plays often share single lines. In this Corneille resembles Shakespeare: both show a subtle use of phrasing and rhythm at strategic moments of action. At rare moments Corneille's phrasing resembles that of Pope, but line endings in his verse are realized with such varied degrees of stress that the whole rarely resembles the somewhat relentless and predictable series of couplets that Pope's verse risks falling into.

Paying attention to phrasing is part of paying attention to the poem. If we listen too closely to the metrical tradition, we end up hearing only the regular *tick-a-tack* of metricality. If we listen to the phrasing and ignore the meter and line ends, we begin to treat poetry as prose. If we listen to the way the poet's phrase weaves its metrical structure or free patterning, we hear something much more obvious, but much more powerful.

Repetition Proper

It only remains to address the most obvious but most ignored element of versification: repetition proper—the repetition of words and phrases. No doubt because it is so obvious, repetition proper has gone unnoticed by treatises on versification. But, as we shall see, transposing repetition proper from one language to another presents its own difficulties. Aimé Césaire's poem "Tam-tam I" begins "à même le fleuve de sang de terre," and the three syllables "à même le" are repeated for the first six lines of the eight-line poem:

à même le fleuve de sang de terre
à même le sang de soleil brisé
à même le sang d'un cent de clous de soleil
à même le sang du suicide des bêtes à feu
à même le sang de cendre le sang de sel le sang des sangs
    d'amour
à même le sang incendié d'oiseau feu
hérons et faucons
montez et brûlez.

(On the very river of blood of earth: on the very blood of
    shattered sun
on the very blood of a hundred stabs of sunlight: on the
    very blood of the fire-beasts' suicide
on the very blood of ashes the blood of salt the blood
    of bloods of love,
on the very blazing firebird blood
herons and falcons
rise and burn.)

(Rees 1990: 816)

Clearly most of the lines owe their pattering to repetition proper, while the final two lines pivot upon the repetition of the word "and" (et), which juxtaposes disyllables in all four words (herons/faucons/ monter/brûler). Does such a poem need meter to ensure that it is foregrounded as a literary work characterized by a heightened attention to form? Surely, when we come to such poems, the opposition between poetry and prose—based as it is traditionally on meter— becomes absurd and meaningless.

In a similar fashion, Ted Hughes's "Examination at the Womb-Door" embraces repetition proper as its organizing principle. Of its twenty lines, eleven open with a question beginning with "Who," seven of which ask, "Who owns ... ?" And sixteen of the twenty lines are answered by the fatal reply "Death":

Who owns these scrawny little feet?	Death.
Who owns this bristly scorched-looking face?	Death.
Who owns these still-working lungs?	Death.
Who owns this utility coat of muscles?	Death.

Who owns these unspeakable guts?	Death.
Who owns these questionable brains?	Death.
All this nasty blood?	Death.
These minimum efficiency eyes?	Death.
This wicked little tongue?	Death.
This occasional wakefulness?	Death.

Given, stolen, or held pending trial?
Held.

Who owns the whole rainy, stony earth?	Death.
Who owns all of space?	Death.

Who is stronger than hope?	Death.
Who is stronger than the will?	Death.
Stronger than love?	Death.
Stronger than life?	Death.

But who is stronger than death?
Me, evidently.

Pass, Crow.

(2003: 218–19)

The rhythm of this poem is not the reassuring rhythm of alternation. There is no relief, no escape; the repetition is relentless. Thudding onwards, the repetition forms part of this incessant incantation. When relief does come, it comes not in the form of syntactic freedom but in the form of alternative repetition. The lines "Stronger than love? / Stronger than life?" move back into repetition proper, which inevitably follows the same syntactic shape and the same accentual pattern. The final stressed syllable even introduces an alliteration (love/life). Poems such as Hughes's and Césaire's are obviously setting up a counter-meter, an alternative form of organization that gives shape and unity, almost a structure, to the poem as a whole.

But this is not new, despite all the celebration of free-verse revolutions. Repetition and parallelism play an important part in the King James Bible and in the Hebrew original, as Meschonnic reminds us in his Bible translations (2001a, 2002, 2003). But we should avoid falling into Jakobson's error of assuming that this alternative patterning constitutes a dominant that replaces the meter. In fact, repetition proper, even of the relentless kind used by Hughes and Césaire, is often found in metrical verse. In Shakespeare's "Sonnet 66," ten of the fourteen lines begin with "And"—the choice is expressive. Opening with "Tired with all these, for restful death I cry," the lyrical subject of the poem goes on to list, one by one, all the things that fuel his world-weariness (1988: 35).

Repetition proper is obviously a significant organizing principle in both metrical and free verse. It does not, however, often organize the whole but rather separates and holds together freer passages of verse. In such instances, repetition proper can be considered to function as a kind of refrain. It is important, though, to distinguish between the way refrains function in metrical and in free verse. In metrical verse they constitute a line verbatim recurring at regular intervals, invariably at the end of a stanza. Brogan notes examples of refrains in the Egyptian *Book of the Dead* and in the Psalms of the Hebrew Bible, as well as in Greek and Latin poetry (Preminger and Brogan 1993: 1018). Found in Old and Middle French as well as in modern French verse, the refrain is often associated with ballads and with oral poetry in general. Indeed, in oral poetry the listeners can be invited to chant the refrain, as in folk songs.

In "La ballade des dames du temps jadis," François Villon ends each stanza with the line "Mais où sont les neiges d'antan" (But where are the snows of yesteryear; 2004: 34). In the English verse of Charles d'Orléans the refrain is often used. In "Oft in My Thought," Charles ends each stanza with "God have her soul, I can say no better". In metrical verse the refrain tends to take its place within the structure and within the framework of expectations. How does this compare to free verse? We might be inclined to assume that in free verse the refrain too is free. But this is not entirely true; often it works as a reminder of regularity. For this reason refrains frequently introduce an element of regularity, metrical or otherwise, into an otherwise free and unpredictably shaped poem. Metrical refrains in free verse work like the versified refrains of children's stories and fairy tales. They break into the flow of prose with examples like "Run, run, as fast as you can / You can't catch me. I'm the gingerbread man."

Examples that run counter to this are not hard to find. T. S. Eliot revolts against the refrain when he ironically elevates the barmaid's call for last orders to a refrain in *The Waste Land*: "Hurry up please it's time" (1969a: 65). More characteristic of the refrain in free verse, though, is Saint-John Perse's use of *palmes* in his "Pour fêter une enfance" (1960: 28). The French word for palms intervenes at strategic moments in Perse's lyrical free verse, often at the beginning of the free stanza, and it is invariably backed up by alliteration in the accompanying words (*plaintes, pentes, pouvait, plus, présent, pleure*).

This short review of repetition proper inevitably introduces new questions for the translator. Traditionally translators consider it their job to translate the meaning of the poem, and to translate the form when the form is clearly defined. But how are they to handle repetition? Often the meaning is translated but not the function. Another series of questions therefore becomes inescapable:

1. Is the repetition essential for the poem as a whole?
2. Does it organize the whole, contributing to the poem's structure or shape?
3. Does it intervene at strategic moments to foreground crucial transitions, openings, or closures?
4. Is the refrain metrical or not? If so, does it maintain or break with the poem's meter? Or does it introduce metricality into a non-metrical context?
5. Does repetition highlight sound patterning, assonance, or alliteration?

There is a naive hermeneutic tradition in translation theory that encourages translators to supposedly extract the meaning, as if form is matter that gets in the way and must be penetrated in order to uncover that meaning. Repetition proper, more than any other rhythmic element, quite simply refutes the form/meaning opposition within which hermeneutics remains imprisoned. The same meaning is presented in the same form, yet that repetition redoubles the expressive force of the poem as a meaningful experience. In poems, what can be redundant in speech and prose becomes a signifying strategy by which we return to a point while rolling on to something new. In a cyclical movement the new grows out of the old, and what unfolds remains full of what still resounds in the memory.

In repetition proper the present is pregnant with the past and full of the future, making the device very apt for hymns to nature and celebrations of the cycles of the cosmos. Perse's lyricism offers a modern celebration of the cyclical with his repetitions and refrains. But Hughes's example reminds us that we should be wary of seeking metaphysics in the forms we ponder. Death, despair, and world-weariness trundle on just as expressively when repeated. In metrical and in free verse, even monotony becomes a motion that awakens us to emotion.

The Orchestration of Rhythmic Elements

All of the examples of poems we have considered demonstrate two things: the absurdity of reducing rhythm to meter and the absurdity of treating rhythmic elements separately. I would ask readers to kindly indulge me if we seem to have strayed from poems as we advanced into the analysis of form. But is there any other way to proceed towards a stable synthesis than by moving through a meticulous analysis of the parts of the poem as a whole?

Breaking up the poem was an inevitable consequence of the object of this study. It would have been possible to give a vastly greater number of examples, and more poems could have been quoted in full. These strategies might have served to illustrate the points more clearly, but doing so would have made this theoretical section into a book on its own, a book of many hundreds of pages, and that is not the object of this book on translation. The second part of this book grows out of the first, but it also breaks with it. In the first part we have considered poetry and form in relation to making sense. The second part will investigate the voyages of poems from one language culture to another.

In this first part I chose to begin by comparing the forms of French and English verse, and this entailed comparing meters. In turn the comparison entailed dividing syllables into stressed and unstressed syllables and meters into types that depend on syllable count and stress count. Rhyme, phrasing, and repetition have all been treated separately. This process of division, of course, inevitably reminds us that we never perceive anything in the poem in isolation. Each time we listen to the poem, what do we find? The complex and subtle—ultimately poet-specific—interaction of rhythmic elements.

This is the style, the rhythm, that Pound claimed was impossible to counterfeit. Each poet has a style of his or her own, and great poets have a style that imposes itself upon the poetic tradition. Poets leave their mark upon their language. The great German linguist Wilhelm von Humboldt knew that poets strike their roots deeply into reality, and that the linguistic community draws its identity from writers and thinkers who open up and cultivate the language system with which we think. French without La Fontaine, Hugo, and Baudelaire; German without Goethe, Heine, and Rilke; English without Shakespeare, Whitman, and Dickinson would be poorer, less able to inspire, harness, and direct creative thought. How the thoughts of those poets have imposed themselves upon the language, impressing themselves on the imagination, is related not simply to what they said but also the way they formulated their thoughts in formally heightened foregrounded verse. If their poetry is memorable, it is because it uses rhythmic strategies that catch the imagination, resounding in the memory of the people and in their speech.

The first part of this book is not an exercise in mere formalism; this adventure into rhythm has taken us far beyond structure. Structure, metrical constraints, and rhyming schemes should not be disparaged. What we must remember, however, is that form is meaningless if it is empty of meaning. For this reason we need a theory of translation that moves beyond division of the poem into form and content. We need to look further than the sign that divides every object of understanding into signifier and signified. Poetry takes us into signifying—a continuous and interactive process of ongoing meaning-making. Movement and organization are inseparable from meaning, just as each of the rhythmic elements works interactively to engender the whole.

Although we have proceeded in our analysis of individual rhythmic elements, this must be considered a provisional perversion. Now we must return to the theory of translation in order to affirm the need to think through what we are doing when we translate. This work will prove far from easy. But what does that signify? Only that we are on the right side of impossible. The difficult task awaits us. Let us clarify our ideas, and theoretical premises, before engaging in the battles that courageous translators fight when they start dismantling poems and creatively putting them back together.

Notes

1. See the frank exchange of views between Attridge (1996) and Cureton (1996).
2. Wesling was a friend of Meschonnic's and exchanged letters with him in the 1980s and 1990s. To my own regret, as a student of Meschonnic's in the 1990s I was unable to induce him to respond to Wesling's and

Cureton's work as they had responded to his. In those years Meschonnic was suffering from two great tyrants: a grave medical condition and a merciless will. That will drove him to publish more than a dozen books on poetics, in addition to his celebrated Bible translations from Hebrew, during the period from his so-called retirement until his death in 2009. That workload left little time for new, unscheduled research projects.

PART TWO

FORM AND MEANING IN POETRY TRANSLATION

CHAPTER 5

Theorizing the Translation of Poetry

> *Le problème des vers n'est pas le vers. Mais le poème. [...] Nerval, et Hugo [...] disaient déjà, presque, des choses semblables: "Je n'aime pas les vers, j'aime la poésie."* (The problem of verse is not the verse line, but the poem. [...] Nerval and Hugo said pretty much the same thing: "I don't like verse: I like poetry.")
>
> (Meschonnic 1999: 307; my translation)

Even from the page, some poems speak to us. We hear a voice that manifests itself in the movement and organization of its words, in the phrases that form and break off, in the distribution of accents, and in the rhymes, the alliteration, and the assonance that form sonorous patterns. This voice is meaningful, of course, but it takes form in the dynamic interaction of the formal elements of which it is composed.

As we have already seen, however, the poem in translation all too often does not speak to us; it mumbles faintly, and we are left deaf and insensitive to the impulse that inspired the original poem. For this reason it is often asserted that the translation of poetry is impossible: the magic of poetry cannot traverse the gulf between languages. Translation kills poetry, or at least so the argument goes. It will be clear by now that this book analyzes the theoretical approaches to translation at the disposition of the translator in order to demonstrate that those approaches hinder the translation of poetry and, more specifically, the transposition of form. That is to say, such approaches build barriers instead of building bridges.

They begin by dividing meaning and form. While it may be useful to make a conceptual distinction between the meaning and the form of a poem, a verse, or a word, the distinction made between those two aspects of one entity is abstract. No concrete division can be made. Pessimistic approaches often reduce all aspects of form to the conventional structures of meter and rhyme. In Part 1, throughout the discussion of the individual rhythmic elements in play and their interactions, I have stressed that this is absurd. The alliterative links between key words, the internal weighting of lines (which makes one pentameter read very differently from the next), run-on lines, and refrains are all aspects of form that contribute to the force and success of a poem. But these elements tend to be ignored when the poem is considered in terms of a traditional metrical form.

The concept of form that results from such reasoning is depersonalized, conventional, and deprived of context. In such a form the voice of the poem is often muffled or lost. So it is hardly surprising that the translation of poetry is often deemed to be impossible. And yet, miraculously, poetry is translated, and often well translated too. The proof is that all the major poetic traditions have been greatly influenced by foreign traditions, largely thanks to the successful translation of poems. The German romantics regenerated their literary tradition with their inspired and inspiring translations of Shakespeare. And how do most readers throughout the world know Lorca and Baudelaire, if not through the works of translators? Such successes are sometimes attributed to divine accident, and nothing in traditional translation theory can account for them. So how can we come to grips with these miracles? If we can succeed in understanding and explaining what works in translating poems, perhaps we will be able to facilitate the task of the translator in the future.

Sadly, a gulf has widened between the theory and the practice of poetry, and while theoreticians are sometimes inclined to impose their approach blindly on the practice of translation, practising translators often claim that theory is useless and pointless. This conclusion is reached by two contrasting avenues. Pragmatists argue that translation is a practice, a practical affair. Others argue that it is an art. Art here is used as an alibi—like intuition and creativity—for refusing to investigate something that is supposed to be somehow impenetrable to theory, untheorizable.

Rather than joining either of these camps—theory or practice—I contend, firmly and patiently, that it is time to theorize practice and practice theory. What steps can be taken, then, towards theorizing the translation of poetry? As the opening chapters have demonstrated, translation theory made considerable advances in the twentieth century, partly thanks to research in the area of linguistics, more specifically in comparative linguistics. In translation between

French and English, for example, works such as those of J. P. Vinay and J. Darbelnet on comparative grammar and stylistics (1977) and Jacqueline Guillemin-Flescher's on comparative syntax (1981) remain useful aids for the transposition of many linguistic elements. Without being specific to poetry, these remain essential to all discourse, and the translator of poetry may well profit from such research. A great deal of progress has also been made in the past forty years in comparative metrics, mainly by Slavic researchers such as Jiří Levý (1963, 1969, 2011), M. L. Gasparov (1996), and Marina Tarlinskaja (1976). In England Clive Scott has provided a sensitive, informed, and creative approach to comparing French and English versification (1990, 1993, 1998, 2000).

A linguistic approach, however, will not help us understand the specific nature of poetry, and comparative metrics does not try to transform the traditional theory of translation, but rather implies an extension of it. That traditional theories cannot help in the translation of poetry is a fact that many theoreticians are willing (often eager) to admit. Poetry, they argue, is not their field. They are concerned with communication, and their concept of language consists of transmission of the message from sender to receiver. The sole purpose of such theory is to deal with problems arising from the distortion of this message in the transformative process of translating. In such a light, all reflection on the act of translating comes to be reduced to a hermeneutics that aims to explicate and to interpret. Danica Seleskovitch and Marianne Lederer offer a good example of this school of thought in their *Interpréter pour traduire* (1984); this line of research provides the theoretical basis for the praxis of translation taught in France. Some theoreticians have also adopted the hermeneutic approach and pushed it to its extreme form. George Steiner advances the idea that all translation is interpretative and then inverts it by postulating that all interpretation is translation. Even he affirms that "When we read or hear any language-statement from the past, be it Leviticus or last year's best-seller, we translate. Reader, actor, editor are all translators of language out of time" (1992: 28–29).

Whether confusing all forms of intralingual interpretation with interlingual translation can advance the theory of translation proper remains to be seen. But the usefulness of the interpretive theory cannot be denied; the success of professional translation schools in training interpreters testifies to the fact that this approach, with its focus on meaning, is perfectly adapted to the translation of an economic text or even a politician's speech. Most theoreticians defending this approach will usually agree, on the other hand, that a different method is required for translating poetry, in which the form is an essential factor.

It is not, therefore, a question of chiding existing theories for their partial blindness, since they do not pretend to teach us how to translate a poem. Rather it is the responsibility of poetics to define this partial blindness—not with the aim of opposing such theories but in an attempt to show their limits. Poetics must mark the boundaries of a theory suited to the specific needs of translating poems. Levý's comparative metrics; the work in English by Derek Attridge, Donald Wesling, and Richard D. Cureton; and the studies in French by Henri Morier and Henri Meschonnic have helped advance the redefinitions of poetics. The key question is, to what extent does our conception of poetics transform our theory of language and our theorization of the translation process? This question proves to be one that translators tend to avoid and that traditional theory resists.

CHAPTER 6

Translating the Sign or the Poem?

As Henri Meschonnic (1972, 1999) argues, thinking within the limits of traditional theories of translation renders us insensitive to that which is specifically poetic. It forces us to consider poetry in terms of the linguistic sign that constitutes the union of two separate things, the signifier and the signified (form and meaning), whereas the poem testifies to an inseparable union of the two. While it is true that the form and the content are inseparable for the most part, our attempts to understand their essential unity have invariably consisted of trying to link up two separate elements. Paradoxically, to link is to divide.

Thinking within the limits of a theory of translation based on the concept of language as communication—that is to say, within the limits of the linguistic sign—we are inclined to consider form in merely functional terms: as the vehicle of meaning, the container of the content. If we accept such a conceptual framework when translating the poem, we are compelled to choose between the form and the content. One is privileged at the expense of the other; one is sacrificed. This is the reasoning that lies behind a translator's decision to translate the poem into prose, as Goethe suggests (1973). It is also behind the decision to retain a certain word to preserve a conventional rhyming scheme. What proves grotesque is that we are doing this for the best of reasons, without actually considering whether the highlighting of such a word contributes towards the signifying process of the poem. Such schismatic thinking can indeed be fatal, and we would be justified in saying it kills the poem, if by that we mean that the resonance of its poetic force is dampened or deadened.

Few thinkers would argue with the idea that sacrificing form is fatal for the poem. The translation of poetry into prose has never been short of critics. What is less evident, however, is that traditional theories of translation that privilege the content at the expense of the form do in fact "deform" our idea of form in poetry. Having established that poetry translated into prose loses its poetry, we are forced to conclude (so long as we remain within the schismatic logic of the linguistic sign) that the poetry of a poem resides not in the content but in the form. This kind of reasoning is sometimes found in translation treatises, but it belongs to a more widespread prejudice born of a desire to compensate for the fact that form is often misprized.

Paul Valéry, the French poet, novelist, and critic, took up this line when he swam against the current of *les vers libres*. Valéry is all the more interesting because he certainly realized the importance of form. "The subject of a work is that to which a bad work can be reduced" (Le sujet d'un ouvrage est à quoi se réduit un mauvais ouvrage), he rightly claimed (1943: 131). But in his provocative aphorisms, Valéry's extreme formalism can be attributed to the fact that he never escaped the form/meaning dichotomy. He therefore felt himself forced to choose between the two. How else are we supposed to interpret his defence of rhyme over reason: reason requires that the poet defends the rhyme over reason—"La raison veut que le poète préfère la rime à la raison" (126)?

The formalist stance in Valéry's work and elsewhere attributes an inherent value to form itself. But such celebration proves paradoxical, a poisoned gift. Form is simultaneously marginalized and privileged: marginalized in the sense that it is reduced to something that is simply decorative, something that embellishes the sense, and privileged in the sense that this decoration comes to be considered as that which is quintessentially poetic.

Translating Form Blindly

Those working with traditional theories of translation are often eager to please the defenders of poetry by paying homage to the form, but we are hardly deferring to the poem by reducing it to its form—the inevitable result of such reasoning. Since, according to the logic of this argument, the poetic is essentially formal, the meaning of the poem is regarded as secondary, all but irrelevant. Celebrating form deforms our impression of the poem and our impression of its voice, since only the manner in which the poem says what it does is considered to be of importance. The same faulty logic can be found in traditional theories of translation, such as those established in France, Britain, and the United States, but it is found equally in the writings of a great many translators who have tried to make explicit the implicit theory that directs their own practice of translation. As we saw in the redefinition of poetic form in chapter 1, the great essayist and thinker Walter Benjamin espouses an idealized notion of form. He posits that "any translation which intends to perform a transmitting function cannot transmit anything but information—hence, something inessential" (1992: 70).

This starting point is fructuous and thought-provoking, like most of Benjamin's essays. But where is he leading us? To compensate for the traditional marginalization of form, Benjamin swings to the other extreme in marginalizing the sense of the poem. Because ultimately he remains within the conceptual limits of the linguistic sign, the meaning for him comes second, something that would inevitably produce horrendous results if this translation theory were put into practice. Unsurprisingly, as a practising translator, Benjamin does not apply his own theory in translating poems.

It is common to find this same marginalization of the meaning of poetry wherever the translation of poetry into prose is criticized. Many translators defend what we might call a formalist translation, privileging form at the expense of meaning. This tradition has resulted in some of the most lamentable deformations of poetry. In an instructive example, the modern American poet Louis Zukovsky tries to justify his English translations of Catullus—translations that the English reader will find difficult to understand without the aid of another English translation at hand—by claiming to remain faithful to the form.

Zukovsky worked for eleven years (1958–69) on a prose translation of Catullus made by his wife, Celia, who marked the metrical distribution of long and short accents in the original (Venuti 1995: 214). His ambition was to render a "homophonic translation" of Catullus that would "follow the sound, rhythm and syntax of his Latin" (215). Given that Zukovsky himself did not understand Latin, it is arguable whether he was in a position to judge the importance of the sound patterning and the movement of the original and their significance to the poem. Furthermore, he seems to have been ignorant of the fact that the quantitative meter does not transpose directly into English; that is to say, it does not render a perceptible structure that can organize the poem (without considerable adaptation into English syllabo-accentual meters). In fairness to Zukovsky, however, readers should be allowed to judge the result for themselves. Here is an example:

> Newly say dickered my love air my own would marry me all
>   Whom but one, none see say Jupiter if she petted.
> Dickered: did my love air could be o could dickered a man too
>   In wind o wet rapid a scribble reported in water.
>
> (quoted in Venuti 1995: 215)

The easy charm of Catullus's light verse seems impenetrably dense in this rendering. Many of the words do not seem to be English and the movement is surprising, irregular; at best it seems to be wholly without organization. But this is not a dramatic free-verse experiment. We can speak of neither innovation nor rupture here. We are not entering into transgression or tension. No patterning or meaningful order is established sufficiently to set up something that might be undermined or attacked. How are we to account for this mess?

The error in Zukovsky's approach is a fundamental one: having divided the poem into form and meaning, he goes on to attribute a privileged status to the Latin form in and of itself, independent of the meaning of the poem. There are three steps involved in this dead-end anti-theory:

1. The rhythm of the poem is reduced to the form of poetry, in other words, to meter.
2. Metrical accentuation is confused with the accentuation of the language.

3. The accentual orders of English and Latin are confused in a translingual celebration of form.

Ultimately the poet commits that unforgivable sin of privileging form at the expense of the poem. The result is a translation with no perceptible structure and whose meaning is impenetrably obscure. How Zukovsky's translation is supposed to function similarly to the original poem is hard to see. In striving to remain faithful to form, he thus betrays the form, the meaning, and the function of the poem.

Such an example clearly demonstrates the absurdity of privileging form. Yet, strangely enough, many have made the same mistake. I would argue with Meschonnic that they affirm the specific nature of poetic translation without following their intuition to acknowledge the specific signifying process involved in poems and to break out of the conceptual framework of the linguistic sign. Not simply a stumbling block for poeticians, translators, and poets, the linguistic sign is a gulf, a gap that threatens to swallow us up, like the puddle that swallowed up Doctor Foster on his way to Gloucester in the nursery rhyme. If you don't watch where you are going, you will fall into the sign.

What I will call the formalist translation has many adherents. Lawrence Venuti in *The Translator's Invisibility* quotes Zukovsky as a model for the kind of translation we should aspire to (1995: 215–16). Given the success that Venuti has had in translation theory in recent years, this recommendation is perplexing. Surely it is necessary to get back to basics and stress that what is at stake in translating poetry is the poem. The poem expresses something that escapes hermeneutics and a reduction to individual elements of meaning—that is, signs. The meaning is essential to the poem as a whole. If this were not the case, the movement of the poem would not be meaningful. The poetry of poems resides in the unity of their form and meaning. Indeed, it is this very unity that makes a poem a poem. The poem is reducible neither to its message (as Benjamin is right to affirm) nor the manner in which its message is formulated, its formal organization. The poem does not "say," it "does," as Meschonnic argues throughout his entire prolific oeuvre (1972, 1982, 1999). The form not only organizes the meaning but also strengthens it and amplifies its capacity for signifying by establishing series or semantic links between formal elements, such as rhymes or alliterative patterning, or between repeated accentual series.

If we reject the tendency to reduce poetry to an essence, be it a formal or a semantic one, if we accept that poetry does not say but does—imposing its meaning, acting upon us in ways that prose generally does not—we will understand that form, though certainly essential to the functioning of the poem, is no more essential than meaning. It is absurd to marginalize the sense of the poem. For what is to be gained by preserving the formulation of a meaning that is arbitrary and uninteresting? Why should we listen to Catullus if what he says is inessential, as Benjamin's and Zukovsky's reasoning would seem to imply?

Form has value solely inasmuch as it plays a role in the poem as a whole. Benjamin and Zukovsky are both sensitive to the specificity of poetic language, but they raise form to an almost sacrosanct status, attributing to it an absolute importance, whereas its importance is purely relative to the poem.

Translating a Poem with a Poem

Because adherents of the formalist approach to translation fail to seize the functioning of the poem as a whole, they are unable to establish a functional hierarchy that organizes the formal and semantic elements of the poem in order of importance. And it is this incapacity that leads them to insist on the importance of transposing details that are often relatively insignificant to the functioning of the poem as a whole. To attach importance to the distribution of accents without listening to what is accented leads to absurd results, as Zukovsky's backfiring experiment demonstrates. Listening to the voice of the poem should help us avoid conceiving form in purely formal terms. It is clearly necessary to understand the form not as a mechanical structure that imposes itself upon a discourse, but as the formulation of the poetic voice in, and by virtue of, its versification, in the largest sense of the word.

The aim of this section is limited. In the Baudelaire and Dickinson case studies in Part 3 we will closely observe the way poems have been transposed from one language to another. My intention here is simply to illustrate the danger of accepting the conceptual framework of the linguistic sign and a translation theory that reduces all language to communication (i.e., the exchange of information). Certainly it is not my intention to imply that the transposition of form is any easy matter, but rather to stress that we cannot engage the necessary difficulties and attempt to find formal equivalents until we have set aside the theory of the sign. Just as we must consider the poem poetically, we need a translation theory that allows us to transpose the poem poetically.

For this reason I agree with Meschonnic (1972, 1978, 1999) that we must abandon the traditional dichotomies and oppositions furnished by translation theory. Extrapolating his approach to the task at hand, I would argue that we cannot conceive the translation of a poem in terms of

- a word-for-word translation;
- a sentence-by-sentence or line-by-line translation;
- a sense-by-sense translation; or
- a form-by-form translation.

Rather, we must conceive of it as the translation of a poem with a poem. This is the point at which Ezra Pound and Meschonnic begin thinking through the problem that Goethe, Valéry, Benjamin, Zukovsky, and Venuti stumble over. To a certain extent Meschonnic's writings on translation constitute an attempt to theorize the same approach that Pound adopted and propagated. Throughout his work, Pound urged a poem-for-a-poem translation (with greater or lesser success), and the fact that we often tend not to distinguish between Pound's translations and his own poems testifies to the fact that such an ambition is not unrealistic.

The ideas of Pound, as with his practice, have had an enormous influence on poetry translation in the English-speaking world. Having said that, the theoretical extrapolation of this basic principle in the work of Pound is very limited when compared to that of Meschonnic. The importance of Pound's ideas on translation can be summarized in three points (Pound 1954):

1. his affirmation of the necessity of translating a poem with a poem;
2. his insistence on the importance of translation for spreading culture;
3. his affirmation of the historical importance of translation as an influence on the literary tradition.

These three points deserve to be asserted firmly, especially in the context of a culture that tends to underestimate the influence of foreign cultures on its own tradition. The situation today has not changed much since Pound's time. In truth, though, there is nothing particularly original about the three principles that he defined. We find, for example, the same three ideas in Antoine Godeau's "Discours sur les oeuvres de M. de Malherbe" (Discourse on the Works of Mr. Malherbe) in 1630 (Ballard 1992: 157). Too often we forget these ideas, and Pound and contemporary critics such as Venuti certainly deserve credit for reminding us of them.

The essays of Pound do not, however, allow us to theorize this ideal practice—the translation of a poem with a poem.[1] Pound was an inspired, innovative, and original thinker, but he was not a rigorous conceptual thinker. In the end the virtue of Pound's writings owes more to faith than to theory (which explains his weakness for metaphors such as "divine miracles").

Translating Form Meaningfully

If we accept that poetry does something just as much as it says something, if we consider poetry not in the schismatic terms of form and meaning but as an enactment of forging sense, then we will be forced to reappraise the task of the translator. No longer will it be a question of translating either/or—either translating what the poem says or translating its formal structure. The translator must create a poem in the foreign language that does the same thing as the original and that functions in the same way. Eugene Nida came close to discerning this objective when he spoke of "dynamic translations" (Venuti 2004: 156–57), but he never escaped the hermeneutics of the linguistic sign as a conceptual framework.

In striving to make the translation do what the poem does, the translator takes as a starting point the poem itself, before dividing it into form and content. The importance of these elements (usually divided into form and meaning) is determined in relation to the roles they play in the functioning of the poem. The translator must reconsider the possibility of rendering those aspects of the poem usually termed formal. As we have seen, however, form itself has multiple and not altogether compatible meanings. We constantly confuse four very different ideas when using this word:

1. the matter or words (the spoken sound or the written word);
2. what I will define as the structure of the poem;
3. what I call the overall pattern of the poem; and
4. what I call the local pattern that emerges at times in the poem.

The matter of words (the spoken sound or written word) needs little explanation. It may come into play in the functioning of the poem inasmuch as phonemes form part of the rhyme (e.g., play/stay). It may also form part of the alliterative patterning of expressive phrases, for example, in the jarring repetition of sounds in Wilfred Owen's gunfire: "the stuttering rifles' rapid rattle" ("Anthem for a Doomed Youth," quoted in Cuthbertson 2014: 200). The sonorous quality of words plays an important role in governing which syllables can form the metrical beat in a poem. In the first line of Shakespeare's "Sonnet 86" (1987: 385), "Was it the proud full sail of his great verse," though both "proud" and "full" carry approximately the same accentual weight, "full" is downplayed (or demoted) to allow the undulating flow of alternating weak and strong syllables.[2] The matter of words matters inasmuch as the poet and the translator must know (or feel) which syllables are stressed, which are unstressed, and, most important, which are stressable (Attridge 1982, 1995).

The structure of a poem might be defined as a conventional configuration that implies rules and the possibility of transgression of those rules. The first strophe of the following poem from Emily Dickinson clearly establishes the structure of the four-beat ballad-style meter that alternates tetrameters and three-stress lines and that usually rhymes only every second line in an *xaya* rhyming scheme.

> I started early, took my dog,
> And visited the sea;
> The mermaids in the basement
> Came out to look at me.
>
> (2016: 311)

As seen in chapter 3, on meter, this structure sets up expectations that will be fulfilled or frustrated. Dickinson often carves innovative ideas from this the simplest of structures. She is, however, also famous for her curious half-rhymes that partially undo her pert little packages of dense meaning.

The overall pattern of a poem is the organizing principle that lends a coherence to the poem as a whole, thereby allowing some free verse to be organized while remaining free of structural rules. This is the kind of organization that Roman Jakobson was trying to find in free verse when he spoke of the "dominant." As already demonstrated, such patterns are found side by side, or rather intertwining, with meter in more regular verse. Patterns might be formed by accentual configurations but they can equally be formed of repetition proper, parallelism, assonance, alliteration, and so forth. Much of the poetry of Saint-John Perse is organized around a loose but powerful principle. His free-verse strophes are invariably limited to phrases of three, four, six, eight, or nine syllables, for example, phrases of a length to be found in individual short verse lines (*vers simples*) or in longer lines (*vers composés*) such as the alexandrine (6:6 or 4:4:4) or the decasyllable (4:6 or 6:4). This principle can be seen—or felt—in the following extract from Perse's prose poem "Exil II":

> Sagesse de l'écume [6], ô pestilences de l'esprit [8] dans la crépitation du sel [8] et le lait de chaux vive![6]

> (quoted in Rees 1990: 649)

For reasons of space I have not quoted Perse at length, but whole free-verse strophes will not contradict the principles set up in the extract above. The elevated tone of the passage and the dominance of clearly metrical verse lines hiding in this prose poetry clearly invite us to give a metrical reading of the lines by stressing the mute *e* where it appears within the phrase. In Perse's prose poems, five-, eleven-, and thirteen-syllable phrases are extremely rare. This principle allows a great deal of variety whilst evoking traditional French verse. For this very reason Perse enjoyed great success in the 1930s and 1940s, when many people were eager to find a kind of classicism in innovation. Pound and T. S. Eliot were looking for a similar way out of rhythmic routines without breaking completely with tradition. Although much successful free verse depends on some kind of patterning to give the poem a kind of wholeness, overall patterning that organizes the alliteration or the refrains of a poem is just as common in traditional metrical verse, as I have already stressed.

Local pattern is the heightened organization of part of a poem, and the success of free verse often depends on it for its expressive eventfulness, although local pattern is just as common in traditional metrical verse. Such patterns might be formed by the same elements that form the general pattern (accentuation, phrasing, repetition, and so on), though they do not persist to give coherence to the poem as a whole. This fact explains why they are sometimes considered stylistic effects.

Eliot's poetry moves in and out of metrical forms, juxtaposing chunks of one metrical verse with those of another, incompatible type to create unnerving cacophonies. He is also a master of the kind of local patterning that free verse often exploits. Alliteration intervenes to highlight certain verses. Rhyme penetrates unrhymed contexts to form heightened, meaningful moments in the poem that would be altogether less salient if those rhymes were found in a context in which the structure of the poem led us to anticipate rhyming. His rhyme surprises and disturbs us rather than reassures us. In "The Love Song of J. Alfred Prufrock," for example, the timid, balding antihero of a parlour-room story debates with himself whether he can muster the courage to court one of the pretty ladies he meets in polite society; his nervousness comes to a shrill peak in the appropriately absurd rhyme of "ices" and "crisis":

> Should I, after tea and cakes and ices,
> Have the strength to force the moment to its crisis?
>
> (1969a: 15)

The French translator Pierre Leyris is very sensitive to such moments in Eliot's verse. He engenders the same kind of local patterning by means of alliteration:

> Devrais-je, après le thé, les gâteaux et les glaces,
> Avoir le nerf d'exacerber l'instant jusqu'à sa crise?
>
> (Eliot 1969b: 15)

The division of the first line of the French version into two six-syllable phrases (a perfect alexandrine) echoes the meter of traditional verse. But does not the absence of that single rhyme in an unrhymed context constitute a considerable loss? The translator is forced to establish a hierarchy of essential aspects of the poem; here the meaning that Leyris preserves is paramount to the absurd crisis that the rhyme crystallizes. Prufrock dreams of romantic dramas but will remain politely sipping his tea, munching his cakes, and scooping up his ice cream. The exact nature of the word that evokes the platitudes of polite society is inconsequential. Whether crisis is linked to ice cream or biscuits, this meaningful effect will be preserved. For this reason I propose the following invention in place of Leyris's:

> Devrais-je, après le thé et gâteaux aux cerises,
> Oser . . . oser pousser l'instant jusqu'à sa crise?

Here the rhyme is preserved. The two lines intervene in a non-structured context as a pair of alexandrines traditionally divided into two six-syllable phrases. Balanced lines paradoxically upset the unbalanced context. The repetition of *oser* (hesitate) also enacts the nervous hesitation of Prufrock. But it is the rhyme *cerises/crise* that mirrors the effect that Eliot excels in provoking.

Notes

1. On the contrary, the ideas of Pound often prevent us from thinking through the implications of translating rhythm, as can be seen in the concept of *melopoeia*, which he defines as "MELOPOEIA: wherein the words are charged, over and above their plain meaning, with some musical property, which directs the bearing or trend of that meaning" (1954: 25). The idea of the musicality of poetry derives from the idea that the arrangement and repetition of like sounds engenders harmony, which is not always the case. It is a formal conceptualization of repetition, an idea that does not start from the essential unity of the form and the meaning but rather invests the form with an absolute, euphonic virtue. Here Pound is leaning towards Valéry and Benjamin. Furthermore, Pound asserts that transposition of melopoeia is impossible except by "divine accident" (25). Rather than advancing theorization of the practice of poetry translation, this assertion leads us to the conclusion that the magic of poetry must somehow be magically translated. While intuitively correct, Pound was often conceptually weak. He thought in inspired fragments—like a poet—without always coherently organizing his impressions.

2. It may seem curious, but though "full" is far stronger than "his" in this line, the latter, because of its place before two stressed syllables, can be promoted into a metrical stress, while "great," a far stronger syllable, can be demoted. Nonetheless, the rising and falling undulating movement is preserved.

CHAPTER 7

Form and Translation

Translating Strategies: Forms of Reformulating

Translating Aims

Clarifying exactly what we mean when we talk about translating form should allow us to avoid those trite paradoxes, such as "formless form" and "structure without form," that some literary critics tend to find deliciously elusive. On closer inspection, such phrases inevitably turn out to be dead ends, not perspectives. They will not help us conceptualize the difficulties of reconstructing a poem in a foreign language. The redefinition of form as having four components (page 161) allows us to consider a poem as either partly patterned (local pattern) or patterned as a whole (overall pattern) without being organized by meter and rhyme.

This redefinition should also attract the attention of translators to more of the aspects of a poet's voice in versification and help them to see beyond conventional structures. We can thus attenuate the opposition between metrical verse and free verse, since formal patterns emerge in both free verse and within the structures that organize metrical verse. Once these clear-cut categories have been adopted, the translator will no longer be able to take refuge in the excuse that free verse can be translated into prose, since it is formless. Rather, the translator's responsibility will be to discern the free poem's organizing principles—if, indeed, there are any at work. The translator will then consider how the free poem works and take into account its meaningful formal patterning.

These distinctions also allow us to examine more closely the traditional opposition between mechanical form and organic form and its relevance to the translation of poetry. "Mechanical form" can be defined as a conventional structure in poetry, the fixed form involving meter and rhyme. It is usually a pejorative term that denotes the organization of uninspired poems in which the structure is imposed. In such a usage the versification is said to be forced upon the voice, or the voice is forced into the versification. Organic form, on the other hand, emerges from within: it is innate. The voice and versification combine in a harmonious whole. Determining exactly the nature of this form may necessitate both great sensitivity and discernment, but recognition that such a thing exists should serve as a reminder that translating the form of a poem cannot be reduced to transposing its conventional structure. Translating the shell would provide only a hollow translation, empty of meaningful patterning. Translators should of course strive to recreate the voice in the versification. Their objective should be to transpose an organic form through an organic translation.

The distinction between organic and mechanical form allows us to identify four different ways of translating poetry, according to the way we treat the form:

1. Semantic translation, which contents itself with transposition of the meaning of the poem.
2. Formal translation, which prioritizes the form and treats meaning as secondary.
3. Semantico-formal translation, which translates the meaning and then imposes a conventional structure on it.
4. Organic translation, which aims at transposition of the voice within its versification, recreating analogous formal configurations in the translation that make sense without running counter to what is expressed in the original poem.

Translators are pragmatists—doers as much as thinkers—and so some examples will no doubt be welcome at this point.

Semantic Translation

Most translators who opt for a rendering in prose do so because they feel convinced that what poets say is more important than the way they say it. They therefore conclude that the former should prevail over the latter if a choice has to be made. The poetic thrust of alliterative patterning, the pulsation of metrical beating, and the meaningful rhymes are all left by the wayside as the road towards the poem's meaning is rebuilt. Perhaps it is unfair to compare translations of Shakespeare's sonnets to the originals, but it is worth considering to what extent the success or failure of those translations is due to the way they are reformulated in prose. This point can be illustrated by contrasting Pierre-Jean Jouve's translation of "Sonnet 71" with the first stanza of the original:

> No longer mourn for me when I am dead
> Than thou shall hear the surly sullen bell
> Give warning to the world that I am fled
> From this vile world, with vilest worms to dwell:
>
> (Shakespeare 1998: 382)

> Ne me pleurez pas plus longtemps, quand je serai mort, que nous n'entendrez la lente lugubre cloche, donnant avis au monde que j'ai fui, du monde vil pour habiter aux vers encor plus vils;
>
> (Meschonnic 1999: 301)

The translation of poems into prose can be defended in bilingual versions as a means of entering the original. They are intended for students who have not yet mastered the language they are studying. The Penguin books of French, Spanish, and German verse aim at this kind of audience (for example, Rees 1990). Jouve's translation does not, however, and his rendering cannot fail to disappoint the reader familiar with the original. The pentameter that so easily lends itself to a solemnly paced reading and the rhyming of "dead"/"fled" and "bell"/"dwell" find no counterpart in the translation. Jouve's is certainly a poetic translation, as the alliterative patterning of "lente lugubre cloche" and "vers encore plus vils" show, but these are ultimately flourishes. Though meaningful in themselves, they cannot replace a structure that organizes the whole and leads the reader to expect the three stanzas followed by the rhyming couplet that characterize all of Shakespeare's sonnets. As a result, Shakespeare's argument is weakened in the French translation.

Formal Translation

The translation that Louis Zukovsky proposes for Catullus (discussed on pages 156–57) might be taken as an example of the formal translation strategy. Individual elements of form are arbitrarily selected and become the hinge upon which the success or failure of the translation depends.

Semantico-formal Translation

The first strophe of Jean Malplate's rendering of Shakespeare's "Sonnet 71" displays an uncomfortable alliance of form and meaning, which is characteristic of semantico-formal translation.

> Ne pleurez plus sur moi lorsque viendra ma mort,
> Quand vous n'entendrez plus la cloche aux sons funèbres
> Avertir ici-bas que j'ai pris mon essor
> Loin de ce monde vil, vers d'ignobles ténèbres.
>
> (Meschonnic 1999: 287–88)

The translator has clearly striven to reformulate the meaning in this stanza and manages to offer one meaningful rhyme, *funèbres/ténèbres*, though anyone familiar with French poetry will recognize this as a couple that Charles Baudelaire had already overused. As such, it functions as a hackneyed poetical reminder of the French romantic tradition. The second rhyme, *mort/esssor*, leads us in entirely the wrong direction physically. *Essor* implies ascension and élan; we are invited towards an elevated inspiration rather than to that final descent, decomposing among the vile worms. The fact that the vile worms have disappeared from Malplate's translation could be due to the undeniable difficulty of rendering the dense formulations found in the sonnets, but it reveals a strategy that goes against the grain of the poem and its meaning. A makeshift strategy is emerging: Malplate renders the meaning and then adds on the rhymes (sometimes with more success than in this stanza), but once he has opted for the rhyming scheme, he is clearly prepared to sacrifice the meaning in what he probably considers mere details. At this point it becomes a question of tacking the meaning onto the form, rather than the other way around. In these instances the semantico-formal translation might be better termed the formal-semantic translation.

Organic Translation

Henri Meschonnic submits Malplate's and Jouve's translations to rigorous scrutiny, along with several others (1999: 298–307). He considers this critique an indispensable prelude to his innovations—an unusual strategy to adopt when presenting one's own version. More commonly, translators opt for vacuous praise or discreet criticisms of their predecessors in the preface to their own work. Sometimes they efface them totally, acting as if they had never existed. Meschonnic prefers a direct attack. His choice may be a mistake, strategically speaking, since criticism does not tend to prepare the reader for uncritical appraisal of the new version. It does, nonetheless, allow us to evaluate to what extent Meschonnic's versions live up to his personal aesthetic and poetic principles. Here is his version of Shakespeare's stanza in "Sonnet 71":

> Après ma mort ne pleure pas plus tard,
> Que bat le glas qui bat morne à mourir
> Au monde vil annonçant mon départ
> Parmi les vers plus vils pour y finir:

> (1999: 281)

Meschonnic opts for an alliterative pattern similar to the one Jouve proposed ("vers encor plus vils"), though he strengthens it by linking the *p*'s in *Parmi* and *plus*. In addition to this he renders "surly sullen bell" with a similar alliterative pattern, "glas qui bat **m**orne à **m**ourir." But the most successful aspect of his translation is surely the fact that it reads simply as four rhyming decasyllables, without resorting to hackneyed rhymes or any other overused poetical expressions.

In Parisian circles Meschonnic is often thought to be mean in his criticism, but, in fairness, his critique always remains intellectual and reasoned, and it bears no resemblance to the covert strategies used by rival translators to nudge one another out of the limelight. His criticism is a direct and necessary extension of his belief that we must practise what we preach, and that we must preach clearly and honestly when we dissect and define what does not seem to work in the efforts of our fellow translators. He believed this is the only way we can make a contribution to understanding the act of translating.

Meschonnic sets up his own efforts alongside those that he criticizes, in order to allow readers to scrutinize them as rigorously as he appraises the attempts of others. In the same spirit, it would be unfitting to refuse to offer some of my own translations after theorizing for so long about the obligations of the translator.

Voices in Foreign Versification

The real test for the organic translation will come in Part 3, in the case studies on translation of Baudelaire's and Emily Dickinson's poems. But after many pages of theory, the reader is at liberty to ask whether the theoretician can give some concrete idea of how he intends these ideas to be applied. The following examples are not supposed to be models for this poetic project. They are simply attempts to reformulate voice in a foreign versification. Only the reader can decide whether the translations work or not.

I gave some examples of translations of Sidney and Whitman in the introduction. These extracts—beautifully sensitive and technically impressive—were intended to indicate the possibilities of organic translation. But in the final analysis we need poems, not extracts. I therefore include here two poems translated by other translators and two of my own translations. With the first two examples I will, of course, comment on what I think each translator is trying to do. In my own translations I naturally have more insight into the complex dynamics that engage the imagination when trying to bring a poem across from one language to another. I offer these four poems as organic translations—translations in which the form and the meaning hold together, not as two pieces of a whole glued together, but as an emotion unfolding in motion.

In the first two examples I present the translation first, before giving the original. This strategy is intended to enable us to consider whether the poems work as poems in and of themselves, before setting them beside the originals and offering them up to comparative analytical scrutiny. For my own translations I take the risk of setting my work alongside the two great poets I am trying to render.

First is Tony (A. S.) Kline's contemporary translation of an unrhymed love poem, "L'amoureuse," written by Paul Éluard in 1923.

The Beloved
She is standing on my eyelids
And her hair is wound in mine,
She has the form of my hands,
She has the colour of my eyes,
She is swallowed by my shadow
Like a stone against the sky.
Her eyes are always open
And will not let me sleep.
Her dreams in broad daylight
Make the suns evaporate
Make me laugh, cry and laugh,
Speak with nothing to say.

(Éluard 2001)

L'Amoureuse
Elle est debout sur mes paupières
Et ses cheveux sont dans les miens,
Elle a la forme de mes mains,
Elle a la couleur de mes yeux,
Elle s'engloutit dans mon ombre
Comme une pierre sur le ciel.
Elle a toujours les yeux ouverts
Et ne me laisse pas dormir.
Ses rêves en pleine lumière
Font s'évaporer les soleils,
Me font rire, pleurer et rire,
Parler sans avoir rien à dire.

(Éluard 2015)

Does "The Beloved" work as an English poem? It certainly works as a free poem. A three-beat line clearly asserts itself in Tony Kline's elegant translation. The parallelism and the repetition are carefully crafted, and Kline foregrounds that repetition by beginning two lines with "Make" where the lines of the original open on different words. This poem would probably be considered free verse, and a two-beat or a four-beat line would probably not disrupt the rhythm. The meaning imposes itself firmly but delicately, unfolding line by line.

In fact the original poem was written in strict octosyllables, inviting a metrical reading that pronounces each mute *e* when it does not fall at the line end. This reading turns out to be somewhat perplexing, however, because the comma after "Me font rire" in the penultimate line clearly invites a trisyllabic reading, making it a seven-syllable line: "Me font rire [3], pleurer et rire [4]." Besides, do we read Éluard's verse today while observing classical metrical constraints? Éluard seems all too close to us, more on the side of free verse. The truth is actually somewhat surprising. In Gilles-Claude Thériault's beautifully sedate and poised reading (Éluard 2015), the classical rules of diction are meticulously applied but pronounced in a deliciously evasive manner. Thériault prolongs the vowels and leaves the hint of an *e*, making *forme, pierre,* and *pleine* clearly disyllabic, although *elle* almost (but not quite) remains monosyllabic. Thériault also reads the penultimate line with seven syllables, without provoking any rupture.

What does this analysis seem to show? That unrhymed verse of the kind Éluard is writing will still work, much in the same way that free verse works, by opting for a patterned repetition of phrases of roughly the same length. Indeed, it seems probable that Éluard's celebration of his love would work equally well as a free-verse poem with lines of between six and eight syllables, that is to say, by allowing a modern reading to assert itself. Dropping the rhyme already takes us a step towards free patterning in French.

Victor Hugo wrote an untitled hymn to nature in 1831 that was published in *Aurore*. A. Lang's translation was collected in a selection of Hugo's poems published with the work of various translators in 1888 (Hugo 2005). If Hugo's poem is slightly more difficult to respond to today, it is probably because the sentiment expressed in it has become alien to us, or rather that sentiment has been marginalized in poetry anthologies. Hugo's poem simply sings the praise of the coming of spring. It is pretty, and for some critics that is enough to condemn it. The pretty fairs poorly in modernist and postmodernist aesthetics. The romantics had already celebrated the sublime, raising it above the beautiful, and modernists and postmodernists tended to assume that the beautiful was either awesome or hollow. That left little place for the kind of delicate musings that Hugo, Heinrich Heine, and Dickinson excelled in. Inevitably the pretty was swallowed up by kitsch, which remained very tangible for both modernist and postmodernist poets and critics. Some readers will, I expect, find it difficult therefore to enter into Lang's rendering of Hugo. But I would argue that neither the poem nor the translation is remotely kitsch. Hugo delicately defines, dissects, and playfully reconstructs the feeling of joy we experience when we see nature set about its work regenerating living things and inspiring fleeting impressions. Readers today may find something quaint about Lang's diction, but on scrutiny only "lo" is archaic. This translation, written more than 120 years ago, reads otherwise as a very direct and successful rendering of Hugo's precise poetic language.

> The dawn is smiling on the dew that covers
> The tearful roses—lo, the little lovers—
> That kiss the buds and all the flutterings
> In jasmine bloom, and privet, of white wings
> That go and come, and fly, and peep, and hide
> With muffled music, murmured far and wide!
> Ah, Springtime, when we think of all the lays
> That dreamy lovers send to dreamy Mays,
> Of the proud hearts within a billet bound,
> Of all the soft silk paper that men wound,
> The messages of love that mortals write,
> Filled with intoxication of delight,
> Written in April, and before the Maytime
> Shredded and flown, playthings for the winds' playtime.
> We dream that all white butterflies above,
> Who seek through clouds or waters souls to love,
> And leave their lady mistress to despair,
> To flirt with flowers, as tender and more fair,
> Are but torn love-letters, that through the skies
> Flutter, and float, and change to Butterflies.
>
> ("How Butterflies Are Born," in Hugo 2005: bk. 1.12)

Vere Novo

Comme le matin rit sur les roses en pleurs!
Oh! les charmants petits amoureux qu'ont les fleurs!
Ce n'est dans les jasmins, ce n'est dans les pervenches
Qu'un éblouissement de folles ailes blanches
Qui vont, viennent, s'en vont, reviennent, se fermant,
Se rouvrant, dans un vaste et doux frémissement.
O printemps! quand on songe à toutes les missives
Qui des amants rêveurs vont aux belles pensives,
A ces cœurs confiés au papier, à ce tas
De lettres que le feutre écrit au taffetas,
Au message d'amour, d'ivresse et de délire
Qu'on reçoit en avril et qu'en mai l'on déchire,
On croit voir s'envoler, au gré du vent joyeux,
Dans les prés, dans les bois, sur les eaux, dans les cieux,
Et rôder en tous lieux, cherchant partout une âme,
Et courir à la fleur en sortant de la femme,
Les petits morceaux blancs, chassés en tourbillons
De tous les billets doux, devenus papillons.

(Hugo 1967: 507)

There is nothing forced about Lang's translation. He neither sacrifices ideas nor embellishes them. He is not a slave to the line nor is he the prisoner of grammar. He gracefully transposes "roses en pleurs" with "tearful roses." And he knows how to use line ends. Where Hugo ends on *déchire*, Lang opens with "Shredded." And how does Lang rhyme? He rhymes "lays" with "Mays" and "Maytime" with "playtime." These are rhymes that resound with the joy Hugo is trying to express. Whether we are open today to such celebrations of spring is another question, but Lang unquestionably does justice to Hugo's varied alexandrines with rhymed iambic pentameters that promote and demote syllables gently to provide a varied movement, supple but strong. This is the pulsation of burgeoning spring.

For the first of my own translations I offer a love sonnet by Pablo Neruda, "Sonnet 6." Like Éluard's love poem, this sonnet will probably better suit modern tastes, though I have indulged myself in a formal experiment by making the free verse more formal.

En los bosques, perdido, corté una rama oscura y a los labios, sediento, levanté su susurro: era tal vez la voz de la lluvia llorando, una campana rota o un corazón cortado.	Deep in the woods, I cut a black black branch and lifted it to my lips to drink its sound. I thirsted for its voice of broken bells, its shattered heart, its rain-tears that resound.
Algo que desde tan lejos me parecía oculto gravemente, cubierto por la tierra, un grito ensordecido por inmensos otoños, por la entreabierta y húmeda tiniebla de las hojas.	From deep within the earth's dark depths an echo reached my ears. I heard its far-off cry, a cry muffled by immense autumns, shrouded in warm wet leaves, dampened by the night sky.
Por allí, despertando de los sueños del bosque, la rama de avellano cantó bajo mi boca y su errabundo olor trepó por mi criterio	And, waking from its vegetable dream, my branch began to sing its song below my lips. Its wayward scent climbed up into my mind
como si me buscaran de pronto las raíces que abandoné, la tierra perdida con mi infancia, y me detuve herido por el aroma errante.	as though its roots, abandoned, with their tips
("Matin, 6," Neruda 1995: 22)	reached out to me like paradise lost, like childhood. And I stood, hurt by the stray scent of that good wood.

The Hispanic scholar will have to decide whether we can hear something of Neruda's voice in my version; whether the alliteration of "**r**ain-tears that **r**esound" appropriately transposes "**ll**uvia **ll**orando," and whether the alliteration of "my **b**ranch **b**egan to sing **b**elow my lips" captures the force of "**b**ajo mi **b**oca."

The English reader will notice that the translation is organized in pentameter lines that rhyme *xaya*. This creates a loose and discreet versification that gives the lines a light pulsation, which seems appropriate for this poem that evokes the murmuring rhythms of woods with rain that falls like tears and singing scents. The rhyme scheme also allows the poem to insist upon key words (sound/resound; cry/sky; lips/tips). In the final lines I have opted for a Shakespearean couplet rhyming *dd*—the clincher—and I have hidden within the lines a free internal rhyme (stood/good) to lend greater force to the sonorous closure of the poem. The closure should also be further aided by the transgression of the rhythmic pattern; up until the final lines I have avoided disturbing the undulating alternation of weak and strong syllables and have allowed more than one unstressed syllable only where they can easily be assimilated into the offbeat. In the last line, in contrast, I use the ultimate contradiction to this alternating stress contour: the double stress. The three double stresses—"stood, hurt," "stray scent," and "good wood"—should serve to announce the end of the poem by slowing down the line and dragging against the anticipated undulating rhythm, while the four rhyming words (childhood/stood/good/wood) organize an alternative local patterning to soften this transgression. The significance of the rhymes should create a moment of heightened poignancy at the poem's end.

Does it work? The Hispanic scholar might object that the original is written in free verse, but if we can translate metrical verse into prose, then surely we must be allowed to translate non-metrical poetry into verse. La Fontaine did not hesitate to versify Aesop. Ultimately, though, arguments can take us only so far in aesthetic appreciation. Only the translated poem can defend itself. Do the rhymes and rhythms hang upon the translation like worn-out hand-me-down clothes, or do they help enact the poem as a meaningful moment? Does the inspired and inspiring energy that engendered Neruda's poem transcend the language barrier to speak to readers of English?

Similar questions might be asked about my translation of Hugo's poem on love, war, and nature taken from his *Contemplations*. It was translated during the buildup to the invasion of Iraq in 2003, at a time when God was being invoked by various camps to justify their desires, positions, and intentions. In this poem Hugo yearns for a very different kind of god than Titan, the god of war. His desire and his intention had a resonance and meaning that I believed might speak to people more than 150 years later. It captures the bravado of warrior rhetoric all the better to pastiche it. Hugo's poem has survived the test of time, and I believe his orality retains the capacity to move us to meaningful meditation. Whether that voice has been reformulated in the versification of my translation, whether the organizing force of form has metamorphosed Hugo's poem into a poem that can speak to the English-reader is not for me to say. But I have certainly tried to capture that same ironic bravado and to move the reader to contemplate another conception of god: *le bon Dieu*, a very French Catholic god who remains close to his creation, a familiar god, somewhat akin to the one Dickinson evokes in some of her more intimate poems on the sublime and the creator.

XVIII	But I prefer the good old God
Je sais bien qu'il est d'usage	It's the habit of the times, I know,
D'aller en tous lieux criant	To run about shouting here and there
Que l'homme est d'autant plus sage	That we are so much wiser now
Qu'il rêve plus de néant;	To have changed our Dream for black despair.
D'applaudir la grandeur noire,	To applaud that great darkness
Les héros, le fer qui luit,	That makes the hero's sword shine bright,
Et la guerre, cette gloire	To honour war and guts and glory
Qu'on fait avec de la nuit;	And all that is made of night.
D'admirer les coups d'épée,	To admire the rapid cut and thrust
Et la fortune, ce char	To admire the chariot named Fortune.
Dont une roue est Pompée,	Pompey rode that chariot well
Dont l'autre roue est César;	but Caesar rolled over him all too soon.
Et Pharsale et Trasimène,	We admire those little Neroes,
Et tout ce que les Nérons	Those tiny tyrannical men
Font voler de cendre humaine	Who drown with men's grey ashes
Dans le souffle des clairons!	The green of clearing, forest and glen.
Je sais que c'est la coutume	These dwarfs with mouths full of froth,
D'adorer ces nains géants	Spray us with their scum and we
Qui, parce qu'ils sont écume,	Take their spit and spray to be
Se supposent océans;	The mighty motion of the sea.
Et de croire à la poussière,	We marvel before the dust of the dead
A la fanfare qui fuit,	Who died glorious deaths without a sound.
Aux pyramides de pierre,	We wonder to see the battlement walls
Aux avalanches de bruit.	That tumble crashing to the ground.
Moi, je préfère, ô fontaines,	Oh give me the fountain, I prefer
Moi, je préfère, ô ruisseaux,	The good old God who loves the bird.
Au Dieu de grands capitaines,	Let us sit by the stream where his lovely song,
Le Dieu des petits oiseaux!	Weaving in the water's current, is heard.

O mon doux ange, en ces ombres Où, nous aimant, nous brillons, Au Dieu des ouragons sombres Qui poussent les bataillons,	Gentle angel, in this shadowful world, Let us love and shine as the stars once shone Before the God of tempest came Driving his armies on and on.
Au Dieu des vastes armées, Des canons au lourd essieu, Des flammes et des fumées, Je préfère le bon Dieu!	See how the Lord of battalions comes With carnage and fire and cannon smoke. Let us seek a Lord who would not wish Our love on this fuming chaos to choke.
Le bon Dieu, qui veut qu'on aime, Qui met au cœur de l'amant Les premiers vers du poëme, Le dernier au firmament!	Give me the god who inspires the poet Who knows that from Him each word is sent His poem sings the birth of the world The stars and the firmament.
Qui songe à l'aile qui pousse, Aux œufs blancs, au nid troublé, Si la caille a de la mousse, Et si la grive a du blé;	The god who provides the thrush with wheat And hears the plaintive quail whose nest Shakes with the thunder of battle below. I love that lord the best.
Et qui fait, pour les Orphées, Tenir, immense et subtil, Tout le doux monde des fées Dans le vert bourgeon d'avril!	Who inspires with immense and subtle music The harmony-lover's heart And engenders a delicate, fairy tale world In the green budding of April's art.
Si bien, que cela s'envole Et se disperse au printemps, Et qu'une vague auréole Sort de tous les nids chantants!	Listen to the sound of that sweet music That takes to the wing when spring comes round You will hear it rising from every nest And up to the heavens will the song resound.
Vois-tu, quoique notre gloire Brille en ce que nous créons, Et dans notre grand histoire Pleine de grands panthéons;	You see, my love, in all we create Our glory shines full bright. In our great history of monuments that obscure our sense of sight,
Quoique nous ayons des glaives, Des temples, Chéops, Babel, Des tours des palais, des rêves, Et des tombeaux jusqu'au ciel;	The world is full of temples and statues To commemorate those that lie below, The tower of Babel rose up high The pyramid hails a dead Pharaoh.

Il resterait peu de choses A l'homme, qui vît un jour, Si Dieu nous ôtait les roses, Si Dieu nous ôtait l'amour!	But what would be left for man in this world If the Lord looked down one day And saw the roses, and saw our love And took them both away?
(Hugo 1967: 552)	(Underhill 2012a: 26–30)

Does the rhythm of the celebration of rousing violence rise up only to be washed away, dismissed by a greater love of beauty? There is such a climax in Hugo's poem, and it serves to satirize the kind of rhetoric of which George W. Bush was fond. If my poem manages with its rhythm, its rhymes, and its alliterations to enact this meaningful satire on war propaganda—the rousing chant celebrating violence—then it will have succeeded. If it fails, it will sound like hollow, insipid call for a better world. Each reader and each reading of the translation is a trial, a test. Do we hear a voice?

The translation of a poem is, and will always remain, a creative act, and there can no more be fixed instructions for it than there can be instructions for writing poems themselves. This is a point that translation theory, with its methodologies and scientific aspirations, is inclined to obscure. Like the definitions already discussed, these translations are offered to help clarify the task facing the translator and the inescapable difficulties that he or she must face. Ultimately the first two parts of this book can only help the translator avoid a series of procedures that will impede successful transposition of the poetic voice and the versification. Just as Pound proposed a series of Imagist don'ts, we might try to establish a series of translation don'ts. Just as Pound's don'ts do not necessarily help us write good poetry but instead help us to avoid writing bad poetry, such translation don'ts will not guarantee success, though they may help us avoid the most lamentable failures.

If we persist in trying to understand the translation of poetry in terms of the linguistic sign, which divides form and meaning, we will inevitably end up privileging either the meaning over the form or the form over the meaning—without having grasped fully what we mean by either term. The poem has always been treated more or less intuitively by translators, who have often been poets themselves. Translators have often met with a great deal of success in responding to the form of poems. After all, the enormous importance of translation as an influence on our literary traditions testifies to the possibility of an organic translation of organic form, to the possibility of rebirth of the poem. Voices do break through linguistic barriers and speak to us, often from the distant past.

Whether or not we can rely on translators to hurdle the obstacles that traditional theory puts in their way is no certain matter, however. No translator can hope to translate a poem well without the intuition, sensitivity, and inspiration that we often attribute to the poet. Nonetheless it must be remembered that even the poet, as soon as he or she dons the cap of the translator, may be inclined to think within the limited confines of the traditional linguistic theory on which translation theory is based: that of language as communication. This way of thinking is perhaps one of the reasons why great poets often make poor translators. In any event, our theory for translating poetry cannot content itself with relying on intuition, sensitivity, and inspiration as the sole guides to good translation, however necessary these qualities might be. Poetics should define exactly what kind of translation we are aiming at and what kind of translation we are hoping to avoid. This book should allow us to take a couple of steps down the path towards demystifying that "divine accident" that Pound calls the successful translation of a poem. In moving on to the Baudelaire and Dickinson case studies, we should be able to put to work some of the ideas discussed as we determine whether individual choices related to rhymes, syllables, and phrasing form part of the dynamics of those divine accidents, and whether certain translation strategies are indeed inspired.

PART THREE

CASE STUDIES

CHAPTER 8

Baudelaires

Baudelaire Today

Few poets can claim to be so prolific in their influence, if not in their production, as Charles Baudelaire. He produced only one major book of verse, and his book of poems in prose was not published in its complete form until after his death. The other work, however fascinating, remains secondary in his oeuvre. The reaction to Baudelaire's writings was a strong one, though, and the great poets and novelists of his day were not grudging in their praise for his achievement. Their letters to the poet bear witness to their joy and admiration. Hugo wrote to Baudelaire to say that "your *Flowers* shine and dazzle like stars" (Guyaux 2007: 250). Flaubert declared he was "enchanted" as he read and reread each line of the *Fleurs du mal* (Guyaux 2007: 165): "You have found [Flaubert told him] a means of rejuvenating romanticism" (166). Flaubert loved Baudelaire's "rawness" (âpreté) and his flourishes of "delicacy in diction" (délicatesses de langage; Guyaux 2007: 165). And, in a curious revelation of his own covert perversion and world-weariness, Flaubert went on to specify exactly what it was in Baudelaire's poetic expression that pleased him: "You sing of the flesh without loving it, in a sad and detached manner that is dear to me" (Vous chantez la chair sans l'aimer d'une façon triste et détachée qui m'est sympathique; Guyaux 2007: 165).

In contrast to the majestic productivity of both Flaubert and Hugo, Baudelaire's body of work remains compact. And it was immediately censored by the literary establishment for his shocking and sacrilegious poems. Nevertheless this French poet, who was born in 1821 in Paris and who died there in 1867, has stimulated a widespread and unabated fascination among poetry-lovers around the world. Not only has Baudelaire been introduced into Russian, Hungarian, Czech, Spanish, and German, he has also had a great impact on the aesthetic imaginations of writers in those languages. His situation remains unique. The editors of *Baudelaire in English,* Carol Clark and Robert Sykes, point out that he was the first modern poet to join the ranks of Horace, Virgil, and other classical writers in the Penguin series (Baudelaire 1997: xiii). Is Baudelaire to be considered a pillar of the literary academy, then? Certainly, but hardly that alone.

Like the traditional publishing houses, the Internet has succumbed to Baudelaire's charm. Project Gutenberg (www.gutenberg.org) provides versions of Baudelaire's revolutionary collection of poems, *Les Fleurs du mal,* in both French and English translation; James Huneker's English translations of the *Petits poèmes en prose* can also be found there, in the collection *The Poems and Prose Poems of Charles Baudelaire*. Numerous other websites, such as PoetryArchive (http://www.poetry-archive.com/b/the_balcony.html), do the same. Above all, the website Charles Baudelaire's Les Fleurs du mal / Flowers of Evil (Baudelaire 2015) gathers together a vast number of translations of Baudelaire, including a few of my own.[1] Young poets, translators, and readers continue to respond to Baudelaire. For example, the contemporary poet and essayist James McColley Eilers has posted his translations on the *Brooklyn Rail*'s InTranslation webpage (Baudelaire 2010), and the blogger Stephen Saperstein Frug offers different English translations for readers to compare (Frug 2011). Internet surfers continue to consider the relative merits of Baudelaire translations, such as Huneker's and Arthur Symons's from the early twentieth century, on sites like LibraryThing (http://www.librarything.com/topic/94717). The various facets of Baudelaire's work and the diversity of poetic interpretations of his oeuvre in English continue to stimulate discussion and debate a hundred years on.

Poets and academics seem to feel an irrepressible tug towards Baudelaire. Britain's leading contemporary specialist of comparative versification, Clive Scott, devoted an entire work to analyzing the act of translating Baudelaire (2000). This fascination says something about the power of Baudelaire's verse, of course, but surely it also bears witness to the potential of poetry translation as a creative adventure. Baudelaire speaks to a wide public of poetry-lovers without estranging himself from the most sensitive specialists or exacting critics, the hallmark of truly great poets such as Shakespeare, Burns, Whitman, Neruda, and Dickinson.

Baudelaire's appeal is all the more surprising since, as Clark and Sykes point out, the "hardest thing for a translator to catch is the sheer simplicity of some of Baudelaire's lines" (Baudelaire 1997: xxvii). As Baudelaire translators themselves, Clark and Sykes are in a good position to appraise the difficulty of the task. Baudelaire has a predilection for commonplace monosyllables such as *grand, beaux, doux,* and *bon,* but as he demonstrates, no word is commonplace when transformed within the dynamic activity of the poem. Just as it is the melody that decides whether a note rings as beautiful, kitsch, or false, it is the phrasing that gives value and meaning to the words within the poem as a whole. Baudelaire's apparent simplicity paradoxically proves anything but simple. His work has what Clark and Sykes rightly call an "inspired plainness" (xxvii), in lines such as "Riche, mais impuissant, jeune, et pourtant très vieux" ("Spleen LXXVII," Baudelaire 1975: 74).

Translating that simplicity is inevitably arduous. Lewis Piaget Shanks, for example, reproduces that plainness without managing to achieve the melancholy monotony of the original in his "—wealthy, but impotent: still young, but old—" (Baudelaire 1997: 92). Roy Campbell manages to maintain something more balanced with his "Grown impotent and old before my time" (Baudelaire 1997: 93). True, Campbell is forced to drop "rich"—not only a semantic loss but also a loss in parallelism. Campbell thereby transforms the quadripartite rising-and-falling movement of the original into a binary rising-falling lament. Robert Lowell, on the other hand, demonstrates that great poets do not always prove great (or consistently great) translators, when he himself completely misses the measured tone and deforms the register of the original, offering "rich / but sterile, young, but with an old wolf's itch" (Baudelaire 1997: 94). Among such versions, James McColley Eilers's comes as a welcome addition: "Rich, but powerless; young, yet feeling wintry" (Baudelaire 2010).

Lowell proves far more convincing at re-enacting Baudelaire's profound simplicity in the opening lines of "Meditation," his version of "Recueillement":

Sois sage, ô ma Douleur, et tiens-toi plus tranquille,	Calm down, my Sorrow, we must move with care.
Tu réclamais le Soir, il descend; le voici,	You called for evening; it descends; it's here.
(Baudelaire 1975: 140)	(Lowell, in Baudelaire 1997: 226)

In Baudelaire the sublime coexists with the commonplace. The abyss can rise out of an ashtray; the gutters can reflect the heavens. Even decomposition and moral decay can be transformed into magical flights of fancy. Conversely, magical flights of fancy often fall, like Icarus—one of Baudelaire's motifs—into dismay and disenchantment. Poetic transports return like a boomerang to torment the poet. Inspiration can transpire to be an impulse that turns in on itself. Elation, in Baudelaire's poems, turns into abuse of himself and others. Indeed, the very flight of fancy and the craving for stimulation in an imaginary realm—however vivid and enticing for Baudelaire—turn out to be the flipside of a much more sombre and morose sensibility, and both reveal much about the poet's relationship to the world of the here and now.

Baudelaire is always complex, always ambivalent, like reality itself and our perception of it. The originality of this quality for a poet of his time is now difficult to grasp. A dynamic tension, a sense of irony, and a heightened sensibility of both beauty and contradictions make Baudelaire a very modern poet. The poems of Keats and Tennyson remain unquestionably beautiful today, but who would call either modern? In contrast to their poems, Baudelaire's imagination seems to have seized upon something crucial and vital in the urban experience. The poet for whom wandering through the city streets and visiting fairs and bars was a meaningful aesthetic adventure offered us a vision of the city that remains meaningful today, and it has reshaped the imagination of those who spend any time reading his work. For poets from Swinburne to T. S. Eliot, and for thinkers such as the great German essayist Walter Benjamin, Baudelaire introduced a new mode of perception and a means of expressing the urban experience.

Nobody is perfect. Capable of misogyny, ingratitude, and reckless indifference to the fates of his friends, given to self-indulgence and attracted to drug abuse and alcoholism, Baudelaire had no shortage of failings. And those failings earned him scathing denunciation from his critics. His mother and stepfather proved to be his first censors, when they decided to place the remainder of his inheritance under the supervision of a lawyer, as if for a child. Baudelaire was treated from then on as a charge, and throughout his life he was thereby considered irresponsible or incapable. Admittedly he had squandered the greater part of his inheritance in his early twenties on his prostitute mistress and other distractions. Dissipation seems to have been central to Baudelaire's lifestyle, and disgust for himself was to become one of the recurring themes in his poetry. He hardly presents an endearing picture, yet Baudelaire was one of those men who could turn vice into virtue (and vice versa).

Like the great postwar British poet Philip Larkin, Baudelaire focuses his scrutinizing poetic gaze on his vices and his vacillations. Part of the greatness of these two poets lies in that rare gift that combines great sensitivity with unswerving honesty. The perspicacity with which Baudelaire dismantles and catalogues the individual cogs and wheels of his bad faith is unnerving. And his portrayal of the rise and fall of his inspiration and his despair remains both engrossing and insightful. Baudelaire oscillates between profound authentic inspiration and banal everyday indifference. He is both blasé and movingly poetic. And while many poets disparage all that is intellectual—siding with the romantics in extolling feeling over reason—Baudelaire invariably proves scrupulous in his self-analysis and acute in his perspicacity. He takes us along with him in his inspirations and then he coldly sets about dissecting them, laying them out in front of us with a now clinical eye. One moment he is striving to seize that vague emotion we feel when observing the sea late on an autumn afternoon, an experience that remains paradoxically penetrating and inviting; the next moment he is observing his own exasperation as the same scene, rising to a crescendo of intensity, begins to bewilder and revolt him. Baudelaire is no Whitman, who loses himself in emotion, and no Shelley, who sustains elation. Like Dickinson he keeps a cold eye fixed on the flights of his emotions. He analyzes in detail the fusion of the artist with the scene, as the "I" and the "thing" become one in perceiving. He reminds us, however, that the artist must also turn his back on the world as the "I" rejects the overwhelming experience of beauty and its immutable intensity.

Not all of Baudelaire strikes us as modern. Certain traits of his can seem risible today. The structures of feeling at the beginning of the twenty-first century are not those of the nineteenth-century French aesthetic sensibility. Chastity seems to us a ridiculous ideal, and inevitably Baudelaire's feminization of nature and beauty often appears quaint and antiquated. Ironically, when Baudelaire inverts such imagery, we are at a loss to understand, as we can no longer follow the feelings he is setting up and tugging apart. The perverted inversion of ideals such as chastity and purity reminds us more of the cheap, tacky advertising for sex websites that pops up on the computer screen when we are online. There can be little doubt that one of Baudelaire's better translators, Aleister Crowley (1875–1947)—the self-styled "Great Beast" and a reputed Satanist—took Baudelaire's Satanism seriously. T. S. Eliot, however, writing around the same time as Crowley translated Baudelaire, considered Baudelaire's Satanism to be an adolescent fixation. Although Baudelaire's contemporary Charles Augustin Sainte-Beuve admitted that Baudelaire had opened up a curious and original space within the French language (Guyaux 2007: 346), Sainte-Beuve had already expressed a sentiment similar to Eliot's.

Baudelaire's main interest for Freudians is his apparent incapacity "to detach himself from the conflicts and habits of adolescence and even childhood," as Clark and Sykes put it (Baudelaire 1997: xix). Freudian and psychoanalytic readings of Baudelaire tend to glorify this point. Paul Larent Assoun sees in Baudelaire's "My soul laid bare" (Mon cœur mis a nu) a precursor of the psychoanalytic conception of sexuality (Wilhelm 1999: 10). Fabrice Wilhelm perceives in Baudelaire's various penchants for paradise, the infinite, the eternal, and the ideal a driving force through which the lyrical subject strives to find the wholeness of the primitive state within the womb (1999: 141). Wilhelm considers Baudelaire to be subject to melancholic behaviour, which he defines as a state in which "the subject is in grieving but does not know the origin of his suffering" (9). Giving his work on Baudelaire the subtitle "The Writings of Narcissism" will be considered by many of Baudelaire's admirers a Freudian backhanded slap.[2] Nonetheless, if the Freudians and Baudelaire's other critics are right in discerning something narcissistic and self-obsessed in his poetry, it can hardly be said to be a quality of either a man or a poet.

Some of Baudelaire's qualities have aged badly and were probably threadbare at best from the outset. When it comes to his religious references, even the language of Baudelaire's defenders appears absurd to us today. It seems ludicrous that an intelligent critic and serious poet such as Swinburne could proclaim "The Litanies of Satan" to be "one of the noblest lyrics ever written" (Baudelaire 1997: xxix).[3] It must be remembered that the dialectics of good and bad, faith and sin, are structural to the world view of the period and essential to the dynamics of Baudelaire's poetry. Swinburne was trying to save Baudelaire from himself. In a post-postmodern world we are far more comfortable with paradox, confusion, and contradiction—even to the point of intellectual and affective complacency. This is one of the reasons that Baudelaire's verse, with its direct language, its lyrical twists, its rapid changes in register and tone, its depth of colouring in emotion, and most of all its enchanting and disorienting moves in pace and rhythm, continues to provoke an aesthetic response among poets, thinkers, and translators from the broadest reaches.

Baudelaire is not the great modern poet who will fashion a modern answer to the classical aesthetics that animated poets up to the time of Goethe.[4] In Baudelaire's poetry a synthesis of the good, the beautiful, and the true will not be found. Yet throughout his work a deeply felt desire for good is expressed. His conception of good is often novel. It includes the artist of the prose poem "À une heure du matin" with his sense of vocation, who strives to produce a few good lines of verse in the early hours of the morning to justify his existence and to prove to himself that he is not the most contemptible of men (Baudelaire 1975: 288). It includes the sensitive lover who ponders the questionable virtue of his mistress. And it includes his lucidly ambivalent descriptions of that languorous, catlike mistress who appropriates the space around her and imposes respect by fuelling a fiery desire that stimulates the imagination of the poet. There is a search for truth in the depiction of both the object herself and the perceiving subject of the experience. Baudelaire is enamoured but rarely deluded.

He never, without exception, falls into kitsch. He prettifies nothing, and there is an unswerving honesty in this and in his relationship with all he desires. Arguably there is less soul in Baudelaire than in Blake, and there is certainly less love of humanity, but Blake was a prophet of another age. He turned in disgust and horror from the dark Satanic mills, and Wordsworth sought refuge in the lakes of Cumbria. But Baudelaire stared the industrial metropolis straight in the face and gave himself over to the sensuous experience, without giving up the intellectual insight of the sensitive artist who grasps experience as a whole and gives it a form. The poet is penetrated by the experience but penetrating in his analysis, and the come-and-go between the individual subject and the city gives rise to a strikingly authentic form of self-conscious alienation.

Byron had something of Baudelaire's ironic distance, but he never developed the urban experience as an art. In truth, Baudelaire was not being arrogant when he claimed in "Les foules" that "It is not given to everybody to bathe in the man-ocean, to enjoy the crowd is an art" (1997: 242–43). "Prendre un bain de multitude" (Baudelaire 1975: 291) captures the vertigo of an estranged individual giving up his space and his individuality, at least provisionally, to join the procession of passing strangers. There is obviously a sensual element in this pleasure—"jouir de la foule" (291)—which is lost by Crowley when he translates *jouir* (literally to take pleasure or orgasm) as "enjoy." This is a timid translation for a self-proclaimed Satanist; nevertheless, Crowley does capture the fusion of feeling and intelligence. However Catholic Baudelaire may be in the architectonics of his oppositions of good and evil, body and soul, and here and hereafter, his spirituality is, like Saint Augustine's, a sensual spirituality. The intellectual and the sensual are inextricably bound together in Baudelaire's imagination and in his imagery.

There is something frigid and unconvincing in Baudelaire's celebration of nature, perhaps because he hated the countryside and was reluctant to leave Paris, though he did agree to work in peace at his mother's lodgings in Honfleur, on the coast of Normandy. Natural things, from the albatross to the sun itself, remained symbols for Baudelaire. He was not interested in the texture of a dead pig's hide, like Ted Hughes, or with the hue of the hawthorn's leaf or its brittle thorns, like Wordsworth. Nevertheless Baudelaire was alive to the beauty of transcendence and, as much as Wordsworth, Emerson, Whitman, or Emily Dickinson, he took the step from the fragment of reality to the transcendental plane. This transcendence forms part of Baudelaire's Catholic world view. There is a continuity between his work and the religious philosophy of Saint Bonaventure and other Neoplatonic Christian philosophers, for whom all creatures and things are vestiges of the Great Artisan's creation. There is also a very real and direct link with the desires of the city-living soul:

excited and frustrated, craving sensual and spiritual satisfaction. These complex and paradoxical desires inspired his quest for beauty.

Eliot and Larkin identified with Baudelaire's scrupulous representation of the city environment and the soul's discomfort and its frustrated striving. The young Larkin admired and translated Baudelaire's "Femmes damnées" (Baudelaire 1997: 210), albeit in a highly idiosyncratic manner, introducing the *Guardian* newspaper to the living room and milk bottles to the doorstep. Both Eliot and Larkin share Baudelaire's capacity for pathos and bathos. All three are moving poets, and often the movement of their poems follows that fall from inspiration. All three know all about having to face up to the crass contours of a mangled reality. But neither Larkin—with his high windows and his melancholy elegies to bosomy English roses, his cathedral cities and his French windows looking down on provincial canals—nor Eliot—with his melancholy musings on lonely men in shirtsleeves staring out of windows, and his celebrations of the currents and torrents of the winding rivers of his childhood—can sustain beauty as Baudelaire can. Once the rupture of reality breaks in on the reveries of Larkin and Eliot, the spell is broken. Baudelaire's genius can hold the beautiful and the ugly side by side, without one annulling the other. That tension is fundamental to modern aesthetics, and Baudelaire gives expression to our experience of modernity. So while Wordsworth and even Hughes often seem escapist, inviting us elsewhere, Baudelaire—who paradoxically remains the poet of elsewhere (*ailleurs*), the poet who celebrates vertigo, gulfs, and abysses—does nevertheless show us a way back to ourselves and the vibrant pulse of our own existence.

There are conceit and deceit in Baudelaire's verse. His musings are meanderings and his logic is contrived, but there is also truth there, and above all a towering lucidity. Unlike so many modern poets both modernist and postmodern, there is beauty too in his poetry. This is not solace for the suffering soul. Larkin's insights into beauty might be considered as such, and so might Auden's and Eliot's. In contrast, Baudelaire's poems present us with a very real, soul-colliding beauty that imposes respect and at times overpowers us. Baudelaire's self-analysis strikes us as modern, but perhaps it is simply great. His poems introduce something approaching that self-conscious apprehension of the world that we find presented so eloquently in Marcus Aurelius's maxims, in Montaigne's essays, and in the soliloquies with which Macbeth, Hamlet, and Lear express their fears and desires.

Scott's Baudelaire

I would have liked to include more poems and fewer extracts in this book but renounced the idea for obvious reasons of space. Clive Scott bends towards the opposite extreme. Devoting a book-length study to the analysis of a handful of translated poems will certainly strike some readers as laborious, and Scott will not escape criticism from readers who see his *Translating Baudelaire* (2000) as something of an inverted preface. Instead of a book of poems with a dozen pages of introduction, we find the opposite. Not all readers will share my enthusiasm in reading Scott on rhythm and translating, but those who find his analysis demanding and exhausting will no doubt have already lost patience with the present project. Criticisms of theorizing the subject to death would no doubt be justified in the case of many authors, but hardly in the case of Scott.

Britain's leading specialist in French metrics and versification, Scott is the author of *Vers Libre: The Emergence of Free Verse in France, 1886–1914* (1990), *Reading the Rhythm* (1993), and *The Poetics of French Verse* (1998). In his book on translating Baudelaire, he offers the antithesis of woolly, verbose rambling on rhythm. Not only is he a highly sensitive reader of Baudelaire and a specialist in French verse, Scott combines his understanding of versification and rhythm with an enlightened use of translation theory. When Scott speaks of foreignizing translation, we can be sure he is not simply jumping onto Lawrence Venuti's bandwagon but meditating on the poetics of work within the contemporary field of translation studies.

Scott's aim is to move beyond the bland and facile domesticating translation that resolves and effaces all difficulties, while at the same time avoiding the tortuous translation that obstructs the reading process. He is looking for a kind of balance. He seeks to illuminate the original through the translation, allowing its imperial presence to linger and resound like an echo within English. At first glance it might seem that Scott is simply rehashing the traditional opposition between literal translation and the glosses of scholars, on the one hand, and functional translation on the other. Eugene Nida defined the opposition between "gloss translation" and "dynamic translation" skillfully and succinctly (Venuti 2004: 156–57). According to Nida, in the first kind, translators "attempt to reproduce as literally and meaningfully as possible the form and content of the original" (156). In the second kind, following Rieu and Phillips, he argues that "the principle of equivalent effect" is paramount (157). In addition, Nida stressed that the function of the translation is central to the ethics and practice of translation; before Skopos theory, he insisted that university students need one kind of translation to aid them in their endeavours and help them engage with the foreign world of the text, while theatre translation requires an entirely different approach in order to make the play work. To a great degree Jean-René Ladmiral positions himself within the dynamics of this opposition when he claims that literal translators are source oriented, while target-oriented translators often make things easier for readers by effacing difficulties and concentrating on ways of making the translated text palatable to a given audience (1994).

Scott, for his part, is certainly navigating within the waters charted by Venuti when he opens *Translating Baudelaire* with a chapter defending foreignizing translation. There is a difference, however. Venuti's demand for foreignizing translations was a call to allow the strangeness of the foreign text to upset the reading habits of the audience, an audience accustomed to certain conventional strategies that aim to make the foreign text appear like one originally written in English. As a reader of Henri Meschonnic who shares that author's sensitivity to rhythm and orality, Scott is not much concerned with disturbing the reader's mode of aesthetic apprehension of the text or with upsetting the canon. When Scott strives for a "firm-bearing rhythm" and a "strong phrasality" in his translations (2000: 160), he is not simply trying to make them work as poems or to break with established practices. He is trying to realize the potential of translation to transform the aesthetic sensibility of readers. And this is a crucial difference.

Venuti sets up translation in opposition to the literary canon. Scott does not. He knows all too well that translation helps constitute, maintain, and transform the canon. It was on the back of translations that meters hitched a ride into our language: the iambic pentameter derives from the Italian decasyllable, and our ballad owes much to French verse (including its very name, which means "a stroll"). Poetry translations transform the conventions of our systems of versification.

And, as Scott points out, "Translations might be looked upon as one of the contributory factors in the emergence of free verse" (2000: 31; see also 1990).

As a translator who had always felt uneasy about the very act of translation, Scott set out to interpret a process that specialists so often speak of in vague, metaphorical, and often incoherent language. Scott was countering contemporaries such as Norman Shapiro, who in 1998 was still speaking about "elegant exercises in idiosyncratic paraphrase," ill-defined "formal constraints," "the richness of . . . music," and "limping meters" in available Baudelaire translations (quoted in Scott 2000: 8). While such commentators struck Scott "as issuing from the pre-history of versification" (9), he hoped to bring greater technical expertise and a more enlightened theoretical approach—inspired by Meschonnic and Antoine Berman—to bear on the project of lucidly analyzing the process of translating Baudelaire's poems.

This was to prove no easy task. At times Scott betrays one influence to serve another cause. When he defends foreignizing translation in the opening chapter, he defines the act of translating as "trying to get a foreign language into your own" (2000: 14). This is the language of Benjamin, Berman, and Venuti. Meschonnic, on the other hand, reminds us that we do not translate one language into another; we translate one text into another text. It is not a question of transforming Greek into Greekish German or English into franglais. The semantic orchestration of the text must be produced. This point was always misunderstood by Ladmiral and his disciples, who insisted on seeing in Meschonnic a *sourcier*, an adept of literal translation, hung up on the form and structures inherent in the source language. Every time Meschonnic's translations failed to coincide with the established norms of contemporary French, Ladmiral supposed he was being faithful to the structure of a foreign language.[5] Meschonnic knows only fidelity to the text and its mode of signifying, not fidelity to French or any other language. In this example Scott seems tempted by a fidelity to language, but he nonetheless proves true to Meschonnic when he stresses the importance of rhythm over meter, and when he affirms that "the rhythmic ear can be re-attuned [and] that alternative rhythmic versions of a language can be explored" (2000: 29). The adoption of the isochronous strong-stress four-beat meter in contemporary French rap—a meter that even the French *comptine* (nursery rhyme) had been unable to assert—proves this point fairly conclusively.

How does Scott translate, then? He engaged in a series of experiments in versified and free verse. As he advanced "in the apprenticeship of translation," in contrast to most of Baudelaire's translators, he became "increasingly persuaded of the benefits of free verse as a translational medium" (2000: 9). Given Scott's background and erudition, this cannot be considered a copout or an easy option. He is not cutting corners by dropping rhyme and meter. On the contrary, like the great free-verse poets—starting with Eliot, who theorized the problem in his *Selected Prose* (1953)—Scott knows that free verse imposes even greater constraints on poets than metrical verse, if the poem is to work as a convincing aesthetic act. Scott's analysis does prove somewhat difficult to follow at times, but his experiments provide interesting results. Indeed, much of the languid rhythm of the opening stanza of Baudelaire's "Parfum exotique" is reproduced in Scott's unrhymed verse:

Quand, les deux yeux fermés, en un soir chaud d'automne,	When, with both eyes closed, in evening-warm, autumnal,
Je respire l'odeur de ton sein chaleureux,	I inhale, the smell of your breasts' warm in-fold,
Je vois se dérouler des rivages heureux	I see slowly unfurl longed-for far-away coasts
Qu'éblouissent les feux d'un soleil monotone.	Dazzled by the glow of a sun unrelenting.
(Baudelaire 1975: 25)	(Scott 2000: 28)

Scott quotes this experiment, somewhat perversely, to demonstrate what is lost in translation. This is part of his project to make the reading of translations a challenging process. Domesticating translation tends to make it appear a rather banal and unchallenging exercise; much of the text's difficulties are curtailed to provide a style that is easily identified and easily assimilated. Scott is rebelling against this simplifying process.

Indeed, something is undeniably lost in this effort: the loss of the rhyme *automne/monotone* (autumn/monotonous), which contrasts so starkly with *chaleureux/heureux* (warm/happy), is regrettable. But ending on a participle ("unrelenting") adds to the onward movement that undulates expressively throughout the English stanza. And the opposition "in-fold"/"unfurl" is inspired, producing what Meschonnic would have called a semantic effect. This meaningful movement is in turn redoubled with the repetition of the *f* in "longed-for far-away coasts."

Although Scott seems not to be concerned about developments in the study of phrasing, his approach to phrasal rhythm bears much in common with principles espoused by Richard D. Cureton, Donald Wesling, and Derek Attridge from the 1990s onwards. As we saw earlier, for these scholars it is the phrase that is fundamentally expressive, not the meter. Meter is thus considered a form of rhythm. Like these scholars, Scott puts meter into rhythm, and not, as is traditionally done, rhythm into meter. Rhythm is not the shading of a forceful meter. Meter is a heightened, conventionalized form of an already fundamentally expressive movement.

For Scott it is a question of discerning and reproducing the tempo, tone, pausing, and stress degree, but he does not advocate an automatic element-for-element exchange; he argues that they should be put back together as the workings of a new whole. This requires what Scott calls "kinaesthetic participation" on the part of the "reading mind" (2000: 30). In Attridge's terms, this means stressing the stress contour over the meter. In Cureton's terms, it means discerning the organizing shapes of phrasing. This action involves responding to the text and anticipating how the reader of the translated text is likely to respond to a given series of phrases, pauses, and stresses and a tempo that is set up, then played upon.

Arguably Scott is setting up a straw man when he defends free-verse rhythms and "the need for broad rhythmic parameters, and for rhythms both responsive and adjustable" (2000: 30) against "over-normativity [which] has transformed meter into a code which merely over-determines verse as verse, . . . far from releasing expressivity in verse" (30). This is the preaching of the free-verse revolution. Any good metrical verse will demonstrate that expressive rhythms are not hindered or hampered by metrical constraints but rather gain by the very tension that is set up by opposing and resolving the stress contour and the pulse of meter. As we have seen, and as we will have reason to study further on, that tension is often apparent in Dickinson's verse. Shakespeare's verse led Wesling (1996) to propose a grammetrics of metrical verse to describe dynamic tension. And once again it is the dynamics of the tension between meter and speech rhythms that Attridge captures with such elegant simplicity with his binary scansion.

Scott is not limited to free verse though, and he proves he is more than capable of translating into rhymed metrical verse, with his translation of "Harmonie du soir" ("Evening Harmony"). But for some inexplicable reason Scott's version sacrifices the structure of the original, the line ordering, and the repetition of lines (imposed by the fixed form). The result is curious, though it might be argued that it does nevertheless work as a poem in its own right.

Voici venir les temps où vibrant sur sa tige	Like censers, flowers give up their fragrant ghosts.
Chaque fleur s'évapore ainsi qu'un encensoir;	Eddies of sound and perfume stir the air
Les sons et les parfums tournent dans l'air du soir;	At evening; and like a monstrance host
Valse mélancolique et langoureux vertige	Your memory shines in me. So I lay bare
	A heart vibrating like a tautened string,
Chaque fleur s'évapore ainsi qu'un encensoir;	A heart abominating bleak despair,
Le violon frémit comme un cœur qu'on afflige;	Which hoards from distant years their everything,
Valse mélancolique et langoureux vertige!	Their every trace of luminous largesse.
Le ciel est triste et beau comme un grand reposoir	
(Baudelaire 1975: 47)	(Scott 2000: 115)

"Luminous largesse" is striking. "Which hoards from distant years their everything" reads like one of Wordsworth's reminders to himself to store images of nature's beauty for contemplation in tough times ahead, in order to counter despair. "Like censers, flowers give up their fragrant ghosts" captures the sentiment beautifully. And "So I lay bare / A heart vibrating like a tautened string" certainly creates an apt image, one that Baudelaire, so sensitive to tension, would have appreciated.

Scott's experiments have the merit of highlighting the search for solutions that many translators either respond to intuitively or simply do not apprehend. If he gives us some of the tools for helping us in our task, then he has done a great service to poetry translation. Analysis of the act of trying to translate the poem is the substance of Scott's book. To move forward, what we require is to define and list some lessons that can be drawn from Scott's experimental and analytic project:

1. Scott stresses the fundamental expressivity of phrasing.
2. He believes that rhythm must be considered both independently of meter and in relation to meter in metrical verse.
3. For Scott, lexical translations that seek to define the meaning of the poem, and then proceed to translate individual words, neglect the fact that central words create powerful clusters of meaning. *Noir* functions like this in the Black Venus poems, and associations of a lexical and sonorous kind are fundamental in the poems' mode of signifying.
4. Perception of the rhythm of the original by the translator and his anticipation of how his own translated text will be perceived and performed by the reading ear is fundamental in the translation process. This is what Scott means by "kinaesthetic participation," and it represents a major contribution to the uncharted territory of the poetics of the process of reading translated works.

Translation Strategies and Overt and Covert Poetics

Scott's scrupulous self-analysis reveals a great deal about his own poetics as a practising translator, but Meschonnic knew that we do not need to read the translators' accounts to understand their poetics—we only need to look at the translated poems. Far from being able to rationally explicate their aims and intentions, most translators provide a rather disappointing list of clichés relating to elegance, fidelity, and the music of verse. And all too often the supposed poetry of the source language is invoked as an alibi to excuse the prosaic quality of the translator's efforts. It is far from clear to what extent bad faith or lack of a clearly defined linguistic metalanguage is to blame for such obscure ramblings. However, it is certain that many translators—even expert ones, even great thinkers, even those who, like Walter Benjamin, are erudite in both translation and thinking—do not seem able to demonstrate what they are doing or how they are doing it.

Meschonnic, in contrast, had a razor-sharp insight into what was going on. A translator who translated the meter without concerning himself about the rhythm, Meschonnic identified as a slave to a formalistic poetics. Translators who heard and who strove to reproduce a moving movement, the rhythm of a voice—those he considered to be great translators. Most contemporary translators, however, tend to opt for prose or a poetical prose with occasional metrical lines when translating both metrical and free verse, and Meschonnic found such laxness tiresome and self-defeating. It may please readers of French who are left with the impression they are reading something poetical, but it bears little in common with the original. And it cannot produce the same degree of force as a poem that transforms its language in some new, dynamic, meaningful way, as poetry has the power to do.

The poetics of Baudelaire's translators transpires clearly enough in the way they handle tone, register, lexis, meter, and rhythm. As Scott rightly suggests, prose translators tend to treat words as isolated bricks in an edifice. For them, precision consists in making sure each brick is extracted from the source language and then replaced in the foreign language. Translators who believe in the prose/poetry dichotomy opt for a metrical translation, but often arbitrarily, so we see tetrameters replacing the octosyllable and pentameters and hexameters replacing the alexandrine. These strategies work well enough. Meschonnic himself opted (somewhat at odds with convention) for the decasyllable when translating the iambic pentameter of Shakespeare's sonnets. Most French translators prefer the alexandrine, the classical French verse line from the seventeenth century onwards. But all of these strategies can be defended, provided the meter does not drive the expression. The expressive rhythm must harness and direct the meter. When too many concessions are made to meter, we tend to fall into doggerel, rat rhyme, or forced verse. And when rhymes are forced, they serve only to highlight the ineptitude of the translator. They certainly do not reassure the reader or add to the harmony of the poem as a whole.

Baudelaire has met with some mediocre interpreters, but on the whole those inspired by his work have managed to bring into English some remarkably moving versions. Even those versions that seem forced and antiquated to us today often prove upon scrutiny to have unsuspected qualities. How shall we impose some order on the great variety of styles and techniques adopted? Three modes of categorization appear useful. A chronological approach is needed; a system of ordering based on the strategies put into play is required; and finally it is important to consider the translated poems in terms of quality. These modes will allow us to escape dogmatic thought and dichotomies set up by adherents of one school or another. A poem or a translation may work despite the theory it seems to uphold, just as a perfectly coherent argument does not necessarily produce a good poem or a good translation. A translated poem may work at different levels; for example, it may be irritatingly archaic in its lexis or syntax but startlingly original in its rhymes. And as Scott's version of "Parfum exotique" shows, something moving in the rhythm can remain even though the meter is dropped. A domesticating translation can shake us with the originality of its images; a foreignizing translation can fall into facility of one kind or another, or it can simply break down and cease to function as a meaningful poem.

Chronology

In the preface to their excellent *Baudelaire in English* (Baudelaire 1997), the editors Carol Clark and Robert Sykes treat the dates of publication of most of Baudelaire's translations in greater detail than I shall here. I will give only a brief account before considering particular translations in detail. English-speaking readers had to wait until 1894, a generation after Baudelaire's death, before the first extensive publication of his poems in English—by a certain "H. C.," who is believed to have been Henry Curwen. Clark and Sykes tell us that "three noteworthy selections and a handful of individual translations" were to be published in the following fifteen years (Baudelaire 1997: xxxii). These included Lord Alfred Douglas's four translations published in 1899, with a further two poems translated in 1909. Frank Pearce Sturm's collection of Baudelaire poems, published in 1906, is considered by Clark and Sykes to be one of the most successful. Thereafter the editors focus on Arthur Symons's translation of 1925 as the next major contribution. Indeed, Symons's Baudelaire offers us a very poetic contribution. This is all the more remarkable because the poetry of his translations contrasts with the harsh appraisal Symons gave of Baudelaire almost thirty years before, in 1893. At that time he spoke of Baudelaire as "an uneasy guest at the orgy of life." Since then his sensibility had opened up to the poet, it seems. Aleister Crowley, the great Satanist, also deserves a mention for his prose-poem translations that appeared in 1928.

These translators might be considered as the first wave. Clark and Sykes try—not altogether successfully—to group them as the English translators. This strategy clearly allows them to affirm that little interest was shown in Baudelaire in the interwar period. The argument goes hand in hand with their promotion of the American interpreters, who take up the torch, as far as the editors are concerned, first with Lewis Piaget Shank's edition, which came out in the United States in 1926, and then with George Hill Dillon and Edna St. Vincent Millay's edition of 1936.

Clark and Sykes have modern tastes. They are hostile to the archaizing poetical touch of the English translators and they are particularly hard on Symons, who remains popular with Internet readers. Clark and Sykes prefer the Americans. They selected thirteen examples—more than for any other translator—from Richard Howard's edition, which came out in the United States in 1982. *Baudelaire in English* makes great reading, and their selections consolidate the line of argument taken by the editors. Nevertheless, although I personally share their tastes to some extent, the Anglo/American opposition breaks down mainly because Baudelaire attracts translators from all over the globe, and many of those who translate him into "English" English turn out not to be English. Sturm, the editors' favourite British translator, is a Scot. True, he translates into an English that sits well with London readers but, in adapting to English English, his Aberdonian dialect is perhaps acting as a counterpoint, making him more sensitive in his use of language. Roy Campbell, from whose work eleven translations are selected, is a South African.

A pattern is emerging here. Clark and Sykes offer a wonderful variety of translators and deserve praise for the efficiency and quality of their project, but they do seem to have a covert aesthetic agenda. They wish to break with the Victorian and the Georgian sensibility, preferring plain, direct, harder-hitting poetry—or even something not quite English—to the archaic language that evokes a poetic tradition of the past. Even Alan Conder's 1952 translation, which was published in England and offered a complete collection of Baudelaire's verse, like Campbell's, does not suit the editors' tastes. Only one of his translations is selected by Clark and Sykes, a translation that nonetheless proves that Conder was capable of translating into simple, efficiently expressive language, very different from those archaic attempts his compatriots were producing at the beginning of the twentieth century (Baudelaire 1997: 65–67).

In recent years James McGowan's complete translation of the *Flowers of Evil*, published in the Oxford World Poets series in 1998 (a year after Clark and Sykes's collection came out), has come to be regarded as one of the major Baudelaire translations (Baudelaire 1998). Clark and Sykes cite two examples from McGowan, a professor at Illinois Wesleyan University. McGowan's collection came more than a quarter of a century after Richard Howard's American translation of the *Fleurs du Mal* in unrhymed verse. Both these collections tend to contradict Clark and Sykes's affirmation that "[f]rom the 1960s onward 'straight' versions of his poems begin to give place to freer more radical approaches" (Baudelaire 1997: xlv). The same must be said of Roy Fuller's half-dozen translations, which the two editors admit combine fidelity with freshness and clarity. They go on to name Peter Dale, Dick Davis, and Alistair Elliot as translators who have recreated "thoughtful and direct versions" (li). Who are the iconoclastic free re-inventors of Baudelaire, then? Clark and Sykes seem to have Robert Lowell in mind. Lowell's controversial and aptly named *Imitations* was published in 1961, and it is hardly surprising, given his stature as a great modern poet, that these translations have given rise to debate ever since.

No selection of Baudelaire translators could hope to compete with *Baudelaire in English*. Clark and Sykes have done a marvellous job of furnishing a spicy selection of thought-provoking translations and juxtaposing styles and manners as they have evolved over the years. Baudelaire's evil flowers have sent their seeds sprouting up throughout the world. The Internet offers a vast array of translations in various languages. Stefan George's translation of *Fleurs, Die Blumen des Bösen,* for example, can be found on the website Internet Archive (www.archive.org), and many Czech sites offer examples of Czech Baudelaires (for example, www.baudelaire.cz).

As for English Baudelaires, the website Charles Baudelaire's Fleurs du mal / Flowers of Evil (Baudelaire 2015) takes up the same task as Clark and Sykes. This site contains translators not included in their collection. Cat Nilan's translations (1999, 2004) could obviously not have been selected by Clark and Sykes, but among other previously published translators of Baudelaire, the site has selected William Aggeler (1954), Jacques LeClercq (1958), and Geoffrey Wagner (1974). Clark and Sykes's edition can be seen as a moment of crystallization in the reception of Baudelaire, but one that will not prevent further projects from sprouting in different directions.

Strategies

Just as it is impossible to include all of Baudelaire's translators in any one study, so is it impossible to do justice to the full variety of strategies adopted to convey in English something of Baudelaire's poetic genius. Nonetheless it is important to try to grasp the various options open to translators and to attempt to establish some order among the diversity of English Baudelaires that exist. A this stage it will become obvious that pigeonholing translators makes little sense. Partisans of polemical approaches to translation are fond of oppositions, but while the simplicity of binary oppositions between glosses and dynamic translations or between domesticators and foreignizers permits meaningful statements about the intentions of translators in general, when it comes down to analyzing given translations, the situation invariably turns out to be much more complicated.

A translator may be both archaizing and foreignizing or archaizing and domesticating. A translator might be free with content but strict in terms of formal constraints. Another translator will prove free in terms of both form and content. One translator may drop rhyme and meter but remain archaizing in terms of diction and syntax. Then again, a translator might be very modern in diction but choose to preserve the meter. Most of all it is important to understand that choices and strategies tend to form in clusters, and it is the interaction of various linked strategies that reveals the specificity of each translator's style. An outline of some trends and tendencies will allow us to distinguish between strategies.

Archaizing Translators
As we can see below, Lord Alfred Douglas's translation of "Recueillement" ("*Sois sage ô ma douleur*"), published in 1909, is predictably archaic compared with Frances Cornford's "Meditation," published in 1976.

Peace, be at peace, O thou my heaviness, Thou calledst for the evening, lo! 'tis here, The City wears a somber atmosphere That brings repose to some, to some distress.	Cease, O my Sorrow, like a child be still, You begged for evening, evening, look, is there: The streets with an enfolding darkness fill Which brings to this man peace, to that one, care.
(Douglas, in Baudelaire 1997: 224)	(Cornford, in Baudelaire 1997: 225)

It is difficult to understand today how a translator could have felt justified in introducing "calledst," "'tis," and "thou." These are the poetical props of the verse of Douglas's time, already archaic and nostalgically otherworldly at the beginning of the nineteenth century. Byron would not have stooped to such diction. When Douglas takes the liberty of introducing a charioteer a few lines on, simply in order to maintain his rhyming scheme, this begins to look very much like a poetic disaster: "Where pleasure drives them, ruthless charioteer, / To pluck the fruits of sick remorse and fear" (225). Where is the charioteer in Baudelaire's lines? Nowhere! A penchant for Homer and the trappings of heroic Greek verse is perverting the translating process.

In fairness to Douglas, however, he is a good rhymer on the whole, as the first four lines prove. Curiously, in 1899 Douglas was working in a much less ornate manner, as his translation of the opening stanza of "Harmonie du soir" proves:

> Now is the hour when, swinging in the breeze,
> Each flower, like a censer, sheds its sweet.
> The air is full of scents and melodies,
> O languorous waltz! O swoon of dancing feet!
> (Douglas, in Baudelaire 1997: 61)

In many respects Douglas proves himself to be a competent and talented translator, and this fact should not be obscured by our distaste for the aesthetics of his times. Our own tastes and prejudices will no doubt appear equally ridiculous to generations to come. Douglas manipulates the meaning skillfully, if freely, rearranging the phrasing in order to establish meaningful rhymes. The art with which he maintains the easy flow of the lines could upset only the most ardent defender of foreignizing translation. Douglas tends to sweeten Baudelaire, though. In "Recueillement," where Baudelaire sends a "moribund sun" (soleil moribund) to sleep under an arch (Baudelaire 1975: 41), to Douglas a "dying sun sinks in the west" (Baudelaire 1997: 225).

We can clearly observe in Douglas's translation the interplay of three converging strategies. He is a metrical translator, an ennobling translator, and an archaizing translator. These strategies prove to be inseparable in his style. He would not think of dropping the rhyme or failing to observe the metrical constraints he sets up. He wants a noble Baudelaire, a poetic Baudelaire. His syntax and his diction opt—when it comes to choosing—for a diction and register that remind us that this is poetry and not everyday speech. No doubt more modern Baudelaires appear closer to us and our times, and perhaps they move us more for that reason. But Douglas clearly does not intend to bring Baudelaire down to our level; he wants to lift us up. The only difficulty with this though is what while Douglas's Baudelaire is noble, not crass, arguably Baudelaire was both.

Meter is part of this ennobling process. Free verse would not achieve the effect Douglas attempts. As Cornford's translation demonstrates, it is not the meter in itself that is ennobling. Lowell's translation of the opening lines of "Recueillement," which we have already considered in this chapter (page 188), demonstrates this point equally well. We can therefore hazard a working conclusion: ennobling translating is by nature metrical, though metrical verse is not necessarily ennobling. Let us try to see if this hypothesis is borne out by other archaizing translations. In the Clark and Sykes collection, these include Arthur Symons, W. J. Robertson, and Aldous Huxley (better known as the author of *Brave New World*).

Clark and Sykes find Symons's versions so unreliable that they accompany them with plain prose translations. This certainly seems fair if we compare "The Beautiful Ship," Symons's 1925 version of "Le beau navire," with the original.

Je veux te raconteur, ô molle enchanteresse Les diverses beautés qui parent ta jeunesse; Je veux peindre ta beauté, Où l'enfance s'allie à la maturité. Quand tu vas balayant l'air de ta jupe large, Tu fais l'effet d'un beau vaisseau qui prend le large,	My desire is to respire thy charms that are divine And all in thee that is more beautiful than wine, All this desire of mine Is to paint the child whose fashions are malign. When thou dost wander thy skirt balances to and fro In the wind's embraces from the seas that flow,
(Baudelaire 1975: 51–52)	(Symons, in Baudelaire 1997: 67–68)

As in Douglas's translations, rhyme and meter converge with the archaizing strategy (consider the use of "thou" and "dost"). "Malign" might have come from Baudelaire, for he had a taste for malicious seductresses, but here it is simply wrong, a mistranslation, a prop used to rhyme the line. And is wine beautiful? Symons thought so, but the idea is totally absent in Baudelaire's verse. "Your kisses are sweeter than wine" was perhaps original when first written in the Song of Solomon of the Old Testament, but it has long since become a cliché. Beautiful wine is simply an inept attempt to preserve the rhyming scheme by rhyming "wine" and "divine." More disconcerting still, Symons prefers to stress the motion of the wind, which he depicts, as a true romantic, as embracing the forms of the skirt. This metaphor induces him to drop the image of the ship heading for the high seas, and we are consequently left at a loss to understand the title of the poem, "The Beautiful Ship."

Symons proves more successful in other translations, and this explains in part the success that his versions had at the time of their publication, and continue to have today, but in the extract above we see the convergence of a series of perverting strategies. Content is sacrificed for form, rhyming is arbitrary, and the ennobling and archaizing tendencies of the translator work on the whole to weaken and dilute Baudelaire, most of all in the attempt to ennoble him and keep him sounding poetical. Meter and rhyme have become accomplices to the crime.

That the archaizing strategy does not necessarily have to produce results like this is demonstrated by the versions of Robertson and Huxley. The opening stanza of Robertson's 1895 "Hymn to Beauty" certainly adopts the archaizing and ennobling strategies— using "thy" and "thou," adjectives following nouns, and "likened unto"— but it does, nevertheless, render the meaning while organizing the poem into balanced but compact lines that rhyme poignantly. Wine is divine this time in both the original and the translation. And good and evil, from Heaven "descended," are "blended" in the translation in both meaning and in sound.

Viens-tu du ciel profond ou sors-tu de l'abime,	Be thou from Hell upsprung or Heaven descended,
Ô Beauté? ton regard, infernal et divin,	Beauty! Thy look demoniac and divine,
Verse confusément le bienfait et le crime,	Pours good and evil things confusedly blended,
Et l'on peut pour cela te comparer au vin.	And therefore art thou likened unto wine.
("Hymne à la beauté," Baudelaire 1975: 24)	(Robertson, in Baudelaire 1997: 35)

Huxley wrote five collections of poems during his literary career and produced an intriguing translation of one of Baudelaire's longer poems, "Femmes Damnées: Delphine et Hippolyte," the title of which he translated more explicitly as "Lesbians." More than thirty years after Robertson's version, this novelist who looked into the future kept slipping back nonetheless into a nostalgic poetical mode with archaisms and lofty syntactic inversions. His version reads: "On cushions deep Hippolyta reclined" (Baudelaire 1997: 206); "twere a sin to throw" (207); and "Hence, lamentable victims, get you hence" (209). For all these poetical frills, however, Huxley's version still has a very direct thrust that it owes partly to its monosyllabic movement, partly to its ominously meaningful rhymes, and partly to his pithy choice of words.

Jamais un rayon frais n'éclaira vos cavernes;	Sunless your caverns are; the fever damps
Par les fentes des murs des miasmes fiévreux	That filter in through every crannied vent
Filtrent en s'enflammant ainsi que des lanternes	Break out with marsh-fire into sudden lamps
Et pénètrent vos corps de leurs parfums affreux.	And steep your bodies with their frightful scent.
L'âpre stérilité de votre jouissance	The barrenness of your pleasures hard and stale
Altère votre soif et roidit votre peau,	Makes mad your thirst and parches up your skin;
Et le vent furibond de la concupiscence	
Fait claquer votre chair ainsi qu'un vieux drapeau.	And like an old flag volleying in the gale, Your whole flesh shudders in the blasts of sin.
(Baudelaire 1975: 155)	(Huxley, in Baudelaire 1997: 209)

Huxley was Symons's contemporary, but while Huxley could at times slip back into a past, Symons was steeped in a nostalgia that made him cling to a worn-out Victorian poetical mode; he wished to anchor Baudelaire in the nineteenth century and make him into a poet he himself could respond to. Huxley, on the other hand, kept dragging his Baudelaire back into the land of the living, with its pleasure in pain, its thirsting lust, parching skin, and awful odours. However much he was seduced by poetical diction, Huxley remained a friend of T. S. Eliot and shared something of his sensitivity to frenetic lust and the stench of the city. Above all, the genius of Huxley's rhyming—linking "sin" with "skin"; "gale" with "stale"; and "scent" with "vent"—is sickeningly (and appropriately) overwhelming.

Metrical Moderns

Translators may refuse the archaizing strategy but want a well-carved metrical Baudelaire who speaks to the heart directly, without the architectonics of inverted syntax and poetical flourishes. Among them are the American translators George Dillon and Edna St. Vincent Millay in the 1930s, and Lowell in the early 1960s. The South African Roy Campbell in the 1950s, and the contemporary English translator Robert Sykes, who co-edited *Baudelaire in English* with Carol Clark, also belong to this group.

Dillon's translations are somewhat pedestrian. Baudelaire's nature engenders "monstrous children"; his nature is ominous and unpredictable. Dillon's nature, in "The Giantess," his translation of "La géante," is overflowing with joy and creativity. The lyrical subject runs and laughs beside his monster muse, this great, growing matriarch and object of his lust. Celebrating his muse blinds Dillon to her sinister side. The ominously ambivalent manner with which Baudelaire caresses his grotesque demigoddess is lost in his translation. Nevertheless, as is often the case, enough of Baudelaire survives in Dillon's plain, straightforward, and at times elegant style to make sure that a powerful poem emerges from the translation process.

Du temps que la Nature en sa verve puissante	In times of old when Nature in her glad excess
Concevait chaque jour des enfants monstrueux,	Brought forth such living marvels as no more are seen,
J'eusse aimé vivre auprès d'une jeune géante,	I should have loved to dwell with a young giantess,
Comme aux pieds d'une reine un chat voluptueux.	Like a voluptuous cat about the feet of a queen.
(Baudelaire 1975: 22)	(Dillon, in Baudelaire 1997: 34)

Dillon's translation is certainly somewhat paler that the original, and it appears difficult from these lines to see why his collaborator Millay admired him so much. Nevertheless the English poem works as a whole; it has a direct impact, and at times wonderful lines break forth, such as "To scale the slopes of her huge knees, explore at will / The hollows and the heights of her . . ." (34).

Dillon and Millay both opt for the hexameter rather than the pentameter. This choice allows them a little more breathing space than the compact ten-syllable iambic pentameter, and in length it resembles the alexandrine more. This last point gives no more justification than for the pentameter, however. Both verse lines replace syllable count with accentual alternation, and the choice of meter ultimately comes down to one of convention. The fact that the pentameter has dominated verse and sonnet translation is no argument against Dillon's and Millay's strategy. Where Baudelaire uses an octosyllabic line, Millay opts for the iambic tetrameter. In the end, though, it is not the structure that counts but its use by the individual poet or translator.

The breathtaking simplicity of Millay's translations echoes the original poignancy of Baudelaire. When the poet dreams of Paris, Millay aptly evokes the "steel and slate" of the roofs of Haussmann's rows of Parisian apartment blocks.

Et, peintre fier de mon génie	And, proud of what my art had done,
Je savourais dans mon tableau	I viewed my painting, knew the great
L'enivrante monotonie	Intoxicating monotone
Du métal, du marbre et de l'eau.	Of marble, water, steel and slate.
("Rêve parisien," Baudelaire 1975: 101)	(Millay, in Baudelaire 1997: 146)

Like the American Millay, the South African Roy Campbell captures Baudelaire's meandering muse in simple, elegant, and direct metrical verse. Campbell takes liberties: he introduces the grimness of the city to get his rhyme, and he transforms *enchantements* into "grace" for the same purpose. But who would deny that a deep understanding of Baudelaire's poetic universe is at work in these inspired manoeuvres? Like any sensitive reader, Campbell knows that Baudelaire will always seek the beautiful in the grim, and that his desire, his lust for enchantment, is twisted and tangled up in spiritual longings. For that reason Campbell's translations invariably work as direct poetic experiences, as the opening stanza of "The Little Old Women" shows well enough.

Dans les plis sinueux des vieilles capitales,	In sinuous folds of cities old and grim,
Où tout, même l'horreur, tourne aux enchantements,	Where all things, even horror, turn to grace, I follow, in obedience to my whim, Strange, feeble, charming creatures round the place.
Je guette, obéissant à mes humeurs fatales, Des êtres singuliers, décrépits et charmants.	
	These crooked freaks were women in their pride
Ces monstres disloqués furent jadis des femmes,	
("Les petites vieilles," Baudelaire 1975: 89)	(Campbell, in Baudelaire 1997: 125)

And what about the English translators? Are they condemned to pace the treadmill towards the archaic? Sykes proves otherwise. But the Scot Frank Pearce Sturm, from Aberdeen, had already demonstrated that it was possible back in 1906 to have a modern Baudelaire. Sturm, however, proves uneven and unpredictable. His "The Balcony" is deliciously poetic, but it is so despite, rather than thanks to, the archaically poetical diction:

> Mother of memories, mistress of mistresses,
> O thou, my pleasure, thou, all my desire,
> Thou shalt recall the beauty of caresses,
> The charm of evenings by the gentle fire,
> Mother of memories, mistress of mistresses!
> (Baudelaire 1997: 47)

How would this read if we could extract the poetry and do away with the poetical frills? Sturm himself is no longer here to answer this question. But if I might be allowed to improvise upon his version, we will see that it takes relatively little effort to purify his verse of the pseudo-poetical and allow the essential beauty of his lines to shine through.

> Mother of memories, mistress of mistresses,
> You are my joy, my kernel of desire.
> Will you remember the beauty of our caresses?
> The charm of evenings by the gentle fire?
> Mother of memories, mistress of mistresses!

This experiment is not a betrayal of Sturm, because he was often poignantly direct in his translations. The following lines from "A Former Life" certainly do not seem contaminated with contrived poetical flourishes. They could easily have appeared in 2006 rather than 1906.

C'est là que j'ai vécu dans les voluptés calmes, Au milieu de l'azur, des vagues, des splendeurs Et des esclaves nus, tout imprégnés d'odeurs, Qui me rafraîchissaient le front avec des palmes Et dont l'unique soin était d'approfondir Le secret douloureux qui me faisait languir. ("La vie antérieure," Baudelaire 1975: 18)	And there I lived amid voluptuous calms, In splendours of blue sky and wandering wave, Tended by many a naked perfumed slave, Who fanned my languid brow with waving palms, They were my slaves—the only care they had To know what secret grief had made me sad. (Sturm, in Baudelaire 1997: 28)

Sykes's metrical Baudelaire of "Mist in Rain" is the antithesis of the archaizing translation, with phrases like "Fag-end of autumn." Compact and sinuous, the translation makes use of triple-stressed, semantically charged units in which the middle stress is demoted to convey the force of Baudelaire's expression: "mud-drenched spring"; "great flood-plain"; "storm-winds sound"; "black rook's wing." The result is a dense and ominously powerful English Baudelaire.

Ô fins d'automne, hivers, printemps trempés de boue Endormeuses saisons! je vous aime et vous loue D'envelopper ainsi mon coeur et mon cerveau D'un linceul vaporeux et d'un vague tombeau. Dans cette grande plaine où l'autan froid se joue, Où par les longues nuits la girouette s'enroue, Mon âme mieux qu'au temps du tiède renouveau Ouvrira largement ses ailes de corbeau. ("Brumes et pluies," Baudelaire 1975: 100–01)	Fag-end of autumn, winter, mud-drenched spring, seasons of sloth, it's you I love and sing who swaddle up my heart and my poor brain in a tomb of air, a shroud of misty rain. In this great flood-plain where the storm-winds sound, where all night long the weather cock whirls round, my soul—which cowered when buds were opening— arches the panoply of its black rook's wing. (Sykes, in Baudelaire 1997: 145)

"Seasons of sloth" renders *endormeuses saisons* wonderfully. "Fag-end of autumn" could have come from T. S. Eliot's "Preludes" or *The Waste Land*, and in such a line resides the Baudelaire that Eliot responded to. Indeed, the soul that cowers when the buds open is the soul that groans that "April is the cruellest month" in the first line of *The Waste Land* (Eliot 1969a: 61). This is a deep reaction to a profoundly heartfelt anti-romanticism, one whose roots reach down into the English poetic tradition and into a shared disgruntled reaction to those unsung days of miserable weather and desolate plains of mud and furrowed fields.

What can we conclude at this point? The distinction between free-verse translators and metrical translators, however useful it first appears, must be broken down and rearticulated. A wealth of different practices emerges within metrical translations, just as the quintessential balance of strategies and tendencies, tastes and aversions found in the creations of each translator must be taken into account and listened to. Each translation harnesses, either harmoniously or disharmoniously, a set of covert strategies that set the poem in motion and make it work or let it fall to pieces as a collection of transposed lines. Sometimes we hear the hollow ring of a demoded English tradition rattling around inside a translation. At other times translators aiming to be modern and straightforward unravel too much of Baudelaire's complexity in their uncomplicated attempts. Conversely, translators eager to offer a harsh and hard-hitting Baudelaire risk effacing the delicious elegance of his poise.

Among the metrical Baudelaires we find archaizers, ennoblers, and sweeteners, just as we find contemporary hard-hitters like Sykes. In many of them we find forceful rhyming and moving rhythms that cannot be reduced to the rule-bound structure of the meter. Most of these translators are responding to Baudelaire, and in the hands of Campbell, Millay, and Sykes, meter forms the organizing framework of a dynamic, meaningful poem. In their hands, line ends are heightened points of expressive force, rhymes make sense, and the flow of lines embodies the meaning. Despite wonderful lines and great images, Lord Alfred Douglas and Arthur Symons at times sacrifice the meaning for the rhyme, and in doing so they sacrifice something of Baudelaire. Campbell and Millay are often free in their rhyming, yet their freedom takes us back to Baudelaire. While Douglas's and Symons's innovations often lead to a dead end all of their own, Millay and Campbell intuitively respond to the imagination of Baudelaire, finding shortcuts and underground passages to his poetic mode of expression.

Prose Baudelaires

Ultimately there is nothing prosaic about Baudelaire, so the very idea of a prose Baudelaire is inevitably something shocking. Even Baudelaire's prose is poetic, as his *petits poèmes en prose* clearly demonstrate in *Le spleen de Paris*, those short pieces that did a great deal to launch the genre (Baudelaire 1975: 275–374). Curiously, the poetry of Baudelaire is so full of moving rhythms, foregrounded orality, idiosyncratic turns of phrase, and striking imagery that once the meter and rhymes are stripped away, some kernel of poetry remains, refusing to be ground down to prose, or at least to what might be called prosaic prose. That is why it is no longer a pleonasm to speak of Baudelaire's non-versified poetry. The question of what poetry survives in a prose translation therefore arises.

Inevitably some readers find Francis Scarfe's prose translations (Baudelaire 1961) disappointing, though a great many lines are elegantly and movingly rendered. Scarfe's unpretentious prose gloss is intended as an aid to English-speaking students of French who are entering into Baudelaire's world, and the work can be commended for doing a good job of making the French text explicit. The whole suffers, but many of the parts give an impression of what Baudelaire intended.

La Nature est un temple où de vivants piliers Laissent parfois sortir de confuses paroles; L'homme y passe à travers des forêts de symboles Qui l'observent avec des regards familiers.	Nature is a temple, in which living pillars sometimes utter a babel of words; man traverses it through forests of symbols, that watch him with knowing eyes.
Comme de longs échos qui de loin se confondent Dans une ténébreuse et profonde unité, Vaste comme la nuit et comme la clarté, Les parfums, les couleurs et les sons se répondent.	Like prolonged echoes which merge far away in an opaque, deep oneness, as vast as darkness, as vast as light, perfumes, sounds, and colours answer each to each.
("Correspondances," Baudelaire 1975: 11)	("Correlatives," Baudelaire 1961: 36–67)

This is prose, but sensitive prose, prose that often reads rhythmically and pauses meaningfully in expressive phrasing. The poem is destroyed; the wholeness is lost. But from the debris of prose, poetry keeps breaking though. It might be called a free translation if we are thinking in terms of versification, but it is not a free-verse translation; free verse still presents a poem, a whole, not an assemblage of poetic parts. For this reason free-verse Baudelaires must distinguish themselves from this type of rendering if they are to defend their poetics and do justice to the expressive potential of their strategy.

Scarfe described his own strategy as a "compromise" between "word for word equivalents for the original, and a desire to render them into something like a prose-poem" (Baudelaire 1972: lx). In *The Penguin Book of French Verse: 1820–1950*, selected and translated by William Rees (1990), the intention is somewhat similar. Rees is all too conscious that prose translation "implies a discipline in the rendering of sense which inhibits the verse-to-verse translator rather less, particularly if he is reshaping the original impulse into a new metrical and rhyming structure" (1990: xxiv), and he is eager to avoid "producing distortion or bathos" (xxiv) as many translators end up doing, in his opinion, in their versified versions. Nevertheless Rees prides himself on aiming at faithful translations that are "a step above the literal" (xxiv). The strategy he adopted strives to produce "decided rhythms and sound-patterns that please the ear, or at least do not displease it" (xxiv). Rees feels that this occasionally gives rise to a "certain equivalent musicality" (xxiv). That is the theory, but what transpires in practice?

Rees proves less reliable in practice than Scarfe. "Meditation," Rees's version of "Recueillement," a poem already considered earlier (pages 188 and 205–6), begins badly: "Be discreet, O my Suffering, and be more placid. You craved the Evening, it comes down; here it is: a dusky atmosphere cloaks the city, bringing peace to some, anxiety to others" (1990: 169). This phrase-by-phrase translation is charmless, to say the least. Besides, *sage* is not "discreet," and "placid" is a curiously insipid translation of *tranquille*, used to address the troubled soul.[6] If this were all Rees had to offer, he would not have a place here, but he proves a sensitive translator in his rendering of other poems. In both "Beauty" ("La beauté") and "Carrion" ("Une charogne"), he responds to Baudelaire by producing something of Baudelaire's sweeping sovereign rhythms in the first and the jarring movement of his exclamations of disgust in the second.

I am beautiful o mortals, like a dream in stone, and my breast, where all have bruised themselves in turn, is destined to inspire in the poet a love that is eternal and wordless, like matter.

I am enthroned in the azure like an unfathomed sphinx; to the whiteness of swans I join a heart of snow; I hate motion which displaces the lines, and I never weep and never laugh.

("Beauty," Rees 1990: 138)

Remember the object that we saw, love of my soul, that fine sweet summer morning: at the turn of a path a vile carcass on a bed strewn with pebbles,

Legs in the air, like a lascivious woman, burning and oozing out poisons, opened in casual, brazen fashion its fuming belly.

("Carrion," Rees 1990: 143)

It would be easy to find fault with these lines by comparing them to the orality and expressive movement of the originals. But this comparison would amount to proving that poetry is more powerful than prose, a bet that is easily won. A more relevant question is, how do such attempts compare with free-verse translations? When prose translations have served their purpose and helped students of French to penetrate the originals, and when readers are looking for something like the same experience French-speaking readers enjoy on discovering Baudelaire, what do free-verse translations provide that is missing here?

Free-Verse Baudelaires

Laurence Lerner's Baudelaire is at times rhymed and versified. His "Spleen II" (Baudelaire 1997: 97) is successful line by line, but the rhyming scheme he chooses is complex and idiosyncratic. Readers will inevitably have difficulty discerning it when a couplet is encased within a series of lines in which the first must await the fifth to find its rhyme. Lerner does not hesitate to interject English references into Baudelaire's poems, such as Dickens's Miss Havisham. Clark and Sykes find this commendable, and although they consider his translations free, they believe Lerner is "almost always successful in rendering the feeling of the poem" (Baudelaire 1997: 88). For this reason Lerner figures among their favourites: they include no less than eight of his versions in their collection. Line by line, Lerner does indeed prove a sensitive and responsive interpreter. Something essential in Baudelaire remains in his final lines of "Spleen II": "But if my streets ran blood, and all the drains / Were gushing blood, it wouldn't thaw the cold / And frozen muck of Lethe in my veins" (Baudelaire 1997: 97).

But what fills the reader with consternation upon discovering Lerner's versions is the fact that they only partially rhyme. A rhyming scheme is set up but not always respected. In this sense Lerner is obviously not adopting a strategy; he is doing the best he can to respect his two masters' meaning and form. Partial rhyming works in a *xaya* rhyming scheme, so it is not too upsetting to find "in" rhyming with "wing" in the second stanza of "Spleen III" (the first rhyme in the following quotation). However, an altogether different effect is made when Lerner rhymes in *axay* form and asks us to accept "sight" and "thought" where we expect a rhyme.

Quand la terre est changée en un cachot humide,	When earth becomes a dungeon, shutting in
Où l'Espérance, comme une chauve-souris,	Hope like a bat that darts and twists and falls,
S'en va battant les murs de son aile timide	Scraping the roof with head or timid wing,
Et se cognant la tête à des plafonds pourris ;	Dislodging plaster from the rotten walls;
Quand la pluie étalant ses immenses traînées	When the interminable lines of rain
D'une vaste prison imite les barreaux,	Are stretched like prison bars before our sight,
Et qu'un peuple muet d'infâmes araignées	And a mute horde of spiders in the brain
Vient tendre ses filets au fond de nos cerveaux,	Wrap their disgusting webs round every thought
(Baudelaire 1975: 75)	(Lerner, in Baudelaire 1997: 101)

Lerner's horde of spiders wrap their disgusting webs around each thought; Baudelaire's spiders cast their nets at the bottom of the brain. Lerner's bats dislodge the plaster on the walls, while Baudelaire's smack their heads against the rotting ceilings. These are improvisations, but improvisations that follow the flow of Baudelaire's strikingly original and morbid mode of expression. As Clark and Sykes claim, Lerner does on the whole reproduce the feel of the original. But breaking with the rhyme structure introduces a jarring, disrupting influence, and this paradoxically upsets the delicate balance of Baudelaire's perverse verse, because Baudelaire's lines flow harmoniously, in stark contrast—in dramatic counterpoint—to the unsettling imagery.

Changes in rhyme can be used as a strategy of surprise, but here we simply feel we are being let down. The lack of rhyme is eventless, semantically speaking. Dropping the rhyme in Eliot's poems signals entry into a new phase of the poem, and often the adoption of a new mode of discourse. This is not the case here, and however satisfying Lerner's translations are at one level, his freed-up rhyming schemes create something of an unsatisfactory halfway house teetering between metrical and free verse.

The American translator Richard Howard adopts a more clearly defined strategy. Strictly speaking, his translations are not in free verse but in metrical verse: blank verse in iambic pentameter. This mode, though it does lack something of Baudelaire's elegant contrast between formal perfection and pitiful whining, allows Howard to convey much of the feeling of the original "La muse vénale" with its ebb and flow of accentual undulation, while preserving the essential images of frostbitten feet, frozen huddled shoulders, the empty belly and the empty purse, and the desire to harvest the stars.

Ranimeras-tu donc tes épaules marbrées Aux nocturnes rayons qui percent les volets? Sentant ta bourse à sec autant que ton palais, Récolteras-tu l'or des voûtes azurées?	Are streetlamps through your shutters stove enough to make your huddled shoulders warm again? When your belly is as empty as your purse, what will you do—harvest the stars for gold?
("La muse vénale," Baudelaire 1975: 15)	(Howard, in Baudelaire 1997: 23)

Elsewhere Howard does have recourse to partial rhyming, but unlike Lerner, once he sets in motion a rhyme scheme, however fragmentary, he respects the rules he has set up. This is the case with his "Artist Unknown," in which three pentameters are followed by a two-beat line with a rhyming scheme of *xaya*:

> Flesh is willing, but the Soul requires
>   Sisyphean patience for its song.
> Time, Hippocrates remarked, is short
>   And art is long.
>   (Howard, in Baudelaire 1997: 26)

In both the detail and the handling of individual lines and images, Lerner's may prove more striking than Howard's versions of Baudelaire, truer to the poet's spirit. This statement does not alter the fact that in terms of strategy, Howard is both consistent and coherent. Lerner sets in motion expectations and then lets his own formal constraints slip. Because Howard clearly announces his strategy and observes the rules he sets in play, there are no disruptions or interruptions in the flow of his verse. In other words, Howard does not get in the way of his translations, while Lerner sometimes does.

The Irish translator James Liddy is far more a child of free verse. His *Baudelaire's Bar Flowers*, published in 1975, gives a radical reading of Baudelaire by recasting him in a gay light. In contemporary parlance we would speak of queer translation, though this strategy should not shock readers. However fresh his versions are, Liddy does respond to a latent and at times ambient homoeroticism in Baudelaire's verse. In terms of form, he sides staunchly with modern free verse. He drops the rhyme and carves up the lines, principally in order to focus on key words at the ends of tapering stanzas: "Blossoming / For us"; "Twin / Mirrors"; "Orgiastic with / Goodbyes."

Nous aurons des lits pleins d'odeurs légères,	We'll have beds full of delicate scents
Des divins profonds comme des tombeaux,	Divans deep as graves
Et d'étranges fleurs sur des étagères,	And beneath more beautiful skies
Écloses pour nous sous des cieux plus beaux.	Strange flowers on the shelves Blossoming For us.
("La mort des amants," Baudelaire 1975: 126)	(Liddy, in Baudelaire 1997: 191)

The loss of the rhyme *tombeaux/beaux* (tomb/beautiful) is unfortunate, and no compensation is provided. Baudelaire-lovers may find the attempt lacking. Nevertheless, this free-verse Baudelaire transmits sufficient of the author to allow the translation to stand up to most English free verse. At times the line breaks, though conventional on the whole in that they follow the syntax, introduce meaningfully delicate pauses and ruptures. How are we to classify Liddy's strategy? Though the translated poem works simply enough, this task proves somewhat more difficult. On one level Liddy is a foreignizer, because his short collection of translations presents a queer Baudelaire. On another level he breaks with the uninterrupted tendency to translate Baudelaire into metrical (if not always rhymed) verse. Is he then a domesticator, pandering to prevailing tastes?

Lines like those quoted above slip snugly into an English tradition of free verse that had been around for three generations when Liddy made his translations. Rhythmically speaking, his work bears much in common with Scarfe's prose translations, which are sensitive to the movement of phrasing. In this sense, a case might be made for calling Liddy a domesticating free-verse translator. For readers of Baudelaire today there is nothing particularly shocking about his translations, and a queer free-verse Baudelaire will certainly find a niche among poetry readers.[7]

A more pedestrian free-verse translator is William Aggeler, whose translation of "Correspondances" was published in 1954 and collected on the website fleursdumal.org.

> Nature is a temple in which living pillars
> Sometimes give voice to confused words;
> Man passes there through forests of symbols
> Which look at him with understanding eyes.
>
> Like prolonged echoes mingling in the distance
> In a deep and tenebrous unity,
> Vast as the dark of night and as the light of day,
> Perfumes, sounds, and colors correspond.
>
> (poem 103, Baudelaire 2015)

It is always surprising to see how powerful Baudelaire remains even in prosaic translations.[8] Enough of Baudelaire remains here to entice and disturb the reader. But as a strategy, Aggeler's mode of translating proves disappointing. Elsewhere his translations run more smoothly in blank verse, but here the movement is not eventful. Indeed, the translation above has little to recommend it, and Scarfe's modest prose translation proves equally sensitive to rhythm, phrasing, and imagery.

Free Translations and Transcreations

Considering freedom in translation inevitably evokes the question of fidelity, and it frames that question within a post-romantic celebration of freedom. Free-verse rhetoric, championing the cause in revolutionary terms, was only a later development. The ideal of fidelity has resisted the celebration of freedom, however. If we want to consider Baudelaire translators within the framework of an opposition between free and faithful verse, we will have to redeploy them. This turns out to be curiously difficult. Most translators consider themselves to be faithful; the question is to define what they are being faithful to. Doing so involves the question of how they define poetry, its essence or its fundamental nature. For some translators an unrhymed Baudelaire will seem monstrous. To others a forced rhyme appears ridiculous. Some refuse to debase Baudelaire's undeniable purity of form and the ardour of his inspired aspirations. Others ridicule those aspirations, allowing the trash and trinkets of his poetical universe to take the foreground and permitting themselves to be drawn into Baudelaire's taste for bathos, his profound existential irony, and his self-indulgent sensuality with its taste for the crass, the filthy, and the perverse.

If we ask which translators are freer than others, then we must inevitably reclassify the players within the categories already outlined. For just as free-verse translators may decide to transcreate Baudelaire—to use poetic inspiration and appropriation—by following their own irrepressible élan, so metrical translators may choose to take liberties with the meaning and the organization of the lines and stanzas, in order to make the matter more flexible and reset the moulds of meter and rhyme.

The free translators follow Pound's dictum that a poem must be replaced by a poem. It must be admitted, however, that many faithful translators are equally animated by this ideal. There is, though, an essential difference. Free translators use the ideal that Pound championed (he merely named it, for it has always existed) in order to justify following their own creative élan. Nida would consider them to be following the logic of the "dynamic translation" (Venuti 2004: 156–57); Ladmiral would speak of "target-oriented translators" (ciblistes; Ladmiral 1994); Venuti would speak of "domesticators." All these commentators understand that something is happening in the act of opening up a poem to alternative courses in the target language, but siding with source-oriented translators against target-oriented translators obscures one essential factor: the diversity of strategies and objectives to be found among free translators. Among the free translators we can list Symons, Millay, Larkin, Lowell, and Seamus Heaney.

Symons, as we have seen, takes liberties that do not appear to stand up to analysis when compared to the original. His improvisations are trite, poetical, and uninspired. His rhymes are often forced, and he feels at liberty to cut ideas and images and introduce his own. To this extent I share Clark and Sykes's feeling of disappointment on reading Symons. Yet he has always been popular; we must therefore conclude that there is still a market for his free poetical Baudelaire. Perhaps it is simply that the specialists are suffering from academic narrow-mindedness and fail to recognize that much of what is essential in Baudelaire does indeed survive in Symons's translations. Critics and later translators tend to allow the demoded poetical diction and blemishes of his versions to mar their experience of the poem as a whole, but most Internet readers of Baudelaire appear to remain sensitive to Symons's creations.

Whatever we decide, we must make a crucial distinction between the strategy of free translation as it is used by Symons and as it used by Millay. Millay and Campbell (to a lesser extent) enter into Baudelaire's imagination. Their improvisations appear to take place within the networks of associations and the aesthetic parameters of Baudelaire's own work. Symons strikes out on his own course, leaving Baudelaire behind. Larkin and Lowell strike out in their own directions too, and there is something deeply Poundian in this. Larkin and Lowell appropriate Baudelaire: they make him enter into their own poetic universes. They grew poetically in encountering and appropriating Baudelaire, just as Pound advocated for the young poet, who should enter into a self-styled apprenticeship by imitating other poets and adopting masks.

Baudelaire-lovers may object to the poetry produced, but our criticisms will ultimately be irrelevant if we refuse to understand that these are not attempts to mirror or to replace the original. These are new paths being taken in the poetry of a foreign land. Baudelaire has survived and will outlive Symons. Lowell's Baudelaire has not whitewashed the original. Symons, Lowell, and Larkin are simply offering their insights into Baudelaire as personal responses, prisms through which to view something of the original. In aesthetic terms, all that we can legitimately criticize is the poetic experience of that prism as a whole. So what do such appropriators produce?

Larkin pushes this strategy of free appropriation to the extreme in a version of "Femmes damnées" that, though it was not published until 1978, was written in 1943, when he was still a student. His version is so far removed that we find only traces of the original, towards the middle of Larkin's poem. For this reason we might more legitimately speak of poetic inspiration and appropriation—transcreation—rather than translation. Certainly Larkin's poem begins in a style very different from Baudelaire's, in a world totally transfigured by mid-twentieth-century Britain.

À la pâle clarté des lampes languissantes, Sur de profonds coussins tout imprégnés d'odeur, Hippolyte rêvait aux caresses puissantes Qui levaient le rideau de sa jeune candeur. […] Étendue à ses pieds, calme et pleine de joie Delphine la couvait avec des yeux ardents, Comme un animal fort qui surveille une proie, Après l'avoir d'abord marquée avec ses dents.	The fire is ash: the early morning sun Outlines the patterns on the curtains, drawn The night before. The milk's been on the step, The *Guardian* is in the letter-box since dawn. […] Stretched out before her, Rachel curls and curves, Eyelids and lips apart, her glances filled With satisfied ferocity, she smiles, As beasts smile on the prey that they have just killed.
("Femmes damnées," Baudelaire 1975: 152–53)	(Larkin, in Baudelaire 1997: 210–11)

Larkin's poetical universe, with its lyrical longings of world-weary postwar Britain, drew a whole generation into it. What has Larkin preserved of Baudelaire, however? He shares with him a taste for lyricism. He has the poet's acute sense of metonymy, his acute sensibility of the tawdry cheapness of everyday reality. He has a lucid eye for perverse intentions and he demonstrates a scrupulous honesty when it comes to owning up to the stories we like to tell ourselves. But Larkin lacks Baudelaire's sensuality, his aesthetic pleasure; he does not abandon himself to pleasure as Baudelaire does. His transcreation leaves the bitter taste of Baudelaire without the sweetness of his sensuality. Larkin seeks to draw Baudelaire into his own aesthetic world, but Baudelaire's love of beauty and his playful pleasure do not take root.

Lowell remains much closer to the spirit of Baudelaire. True, he "cuddles" the insensible blank air in his translation of "Le gouffre," a poem about the fear of open spaces that Baudelaire shared with Pascal. This is a tenderness that is absent in Baudelaire's angst; his lyrical subject is confined ("l'espace affreux et captivant"), trapped in anguish, not amorous or cuddly. This is not the only remarkable change. Baudelaire's "jealous love of nothingness" (my translation) simply disappears in Lowell's version, and Lowell transforms *Êtres* into "form." Notwithstanding these significant shifts, and despite the reorganization of phrasing and sentence structure, Lowell's appropriation of Baudelaire is powerful and meaningful. And we do enter into his angst when he faces the gaping gulf he sets before us.

[...]	[...]
En haut, en bas, partout, la profondeur, la grève,	Above, below me, only depths and shoal, the silence!
Le silence, l'espace affreux et captivant...	And the Lord's right arm traces his night-
Sur le fond de mes nuits Dieu de son doigt savant	mare, truceless, multiform.
Dessine un cauchemar multiforme et sans trêve.	
J'ai peur du sommeil comme on a peur d'un grand trou,	I cuddle the insensible blank air, and fear to sleep as one fears a great hole.
Tout plein de vague horreur, menant je ne sais où;	
Je ne vois qu'infini part toutes les fenêtres,	
Et mon esprit, toujours du vertige hanté, Jalouse du néant, l'insensibilité.	My spirit, haunted by its vertigo, vague, horrible, and dropping God knows where...
Ah! ne jamais sortir des Nombres et des Êtres.	Ah never to escape from numbers and form!
("Le gouffre," Baudelaire 1975: 142–43)	(Lowell, in Baudelaire 1997: 227)

Formally speaking, Lowell is no more faithful to the original than he is to the content. Lowell is a poet. He does not feel bound to sacrifice form to content or vice versa. In all fairness, though, Lowell, who made his mark with his great blank verse, is no great rhymer. Like Wordsworth, his expressiveness belongs to the elegant poise and the surprises he provides through rhythm and imagery. His rhyming has nothing of the sting or surprise of the great rhymers such as Byron, Larkin, and Pope. This point must be set against him, since Baudelaire was certainly a formidable rhymer who knew how to ridicule with his rhymes. Like Byron's, Pope's, and Larkin's verse, the satirical sting of Baudelaire's poetry owes much to his rhyming.

Lowell, on the other hand, rhymes "arm" with "form." After "air" we must wait five lines to find its rhyme, "where." *Êtres* is transformed into "form" but not, as Symons would have done, for the sake of rhyme; or at least if Lowell does intend a rhyme, he must mean it to rhyme with "multiform," six lines earlier. Perhaps the clumsiest solution in this rhyming scheme is the opening one, in which Lowell commits the primary faux pas for poets: rhyming "side" with "side" without any homophonic surprise. As for the versification, this is free verse without that freedom proving particularly fortunate. But as domesticating free-verse appropriation, it will certainly not be found lacking. The meaning and the movement of the lines—Lowell's twin strengths—are powerfully expressive. The same hesitating pulsation is felt in the broken syntax. Baudelaire's lines lead us towards uncertainty ("menant on ne sait où"), while Lowell's line leads us on, "dropping God knows where . . ." The ellipsis leads us to the brink in his translation. Lowell ends lines on crucial words (hole, vertigo), and after them even the window hangs precariously, ominously, at the end of the line . . . as it should.

Edna St. Vincent Millay tends to cleave to Baudelaire when she can. When she improvises at the level of the phrase or the stanza and at times juggles with images and ideas, it is invariably in order to render the poem as a whole that works successfully. Because she is a highly sensitive and skillful translator, she often feels no need to improvise. Indeed, her rhymed translation "The Mercenary Muse," from 1936, is no freer than Howard's blank-verse version quoted earlier (page 219).

Ranimeras-tu donc tes épaules marbrées Aux nocturnes rayons qui percent les volets? Sentant ta bourse à sec autant que ton palais, Récolteras-tu l'or des voûtes azurées?	Think: when the moon shines through the window, shall you try To thaw your marble shoulders in her square of light? Think: when your purse is empty and your palate dry, Can you from the starred heaven snatch all the gold in sight?
("La muse vénale," Baudelaire 1975: 15)	(Millay, in Baudelaire 1997: 22)

Where the movement of the lines requires some nimble steps, Millay effortlessly reshuffles the ideas and the images in order to concoct a coherent mood. The short lines of "L'invitation au voyage," with its swift rhymes, present a very real difficulty for maintaining the mood while preserving the meaning. Millay's solution is admirable: elegant and free, without that freedom tugging against the will of the original poem.

Les soleils mouillés	Charming in the dawn
De tes ciels brouillés	There, the half-withdrawn
Pour mon esprit ont des charmes	Drenched, mysterious sun appears
Si mystérieux	In the curdled skies,
De tes traitres yeux,	Treacherous as your eyes
Brillant à travers leurs larmes.	Shining from behind your tears.
Là, tout n'est qu'ordre et beauté,	There, restraint and order bless
Luxe, calme et volupté.	Luxury and voluptuousness.
("L'invitation au voyage," Baudelaire 1975: 53)	(Millay, in Baudelaire 1997: 73)

For the sake of rhyme the lines are reorganized. Millay's sun is withdrawn and drenched where Baudelaire's are merely sodden (mouillés). The whole movement of withdrawing into the narcissism and luxury of reverie is implicitly Baudelairian, and the movement of that mood is what inspires Millay's improvisation. Once more, when Millay introduces the blessing of luxury and voluptuousness, she is responding to the tension in Baudelaire's poetics that extols restraint, order, and perfection on the one hand and, on the other, the act of letting loose the senses and giving in to pleasure. There is a freedom in this kind of translating that is paradoxically faithful.

Unlike Lowell, the further Millay moves from Baudelaire, the more she spirals into something essential in his poetry. Lowell has taken leave of Baudelaire's poem and is concerned with spiralling outwards into his own creative appropriation. What makes his translations successful both as poems and as translations is that, curiously, the more he spirals outwards, the more he recreates something essential in Baudelaire himself. Lowell expands Baudelaire's potential; Millay moves more profoundly into the centre of his sensibility and his imagination.

Seamus Heaney, like Lowell, is a successful poet. When Heaney appropriates Baudelaire, he brings him into the sphere of his own poetic universe. Like Lowell's "Abyss," Heaney's "The Digging Skeleton" is inspired by the mood of the original, but that mood is transformed by his own sensibility. Baudelaire is being drawn into Heaney's lyrical universe: there are no navvies in Baudelaire's poem, and the labourers are not digging with their spades into an "unrelenting soil." Neither are the spectres a "gang of apparitions." This is a Northern Irish transcreation of Baudelaire: he is being displaced into a specifically Anglo-Irish class conflict. All of the earthy song of the soil, so pungent in Heaney's verse, is brought to bear in this transcreation. Unlike Millay, Heaney is growing through Baudelaire, not confining himself within the sphere of that second, adopted self.

The Digging Skeleton
after Baudelaire

[...] Flayed men and skeletons
Digging the earth like navvies.
ii
Sad gang of apparitions,
Your skinned muscles like plaited sedge
And your spines hooped towards the sunk edge
Of the spade, my patient ones,

Tell me, as you labour hard
To break this unrelenting soil,
What barns are there for you to fill? [...]

(Heaney, in Baudelaire 1997: 135–36)

Formally speaking, this poem is a far cry from Baudelaire. The formal perfection of the original reinforces the aesthetic distance; it enacts the coldness of scrutiny. Baudelaire is fascinated by individuals, with *le peuple* and with crowds, but his empathy is rarely tinged with sympathy. In its place Heaney is reaching out towards the ancient labourers that he imagines. His own poetry has no need for rhymes, so he sees no need for them here. While Baudelaire stands back from the workers and looks down upon them, Heaney responds to them as industrial pastoral figures; he embraces them and makes their sensitivity his own. Rhyme would only get in the way.

A Wealth of Strategies

This concludes our overview of the vast array of responses to Baudelaire's poems and his poetics. What are we to retain from the examples we have delved into? Categorizing translation strategies is helpful as long as categories are not thought of as rigid restrictions. As we have seen from the translations, strategies are flexible. Often multiple strategies fuse; for example, archaizing translators invariably opt for rhyme, meter, lofty diction, and a syntax that is closer to Latin and French than to the phrasal verbs and monosyllables of English's fundamentally Germanic prose. The analysis so far has set up a series of oppositions:

- metrical/free
- rhymed/unrhymed
- literal/dynamic
- foreignizing/domesticating

I would maintain that these oppositions enable us to discern fundamental strategies adopted by translators. Such dichotomies, however, soon break down, and they will be of no use if we consider them as hard-and-fast oppositions within which to confine translators. Translators may fit into one category, but that does not necessarily mean they will not fit simultaneously into another. Translators are creators. They are juggling a set of balls and they are not necessarily consistent; they may prove less than reliable in their skill from one poem to the next. The "divine miracle" in poetry translation that Pound spoke of is of little use as a conceptual tool or a working principle, but it does, nevertheless, tell part of the truth about translating. Intuition—that shadowy term—refers to the delicate feeling of balance that sensitive translators experience when something fits together, forming a whole with multiple shades of meaning and interacting dynamic forces. Often translators are at a loss to understand why they chose a particular word or decided to follow the flow of a certain form of phrasing. And when a translation works, they may find it difficult to explain exactly why it works. This difficulty is, I concede, frustrating for readers and students, but it is one that must be admitted. Theory helps, but it has its limits.

In place of tidy oppositions, we have an untidy, tangled set of meaningful responses and attempts. What the free-verse translators prove is that, as Eliot puts it, there is no freedom in art—there is only good poetry, bad poetry, and poetry that is not poetry at all. Among the free-verse poets we find those who drop the rhyme but maintain the meter (as in blank-verse translations), and those who drop both the meter and the rhyme but remain attentive in the way they carve the phrasing. Even the prose translators tend to do this, though they tend to do so in order to embellish the part without concerning themselves with the movement of the poem as a whole. The metrical translators prove that meter is not enough and that phrasing must be taken into account, for rhyming and maintaining the meter at the expense of the poem, its meaning, and its mood can prove catastrophic.

Polemicists and dogmatists looking for an either/or theory of translation will no doubt find this disconcerting. Students looking for an instruction manual on translating poems will inevitably be disgruntled by this contrastive study of stylistic and semantic responses. This cannot be helped. As I have argued throughout this book, thinking within the limits of schematic binary oppositions such as form/content and free/faithful will prove to be a dead end, not a path to any real, practical solutions regarding the subtle question of the translator's aesthetic response to the poetic universe of any poet of interest.

Ultimately translators concoct their own special brand of strategy. They cannot be pigeonholed into one single category, for often they will fit into several categories at once. In distinguishing between strategies, the point is that each of these aesthetic and poetic approaches acts as a pole of attraction. But in the complex dynamics that make up the sensibility of each translator, various poles of attraction may be at work. This makes it impossible to limit any one translator to a given specific category. Binary oppositions may prove useful provisionally as conceptual tools for categorizing translators point by point, but their explicative power is limited. And dogmatic expectation that a translator must and will remain the servant of any set of given constraints is ultimately naive. In the final analysis it must be remembered that translation is indeed complicated. In translating, various strategies will be adopted and combined, often to be abandoned with a new poem that appears to call for a different kind of response.

Successful Strategies

Symons's popularity only goes to show that what the critics dislike, the public will often welcome and praise. This is not surprising. Critics compare efforts, while the public responds to one work at any given time. Baudelaire in translation—in whatever version—can be considered a success inasmuch as the version created is often more intriguing, more beautiful, and more moving than many poems being written today in English. Great writers assert their greatness in translation, even if the gem they produce seems at times to have had some of its facets ground away. Much of Baudelaire is not lost in translation. For similar reasons, the main stage of the prestigious Festival d'Avignon hosts Shakespeare more than any other dramatist. The French have yet to produce a playwright of his genius (not to belittle their literary heritage); they find that Shakespeare excels at penetrating life's mysteries and staging life's dramas for them, in their translations. This preference explains why writers such as Shakespeare and Baudelaire continue to have such a profound influence on other cultures. Their success asserts a simple truth that pessimists and academics often seem to deny: translation works, in the literal sense of the term—translations continue to work upon a living foreign literary heritage.

For this reason, the vast array of Baudelaire translators who can be found on the Internet, in published volumes, and collected together in Clark and Sykes's edition can be considered successful, to a greater or lesser extent. Which are most successful? Such a question can be answered only by the individual reader, and that answer will speak volumes about the reader's conceptions of poetry, of beauty, of form and meaning. The response will be motivated by a theory of language, albeit unwitting and unanalyzed. The gut reaction to poems, whether we open up to them or reject them, is a staunch and unwavering response that reveals what we think is or is not acceptable. This reaction does not alleviate the obligation of criticism to make a reasoned response to the various ways in which translators engage with the poem. It is important to recognize, however, that criticism is confession, inasmuch as critics expose the limits of their own sensibility when they respond to poems and their translations. How are we to proceed in evaluating these Baudelaires, then?

After examining the translators in terms of their poetic force, their sensitivity to Baudelaire's imagination and their capacity to draw us into it, and their talent for negotiating rhymes and meaningful sound patterning, four stand out: Sturm, Campbell, Millay, and Sykes. In the single poem by Sykes included in the anthology he co-edited with Clark ("Mist in Rain," page 213), his dense and expressive language finds a perfect balance between morose monotony and elegant rhythmic harmony. And he masters Baudelaire's artful use of startling jumps in register, from buds opening up to the empresses of the weather to the morbid moaning of the soul.

Sturm, Millay, and Campbell share a capacity to respond to the various registers of Baudelaire's poetry, and this allows them to respond to a vast array of very different poems, something that I personally cannot imagine ever being able to do as a translator. These translators are at home in meter but do not reduce rhythm to meter. They allow meter to emerge from expressive phrasing without those contortions we associate with forced versification. They all prove skillful rhymers, and their rhymes give a greater depth to the way the poem makes sense. Although their translations stand as poems in their own right, they do not mask the originals or dart off on their own tangents. They serve both as poems in English and as ports of entry into Baudelaire's imagination. And that imagination has been so deeply penetrated by these three translators that even when they take liberties with his lines, they do so in a way that we feel Baudelaire might have approved—not because he was Baudelaire and what they are doing resembles him, but because they have uncovered some of the forceful poetic feeling he was tapping into as he wove his verses.

Tastes vary from person to person, just as tastes vary with the times. Readers must make up their own minds, and the themes of the poems will affect their choices. I offer the following extracts as examples of how the equilibrium of various formal elements and the handling of meaning and mood can be managed successfully by outstanding translators, translators who reaffirm that translating is truly possible. In these passages we hear various facets of a Baudelaire whose force is undiluted.

> Space rolls to-day her splendor round!
> Unbridled, spurless, without bound,
> Mount we upon the wings of wine
> For skies fantastic and divine!
>
> Let us, like angels tortured by
> Some wild delirious phantasy,
> Follow the far-off mirage born
> In the blue crystal of the morn
> (Sturm, "The Wine of Lovers" [1906],
> in Baudelaire 1997: 157)

A sputtering gazetteer, who thinks he casts a light,
Says to his readers drowned in paradox and doubt,
"Where do you see him, then, this God of Truth and Right?
   This Savior that you talk about?"

Better than these I know—although I know all three—
That foppish libertine, who yawns in easy grief
Nightly upon my shoulder, "All right, you wait and see;
   I'm turning over a new leaf!'"

                  (Millay, "The Unforeseen" [1936],
                          in Baudelaire 1997: 215)

I'm like the King of some damp, rainy clime,
Grown impotent and old before my time,
Who scorns the bows and scrapings of his teachers
And bores himself with hounds and all such creatures.
Naught can amuse him, falcon, steed, or chase:
No, not the mortal plight of his whole race
Dying before his balcony. The tune,
Sung to this tyrant by his pet buffoon,
Irks him.

   (Campbell, "Spleen" [1952], in Baudelaire 1997: 93)[9]

   Such translations give us an idea of the transports of Baudelaire's aspiring soul, of his capacity for pitiless satire, and of his world-weariness and equally pitiless self-satire. But they do more than that. They bring Baudelaire's world into English. In this sense they take us beyond the dichotomy between domesticators and foreignizers. They help transform the English-speaking imagination by bringing into its world view a foreign sensibility to make its own.

The Whole Poem

It would be impossible here to give a fuller account of the different strategies involved in translating Baudelaire. This overview remains somewhat fragmentary, of course. Ultimately the value of each strategy can be intuited or ascertained only by considering the poem as a whole. This restriction has not been addressed for obvious reasons of space, and because Clark and Sykes and the Baudelaire website (fleursdumal.org) have done such a wonderful job of collecting and juxtaposing various translations of Baudelaire's poems. Nevertheless, it should prove worthwhile to end by comparing several complete versions of the same Baudelaire poem to determine if, and how, various strategies work in the translated poem as a whole. This approach also enables me to interject one of my own translations. As I have already stressed, the critic should not hide behind the imperial distance of the censor. Translators are free to criticize their colleagues, but they should, in fairness, offer up their own attempts for criticism too. For this reason I present my own version first and then allow readers to compare it with six other versions of Baudelaire's "Les plaintes d'un Icare."

Les plaintes d'un Icare

Les amants des prostituées
Sont heureux, dispos et repus;
Quant à moi, mes bras sont rompus
Pour avoir étreint des nuées.

C'est grâce aux astres nonpareils,
Qui tout au fond du ciel flamboient,
Que mes yeux consumés ne voient
Que des souvenirs de soleils.

En vain j'ai voulu de l'espace
Trouver la fin et le milieu;
Sous je ne sais quel œil de feu
Je sens mon aile qui se casse;

Et brûlé par l'amour du beau,
Je n'aurai pas l'honneur sublime
De donner mon nom à l'abîme
Qui me servira de tombeau.

(Baudelaire 1975: 143)

The Lament of an Icarus

The lovers of whores are happy in love.
Languid, refreshed, they love at their ease.
While my arms are broken because I dared
Embrace the mists above the seas.

The peerless stars that blaze
At the edge of the edge of the skies
Drown my sight till the memory of suns
Is all that fills my eyes.

In vain, I wished for space,
To find the edge and the in-between.
Instead, my wings begin to break
Under a fiery eye unseen.

And burned for my love of beauty,
I shall not know the honour, the bliss
Of giving my name to the grave,
I make of this the great abyss.

(Underhill 2012b: 287–88)

The Lament of an Icarus	**Complaint of an Icarus**
Those men who cuddle whores for love Are sated by their darlings' charms, But I have only tired arms From having hugged the clouds above.	Those who love whores are well-endowed, Spry, and well-fed, and cheerful-spoken. But, as for me, my arms are broken From trying to embrace a cloud.
Thanks to the stars, the matchless ones That flame within the depths of the skies; All I can see with burnt-out-eyes Are dark remembrances of suns.	To what two peerless stars have done That kindle in the farthest skies, I owe it that my burnt-out eyes Know only memories of the sun.
In vain, I've tried to find the heart Of space, to venture deeper, higher; Under who knows what eye of fire My weary wings will break apart;	In vain I've tried to find the pole And the equator-line of space. I know not by what burning gaze The wings were molten from my soul.
And burned by love of beauty, I Will not achieve my poignant wish, To give my name to the abyss, The tomb below to which I fly.	By love of beauty singed, I fall Yet fail the honour and the bliss To give my name to the abyss Which serves me for my tomb and pall.
(McGowan, in Baudelaire 1998: 345)	(Campbell [1952], in Baudelaire 2015)

McGowan and Campbell offer masterful translations; I am not sure I would have ventured to translate the poem, had I known of them. Both manage to convey something of Baudelaire's profound simplicity. Their phrasing is balanced, the words they foreground in end rhymes—for example, "heart"/"apart" for McGowan and "pole"/"soul" for Campbell—are powerfully meaningful. Both translators experiment with half-rhymes—"wish"/"abyss" for McGowan and "space"/"gaze" for Campbell—but once again the effect is full of meaning. I must admit feeling somewhat dismayed on learning that Campbell had already discovered the rhyme "bliss"/"abyss," for which I prided myself when I first translated this poem back in 1997.

I opt for an *xaya* rhyming scheme, which affords me greater freedom and allows me to remain closer to the original. This is a poem about exploring space, but I find myself disoriented when reading Campbell's and McGowan's renderings of "En vain j'ai voulu de l'espace / Trouver la fin et le milieu," which I translate simply as "In vain, I wished for space, / To find the edge and the in-between." Is the heart "higher," or not, rather, "deeper"? Freeing up the rhyming scheme also allows me to foreground the words placed at the ends of lines. In a sense these alone tell much of the story of this Icarus of Baudelaire's: "love"/"ease"/"dared"/"seas"; "blaze"/"skies"/"suns"/"eyes"; "space"/"between"/"break"/"unseen"; "beauty"/"bliss"/"grave"/"abyss." The free internal rhyme on "this" redoubles the rhyme "bliss"/"abyss," while the space in my final line invites a pause in the reading, thereby enacting the gulf evoked by the abyss.

Jacques LeClercq offered his own rhymed version in 1958. Scarfe, of course, proposed a prose version, in 1961.

Laments of an Icarus

Lovers of harlots are happy, cheerful, and satisfied; but as for me, my arms are racked through embracing clouds. It is thanks to the incomparable stars which blaze in the sky's remotest depths, that my burnt-out eyes can see nought but memories of suns.

Vainly, have I sought to discover the end and the centre of space: beneath I know not what eye of fire I feel my wing dissolve, and scorched by the love of beauty, I shall not have the sublime honour of giving my name to the bottomless pit which will serve for my tomb.

(Scarfe, in Baudelaire 1972: 247)

Plaint of Icarus

Lovers of prostitutes, in crowds,
Are sated and content and cheery,
But as for me, my arms are weary
Because I have embraced the clouds.
Thanks to the stars—O peerless ones!—
That flame deep in the boundless sky,
My burned-out eyes can now descry
Only the memories of suns.

In vain I sought to trace and fit
Space in its mid and final stance
I know not under what hot glance
My wings are crumbling bit by bit.
The love of beauty sealed my doom,
Charred, I have not been granted this:
To give my name to the abyss
That is to serve me as a tomb.

(LeClercq, in Baudelaire 2015)

Scarfe's prose fairs badly in contrast to McGowan's and Campbell's versions. But McGowan (writing in 1998) appears to have borrowed from Scarfe "burnt-out eyes"—a beautifully apt phrase, rhythmically compact. In Scarfe's version the quest for "the end and the centre of space" is rendered with simple elegance. The alliteration of "The lovers of **h**arlots are **h**appy" also gives a jaunty contrast to the damned aspirations of Icarus. And "bottomless pit" gives an aptly biblical tone to this neo-romantic Christianized Icarus.

LeClercq's version is somewhat lopsided. His decision to preserve the *abba* rhyming scheme forces him to introduce "crowds" (from where?) to rhyme with "clouds." And in rhyming "O peerless ones!" with "suns" he highlights the stars at the cost of the other major actor in this scenario: the sun that will singe and disintegrate Icarus's wings. This is not an ode to the stars but a poem about Icarus being burned for his aspirations. In LeClercq's version "stance"/"glance" is a forced rhyme, and one that obscures the scenario. Is space standing somewhere? Perhaps it may be said to *lie* somewhere, but defining space is not easy; it proves difficult to seize and conceptualize in Baudelaire's poem as well. Likewise the sun is burning down relentlessly, cruelly; it does not glance casually in Icarus's direction. Though the melting of the wax of his wings may take some time, adding to the suspense of the scenario, "crumbling bit by bit" has a casual tone that does not capture either the drama or the danger. On the other hand, LeClercq does manage to end on the rhyme "doom"/"tomb." Despite the archaic "descry," "That flame deep in the boundless sky, / My burned-out eyes can now descry" is a wonderful couplet, one that intensifies the attraction and the danger of Icarus's flight into the skies above.

Twenty years apart, William Aggeler (in 1954) and Geoffrey Wagner (in 1974) offer free-verse translations of Baudelaire's "Les plaintes d'un Icare."

The Complaints of an Icarus

The lovers of prostitutes
Are happy, healthy, and sated;
As for me, my arms are weary
Because I have embraced the clouds,

It is thanks to the peerless stars
That flame in the depth of the sky
That my burned out eyes see
Only the memories of suns.

I tried in vain to find
The middle and the end of space;
I know not under what fiery eye
I feel my pinions breaking;

Burned by love of the beautiful
I shan't have the sublime honor
Of giving my name to the abyss
That will serve me as a tomb.

(Aggeler, in Baudelaire 2015)

The Lamentations of an Icarus

The lovers of prostitutes are
Happy, cheerful, well-fed;
As for me, my arms are broken
Through having hugged the clouds.

It is thanks to the incomparable stars,
Blazing in the depths of the sky,
That my devoured eyes see only
The memories of suns.

In vain I wished to find
The center and the end of space;
I know not under what fiery eye
I feel my wings breaking;

And burnt up by love of beauty,
I shall not have the splendid honor
Of giving my name to the abyss
Which will serve as my grave.

(Wagner, in Baudelaire 2015)

Possibly, considered on their own, these two translations might seem noteworthy, but in comparison with the other versions, they inevitably appear to be lacking. Indeed, it is difficult to see how these free-verse translations offer us anything that Scarfe's elegant prose does not. True, the line ends do allow the translators to stress key words—"beautiful"/"honor"/"abyss"/"tomb" for Aggeler and "beauty"/"honor"/"abyss"/"grave" for Wagner—but Wagner ends lines clumsily with "are" and "only." His rendering of Baudelaire's satiated patrons of whores as "well-fed" appears to result from a somewhat ridiculous misunderstanding.

Free verse is going strong as an expressive medium, proving again and again that rhythm cannot be reduced to meter and that expressive phrasing is what meter harnesses—and, ultimately, what matters. Free verse proves that when versified poetry fails to be rhythmically interesting, it falls into mechanical routine. But neither Aggeler nor Wagner seems to do justice to the medium of free verse here. It is curious to observe that while it became common practice to render metrical verse as free verse in translations of the postwar period, the most recent versions of Baudelaire are, like the first ones, written in rhymed verse. Perhaps Baudelaire's poise and perfection invite an elegant response in which to encapsulate his lyrical longings and his rummaging around in the grime and slime of city existence.

This concludes our case study on re-creating Baudelaire's voice and his versification. No one strategy can be applauded and approved. Baudelaire breaks through into English in rhymed and unrhymed verse, in meter and in prose. The greatest translators—Millay, Sturm, Campbell, and Sykes—do opt for rhymed metrical verse, but it would be interesting to see what they would have produced in a free-verse form, for it is the master, not the tool, that is at the origin of their success. They help us to break into Baudelaire's lyrical universe, while others who use the same tools fail. They break in with their own tastes and strategies, often distracting us with inappropriate rhymes: they complicate simple phrasing. Why? Apparently, in order to observe the constraints of the versification to which they enslave themselves.

Great translators are like dancers. The easier they make their work appear, the more their graceful and expressive innovations bear witness to the inspiration that constitutes the real work of poetic creation. In the final analysis, the success of Baudelaire in English remains the most direct response to those who claim that translating verse is impossible. Even Baudelaire's less talented interpreters continue to enjoy success when they perpetuate something of the poet's lyrical élan. In the following case study, we shall turn to an American poet and see to what extent her translators help French readers open up to a new sensibility.

Notes

1. My own translations of Baudelaire's poems—"Muse vénale," translated into Scots, and "Abyss" and "The Giantess," translated into English—can be found on the website Charles Baudelaire's Fleurs du mal / Flowers of Evil, see fleursdumal.org. (Baudelaire 2015). *The Pathhead Review*, edited by Tom Hubbard, also published my version of Baudelaire's "The Fall of an Icarus" (Underhill 2012b). *Scottish Spleen*, a selection of Baudelaire's poems in prose with translations from various Scottish poets and translators, edited by Tom Hubbard and James W. Underhill, includes translations from both editors (Hubbard and Underhill 2015).
2. Freudian and psychological readings of poetry are problematic for both aesthetic and spiritual reasons. They tend to dissect the poet's world in order to penetrate and comprehend it, but the critics who adopt this approach inevitably find little place for appreciating the moving beauty of the poems or the lyrical longing found in much poetry, romantic poetry in particular. Critics steeped in the Freudian and psychoanalytic schools demonstrate these limits in their attempts to understand and define Baudelaire. This shortcoming poses the question of the raison d'être of such criticism. Is Freudian criticism a celebration of the author or is it rather the expression of an obsessive fixation with the poet's fixations? Baudelaire's poetry does yearn to move beyond the sphere of the petty, self-centred self. Inspiration and the poet's dialogue with his soul are central in many of his poems. Can psychoanalysis take this on board, however? As Jung puts it, psychology (etymologically "the study of the soul") is a science for those who do not believe in the soul.
3. Swinburne's admiration of the Marquis de Sade is simply one more layer in the absurdity of this attempt to set up Baudelaire as a paragon of virtue.
4. That we consider Goethe at times to be a romantic and at times to be a classical poet is revealing. Ultimately, like Wordsworth,

Goethe had a foot in both worlds, the modern one and the *ancien régime*. This dichotomy explains why he craved, in his poetry and in his aesthetics, a modern—what might be called I-centred—consciousness that remained nonetheless timeless and impersonal and, paradoxically, universal but deeply personal. It also explains why both Wordsworth and Goethe were exposed to harsh criticism by the generation of poets that followed them, who had little sympathy for classical ideals and the poet's striving for the universal.

5. Meschonnic always insisted that the poems he translated—and most of all the Bible—were not written in conventional language and must not be watered down into a tepid translation that corresponds to transient linguistic tastes. Meschonnic believed it was the working force of the text as a meaningful signifying activity that should be discerned and re-enacted in the translation. This approach can lead to inspired translations that transform the target language. Meschonnic, in his works and conference papers, often quoted the King James version of the Bible as such a translation.

6. In Baudelaire's objectification of the self, nature, and women, there is invariably some intuition of the dynamics of what the Chinese define in terms of yin and yang: a dynamic opposition/coupling in which the passive is powerful, inviting, enticing, and full of mystery, not the placid object subjected to male desire and active male celebration in the Victorian and post-Victorian sensibility.

7. This description leads to a curious paradox: foreignizing has begun colluding with domestication. As long as poetry stays clear of mainstream literature and cultivates a space for the alternative, anything that sounds odd risks being considered poetic by readers whose tastes are acclimatized to modernist and postmodernist poetics.

8. Aggeler navigates between blank verse and prose rhythms, but this proves a dubious strategy, because blank verse needs to be sufficiently assertive to induce the reader to promote and demote syllables in order to maintain the metrical beating. In Aggeler's verse, as the quotation demonstrates, we lose track of the five-beat meter and find ourselves slipping into four-beat lines. We consequently tend to allow the stress contour to impose itself irrespective of Aggeler's intentions. This change allows free verse, not blank verse, to predominate in reading his versions.

9. It is not possible in this book to enter into the poetics of the Scots Renaissance, but it is worth quoting the contemporary Scots poet James Robertson's powerful transcreation of Baudelaire's lines:

I'm like a lairdie in Lochaber, or somewhaur juist as wet:
A tweedy rich *im*potentate, young, yet past his sell-by-date,
Sneerin at the bou and scrape o factors,
Bored wi his dugs an paycocks, pigs an tractors […]
                                        (Baudelaire 2001: 5)

CHAPTER 9

French and German Emily Dickinsons

Introducing *une Emily Dickinson française*

Great poets like Shakespeare and Baudelaire make themselves heard in the end, we like to believe, though they do not always fit comfortably into the established tastes of their times and are not necessarily supported and promoted by those in power in the state or the publishing industry. Often we see their value more clearly in hindsight. To us Shakespeare towers above his contemporaries, although he himself held those contemporary poets in great esteem and spoke of them highly. Who remembers George Chapman, the rival poet Shakespeare paid tribute to in "Sonnet 86," with "the full blown sail of his great verse" (1987: 385). Chapman and his *Iliad* translation are forgotten today by all but a few scholars, while Shakespeare dominates throughout the world as an almost universal reference in poetry. Greatness dies with some poets, while the greatness of others outlives them. On rare occasions poets come alive to us after their deaths.

Emily Dickinson's poetic treasure was not dug up until after her demise. Like many poets and thinkers—like Nietzsche, one of the twentieth century's most quoted philosophers—Dickinson's fate is somewhat paradoxical. Both belonged very much to their times, but in their own times they were not granted an ounce of the recognition we now freely accord them. Despite her abstruse reasoning, her frequent obscurity, and her startling images, the unmistakable voice of Dickinson, with its simple but profound verse, has attracted interest throughout the world. French readers did not discover her for three generations after her death, but since the 1950s translators in France have devoted great energy to rendering her poems in their language. If the past fifteen years is anything to go by, Dickinson's voice is likely to live on in French in the translations of Philippe Denis (Dickinson 2003), Claire Malroux (Dickinson 1989, 2007a), Patrick Reumaux (Dickinson 2007b), and finally Françoise Delphy, whose monumental project was brought to a close with the publication of the complete 1,789 poems in French translation (Dickinson 2009).

What do these various translations have to teach us about the relationship between voice and versification? Like our Baudelaire case study, this one will consider the various aesthetic trends, individual choices, and implicit translation strategies that are at work in the transpositions of Dickinson's poems. In the various responses of translators we will observe a wide variety of technical strategies and lexical choices. We will be able to uncover diverse underlying principles proclaimed and defended, or tastes and bents that are implicitly identifiable in the intuitive choices and aesthetic strategies adopted. Studying the translation of poems moves beyond the sphere of conscious reasoning and lucid analysis. The latter will always form part of the translation process, but many of the choices made and the preferences displayed reveal aspects of the translators' ideas, feelings, and sensitivity to poems, some of which they are only dimly aware of.

Understanding what motivates a translator to opt for rhyme and meter or free verse requires a rigorous attention to the poem and its translation. Understanding the way each translator handles the meaning of words and phrases requires a similar rigour. This painstaking study of phrasing, accentuation, rhyming, and repetition becomes meaningful when it allows us to demonstrate the way the translator and the poet meet—or fail to meet—in the translation process. The contribution of comparative versification to translation studies shall be evaluated in terms of how much it shows that technical, theoretical, linguistic, aesthetic, philosophic, and even religious questions are tied up in that encounter or that failure to meet the poet.

Like Baudelaire, Dickinson appeals to both male and female readers and translators. She was established in the French poetry tradition by three male translators, however. Between 1956 and 1970, three translation projects took shape. Pierre Messiaen (Dickinson 1956), Alain Bosquet (1957), and Guy Jean Forgue (1970b) all show a feeling for Dickinson. Despite individual differences, all three share the same desire to produce a French Dickinson that is palatable to the French reader: a readable, comprehensible Dickinson. We have already discussed Forgue's translation (in the introduction and chapter 1), and we shall have occasion to do his work more justice shortly. These three initial projects are academic and pedagogical, but they remain poetic responses to the poet. All three aim to present French readers with a broad selection of the poems collected by Thomas H. Johnson (Dickinson 1963) and allow their readers to enter the dense, enigmatic, and often obscure writing of a poet fascinated by paradox.

Those qualities of Dickinson in themselves entail an implicit strategy. The nature of the poet seems to beg for a certain reading translation. The translators thus seek to clarify what is obscure, to make understandable what cannot be understood. They make choices where the poem is ambiguous or where the poet's own ambivalence becomes tangible. This is a hermeneutic approach, but one that is linguistically informed, since the target language often forces the translator to choose an abstract or a concrete term where the source language allows the poet to combine these two aspects.

Evidently none of the three translators tries to replace a poem with a poem. The translation strategy they adopt does not involve equivalence. No doubt the translators all feel they are introducing Dickinson into French free verse. But they all drop the meter, the so-called common meter that structures most of Emily Dickinson's work: a four-line stanza (usually iambic) that alternates four-beat and three-beat lines, as in the following example from Messiaen (scansion is added according to Attridge 1982, in which B = beat and o = offbeat):

"Heaven" —is what I cannot reach!
  B   o B o B o B
The Apple on the Tree,—
  o B o B o B
Provided it do hopeless—hang—
  o Bo Bo B o   B
That "Heaven" is to me.
  o   B o   Bo B

Le Ciel, c'est ce que je ne puis atteindre!
La pomme sur l'arbre,
Pourvu qu'elle pende inespérée,
Cela, c'est le *Ciel* pour moi.

(Dickinson 2016: 162)   (Dickinson 1956: 71)

In their work, all three translators aim to catch the meaning and reconstitute it. Messiaen's interpretation above does indeed allow the reader into Dickinson's strange world. Both the idea and the emotion are perfectly represented: the subject of the poem aspires to transcendence but is enclosed by the world. Heaven appears so impenetrable that anything out of reach is consequently, by a metonymic sideways shuffle, transformed into a celestial object. The apple of this world is transported into the world beyond.

In his commentary on Dickinson's metaphysics, Bosquet finds that her work oscillates perpetually between sadness, a vital principle, and exaltation, a life principle very close to that vital sadness . . .

> everything is foreboding (though one does not know of what), everything is a wonder (that does not materialize) and everything becomes subject to extreme doubting (which allows us to question the meaning of our very questions).
>
> (Dickinson 1957: 55; my translation)

By reconstituting the meaning of this poem Messiaen invites us to enter Dickinson's space, a world animated by the desire to reach another level, a spiritual plane.

Similarly, Bosquet's next poem invites us to experience—to live out—time the way Dickinson experiences it.

If I should die—	Si je mourrais,
And you should live—	Si tu vivais,
And time sh'd gurgle on—	Et que le temps continuât de glouglouter,
And morn sh'd beam,	Le matin de briller,
And noon should burn—	Le midi de brûler
As it has usual done—	Comme à son habitude,
(Dickinson 2016: 60)	(Dickinson 1957: 113)

Entering the time of this poem means entering the routine that has midday follow morning and implies that time can be represented as a liquid. This may seem commonplace; we know that time flows, as it were. But it is through the use of the word "gurgle," which evokes both a brook and a sound made with the throat, that Dickinson catapults us from the plane of abstraction into a tactile experience of things. With this one word Dickinson overturns our conceptual frameworks, our routines, our habits. Bosquet does a marvellous job preserving this word as *glouglouter*, an onomatopoeia that helps evoke the repetition and the routine in which we find ourselves caught up. The rhythm of the lines is also consolidated by the parallelism preserved in "Le matin de briller, / Le midi de brûler," and parallelism is introduced where it is absent in the original, in the opening lines, "Si je mourrais, / Si tu vivais."

Dickinson's contemplation of birds and brooks, twilights and Paradise firmly enroots her in a transcendental romantic tradition. Elsewhere, however, Dickinson is somewhat more romantic. But the question of her romanticism invites another question when it comes to welcoming and assimilating her poetic consciousness into the French tradition: are French readers in need of another romantic poet? Our translators appear to believe so. Indeed, what we find in Dickinson's work exists nowhere else in the French romantic tradition, to my knowledge. Translating Dickinson does not come down to warming the leftovers of Alphonse de Larmartine or rehashing Victor Hugo. Dickinson's translators are offering to open French eyes to another romanticism.

In Dickinson's work the celebration of the world of creation is as ecstatic as in Hugo.[1] But where Hugo's genius lies in the grandeur of his sensibility and his capacity to uplift his own soul in his praise of creation—when he listens to the stars murmuring their thousand harmonies—it is in the contemplation of small and obscure things that Dickinson's strange and striking originality emerges.

It would be unfair to overstate the case and to set up the romantics as escapists, who seek a way out of the ugliness of everyday existence into the sublime beauty of a transcendence untouched by ordinary life. Like Wordsworth, Hugo was acutely sensitive to the grit and grain of nature. Not for them the symbolism of Coleridge, Shelley, and Eliot, in whose poems birds all too often become archetypes, icons, representations of other things, symbols. Hugo invites us to watch "the robin, the greenfinch, the warbler and the dove" twittering amid the branches (2005: 543). And yet, as a poet who is "taken with shadow and azure blue" (532), Hugo does not open our eyes to the world that Dickinson presents. He has an eye for the sublime, the obscure, and the grotesque, but he seems unable to see the beauty of God's creation in its more repugnant creatures. This is precisely the perverse beauty that Dickinson invites us to contemplate, here translated by Messiaen and Forgue:

The Bat is dun, with wrinkled Wings— Like fallow Article— And not a song pervades his Lips— Or none perceptible.	La chauve-souris est gris sombre avec ailes ridées Comme un fragment de glèbe; Aucune chanson ne parcourt ses lèvres, Aucune chanson perceptible.	Chauve-souris gris-brun, ailes ridées, Article défraîchi! Pas un chant ne sort de ses lèvres— Rien qui se fasse entendre.
His small Umbrella quaintly halved Describing in the Air An Arc alike inscrutable Elate philosopher.	Son petit parapluie, drôlement partagé en deux, Décrit dans l'air Un arc également insondable— Philosophe altier!	Son menu parapluie, bizarrement coupé, Décrit dans l'espace Un arc tout aussi mystérieux: Transport philosophique.
Deputed from what Firmament— Of what Astute Abode— Empowered with what Malignity Auspiciously withheld—	Envoyée par quel firmament De quel ambigu séjour, Messagère de quelle malveillance Favorablement ajournée.	Délégué par quel firmament, De quel séjour sagace, Chargé de quelle malveillance Par faveur—contenue?
To his adroit Creator Ascribe no less the praise— Beneficent, believe me, His Eccentricities—	À son adroit Créateur N'en attribue pas moins louange; Bienfaisantes, crois-moi, Ses excentricités.	A son habile Artisan N'en rendez pas moins l'hommage: Elles sont bonnes, croyez-moi, Ses excentricités.
(Dickinson 2016: 596)	(Messiaen, in Dickinson 1956: 103)	(Forgue, in Dickinson 1970b: 227)

How do the French translators handle this quintessential romanticism? The two translators above open up to us three aspects of Dickinson's world. First they show us celebration of the sublime through contemplation of the grotesque and ridiculous. Celebrating the swallow, as Shelley does, is standard practice in romantic poetry, just as Milton's melancholy nightingale had become something of a lame poetic cliché by the time Coleridge set out to debunk it in his poem "The Nightingale" (2001: 953). Celebrating the bat, on the other hand, is flirting with the absurd. Dickinson has a wry sense of humour, something akin to Robert Burns's. Where Burns philosophizes on the destruction of a mouse's home and writes odes to the louse, Dickinson seeks the harmony of God in a dank and murky cave. When Dickinson goes on to turn the bat's wings into an umbrella, we are brought down with a bang (and a touch of bathos). This is more than a simple rhetorical trope or capricious turn of phrase; it is a poet-specific mode of representation. The concrete world asserts itself as if to contest the separateness of the spiritual world, thereby forcing upon us an uncomfortable fusion of the two.

Dickinson juxtaposes extremes in order to show that God embraces, includes, and contains all extremes. This involves a certain ambivalence. Following this logic, if humanity cannot reach God, then God must be excluded from the world, pushed from his creation. At the same time, since he is impenetrable, he cannot be represented as part of the world. For Dickinson, God often appears to be almost a curiosity, an eccentric. The disconcerting familiarity with which she treats God is typical of her entire work. Like Hugo's "bon Dieu"—a tender, familiar God—Dickinson's eccentric God is close. In her poems we find meetings with a God-father, God-uncle, or God-acquaintance, someone who comes for tea. Dickinson likes to bring God down to our level. This is her blasphemous side, a side Forgue remarks upon when he suggests Dickinson was a strange example of a fundamentally Calvinist mind (Dickinson 1970b: 31). In her poems, though, it is often simply a question of breaking free of hollow otherworldly idols and icons, a fundamentally Protestant mode of feeling.

The representation of God introduces the question of world views to the translation process. To use the term "Calvinist" in France today is to position oneself in a secularist space that treats Protestant faith with condescension. Like Forgue, the prolific contemporary translator Claire Malroux also appears to regret the fact that Dickinson seems "unable to give up her faith" (incapable de renoncer à la foi; Dickinson 2007a: 23). This comment merely serves to show the gulf that separates Dickinson from her translators. Faith is crucial to the poetry of this Protestant poet. By reducing God to the status of an eccentric, she makes us meditate on God's place in the world, his location in the metaphysical order. Her ambivalence derives from her paradoxical and ultimately self-defeating attempt to raise herself up to God's level through contemplation of his works. This proves impossible, but the striving remains meaningful: since she can neither imagine nor conceive of God, she is condemned to imagine him in terms that are absurd. The mind cannot grasp God, but the imagination can intuit him and perceive his intentions in his works, however strange they are. And what makes Dickinson unique is that she reminds us that God made not only the lion and the lamb of which Blake spoke, he also made the grotesque and the absurd—Dickinson's bat, Burns's louse.

While Forgue demonstrates that he is little inclined to engage with this Calvinist faith (Dickinson 1970b: 31), he manages nevertheless to enter the spirit of the poem quoted above. Like Messiaen he maintains the word *excentricités*. And he translates "adroit Creator" as "habile Artisan," thereby reinforcing the idea that we can contemplate the divine through the works of God. Messiaen makes a more banal choice: "adroit Créateur." Forgue feels the gap between the everyday world and the heavenly world, that gap between the angels and animals sent by God on the one hand, and the bureaucratic world of work on the other, introduced by the word "deputed" in the line "Deputed from what Firmament," which he renders as "Délégué par quel firmament." He has an ear for the disconcerting irony that resides in Dickinson's lexical juxtapositions. Messiaen's version once more disappoints with his choice, "Envoyée par quel firmament." Both translators give an approximate version of "Like fallow Article": "comme un fragment de glèbe" (Messiaen) and "article défraîchi" (Forgue).

On the whole, Forgue's lines are more striking than Messiaen's, whose work remains close to the original. Messiaen explicates the poems; he consequently renders an eight-syllable line with fourteen syllables. When we examine Messiaen's version of "The Bat is dun, with wrinkled wings" (La chauve-souris est gris sombre avec des ailes ridées), we see that Messiaen interprets the idea where Forgue internalizes it and manipulates it in his own manner. Messiaen repeats the line mechanically, setting it unit by unit in the same order in which he finds it.

Indeed, all three translators display an almost religious respect for the line itself. This is a cardinal strategy in contemporary French poetico-academic translation—the translation of volumes of poems for student readers. As we shall see, Delphy's *Poésies complètes* (Dickinson 2009) marks a return to the line-by-line principle of poetico-academic translation. In the case of these three translators, we can also account for their adherence to line-by-line translation as intuitive conformity to the aesthetics of their time, with its predominance of free verse. It does not demonstrate any aesthetic receptivity to Dickinson's poems. On a superficial level this may pass for fidelity to the source text, but an analysis of the way Dickinson's rhythms work soon dispels this impression.

Dickinson often uses run-on lines that do not always break into quatrains, as we see in the manuscripts of her poems (Emily Dickinson Archive, http://www.edickinson.org). It is not so much her lines that are meter-bound as her phrasing. The syntax cuts the discourse into four-beat and three-beat lines (or the seven-beat phrase found so often in the ballad that divides gracefully into 4:3). Dickinson's rhythmic playfulness resides in the way she sets up a dynamic tension between the syntax and the meter, using punctuation to astonish and disconcert the reader by upsetting the movement, and the logic of what can become an almost monotonous harmony in much of the metrical verse of her period. The four-beat rhythms of the hymns of her time always play softly but surely in the background of her poems, but in the foreground, tension and unease are generated by pauses, breaks, oppositions, and appositions.

Bosquet is more successful than Messiaen in avoiding what Malblanc calls dilution, or the "dispersal of one 'signified' into several 'signifiers'" (1968: 5; my translation). For example, Messiaen translates "dun" as "gris sombre," and "quaintly halved" as "drôlement partagé en deux." Otherwise Bosquet is less successful than Forgue in what Malblanc calls concentration: "the concentration of several signifieds on a small number of signifiers" (1968: 5; my translation).

In terms of rhythm, Messiaen sometimes falls into using what Hegel would call "the prose of the world" (Rose 1995: 140), a movement devoid of harmony and grace, the blissful metaphysical order that romantics such as Shelley and Hugo cherished and sought to evoke in their poems. Bosquet occasionally falls into the same prose-like lines as Messiaen. Forgue tends to maintain the dashes more faithfully, with "Those—dying then" (Dickinson 2016: 368) being translated as "Ceux qui mouraient—alors—" (Dickinson 1970b: 266). But this is not always the case; at times he completely erases them. For the poem that opens with "The Brain—is wider than the Sky" and which he translates as "Le cerveau déborde le ciel," Forgue removes a total of twenty dashes (Dickinson 2016: 273; 1970b: 156). On the other hand, the rhythm of his syntax, and especially the appositions he uses, echoes the movement of Dickinson's lines—a jerky, fitful movement that creates unexpected breaks. He thereby succeeds in reproducing a poetic practice that makes us focus on each word. By introducing a dash in the first and the last lines of the poem below, Forgue marks two expressive breaks that do not exist in the original but nevertheless correspond perfectly to the activity of the poem.

Water, is taught by thirst.	On apprend l'eau—par la soif,
Land—by the Oceans passed.	La terre—par les mers franchies,
Transport—by throe—	Les transports, par les affres,
Peace—by it's battles told—	La paix—en comptant ses batailles,
Love, by Memorial Mold—	L'amour, par une image à garder,
Birds, by the snow.	Et les oiseaux—par la neige.
(Dickinson 2016: 61)	(Dickinson 1970b: 57)

The three translators clearly have a student readership in mind, for they feel entitled to include a number of pedantic remarks. According to Bosquet, "the writing is capricious, and often careless" (Dickinson 1957: 52; my translation). Forgue praises Dickinson's ability to "revitalize vocabulary and syntax" but he regrets that there is not more "syntactic rigour." He concludes, "In sum, Dickinson has the gift but not the breath; she is a poet of fragments" (Dickinson 1970b: 36, 37, 32; my translations).

In a strange inversion of the translator-as-servant role, the three take evident relish in admonishing the poet in the tone of a teacher deriding his students as he hands them back their graded homework. Messiaen cites Higginson when he mentions "the formal irregularity." Citing the "comments of many English and American critics," he finds that Dickinson masters the meter, but regrets that her "grammar is not always correct" (Dickinson 1956: 58; my translations). Like Forgue, he finds that she is "short of breath" (58). As for Forgue, he is astonished to find "satirical poems, observations that blind like lightning" next to "delicacies," "affectations," and "other such nonsense" (Dickinson 1970b: 18–19; my translations).

The three translators are faithful to their projects: to make Dickinson accessible. They find it hard to forgive obscurities and imprecisions, as well as grammatical mistakes and errors of style, but they display a certain indulgence, a tolerance that verges on condescension. There is little that is new in these remarks; they are recycled impressions that can be found throughout the critical literature written on Dickinson's work over the past century. First it was her use of assonance (half-rhyme) in the place of rhyme that was at issue. Her handling of fixed forms was judged inadequate. A journalist writing in the *Saturday Review* on 5 September 1891 thought Dickinson showed "considerable imaginative power" but that these qualities were "separate from merits of form" (Wetzsteon, quoted in Dickinson 2004: 332). Further, he said, some of the poems in the collection he had seen could hardly be described as being "in verse."

Small wonder that our French translators should take up such received ideas and apply them in their own particular ways as they translated Dickinson's poems. However, when it comes to criticism of form and style, two things need to be kept in mind: Dickinson never tried to have the vast majority of her poems published. Her friends and family took on that task. So there is no way of knowing if she considered them ready for publication or if, on the contrary, she viewed a large number of them as failed attempts, works in progress, or fragments.

More importantly, contrary to what the critics have often maintained, Dickinson masters meter perfectly. Indeed, it is because she so mastered the solid binary movement of the rhythms of the Protestant hymns of her time that her poems continue to resonate in our ears and in our emotional memories today. Unfortunately our three French translators are challenged in this respect. Rhythm is not their strong point; they are primarily interested in the meaning. Nothing in their interpretive approach can help them "hear" the poem. They interpret the poems, and in something that is no longer a metaphor, they interpret them with the instruments of their own poetic sensibilities. But orality cannot be analyzed. It does not fit into categories and concepts; it can be perceived or intuited only when, as a part of the whole moving experience of the poem, it unfolds in rhythmic repetition and in flowing, meaningful energy. Orality is heard. Consequently the emphasis on rhyming words in Dickinson's poems is lost in their translations. The alliterations and assonances—echoes of the semantic activity and poetic imagination that connect and juxtapose ideas—are entirely missing from these three translation projects. The energy and efficacy of the French translations suffer from these losses. What the poems do, the French versions, more often than not, fail to re-enact.

In short, it is evident that Bosquet, Messiaen, and Forgue do not try to replace the English poems with French poems. Theirs is a poetic project, but a poetico-academic one rather than a poem-for-a-poem project. Each translator simply tries to recreate the meaning.

This in itself is laudable: Dickinson is impenetrable for anyone who hasn't mastered English, and she is judged difficult to grasp for many students of the language who seek to go deeper than the surface charm that satisfies the wider audience. Besides, since every translation attempt enriches our understanding of a piece of writing, the work of all three translators helps us to penetrate more fully and deeply into poems that appear at first (and even at second) sight, perplexing and confusing with their abstractions and quirky syntax. As the translators remould these meanings into a different form, we see the poems in a different light. For this reason, despite its detractors, the poetico-academic project obviously serves a purpose and is therefore probably here to stay. Indeed, it might be argued that it reaches its logical conclusion in Delphy's translation of the complete poems (2009).

No translation erases the original. To argue that these translators betray or distort the original is, therefore, to dabble in metaphors. Dickinson in English remains untouched by her French translations. And the French tradition is indebted to these artisans for their labour and the pains they have taken to make her work known and to bring her into the literary purview of French readers. Nonetheless, they sing a Dickinson without music. They speak to us from a world of the hard of hearing. The form of Dickinson's poems and their orality are left on the other side of the Atlantic.

Gender and Personification

Fidelity as a concept is vague and ill-defined, but up until now we have been navigating between three forms of fidelity: fidelity to the poem, fidelity to the poet, and fidelity to poetry. When Forgue and Bosquet do a line-by-line translation, they no doubt feel they are being faithful to the poem and to the poet. I would contend that this demonstrates rather a fidelity to a certain idea of free verse: the belief that the poetry lies in the verse line. Metrical and non-metrical English verse, on the contrary, is flexible with verse lines. Lines are often manipulated, with inversions being introduced in order to leave certain words hanging at the ends of the lines. This syntactic manipulation is something that many free-verse translators of French and English fail to notice.

All three translators are sensitive to the diction of the poet, and this awareness accounts for choices such as Forgue's "habile Artisan" and Messiaen's "adroit Créateur." They show an intuitive fidelity to Dickinson's religious world view. Forgue's choice to preserve dashes, however sporadically and erratically, demonstrates a sensitivity to the movement of images in Dickinson's verse. This strategy is being faithful to the poem. A vast number of translations, however, show that striving to remain faithful to poetry can induce translators to forget both the poet and the poem.

When we translate a poem, we translate a poet and his or her language. A poem confronts us with a fundamental set of constraints that cannot be forgotten: the grammatical constraints of the language. No amount of intuition can allow us to pole-vault over these constraints. Henri Meschonnic is no doubt right to insist that we translate the text, we do not translate the language. We translate the Bible, not Hebrew. We translate Baudelaire, not French. This is an important principle, and it should enable us to escape the pernicious mode of thinking that encourages us to make concessions to the grammar of the target language, while the poet feels at liberty to break the rules of his or her own language's grammar and innovate in collocations.

Nonetheless grammatical rules must be negotiated. This point raises the question of language-specific grammar. French grammar does introduce constraints that English does not, and this will affect the representation of ideas and emotions in Dickinson's poems. The most obvious constraint that must be negotiated is gender. This adaptation proves especially tricky, since Dickinson makes great use of personification and has her own peculiar ideas about the gender of religious figures, abstract nouns, and everyday things.

Little attempt is made by Dickinson's translators to render her gendered personifications, however. Where Death is masculine in her poetry, it becomes feminine, *la mort*, in these early translations. The translators conform to the French language and not to the spirit of the poet, who enters into a relationship with death when she uses the masculine. The encounter with death is an intimate affair for Dickinson.

Because I could not stop for Death— He kindly stopped for me— The Carriage held but just Ourselves— And Immortality.	Comme je ne pouvais m'arrêter pour la mort, Aimablement, elle s'arrêta pour moi; La voiture ne contenait que nous deux Et l'Immortalité.
(Dickinson 2016: 239)	(Messiaen, in Dickinson 1956: 133)

Clearly, maintaining a masculine death in French would require something amounting to grammatical gymnastics, but one could imagine trying something like *le pouvoir mortel* (the power of death) or *ce pouvoir, la mort* (this power death). Speaking of *le destin mortel* would enable the translator to preserve the male–female encounter in which the woman, the lyrical subject, is invited to join a courteous Death, clearly Dickinson's intention.

God, who in the languages of Christian cultures is masculine,[2] presents translators with fewer problems. Nature, however, is another story. Personified in Dickinson's work, it is sometimes clearly gendered and sometimes asexual. She personifies the month of March, who becomes an acquaintance, but its sex remains ambiguous or unimportant. This is not Mars, the god of war. The same occurs when nature appears in English with the capital letter of a proper noun. As already mentioned, Bosquet criticized the capricious aspects of Dickinson's writing (Dickinson 1957: 52), and he seems to agree with Messiaen's comments on her grammar. At any rate, in the following example he is unwilling to break the rules of French grammar, and he thus feels obliged to preserve the feminine character of *nature* in French by introducing the article *la,* even though nature (much like March) is not sexed in Dickinson's poem but does constitute a proper noun, a personification. Given the obvious intention of personifying and relating these two terms to each other or, rather, of binding them in a relationship, the feminization of *nature* in French is unfortunate. Equally, making March masculine introduces an unwelcome sexual ambiguity when Bosquet translates "Oh March, Come right upstairs with me."

Dear March—Come in—	Entre, cher Mars!
How glad I am—	Combien je suis content!
I hoped for you before—	Je t'attendais.
Put down your Hat—	Pose donc ton chapeau,
You must have walked—	Tu as dû tant marcher—
How out of breath you are—	Tu es à bout de souffle!
Dear March how are you, and the Rest—	
Did you leave Nature well—	Cher Mars, comment vas-tu?
Oh March, Come right upstairs with me—	Et tout le reste?
I have so much to tell—	Tu as quitté la Nature en bonne santé?
	Oh! Mars, montons vite à l'étage,
	J'ai tant de choses à te dire!
(Dickinson 2016: 577)	(Dickinson 1957: 85)

Malroux: A Voice That Hears and Responds

We had to wait for Claire Malroux, who began her twenty-year project to translate Dickinson back in the late 1980s, for a translator who would respond to the orality of Dickinson's voice. Malroux responded to Dickinson's poetic world just as her predecessors had, but she heard something in the movement and the organization of the poet's voice, something in her versification, that former translators had not rendered. Dickinson has many French voices today, but since her first volume of translations was published by Belin in 1989,[3] Malroux's voice has asserted itself as the most poetical and most resonant of the French Dickinsons. Unlike those of our first three translators, Malroux's versions of Dickinson certainly enact an encounter.[4] Let us compare one of her translations with Messiaen's version.

Come slowly—Eden!	Viens doucement, paradis terrestre !	Viens lentement—Eden!
Lips unused to Thee—	Les lèvres qui ne sont point accoutumées à toi	Des lèvres encore novices—
Bashful—sip thy Jessamines—	Sucent, timide, tes jasmins;	Chastes—hument tes Jasmins—
As the fainting Bee—	Ainsi l'abeille pâmée,	Comme l'Abeille pâmée—
Reaching late his flower,	Atteignant tard sa fleur,	À sa fleur parvenue tard,
Round her chamber hums—	Bourdonne autour de la chambre,	Bourdonne autour de son calice—
Counts his nectars—	Compte ses nectars, entre	En recense les nectars—
Enters—and is lost in Balms!	Et se perd dans les parfums!	Pénètre—et se perd dans les Délices.
(Dickinson 2016: 121)	(Messiaen, in Dickinson 1956: 115–17)	(Malroux, in Dickinson 1989: 33)

Without wishing to denigrate Messiaen's attempt, we find that, if we read the two French versions aloud, something of the rhythmic intensity and poetic power that is so audible in Dickinson's verse is echoed in Malroux's version. Messiaen's translation pales by comparison.

Messiaen cannot be dismissed as simply a dusty academic insensitive to poetry. His version offers some happy finds. The delicate mixture of salient and subtle alliteration works well at times: "Sucent, timide, tes jasmins" and "se perd dans les parfums!" But in general, much of Dickinson's orality is lost in crossing the Atlantic. Malroux, in contrast, preserves the rhythm of Dickinson's poems that invite significant hesitant pauses in the reading process. She reproduces the capital letters (which also act upon the way the lines are read). Malroux's phrase is abrupt and piercing. If she fails to maintain the rhyme in the first stanza, her second one does rhyme, allowing an interesting rapprochement between "calice" and "Delices." Moreover, her alliteration links penetration with wild abandon, "Pénètre—et se perd dans les Délices." The attraction to paradise—a carnal, sensual desire—loses none of the charm of the original; the spiritual experience remains a form of ravishment.

Malroux's translations harness and bind together the sound patterning and orality of the original poems. This is as much a semantic as a formal mode of expression. Malroux is listening to the unfolding of meaning in Dickinson's poems. Clearly she is aspiring to the translation strategy of replacing a poem with a poem. She translates into a different form of poetry—contemporary French free verse—but she is responding to Dickinson's voice. Where Forgue responds to Dickinson's world view, Malroux takes a step further, seeking to re-enact sound patterning that is characteristic of the poet. That is to say, when she finds it impossible to maintain the semantic links set up in Dickinson's meaningful alliterations, assonances, and rhymes, she seeks to compensate for these losses by setting up sound patterning reminiscent of Dickinson's poetics. Malroux drops "Debauchee of Dew" in the following lines, for example, but she links *Rosée* and *été*, thereby using line-end assonance to underscore and body forth Dickinson's romanticism.

Inebrate of Air—am I—	À moi—Soûleries d'Air—Orgies de Rosée—
And Débauchee of Dew—	Aux jours sans fin de l'été
("I taste a liquor," Dickinson 2016: 135)	(Malroux, in Dickinson 1989: 33)

Elsewhere Malroux invents alliteration that is not found in the original but which redoubles the force and meaning of her translations. Thus she translates "To see the little Tippler / From Manzanilla come!" as "Pour voir, de Manzanilla venue— / **P**asser la **p**etite **P**oivrote!" (Dickinson 1989: 33).

Malroux does not maintain all of the dashes in the original poems, and like her three predecessors she tends to stick to line-by-line translations. At times, indeed, it must be admitted that Malroux is no better than Forgue at his best (which is no criticism!). The following translation demonstrates Forgue's sensitivity to orality in his inspired translation.

The Soul selects her own Society—	L'âme choisit sa compagnie	L'âme choisit sa Compagnie—
Then—shuts the Door—	Puis se calfeutre.	Puis—ferme la Porte—
To her divine Majority—	Dans sa pluralité divine	À sa Majorité divine—
Present no more—	Plus d'intrusion.	Ne présentez nul autre—
	Impassible, elle voit s'arrêter les carrosses	
Unmoved—she notes the Chariots—pausing—	A son humble porte—	Impassible—elle voit les Chars—faire halte—
At her low Gate—	Impassible, un Empereur fût-il à genoux	Devant son humble Grille—
Unmoved—an Emperor be kneeling	Sur son paillasson.	Impassible—un Empereur fût-il à genoux
Upon her Mat—	Je sais qu'au sein d'un vaste peuple	Sur le tapis du Seuil—
	Elle a choisi—un Etre,	
I've known her—from an ample nation—	Puis obturé son attention Comme un caillou.	Je l'ai vue—dans une ample nation—
Choose One—		En élire Un—
Then—close the valves of her attention—		Puis tel un Minéral—clore les Valves De son attention—
Like Stone—		
(Dickinson 2016: 218)	(Forgue, in Dickinson 1970b: 73)	(Malroux, in Dickinson 1989: 71)

Notwithstanding the preceding example, Malroux manages to sustain successful adaptation of meaningful sound patterning in her versions. As French free-verse poems, they work. Examples such as following can be found at random when browsing Malroux's collection.

It's easy to invent a Life— God does it—every Day— Creation—but the Gambol Of his Authority—	Il est aisé d'inventer une Vie— Chaque jour—Dieu le fait— La Création—simple Gambade De son Autorité—
It's easy to efface it— The thrifty Deity Could scarce afford Eternity To Spontaneity—	Il est aisé de l'effacer— L'économe **D**éité Ne pourrait guère au Spontané Offrir l'Éternité—
The Perished Patterns murmur— But his perturbless Plan Proceed—inserting Here—a Sun— There—leaving out a Man.	Les formes Abolies **p**rotestent Mais Son **P**lan Im**p**assible Se **p**oursuit—il insère Ici—un Soleil— Là—il omet un Homme.
(Dickinson 2016: 375)	(Malroux, in Dickinson 1989: 207–08; emphasis added)

This orchestration of sound patterning, which appears to come so easily to Malroux, is not accidental. "Inventer une vie" and "Ici—un Soleil" might be happy accidents, but the consistency with which Malroux fashions meaningful sonorous links is impressive. And this practice is nourished by a reasoned strategy. Unlike many of Dickinson's critics, Malroux admires the poet's versification. She praises her virtuosity in rhyming[5] and she analyzes and interprets the significant density of sound patterning. This is partly what enables her to make a poetic response to the poems of Dickinson.

Voices after Malroux

How should we order the translators who come after Malroux, or after she began her translation project more than two decades ago? Philippe Denis's project, first published in 1986 (Dickinson 2003), is less ambitious than Forgue's or Malroux's. In a collection of forty-seven poems, he maintains the dashes but follows a strict line-by-line reproduction of the meaning. Unlike Malroux, he does not appear to have internalized and assimilated the meaning sufficiently to refashion it in his own poetic response to Dickinson's poems. Consequently the lines end somewhat arbitrarily with the words that French syntax and grammar dictate. The abrupt pauses are partially maintained, but Dickinson's inversions and the words she leaves hanging—precariously—are not to be found in his verse.

The least interesting of Dickinson's translators is probably Odile de Fontenelles, who laboured to render the meaning of twenty-six unpublished poems (Dickinson 1997). The project can be considered a success if we accept that specialists and students gained access to poems hitherto unknown in France. But the translations are laborious affairs of little aesthetic value. The following example should serve to prove this point.

'Twas my one Glory—	C'était ma seule Gloire—
Let it be	Qu'on s'en
Remembered	Souvienne
I was owned of Thee—	J'étais possédée de Toi—
("Poem 1028," Dickinson 2016: 469)	(Fontenelles, in Dickinson 1997: n.p.)

The translator clearly aspires to a literal line-by-line translation, even to the extent of separating the reflexive verb "s'en / Souvienne." In the hands of Forgue or Malroux we might be inclined to believe that the translator is trying to introduce an expressive break, intended to drag out the act of remembering and leave the lyrical subject caught off-balance, ill-at-ease—in the gap—seeking solace in the past. But Fontenelles' translations seek only to reproduce the lexis and the syntax of the lines, and all concessions or manipulations prove to be motivated by respect for the English verse line or for French grammar, rather than metrical, rhythmic, poetic, or expressive considerations.

Patrick Reumaux, on the other hand, proves sensitive to sound patterning and orality in his translations (first published in 1998; Dickinson 2007b). In the following stanza, Reumaux leaves "pensée avortée" hanging at the end of the verse line and links it with assonance to both "Pensée" and "Année." Like Malroux, Reumaux is responding to the poem here, but in doing so he is responding to the poetics of Dickinson rather than to the individual poem; as we can see, neither rhyme nor alliteration is to be found in the original stanza.

A Thought went up my mind today— That I have had before— But did not finish—some way back— I could not fix the Year—	Aujourd'hui m'est venue à l'esprit une **Pensée**— Que j'ai déjà eue— Il y a un moment—une **pensée avortée**— Je ne sais plus de quelle **Année**—
(Dickinson 2016: 366)	(Reumaux, in Dickinson 2007b: 173; emphasis added)

Similarly, as we can see in the next extracts, in response to Dickinson's reflection on death, which begins "Because I could not stop for Death / He kindly stopped for me," Reumaux compensates for dropping the alliterative link between "labor" and "leisure" with alliteration: "**p**ressait"/"**p**ensums"/"**p**asse-temps."

We slowly drove—He knew no haste And I had put away My **l**abor and my **l**eisure too, For his civility—	Nous conduisions lentement—rien ne La **p**ressait J'avais mis de côté Mes **p**ensums, mes **p**asse-temps aussi, Vu Sa Civilité
(Dickinson 2016: 239; emphasis added)	(Reumaux, in Dickinson 2007b: 175; emphasis added)

Reumaux manipulates the phrasing of his verse skilfully to reproduce something approaching the curiously erratic and delightfully intelligent manner so characteristic of Dickinson. Let us take his translation of the first stanza of "Poem 654":

A long—long Sleep— A famous—Sleep— That makes no show for Morn— By Stretch of Limb—or stir of Lid— An independent One—	Un Long—long Sommeil—un Merveilleux—Sommeil— Qui ne tient pas compte du Matin— En Étirant un Membre—ou en soulevant une paupière— Un Somme indépendant—
(Dickinson 2016: 232)	(Reumaux, in Dickinson 2007b: 159)

How daring—and yet how apt—to begin the last line with *Un*, drawing out the phrase and inviting us to marvel at this marvellous sleep.

Although Reumaux proves less consistent than Malroux, he nonetheless sets himself apart from Bosquet, Messiaen, Denis, and Fontenelles in refusing, like Malroux, to be satisfied with rendering the meaning of the poem. Without betraying that meaning, the two translators consolidate the poetic impact of the meaningful movement of the poem. They re-enact an orchestration of sound patterning that cannot be divorced from the voice of the translated poem. In this sense they achieve something akin to organic translations in which the voice and the versification prove inextricable, while their predecessors aspire only to poetically transcribe in French the meanings they have deciphered. Malroux's and Reumaux's translations work: they are poetic responses to poems. Whether these new poems reproduce the moving emotion of Dickinson's voice remains open to question. This point will be taken up when we compare our French translators with the wonderful German translator Gertrud Liepe. Before that, however, we cannot afford to neglect the impressive project of Dickinson's latest French interpreter.

Delphy's Return to the Academy

It is difficult to do justice to Françoise Delphy's translation project in a case study like this one, which can of necessity offer only an overview of the various translators' approaches and strategies. By quoting individual poems it is easy to pick holes in Delphy's translations and find fault with her poetics. Delphy, however, does not set out, like Ezra Pound or Henri Meschonnic, to refashion a handful of poems that inspire her. She labours to produce a clear and readable edition of Emily Dickinson's entire poetic output. Unpublished in her time and not collected in English until Johnson's 1955 edition (Dickinson 1963), this entire œuvre has now been offered up to French readers.

Delphy's is a hermeneutico-poetic project. While readers and scholars might find surprising the claim she makes in her translator's note (Dickinson 2009: xxviii) that a mere five percent of Dickinson's poems are truly obscure (*hermétique*), Delphy does succeed in rendering translations that clarify what is ambiguous in the original. The simple profundity of Dickinson's verse comes through in her translations, as we can see in the following lines.

If you were coming in the Fall,	Si tu venais à l'Automne,
I'd brush the Summer by	Je balaierais l'Été
With half a smile, and half a spurn,	Avec un demi-sourire, à demi dédaigneux,
As Housewives do, a Fly.	Comme les Ménagères font, d'une Mouche.
(Dickinson 2016: 188)	(Dickinson 2009: 326)

Delphy respects the use of capital letters, the dashes, and other aspects of Dickinson's verse. Like Forgue and Malroux, she is sensitive to the poet's elliptical style. And she knows all too well the significance of her concise allusions. These are questions she considers in her translator's note (2009: xxviii), and her translations throughout this heavy volume bear witness to her sensitivity to these aspects of Dickinson's poetics.

But Delphy's aim is obvious. She aspires above all to produce a translation of the meaning. As she puts it in her translator's note, "I wanted to remain as faithful as possible to the literal text of the original" (J'ai voulu rester aussi fidèle que possible à la littéralité de l'anglais; Dickinson 2009: xxviii). Her reasons, from our point of view, prove somewhat disappointing and anti-analytical. Since she makes no distinction between rhythm and meter, her claims remain rather vague and generally unhelpful. Delphy asserts that "keeping the rhythm of the Dickinson poem is impossible," but it remains uncertain as to why this might be. Is it because, as she claims, "English is more rhythmic (plus rythmé) than French" (xxviii; my translations)? Or is it because of something proper to Dickinson's own specific rhythm? Delphy offers no real answer but states that, since translating the rhythm of Dickinson's poems is impossible, "I have preferred to give a rhythm proper to, or more appropriate to, French" (donner un rythme propre au français; xxviii; my translation). We are clearly back in the theoretical Dark Ages, when translators proved so reluctant to theorize and distinguish between the accentuation of the language, the movement of the phrase, the structured order of meter, and the patterning of free verse.

In order to verify whether Delphy succeeds in reproducing "an appropriate rhythm," we must in fairness consider one of her translations of a poem as a whole.

I lived on Dread—	J'ai vécu de Terreur—
To Those who know	Pour Ceux qui connaissent
The stimulus there is	L'aiguillon du
In Danger—Other impetus	Danger—Toute Autre impulsion
Is numb—and vitalless—	Est léthargique—sans vitalité—
As 'twere a Spur—upon the Soul—	Comme un Éperon—sur l'Âme—
A Fear will urge it where	Une Peur la poussera où
To go without the spectre's aid	Aller sans l'aide Du spectre
Were challenging Despair.	Serait défier le Désespoir.
(Dickinson 2016: 247)	("Poem 498," Dickinson 2009: 469)

As elsewhere, Delphy elegantly renders the meaning of the poem, paying attention to capitals and syntactic breaks. Leaving "où" (where) hanging at the end of the line in the second stanza means cutting up "où / aller" (where / To go). But the translator is following Dickinson, and the effect sets up a delicately precarious enjambment. Alliteration asserts itself in the second stanza: "**P**eur la **p**oussera" and "**d**éfier le **D**ésespoir." This makes the second stanza much more interesting than the first, and Delphy does at times offer compact lyrical lines. However, on the whole this appears to be rather more by accident than by intention. Certainly the alliterations mentioned appear fortuitous; nothing in the other poems suggests there is an intention to work on sound patterning of either a formal or a meaningful kind. As for the French rhythm that Delphy claims to offer in place of the untranslatable rhythms of English and the rhythm of Dickinson's poems, it seems difficult to determine what she has in mind. Her verse is not metrical, nor does it tend to gravitate towards metrical lines in the free alternation that Malroux and Forgue achieve.

Form, rhythm, and the meaningful organization of movement and sound patterning all seem to have been sacrificed in Delphy's ambitious hermeneutic project—sacrificed at the altar of the poem's meaning. At times this focus makes her verse sound like Bosquet and Messiaen at their worst. Certainly the poignantly concise, crafted metrical verse of Dickinson seems to have been left far behind in translations such as the following one.

Have any like Myself Investigating March, New Houses on the Hill descried— And possibly a Church— That were not, We are sure— As lately as the Snow— And are Today—if We exist— Though how may this be so?	Est-ce que d'autres comme Moi, Investiguant le mois de Mars, Ont aperçu de nouvelles Maisons sur la Colline— Et peut-être une Église— Qui n'étaient pas là, Nous en sommes certains— Ces derniers temps de Neige— Et aujourd'hui sont là—aussi vrai que Nous sommes en vie— Mais comment est-ce possible ?
(Dickinson 2016: 362)	(Dickinson 2009: 362)

This is clear but laborious prose, a rhythm born of an entirely different hemisphere from the one that nourished Dickinson's poetic sensibility. Gone are both the structure and the tension. Gone are the compact packets of meaning that Dickinson juxtaposes line by line. And the Protestant hymns that play behind all her verse, announcing an uneasy, quizzical celebration of creation and perception, have entirely vanished.

At her best, Delphy offers eloquent prosaic translations that encapsulate the quirky but arresting meaning of Dickinson's reflections, as in the following version.

Our little Kinsmen—after Rain In plenty may be seen, A Pink and Pulpy multitude The tepid Ground upon. A needless life, it seemed to me Until a little bird As to Hospitality Advanced and breakfasted— As I of He, so God of Me I pondered, may be judged, And left the little Angle Worm With modesties enlarged.	On peut voir en grand nombre, Nos petits Cousins—après la Pluie Multitude Rose et Charnue Sur la Terre tiède. Vie inutile, me semblait-il Jusqu'à ce qu'un petit Oiseau Comme devant l'Hospitalité S'approche et déjeune— Il se peut que Dieu Me juge, Comme je Le Juge, pensai-je Aussi quand je quittai le petit Ver de Terre J'avais gagné en Modestie.
(Dickinson 2016: 436)	("Poem 932," Dickinson 2009: 839)

"J'avais gagné en Modestie" is elegantly compact, a balanced octosyllabic line that breaks up 4:4 if we wish to render it in an expressively slow, pondering rhythm. "Vie inutile, me semblait-il" follows the same pattern and maintains Dickinson's parallelism. "Terre tiède" offers an effective alliteration. And "Multitude Rose et Charnue" is a beautiful line, even if it lacks Dickinson's characteristically palpable alliteration in "A Pink and Pulpy Multitude."

In general, though, Delphy has difficulty rivalling Forgue, and she is certainly no match for Malroux at her best. In translating the following famous stanzas, Delphy's verse compares unfavourably with those of her predecessor and her contemporary.

> Because I could not stop for Death—
> He kindly stopped for me—
> The Carriage held but just Ourselves—
> And immortality.
>
> We slowly drove—He knew no haste
> And I had put away
> My labor and my leisure too,
> For His Civility—
>
> (Dickinson 2016: 239)

Puisque je ne pouvais m'arrêter pour la Mort— Ce Gentleman eut la bonté de s'arrêter pour moi— Dans la Voiture il n'y avait que Nous— Et immortalité. Nous roulions lentement—Il n'était pas pressé Et j'avais mis de côté Mon labeur ainsi que mon loisir, En réponse à sa Civilité—	Pour Mort ne pouvant pas m'arrêter— Aimable il s'arrêta pour moi— Dans la Calèche rien que Nous deux— Et l'Immortalité. Lent voyage—Lui était sans hâte Et j'avais renoncé À mon labeur, à mes loisirs aussi, Pour Sa Civilité—
(Delphy, in Dickinson 2009: 451)	(Malroux, in Dickinson 2007a: 147)

With her compact lines, idiomatic and familiar, Malroux manages to evoke something of that strange intimacy that Dickinson depicts here between the reluctant dying individual and the death that comes to welcome all of us in the end. She does not hesitate to make death masculine, where other translators bow down to the grammar of the French language. And as for sound patterning, though Delphy does manage to preserve the *l* in "Mon labeur ainsi que mon loisir," Malroux, for her part, has already set the scene for this alliterative effect and the binary parallelism of the line three lines before, with a similarly alliterative line linking the *l*, which likewise sets up a balanced apposition: "Lent voyage—Lui était sans hâte."

What are we to conclude? Clearly Malroux is responding to the poem, where Delphy is simply rendering the meaning. Malroux's response shows that she listens to the movement and the organization of both the poet's and her own verse. And where she can, Malroux binds together rhythmic effects to generate a much more expressive response, one that holds together the poem as a whole and that holds together, in inextricable unity, the meaning and the form of her reformulations.

Delphy's achievement should not be underestimated, and if it inevitably invites criticism, then that should not obscure the fact that she alone has had the courage and the determination to take on the complete works of Dickinson. Her efforts will no doubt be appreciated by students and scholars, and readers in general will enter into Dickinson's world thanks to her versions. But the voice that is heard in Dickinson's versification does not break through into French. And the voice that makes itself heard in the movement and organization of her lines, is—however interesting and however perplexing and arresting—the voice of prose.

Should we be surprised by this return to a poetico-academic translation strategy after two decades, during which Malroux's versions asserted themselves in the French tradition? Perhaps not. The sheer volume of work involved must have tempted Delphy to be more modest in her aspirations. Something more curious, more sombre, is at work here too. For although it seems impossible that Delphy could have ignored or failed to consult the versions of Forgue and Malroux, both of which are well established, she makes no mention of them in her translator's note. It is difficult to interpret this as anything other than an indirect insult, given the fact that both Forgue and Malroux have made a great impression on French readers. Are we supposed to believe that Delphy has not found the time to look at the work of the other translators? Whatever the case may be, no attempt is made to define how Delphy intends to position herself in relation to her predecessors. She does not mention what she appreciates or dislikes in their versions. Nor does she suggest what motive she has in seeking to oust or replace them. For Delphy, Forgue and Malroux simply do not exist.

In a very different vein, Meschonnic tends to criticize in great detail (and with evident relish) the translators he is competing with when he offers his versions of the books of the Bible and Shakespeare's sonnets. One might argue that this is a clumsy strategy that in no way predisposes us to appreciate the beauty or erudition of his efforts. Perhaps, but Meschonnic's strategy at least has the virtue of being more honest than Delphy's. Meschonnic's response is an intellectual one, not an emotional one. He critiques; he does not reject. Delphy effaces; she acts as if her versions come from nothing, though it seems impossible that she could fail to have been influenced by the work of translators who came before her.

Whatever her motives might be, Delphy boldly presents an entirely different project from the one Malroux offers. Her return to a hermeneutic response is, poem by poem, disappointing, but as a whole, the enormous effort that she has put into producing 1,789 versions will certainly have an impact on the way readers understand Dickinson in French. Delphy undeniably broadens the horizons of French readers, inviting them into that curious world that Dickinson opens up. In Delphy's version of that world, we hear little of the poetry of Dickinson's voice, but her images and ideas and her curious phrasing assert themselves in a style very unlike anything being produced in French poetry today. Malroux at her best far surpasses Delphy's individual efforts, but no one can always be at their best. Malroux herself at times falls back into prose and, understandably, she has yet to take on the collected works. The fact that Delphy brushes her aside in her translator's note might very well serve as the impetus Malroux needs to set her off on that endeavour. Certainly she is both aesthetically and technically better equipped for re-forging the versification of Dickinson's poems into powerfully expressive verse. Delphy hears what the voice says but does not listen to the timbre or the texture of the voice that speaks. Ultimately Malroux hears a voice, and if Delphy does not, perhaps that explains to some extent why she fails to hear what Malroux is doing in her versions.

Malroux's Missed Rhythms

Malroux's interpretation of Dickinson's voice shows greater insight than her predecessors. Others knew well enough that Emily Dickinson's verse was built upon the common meter, pounding out four-beat and three-beat lines (with implied offbeats), the meter of those Protestant hymns made famous by Isaac Watts (Dickinson 1956: 58; 1970b: 35). There is a crucial difference between what Messiaen and Forgue grasp and what Malroux discerns. Malroux does not confuse meter and rhythm—the interaction of the phrase (the breath of the poet) and the meter that encases and structures it. Consequently the reflections in Malroux's preface show none of that pedantic condescension that Bosquet and Messiaen allow themselves. Messiaen is disappointed by the poet's form, which is always "short, and somewhat monotonous," in his opinion (Dickinson 1956: 59; my translation). In contrast, Malroux hears a voice in Dickinson's metrics that she finds "supple and flexible" (souple), and she hears "various rhythmic phrases within that mould" (variation des groupes rythmiques à l'intérieur de ce moule; Dickinson 2007a: 27; my translations). Malroux finds that Dickinson's practice of replacing rhymes with assonance and introducing dashes "marks the breathless means by which the poet shows the discontinuity of a bogged-down way of thinking that moves forward in leaps and bounds" (met en évidence la démarche haletante du poète et révèle la discontinuité d'une pensée comme agglutinée qui procède par bonds; 27; my translation). For Malroux that discontinuity is the very quality that makes Dickinson's poetry modern. The dash, she claims,

> surprises both the breath and the meaning, weaving new combinations between lines and segments of lines that it separates, right to the end, a pause dragging the poem out towards infinity, or which stops it dead in its tracks (surprend le souffle ou le sens ... tisse de nouvelles combinaisons entre les vers ou segments de vers qu'il sépare, jusqu'au dernier d'entre eux, point d'orgue qui prolonge à l'infini le poème ou cassure qui le brise net; 28; my translation).

What Malroux eloquently describes, we do experience on reading Dickinson in the English original. But what about Malroux's translations? She certainly captures Dickinson's discontinuity. In this sense she is, by her own definition, a modern translator. Her aesthetic sensibility is inspired by Stéphane Mallarmé (1842–98) and T. S. Eliot.[6] But this raises a question: what is broken or disrupted in her translations? Ultimately nothing, because the moulds Dickinson is grating against and breaking out of do not figure in Malroux's versions. The meter of her verse never gets sufficient hold on the translation to set up rules and expectations. And without them, rule-breaking is excluded. There is an aesthetics of transgression in Malroux's poetics, but no actual scope for rupture in her freely flowing verse. Without continuity there can be no discontinuity. The line cannot liberate itself from free verse.

To this extent, although Malroux's voice is the French voice that has made itself heard most resonantly among Dickinson translations, that voice turns out to be of quite a different timbre than the voice that Malroux hears and understands so clearly in Dickinson's poems. The solid framework of Watts's hymns, with their thumping four-beat rhythms, is entirely absent in her French verse. Comparing the movement of her translations with Dickinson's verse requires the help of Attridge's binary scansion (1982), which we have already relied upon and which crucially differentiates metrical beating and stress contour.

If we are to make any real headway in distinguishing between Forgue and Malroux and in understanding how Delphy abandons tension and Malroux only partially achieves an aesthetic realization of her own declared poetics, we must return to the analysis of syllable stress, promotion, and demotion. It is not a question of returning to form but of seeing how dynamic accentual movement sets in play moving and metaphysical forms. Without rigorous stylistic analysis of the kind we find in Henri Morier (1961), Alex Preminger and T. V. F. Brogan (1993), Derek Attridge (1982), Richard D. Cureton (1992), and Henri Meschonnic (1982), we will inevitably fall back into a metrical Middle Ages, when essayists such as Alexander Pope and Paul Valéry liked to muse on vague emotions without the analytical tools required to make sense of our subtle and elusive, but all too poignant, responses to poems.

As we saw in the chapter 3, Attridge's revolutionary scansion distinguishes among syllables that are stressed, unstressed, and stressable in order to demonstrate how those syllables fill metrical positions as beats and offbeats (1982). This point reminds us that we must examine the metrical manipulation of syllables that promotes stressable or unstressed syllables into beats and demotes stressed syllables in order to make them work in weak positions between stressed syllables, as offbeats. Free verse has proven its worth as a movement by opening up new horizons for rhythmical experimentation, but it has not necessarily trained the modern ear to discern the subtle shading of accentuation that is omnipresent in even the strictest metrical lines, such as in sonnets and nursery rhymes. It is not certain that the free-verse culture has equipped translators sufficiently in that rhythmic apprenticeship that the great free-verse proponent Pound dreamed of. Indeed, the French translators considered here appear to be wary of technical analysis. Whether they all understand the way meter functions in Dickinson's verse remains unclear.

Entering into the technical details of metrical manipulation will allow us to clearly discern some of the facets of Dickinson's poetics that have been evoked in confused and impressionistic terms by translators and critics alike. This analysis should enable us to grasp something of the specific timbre of her poetic voice, a voice that is at once startlingly original while remaining, on the whole, metrically traditional. Take the following lines, in which the beats (B) and the offbeats (o) can be felt as they emerge from the stress contour of stressed (+s), unstressed (−s), and stressable syllables (s):

```
        −s  s  −s   +s      +s    −s  +s
        As from the Earth the light Balloon
        o   B  o    B    o   B    o   B

        +s +s −s    −s −s +s
        Asks nothing but release—
        o   B  o    B   oB

        −s +s−s     −s  s     s   s +s
        Ascension that for which it was,
        o   B o  B  o       B   o   B

        s  +s −s  +s −s  s
        It's soaring Residence.
        o   B  o   B o B

        −s  +s−s  +s   −s +s −s   +s
        The spirit looks upon the Dust
        o   B o   B    o B  o     B
```

```
   s  +s −s      s  s  +s
That fastened it so long
  o  B  o      B  o  B

    s    +s   −s +s −s
With indignation,
   o  B  o  B  o

 s  −s  +s
As a Bird
 B  o  B

−s +s −s    −s −s +s
Defrauded of its Song.
 o  B  o    B  o  B
```

(Dickinson 2016: 650–51)

In many respects this is standard metrical verse. Series of three unstressed syllables centring around "it"—in "That fastened it so long," for example—allow promotion of the internal syllable. In the same way, series of triple-stressed syllables allow the inverse process of demotion, the weakening of the internal syllable ("Asks" in "Balloon / Asks nothing," for example). Rhythmically speaking, we find ourselves in the four-beat ballad meter that respects scrupulously the seven-beat line, which divides 4:3 and invites the reader to mark a pause, both syntactically and metrically, thereby enacting an implied offbeat at the end of alternating three-beat lines. In the penultimate line of the poem the four-beat line is divided in two, inviting the reader to pause. This is a delicate effect but, metrically speaking, it in no way contradicts the movement of the poem or introduces rupture or dissonance. It simply serves to slow down the reading in anticipation of closure.

Dickinson is always ambivalent, even in her ecstasy and her exhilaration. Here she aspires, soaring upwards, but her choice of the balloon metonymy for the soul implies bathos; release sends the balloon-soul soaring upwards with a sense of indignation and resentment at what is lost on leaving the earth. Like her predecessors, Malroux seizes the meaning of these lines. But the movement of inspiration escapes her, just as the balloon escapes the earth. Malroux's French verse shows no metrical impulsion; it lacks the original's dynamic regularity and the pauses that tug delicately against order. And for this reason, it is no longer clear whether the mute *e* should be pronounced.

Comme de la Terre le Ballon léger	9/11
Ne demande que sa libération—	9/10
L'ascension vers sa raison d'être,	8
Son essor, Résidence.	6
L'âme considère la Poussière	7/9
Qui l'a liée si longtemps	7
Avec indignation,	6
Comme un Oiseau	4
Frustré de son Chant.	5

(Malroux, in Dickinson 2007a: 349–51)

Malroux's lines will please many French ears with their lyrical charm. But this turns out to be part of the problem: the English lines are *not* pleasantly reassuring. They tug us towards transcendence. The meter forms part of a metaphysical movement, a spiritual trajectory. It reaches towards God. In Malroux's French free-verse poem, the balloon liberates itself from earth, but the lines, liberated from order and predictable organization, simply invite us towards an aimless reverie. We are taking flight towards Baudelaire's *ailleurs*, towards Larkin's high windows, the lyrical beyond that the romantics celebrated. These are modern balloons. Dickinson may step out into the woods but she never turns her back on the Church, tradition, and the rhythms of religious order with its celebration of a Divine Order. Dickinson is reminding us of the reasons why we prize ascension: as an earth-escaping leap of the soul. In this she remains, as Malroux so clearly perceives, faithful to the Calvinist faith that shaped her morality, her aspiration, and her aesthetics.

Malroux is a modern translator from the French free-verse tradition. She could instead have chosen to translate Dickinson into alexandrines like those of Hugo or Corneille, to sing and celebrate creation. Technically nothing opposes such a strategy. But she chose not to; that choice would have gone against the grain for Malroux and prevailing tastes in French today. Why? French contemporaries like to believe that poetry is by nature free. There is something vaguely irritating for French readers in Dickinson's relentless, hymn-like rhythms. Hugo seems to belong to another age, and to my knowledge no French students today read Corneille for pleasure. Meter has gone out of fashion and, apart from period-piece translations, the alexandrine is no longer welcome. In French Shakespeare translations, it is the poignant, expressive free rhythms of Jean-Michel Déprats that have asserted themselves over the past two decades. In contemporary verse, at any rate, the alexandrine is tolerated and appreciated only if it emerges spontaneously as a traditional refrain and then fades away as other rhythms take over. In this light Malroux's choice to free up Dickinson's rhythms can be seen as an attempt to modernize Dickinson as much as an easy way out. She makes Dickinson more palatable to French readers who are ill at ease with their own classical metrical tradition.

What is untranslatable often transpires to be what an age refuses to hear, more than what is linguistically or technically impossible. For many years it was maintained that isochrony was unthinkable in recitations of French poems or in spoken French.[7] But French rap rhythms broke away from tradition by asserting their strong-stress meters. Even at the very fundamental level of accentuation, language often proves more flexible and permeable than expected. Nevertheless, something that Antoine Berman would have called the *étrangété* (1985; Venuti 2005) of the text in Dickinson's verse resists translation into contemporary French, and that is faith. Hugo's faith is rarely discussed in class by teachers today. His romantic faith in harmony with the universe seems quaint and attractive, but only in the same way that Californian New Age versions of Zen, Tao, and the art of living have spread throughout French culture today.

Dickinson's faith, her prayers, her perplexity, and her dialogue with her soul are of an entirely different order, however. They resound within a very different world, and they force us to enter that world and to follow the lyrical subject's path in seeking an exit from the physical and an entry into the metaphysical world. This is the cultural, which cannot be assimilated, as Meschonnic reminds us when he speaks of the difficulty of translating poems. His reminder that we should not confuse the untranslatable with the untranslated is relevant here. The untranslated Dickinson is a Christian voice that sings in tune and in time—but not always in tune and not always in time—with the Protestant hymns of her times.

Malroux is a remarkable translator who shows great sensibility of Dickinson's world. She is attracted to that world and she praises it with a lucid understanding. She speaks of "those moments of terrestrial joy that she [Dickinson] exalts, the moments of epiphany that she experiences," and she argues that without them, Dickinson's poetry "would lose both its contours and its depth" (Malroux 2007a: 23; my translation). But Malroux remains a stranger to that world, however much she marvels over it. She gravitates towards it without entering, and without truly desiring to penetrate it. Malroux remains in this sense a spectator, where Dickinson is crucially a perplexed and protesting believer. This difference explains to some extent Malroux's atheistic aesthetics. Though Malroux does not appear to believe in the celebration of creation that Hugo and Shelley espoused, she does show an inverted spiritual craving. Only it is the return to earth, the collision with the physical, that excites and ravishes Malroux. She does not believe in the elevation of believers to their god; on the other hand, she is very much enamoured of the fall.

These predilections make Malroux all too modern and all too tangled up in the movement of post-Christian thought and feeling. Like Dickinson's soul-balloon, she might rise up, but only the deflation of inspiration sounds real to Malroux—the fall is inevitable, the fall is real. God is, but only in the sense that God is dead. In a revealing remark, Malroux regrets Dickinson's faith, despite her rebellious spirit. The translator manifestly approves of rebellion, no doubt because rebellion is on the side of freedom, and for her, freedom is on the side of poetry. But, as already noted, she laments that Dickinson appears "incapable of renouncing her faith." This is not the kind of objection to faith that stands on moral grounds; Malroux appears to disapprove of Dickinson's faith on aesthetic grounds. Believing in God is in bad taste. That is a faith from which Malroux and her French readers are excluded. There is something tragically inappropriate in the movement of Malroux's elegant offering: her *invitation au voyage* invites the soul to a very different destination, and it is the movement of her verse that invites French readers. Dickinson never ceases to celebrate the cosmos and to sing of creation, even when her chant is disenchanted. Paradoxically, Malroux's successful lines miss the beat that Dickinson's heart misses when her undulating rhythm evokes the longing of the striving soul with its palpably physical élan. The physical nature of Dickinson's metaphysical élan still remains to be introduced in French; she still awaits her French Liepe.

What Liepe Hears

The meeting of Emily Dickinson and the German translator Gertrud Liepe produced one of those great encounters that verse translation can bring about. In 1970 Liepe published a large selection of Dickinson's poems in Stuttgart with the publishing house Philipp Reclam. Like those of her French counterparts, her translations show a great sensibility of Dickinson's lexis. Like Edna St. Vincent Millay, Frank Pearce Sturm, and Roy Campbell in their organic translations of Baudelaire, Liepe enters into her poet's world view, and when she re-emerges in her own tongue, she finds a language in accord with the American poet's outlook.

Like those great Baudelaire translators, Liepe effortlessly reshuffles ideas and images in order to concoct a coherent mood. When she improvises, Liepe remains in harmony with Dickinson's world and in pace with the trajectory of her ways of thinking and feeling. Like Dickinson, Liepe gropes her way towards her startling revelations, perceptions, and perplexities. Where Dickinson writes "I robbed the Woods—The trusting Woods," Liepe innovates with "Ich plünderte die Wälder— / Die vertrauenden Wälder" (Dickinson 1970a: 10–11). "Plündern" (pillage) dovetails perfectly with the poem.

Like Malroux, Liepe enters into the organization of ideas and the unconscious patterning of Dickinson's thinking. She intuits its oppositions and juxtapositions, and she jumps to match the poem's erratic coupling of ideas. She sets up the contrasts between words, perplexing the reader with distorted improvisations on collocations from everyday speech. In this way Liepe avoids that fault so characteristic of bad translations that aspire to sound natural, something that Messiaen, with his didactic professorial tone, inevitably falls prey to. Messiaen is a target-oriented translator who tailors a radically personal poetics into appropriate French diction. Liepe, on the other hand, preserves and improvises on Dickinson's quirky innovations. This is not how she surpasses her French counterparts Forgue and Malroux, however. It is in the movement and organization of her versification that Liepe excels.

Liepe does not limit herself to a line-by-line translation, like Denis and Messiaen, and that allows her to use line ends for expressive effect. It allows her to reshape the movement of the lines and insist on expressive pauses. Most of all, freeing up the syntax allows her to enter Dickinson's style by reshaping the phrase in order to make line ends rhyme. Unlike the French translations, Liepe's translations rhyme, and rhyme well.

This strategy forms part of an ambiguous and ambivalent poetics that is proper to Dickinson and that Liepe successfully restages. The form of the romantic poem celebrating creation is forged anew, but there is an implicit critique of that romanticism. The lyricism that is sung in Liepe's versions of Dickinson's poems is not the unequivocal ecstasy of the religious tradition of Hugo, nor is it close to Shelley's Neoplatonism, with its perception of the pure transcendental forms of hidden reality. Dickinson's romanticism is a kind of thinking and feeling in perplexity. This explains the precarity of her line ends, her pauses, and the meaningful gulfs that open up when unusual words are juxtaposed. Dickinson has something akin to the lucid ecstasy of Saint Teresa of Ávila, the Spanish nun and founder of a monastic order who was said to be visited by the angels, and who felt the penetrating force of spiritual inspiration in both her heart and her entrails. In Dickinson there is pain in inspiration, but also, almost perversely, a certain prose. This ambivalence forms part of Dickinson's practice of re-enchanting the world of everyday things and elevating the commonplace to a transcendental plane. Conversely, she doesn't hesitate to bring the metaphysical back to the physical reality of everyday life in an act of bathos. She preserves, reasserts, and even consolidates oppositions and frontiers while she undermines them ironically and controverts them.

In the following poem, "Besides the Autumn poets sing," instead of singing the poetry of springtime, Dickinson sings the prose of autumn. She lists pleasant, pretty things—for example, a squirrel scampering about in the fog and mist—but she moves beyond facile celebration of an azure-blue sky, the colour of Christ's robes, in contemplating her own, very real world of autumn prose. This is how Dickinson invites us into the movement of celebration to scale the stairs of everyday life towards the divine. As Liepe intuitively knows, meter is part of that metaphysical movement, and that is what makes her rhymed metrical translation so much more than a reassuring melody or an exercise in technical style.

Besides the Autumn poets sing	Neben den Herbstpoeten singen
A few prosaic days	Einige prosaische Tage
A little this side of the snow	Ein wenig diesseits von dem Schnee
And that side of the Haze—	Und jenseits vom Dunst im Hage—
[...]	[...]
Perhaps a squirrel may remain—	Vielleicht bleibt noch ein Eichkatz—
My sentiments to share—	Meine Gefühle zu stillen—
Grant me, Oh Lord, a sunny mind—	Gib mir, o Herr, ein sonnig Gemüt—
Thy windy will to bear!	Für deinen windigen Willen!
(Dickinson 2016: 82)	(Dickinson 1970a: 21)

In fairness to our French translators, it must be remembered that German meters are closer to English ones. Indeed, accentuation is one of those fundamental facts of languages that reminds us of their origin. English in this sense is clearly a Germanic language. As I argue in my discussion of Christoph Küper's metrics in chapter 3 (see page 97), there is a very real possibility of transposing the binary scansion of Attridge to German metrics. Whether German specialists concur on this question remains to be seen, but one thing is certain: rule-bound conventional systems such as meter take on much the same form in both modern German and modern English. This fact inevitably facilitates the transposition of meter at a formal and theoretical level. Syllable count proves important in German verse; often it plays a greater role than it does in the free strong-stress verse of the English or Scottish ballads. Nonetheless, in both German and English, meter clearly depends more on accentual beating and the undulating alternation of weak and strong syllables. If we apply Attridge's scansion (1982) to Liepe's verse, we can discern its clearly metrical nature.

Neben den Herbstpoeten singen
B   o B   oBoBo

Einige prosaische Tage
B   o B o   Bo

Ein wenig diesseits von dem Schnee
o   Bo   B o   B o   B

Und jenseits vom Dunst im Hage –
O   B   o   B   o   Bo

[...]

Vielleicht bleibt noch ein Eichkatz –
o   B   o   B   o   B   o

Meine Gefühle zu stillen—
B   o   B   o   B o

Gib mir, o Herr, ein sonnig Gemüt—
B   o   B   o   B   o   B

Für deinen windigen Willen!
o   B o   B   o   B   o

Something approaching the strong-stress ballad rhythm asserts itself in Liepe's translation. This makes the verse resonate more fully in the ears of German readers who are familiar with their own folk poetry. Her verse proves flexible, allowing multiple unaccented syllables between the metrical accents, the beats.

Küper, in his *Sprache und Metrum* (Language and Meter, 1988), would scan these lines otherwise, using / to mark accents and X to mark unaccented syllables. Nevertheless, as readers will remember, Küper has integrated the ideas of promotion and demotion in his German scansion, and he would no doubt come up with a scansion that conforms more or less to the one I suggest here.

On a formal, linguistic level, it is clear that things are easier for Liepe than for her French counterparts. We should not, however, underestimate Liepe's achievement, because the technical success of a translation is always secondary. The various metrical archaizers, metrical ennoblers, and metrical sweeteners, with their formal translations of Baudelaire's poems, should have made this patently clear. Many verse translations end up as tiresome doggerel, versification in the worst sense of the term. The question is, do Liepe's poems move meaningfully? Or has she, like the metrical sweeteners, privileged the form at the expense of the content? Has she imposed a mechanical structure on the dismantled and reassembled meaning? Do Dickinson's ideas organize themselves meaningfully in their new German form?

The French translators stopped short of this question. Delphy and Malroux both contend that translating English rhythms is impossible. But our comparative versification should have unmasked this as a spurious prejudice, one that focuses on neither linguistic form nor poetic function. It is not the lack of the tetrameter or the pentameter in French that renders French translations less expressive. It is the formulation of the form that makes sense. It is the way the voice inhabits the verse that matters.

Death poses less difficulty than faith for French readers and critics. Death, as we know, is one of Dickinson's preoccupations, and negation, more than the celebration of creation, is altogether more in phase with modernist and postmodernist aesthetics. But it is far from certain that Malroux, Forgue, and their fellow translators read the same meaning into death and negation that Dickinson does. In "Poem 1551" Dickinson upbraids God for his absence and for taking back into his divine eternity the souls of the living. Malroux appears to read a resistance to faith itself in this protest (Dickinson 2007a: 17). As Forgue knew, Dickinson was above all else a Protestant, and her protest could turn against God himself. This is what Forgue means when he suggests that Dickinson showed "a sort of blaspheming masochism" (Dickinson 1970b: 31). Her feelings of helplessness and impotence in the face of mourning contaminate her conception of God, whose divine hand is amputated in her representation of the all-powerful presence.

In contrast to the French translators, Liepe produces a translation that reproduces the biting irony of Dickinson's verse.

Those—dying then,	Jene—die damals starb**en**,
Knew where they w**ent**—	Wu**ßten** wohin sie ging**en**—
They went to God's Right **Hand**—	Sie gingen zu Gottes rechter H**and**—
That Hand is amputated now	Jene Hand hat man abgenomm**en**
And God cannot be found—	Gott hat sich fortgew**andt**—
(Dickinson 2016: 638)	(Dickinson 1970a: 175; emphasis added)

The German rhyme "Hand/fortgewandt" that links the third-last and last lines underscores the maiming of Dickinson's demoted deity—God has gone on his way. This is the end of the "good news" that the New Testament proclaims. This rhyme is all the more striking since neither the assonance that sounds at the ends of Liepe's lines (with "-en") nor her rhymes can be found in the original poem. Like Malroux at her best, Liepe is working within the framework of Dickinson's poetics, innovating in the spirit of her sound patterning, linking ideas together to make the poem more expressive. Malroux remains what I have called a free-verse domesticator, trimming Dickinson's metrics to contemporary tastes and downplaying the metaphysical angst that rhythmic tension engenders. Liepe instead approaches the ideal of organic translation, in which the voice resounds within the rhythmic patterning of the versification.

Her search for God proves to be a laborious quest, but for Dickinson it remains a quest, as seen in "Poem 1564." Liepe's translation introduces rhymes that consolidate the impression of hymn-like rhythm so characteristic of much of Dickinson's verse. Liepe's lines sing their celebration of the world while never failing to question the relationship between man and God (or woman and God). With a wonderful effect of ambivalence, the rhymes that help frame the following lines stress what is negated: "ohne Angst"—fearlessly, painlessly, the soul leaps across the mystery.

Pass to thy Rendezvous of Light,	Geh zu deinem Rendez-vous mit dem Licht
Pangless except for us—	Ohne uns—ohne **Angst**—
Who slowly ford the Mystery	Während wir das Geheimnis durchfurchen
Which thou hast leaped across!	Das du überspr**angst**!
(Dickinson 2016: 729)	(Dickinson 1970a: 175; emphasis added)

Rhyming "Angst" and "übersprangst" (leaping across) shows the genius of the translator in perfectly mirroring Dickinson's half-rhymes and the inspired patterning characteristic of her verse. Liepe's is a meaningful rhyme worthy of the great metaphysical poet George Herbert (1593–1633), who strove to enter into harmonious communion with the divine presence by rhyming harmoniously, to echo the order of the divine cosmos. Celebrating God in rhymes is an act of union in itself, and Liepe mirrors the practice to which Herbert aspired (and Eliot craved) when she rhymes her lines in the same inspired way as the poet she translates.

At times the language seems to conspire with Liepe to make translating seem simple.

Beauty crowds me till I die	Schönheit bedrängt mich bis ich sterbe
Beauty mercy have on me	Schönheit sei gnädig mit mir
But if I expire to-day	Doch wenn ich heute scheide
Let it be in sight of thee—	Sei es im Anblick von dir—
(Dickinson 2016: 662)	(Dickinson 1970a: 185)

Nobody is perfect, as they say, and Liepe does not always manage to sustain her inspired response to Dickinson's poetry. In the following poem, the loss of the rhyme is regrettable. The effect of the rhymes in the English original sets in play a kind of ironic anti-hymn. Nothing in the translation, however, engenders the mood of Dickinson's meaning.

Title divine—is **mine**!	Der göttliche Titel—ist mein!
The Wife—without the **Sign**!	Frau—ohne das Zeichen!
Acute Degree—conferred on **me**—	Augenblickswürde—mir verliehen—
Empress of **Cavalry**!	Kaiserin von Golgatha!
(Dickinson 2016: 701; emphasis added)	(Dickinson 1970a: 141)

Rhyming "me" with "Cavalry" is characteristic of Dickinson, and Liepe offers nothing in its stead to mirror the rhyme in this poem, which satirizes the act of union with an absent presence who affords neither status nor comfort to the married partner.

On the whole, however, the verse of Liepe's translation resounds with a solid, reassuring metrical movement that not only structures the poem as a whole but allows the meaningful foregrounding of ideas, significant links made in the forceful act of expression using sound. In Dickinson's and Liepe's lines, we find a poetry of ecstasy that carries us away. The poem rocks us gently, nudging us to the brink of bliss, towards a spiritual encounter. At times it offers us transcendence; at times it opens up the abyss of confusion, contradiction, and loss, leaving us puzzled, perplexed, or profoundly moved. Not all readers are sensitive to such an invitation, and even Malroux, whose sensibility of Dickinson's aspirations is acute, resists that invitation. This is the crux of our comparative versification, and the test of its usefulness for translation studies. Differentiating between Liepe and Malroux—two wonderful translators—helps us ask the crucial question about this difficult art: how does the voice emerge in the versification? Liepe reaches beyond Malroux, not because she grasps that Dickinson's verse is a poetry of revelation, but because she perceives that revelation is revealed as much in the movement as in the meaning.

Dickinson is a poet, and a poet of meters and measures. As she herself puts it in "Poem 657," she lives in poetry, "in a fairer House than Prose." She lives within the imagination, within the possible, and her imagination moves in measured movement. In the act of creation (an intellectual act), Dickinson demonstrates that the mind belongs in the spirit. She sings the spirit and she enters into her ecstasy (or seeks to enter it) in entering into poetry. Dickinson could not conceive of a free-verse or prosaic celebration of creation. Nor would she have appreciated a meterless rumination upon the mind that she affirmed was greater than the sky. Prose—unorganized or uninspired in harmonious form—would be inappropriate; its lack of metrical order would fail to echo the divine order. The mind was a gift from the divine mind, the spirit of God. Meter forms part of the bond that links mind to spirit, inviting us to intuit God's presence. Liepe responds perfectly to this inspired poetry.

I dwell in Possibility— A fairer House than Prose— More numerous of Windows— Superior—for Doors—	Ich wohne in der Möglichkeit— Ein fensterreiches Haus— Viel heller als die Wirklichkeit Mit Türen—ein und aus—
Of Chambers as the Cedars— Impregnable of eye— And for an everlasting Roof The Gambrels of the Sky—	Mit Kammern wie die Zedern— Dem Auge unsichtbar— Und als ein ewigliches Dach Des Himmels Giebelschar—
Of Visitors—the fairest— For Occupation—This— The spreading wide my narrow Hands To gather Paradise—	Besucher—die allerschönsten— Meine Berufung—dies— Die schmalen Hände weit zu breiten Zu ernten Paradies—
(Dickinson 2016: 233)	(Dickinson 1970a: 107)

The only criticism that can be made is that Liepe's translation drops the prose of the world, of which her compatriot Hegel spoke so eloquently (Rose 1995: 140). Opting for the word "Wirklichkeit" (reality) is a step down. Liepe makes up for that somewhat when she translates "gather Paradise" in the final stanza as "ernten Paradies" (harvest Paradise).

Liepe makes the leap of faith and writes from within Dickinson's poetics and from within her world view. Malroux sings Dickinson beautifully, but she sings another poetry, with another voice—more sober, more modern, more skeptical. Ultimately, Malroux is more tempted by prose of the world. True, Dickinson herself will meet Malroux on the road halfway to that "house of prose," but she resists it. She cleaves to the divine presence. Even in her most unsettled moods, in her most perplexed states, she chips and chisels her way through the walls of prose in order to break into inspiration.

It will be clear, then, that prose cannot be considered simply a style of writing. Style is not a simple aesthetic question; it is a metaphysical stance. You take your place, either in poetry or in prose. Prose opposes poetry to this extent at least, for all the innovations of free verse.

Within Dickinson's aesthetics, prose opposes transcendence. Dickinson does not sing an unequivocal inspiration—she is no Whitman. In some respects she is closer to Herbert and Eliot in their ruminations on doubt and spiritual crisis. She refuses to exclude doubt and dejection from belief, and this makes her different from poets who, like Hugo, maintain the schism between the real and the ideal, the suffering of this world and the beatitude of the next. Her sublime is always tinged with shadow. The sad "Empress of Cavalry" is a very real dimension of her faith and her sensibility. Modern readers often fail to respond to some of her darker poems, but even her most sombre ones are always tinged with faith, and that makes many of them authentic celebrations of the joy of existence. In contrast to Baudelaire's half-hearted celebration of the reality that lies beyond the symbols of nature, which speaks to him in confused speech in his "Correspondances," Dickinson possesses that capacity to marvel over the sparrow and the earthworm and contemplate their place within the divine order. This was no less a part of her than her doubt, and it forms one of the main pillars of her house of poetry. In verse she gives herself to an orgy of the senses as a "Debauchee of Dew." The voice that sings the senses and murmurs the doubts of a tortured, aspiring mind makes itself heard in Liepe's versions. Like Dickinson's, Liepe's lines reach out to the world, and that world is both palpably physical in its metaphysical sphere and metaphysical in its earthy physical immediacy. Malroux's response is spiritual, subtle, sensitive, authentic, and poetic. A rhythmic dimension that is as metaphysical as it is physical makes her response to Dickinson a reformulation, however, whereas Liepe's translation takes us into an encounter. Juxtaposing the French and German versions with the original "Poem 214" should help make this point.

I taste a liquor never brewed—
From Tankards scooped in Pearl—
Not all the Frankfort Berries
Yield such an Alcohol!

Inebriate of Air—am I—
And Debauchee of Dew—
Reeling—thro endless summer days—
From inns of molten Blue—

When 'Landlords' turn the drunken Bee
Out of the Foxglove's door—
When Butterflies—renounce their 'drams'—
I shall but drink the more!

Till Seraphs swing their snowy Hats—
And Saints—to windows run—
To see the little Tippler
From Manzanilla come!

        (Dickinson 2016: 135)

Je goûte une liqueur jamais brassée—
Dans les Chopes de Perle taillée—
Nulle Baie de Francfort ne saurait
Livrer Alcool pareil!

À moi—Soûleries d'Air—Orgies de Rosées—
Aux jours sans fin de l'été
Je titube—sur le pas des cabarets
De l'Azur en Fusion

Hors de la Digitale, boute,
'Aubergiste,' l'Abeille ivre—
Papillon—renonce à ta 'goutte'—
Moi je boirai plus encore !

Les Anges agiteront leur neigeux
   Chapeau—
Les Saints—à la vitre accourront—
Pour voir, de Manzanilla venue—
Passer la petite Poivrote!

    (Malroux, in Dickinson 1989: 33)

Ich koste niegebrauten Trank—
Aus Krügen in Perlen gespeist—
Nicht alle Frankfurter Beeren
Ergeben solch einen Geist!

Berauscht von Luft—bin ich—
Und verführt von Tau—
Taumle—den endlosen Sommertag—
Aus Schenken von Schmelzendem Blau—

Treiben die 'Wirte' die trunkene Biene
Von des Fingerhuts Tür—
Entsagt der Schmetterling—seinem
   'Schnaps'—
Ich trinke mehr dafür!

Bis Engel die schneeigen Hüte schwingen—
Und Heilige—am Fenster stehen—
Den kleinen Trunkenbold
An die—Sonne gelehnt zu sehn—

    (Liepe, in Dickinson 1970a: 27)

The Untranslatable and the Untranslated

It is argued that each generation gets the politicians it deserves. Perhaps that is true of translators and translation theory too. Our period no longer belongs to George Steiner with his hermeneutics of translation (1975). It belongs to Lawrence Venuti (1995, 2004) with his concept of ethnocentric translation and the poetics of postmodernism. In a way it no longer belongs to Antoine Berman, who inspired Venuti, or to Meschonnic, who taught Berman most of his key concepts. Yet Meschonnic was no doubt right in believing that each period translates what it can. It answers what it can hear, what it can understand.

To assume that Dickinson's first translators failed to understand her would be grotesque and unfair. They grappled with the poet and dragged her into the French tradition, which was hostile to many facets of her poetry. Those first translators strove to understand her more than anything else. Yet in seeking to penetrate her meanings and extract the sense of her verse, they failed to perceive the meaning of the movement of her verse. They had little sense for rhythm and they failed to understand Dickinson's rhythmic sensibility, or the way her rhythms enabled her to enter into phase with and move her English-speaking readers. Forgue understood better than his predecessors the poetics of rupture and dissonance, but neither he nor Malroux perceived the necessity of structure and order for either the poetics of the poet or the metaphysics that she espoused. The very protest that she made in resisting order proved impossible and even inconceivable for them without the order that meter erects.

In a sense, each translator understands something of Dickinson. This is the lesson that translation critics like ourselves must bear in mind. After they are finished with evaluation, critics—with their judgmental, appraising, analytical minds—would do well to return to the works of the translators, simply to listen to all the wonderful fragments and phrases that do break through into a foreign tongue. Critics must inevitably show a painstaking attention to detail, but this should not blind them to all the facets of the poet that have been re-carved, even in translations that disappoint at one level or another. Each of Dickinson's translators passes on an interpretation of many of the facets of the poet. Their work enriches the French tradition. Native speakers of English may be skeptical, but it is thanks to the work of translators that playwrights such as Shakespeare and poets such as Whitman, Donne, and Dickinson have become part of the French tradition and resound within the French imagination. Each translator has appropriated Dickinson, but since the entire English-speaking world has not been expropriated, it would be silly to cry theft. Ultimately nobody has been robbed, nobody has been betrayed.

As a creative response, translation nonetheless depends on the ear we lend to the poet. This point forms part of the aesthetics of Berman's and Meschonnic's translation poetics. A voice should respond to a voice, a poem should be offered when reacting to a poem. These actions involve reaching out into the foreign and resisting the moulds that contemporary trends and fashions promote and consolidate.

Liepe has a lesson to teach the French translators: responding to Dickinson means reaching beyond the skepticism of our times and beyond the poetics of free verse. It means reaching out towards the spiritual adventure of a spirit that refuses to live in the house of prose. That is a challenge. Delphy has opened up new horizons for French lovers of Dickinson's poems, but she does not know what to do with her poetry. Perhaps, in the years to come, a poet will answer Dickinson's resolute resistance to the house of prose with a kind of poetry in French that echoes the poet. That is certainly a challenge, but if our study of voice and versification has proved anything, it should by now have shown that translating poetry is indeed possible. New translations, like those of Millay and Liepe, keep pushing back the boundaries of what we conceive of as the translatable.

Notes

1. Hugo's voice is anything but simple and naive. Unlike Baudelaire, he tends to lift up the reader from the crassness and confusion of the workaday world into an unequivocal celebration of existence and creation. Unlike Dickinson's poetry, in which transcendence usually implies tension and poetic inspiration is problematical and perplexing, Hugo's inspirations always open the door to transcendence as a solution. The following poem, "C'est le Seigneur, le Seigneur Dieu!" makes this movement clear.

Extase
J'étais seul près des flots, par une nuit d'étoiles,
Pas un nuage aux cieux, sur les mers pas de voiles.
Mes yeux plongeaient plus loin que le monde réel.
Et les bois, et les monts, et toute la nature,
Semblaient interroger dans un confus murmure
    Les flots des mers, les feux du ciel.

Et les étoiles d'or, légions infinies,
À voix haute, à voix basse, avec mille harmonies,
Disaient, en inclinant leurs couronnes de feu;
Et les flots bleus, que rien ne gouverne et n'arrête,
Disaient, en recourbant l'écume de leur crête:

"C'est le Seigneur, le Seigneur Dieu!"

(Rees 1990: 43)

2. The gender of God is of course subject to socio-historical constraints. Societies invent spiritual hierarchies along the same lines as the social hierarchies that organize their lives. In recent years feminist translators have been contesting masculinist translation strategies. See Luise von Flotow's fascinating work on feminist translations of religious texts (1997) and Rim Hassen's similar work on women translators of the Koran (2011). Meschonnic's extensive notes to his translations of books of the Hebrew Bible also provide much evidence that translators have tended to eliminate the feminine, and most of all the feminine side of God (2001a, 2002, 2003). Forgiveness is perceived by Jonah, for example, as a maternal trait, something that is invariably effaced in English and French versions of the Old Testament, which are, of course, often filtered through Latin. Dickinson tends not to contradict or critique gendered references to the masculine Christian God, but her playful irony does undermine the idea of a lofty power that towers above us. Much in the same way that wives and children ironically mock the father figure, God is subject to playful parody by Dickinson. She pokes fun at the patriarchal divine presence even while evidently revering him.

3. This edition would be enlarged by the later Gallimard edition (Dickinson 2007a).

4. In recent years feminist rereadings of literature and challenges to translation studies as a discipline have raised many valid and urgent questions. But riding on the wave of such political reappraisals was the celebration of *écriture féminine* and, by extension, the female translator (see Jones 2008). In the framework of such debates the female translator

could be seen as a doubly marginalized figure, both as a woman and as a translator. A naive reader might suppose that it is because Malroux is a woman that she demonstrates greater sensitivity than her male predecessors to Dickinson's orality. This would seem to be disproven, however (as I argue in Underhill 2011) by the fact that Patrick Reumaux's 1998 translation (Dickinson 2007b) bears much in common with Malroux's, while Françoise Delphy's project (Dickinson 2009) is closer to the translations of Forgue, Bosquet, and Messiaen. Nevertheless it is understandable that some readers might be tempted to believe in some kind of feminine encounter when we examine Malroux's versions of Dickinson.

5. Malroux speaks of "extrême virtuosité des rimes . . . se terminant par des occlusives labiales et . . . par des dentales" (Dickinson 2007a: 400).
6. For more on the rhythms of rupture in Eliot and their metaphysical implications, see Underhill 2006b.
7. French chanting, in the form practised in religious ceremonies, for example, depends on the lengthening of vowels and insists on what Morier calls the "horizontal accent" (1961: 19–27), but it does not require that beats return at regular intervals.

CHAPTER 10

A Final Word

Like translating itself, reading this study of voice and versification may well have proven to be hard work. My intention from the beginning to the end, and at every step along the way, was to insist that however hard it proves, translating poems is possible. Part of my task involved demonstrating that theories and approaches to translation often distort this fact. What translators do, theory often refuses to acknowledge, and when it comes to metrics and versification, theories often get in the way rather than opening up the way to creative responses to poems. Instead of offering to enlighten translators with lucid ideas, useful concepts, and well-defined terms, theories often lead to confusion and pessimism and into a sterile state in which we no longer apprehend poems, either as readers or as translators.

A whole tradition reduces poems to poetry and poetry to form. Stylistics and poetics are not innocent in this process of schematic reductionism and sterile abstraction. Often theories send us in unhelpful directions. In recent decades translation theory has tended to promote the political—for example, in the defence of gender, queer studies, or the alterity of the foreign text—at the expense of poetics. In themselves, such approaches are opening up new avenues of thought. Translation studies is certainly a crucial field for such questions, being a crossroads for academic disciplines. Debates are vibrant and vital. Nevertheless, as an indirect consequence of these political pursuits, cultivating an ear to apprehend the moving rhymes and rhythms of poetry, free or metrical, has mostly been neglected. The importance of rhythm is obvious to each generation, and this generation, in both French- and English-speaking countries, is no less aware of the importance of rhythm—in music, in songs, in speech out on the streets. But bad theory and a change in literary tastes have tended to deaden curiosity about analyzing rhythm, and inevitably this has not helped us to formulate a rigorous or even relatively reliable means of describing and analyzing it. Theory, in poetics and translation theory at least, is proving less inclined to listen to the poem.

I originally intended to include more poems and fewer extracts. I would have liked to include more case studies. But the patience of editors and readers is not elastic, and 600-page books are no longer welcome (if they ever truly were). This academic treatise has moved swiftly through a vast array of approaches to translation theory, poetics, and the versifications of different languages. I have endeavoured to take readers beyond existing theories and approaches. Derek Attridge, with his theory of metrics; Henri Meschonnic, with his theory of the poetics of translating; and Jiří Levý, with his comparative versification, have aided me in this task. I have laboured to move beyond form, beyond meter, and beyond the dichotomies that provisionally prove useful in ordering the approaches of translators but break down when we begin to analyze what actually goes on in practice.

In moving beyond form, I was not aiming at a nebulous beyond, reaching into the world of escapists and romantics. I was focusing on a resolutely pragmatic goal: I intend this work to help us to return poems when translating. First, we must prevent the poetics from perverting our apprehension of poems. Next, we must prevent translation theories from dictating procedures that prove inappropriate for handling the delicate dynamics of the poem. Accomplishing these goals has entailed reappraising what is involved in thinking through the process of translating poems.

There is an unresolved cold war going on between theory and practice. On one side, intuition denounces analysis; on the other, analysis despairs of intuition's woolly subterfuges that pose as explanations. Practising translators can't see the point of theory, and theoreticians disparage and despair at the lack of conceptual rigour of practising translators, at least when explaining their practice and principles. Standing with Levý, Attridge, Meschonnic, and Clive Scott, I believe in a theory that informs practice, by rigorously analyzing my own mode of translating and in scrutinizing the efforts of others. This means thinking through practice and putting into practice principles that correspond to poems. This theory cannot be simply applied. It is more a mode of thinking and feeling, the sensibility required for translating as an art. It is a response, an apprehension of the poem.

But speaking of sensibility and art does not mean we should abandon theory or learning the art or the trade of translating. Learning to apprehend poems is something that can be cultivated, and this book has made as cogent a case as possible in arguing that rigorous analysis of the rhythmic elements can help develop our poetic sensibility. This remains very much a Poundian stance. The act of translating can be clarified with lucid and rigorous conceptual analysis, but can we teach people to translate poems? That remains to be seen. We can, however, introduce students to the difficulties involved in translating poems, and this act in itself is worthwhile.

Poetry has something of profound importance to teach us about language. Language cannot be reduced to communication, to meaning. And meaning, and what we express, cannot be reduced to the expression of intentions. Often we move people without knowing why or how. Poetry highlights the modes of expression inherent in rhythm, repetition, stress, intonation, and . . . dramatic pausing. Translators must respond to those linguistic modes of expression. They must face up to the fact that foreign languages move differently and that foreign poets mobilize and marshal the elements at their disposal in unique ways of their own. If the voice of a poet makes itself heard in a foreign language, it is by utilizing the resources of that language. Great poets invariably transform their own languages, not only with their diction and their own personal idiolect but also by the way they shape phrasing, repetition, and sound patterning. This is the voice that can be heard in a poet's versification. This is the voice that is worth translating.

If we have spent so much time defining and disentangling theories related to the syllable and the stress, and if we have pondered the complexities and the ramifications of meters, rhythms, and rhyming, it was to rescue form from a formalistic conception of those elements. If versification is to be of any use, it must help us discern how voices make themselves heard in poems. It must show why meaningful words become powerfully moving. This battle must be fought within stylistics and poetics as disciplines. Inadequate theories of metrics tend to put students off poetry, and certainly such theories put them off analyzing poems. This is partly because those pseudo-theories fail to represent and explain what readers feel when they read or hear poems. This situation makes the cause of comparative versification all the more an uphill struggle. Two things offer hope: poems continue to be translated—and well translated, too—and translators frequently feel the urge to explain what they are trying to achieve in their attempts.

Inevitably a work like this one, one that tries to carve out a new field of scholarship or to retrace the outlines of a poetics that has fallen by the wayside, will be critical by nature. I make no apologies for this. We cannot compare translations without betraying our opinions and our sympathies. We respond to poems, and if poetics is of any use, it makes itself useful by explicating the reasons for our aesthetic responses. In all of the fields covered, from metrics and comparative versification to translation theory, it has been necessary to take a stance. My stance has been to defend the poem—the individual poem. My goal was to explain how it can live on in a foreign tongue and in a foreign tradition. I have inevitably been led to criticize a great number of translators. If thinkers and translators truly care about translating poems (as I believe they do), then they will not take sincere criticism badly. They will judge this work not so much in terms of the criticisms I have made of their approaches and efforts as in terms of the steps I have managed to take in thinking through the difficult task in which we are all engaged.

Before us and beyond us lies the poem. Translating it will always remain somewhat mysterious. Inevitably, if we abandon intuition, we will fail to intuit the whole. We will find ourselves stranded in the midst of the fragments that analysis leaves us. Poems move. They move us because they move dynamically. If there is a life in them, it is because we hear a voice in the versification of the poem. This is the metaphysics that animates the matter of poems and elevates the parts to something that transcends them.

True, we have spent many pages dismantling the poem and striving to understand how translators put it back together again. This analysis of details helps explicate the intuitive synthesis that constitutes our impression of the poem. Those who refuse to accept that there is any point in pulling poems apart will have lost patience with the present endeavour long ago. For my own part, I have little sympathy for the anti-theory faction among poetry-lovers. I believe that love entails contemplating the perfection of the parts and the way they fit together as a moving whole. There is a mystery in that contemplation, a profound encounter. It begins and ends in listening. Good translators speak to us in their translations, those newly sprung poems. And like those people we enjoy speaking to, good translators speak to us because they know how to listen.

Glossary

APPROPRIATORS Translators who take the poem and assimilate it as their own poem. What they are trying to do with it, they alone know. The value of their translation appropriation depends on the power and the originality of what they do with the original poem. There is little point in asking, therefore, what is left of the original poem. What counts is what is created. Appropriation is closely linked to transcreation, although in many transcreations an attempt to give a new voice to the original poem is sustained. In appropriation, the original is often taken as raw material, a source of inspiration, not as an aim. *See also* Transcreators.

ARCHAIZERS Translators who show a predilection for archaic words and syntax. They appear to believe that poetry is a thing of the past, and that if translations sound passé they are somehow more poetic. Archaizing translation was common in Britain from the middle of the nineteenth to the middle of the twentieth century. It has since gone out of fashion, and the translations of that period often sound pompous and ludicrously outdated to us today. Because archaizing in poetry and translation is subject to fashion, however, it may come back into vogue in one form or another.

BEAT Also known as metrical accent or ictus, the strong point in an undulating movement. The beat returns between offbeats. Derek Attridge borrowed the term from music (1982). Although no one would read a poem to the metrical beating of a metronome, the idea of the beat entails what might be called a perceived regularity. In all stress-based meters, and especially in the strong-stress meters found in the folk ballad and in contemporary rap, the beat appears to return at regular intervals. Though this perceived regularity does not bear up to metrical analysis, the fact that we perceive it is crucial. Metrical beating makes metrical speech appear regular; readers and listeners partake in this heightened regularity, something very different from ordinary speech with its free, undulating rhythms. This experience is true for speakers of English and other languages with strong word stress, such as German and Russian. *See also* Offbeat.

CADENCE The free undulation of strong and weak syllables that is highlighted or foregrounded in much free verse but defies traditional scansion. Unlike meter, the cadence neither engages the reader in a metrical contract nor depends on the reader's metrical competence. In free verse that does not set up metrical beating, a cadence can often emerge, as in the verse of Ezra Pound and William Carlos Williams, only to disappear. It is the constant of Walt Whitman's verse, which defies all attempts to scan it metrically. *See also* Meter; Metrical Competence.

CLITIC GROUP Also known as the clitic word, the clitic group forms around the main syntactic accent in a series of words and functions as a semantic and intonational unit. Clitics fall into proclitics and enclitics. In "I love you" and "*Je t'aime*," the focal points are "love" and *aime*, but while English clitic groups often have both proclitics and enclitics (as is the case here), French clitic groups tend to have only proclitics. This tends to affect the way we perceive French rhythm as rising and falling and English rhythm as more varied and undulating. This variety is clearly perceived at all levels of English speech, prose and poetry. The following sentences can be divided into three clitic groups:

> I should / have come / yesterday.
> That guy / over there / is annoying me.

CLUMSY RHYME   A rhyme that draws attention to itself because of its contrived and forced character. Clumsy rhyme does not simply heat up leftover rhymes, as hackneyed rhyming does; it makes no sense at all, pointlessly foregrounding arbitrary links between words. Often clumsy rhymers make things worse for themselves by putting the weakest word second, as in rhymes like "hand"/"and" and "day"/"hey!" *See also* Formal Rhyme; Hackneyed Rhyme; Meaningful Rhyme; Rhyme.

CRITICISM   An intellectual activity in translation that involves analyzing the work of translators and theoreticians in order to discern their objectives (covert and overt) and to clearly delineate the limits of their reasoning and practices. Criticism should be distinguished from strategies of rejection and effacement. In criticizing a translated poem, we must discern the implicit aesthetics and the concept of language that are demonstrated in the choices the translator has made to preserve or privilege various facets of the original poem. *See also* Unconscious Aesthetics.

DEMOTION   The process of weakening the weight and length of a stressed syllable in a weak position in an undulating stress-based or strong-stress-based meter, explicated by Derek Attridge in the binary scansion he introduced (1982). Contrary to traditional explanations, strong syllables that do not carry the beat of the meter are never deprived of stress and cannot function as unstressed syllables. They are meaningful and they are not denied their meaning by a metrical reading, but the foregrounding of the undulating meter simply does not render them salient. In the opening lines of Shakespeare's "Sonnet 86," "full" in the first line and "too" in the second are demoted, despite their meaning:

> Was it the proud full sail of his great verse,
> Bound for the prize of all-too precious you, [...]
> (1987: 385)

These lines present what is called in traditional metrics a first-foot inversion, which is commonplace in the most metrical of iambic verse. Both would probably be read /XX/. An alternating reading (X/X/) is possible but would sound pedantically metrical. All the meaningful words can be stressed in the first line (Was, proud, full, sail, his, great, verse) and the second (Bound, for, prize, all, too, pre-, you), simply emphasizing the stress contour that underlies the meter. In both lines the meter counters the stress contour and the emotive reading it permits, by grading the stresses, highlighting the beats, and demoting the stressed syllables between them. If we choose to foreground the stress contour and attract attention to "too" in the second line, we are encouraged to redouble the relative stress on both "all" and "pre-," thereby creating a semantically charged line, heavy with meaning, but one that does not contradict the metrical pulse of the meter. *See also* Meter; Promotion; Stress Contour.

DIAERESIS The pronunciation of successive vowels as separate sounds and not as a diphthong (for instance, Chlo-ë or co-operate). Given that syllable count is more important for French verse, the manipulation of individual syllables is often more marked in it than in English verse. *See also* Elision; Synaeresis.

DOMESTICATING TRANSLATION One side of the concept of translation that Lawrence Venuti helped promote in English-speaking countries from the mid-1990s onwards (1995, 2004). It refers to the process by which translators adapt both consciously and unconsciously to the target language, the target culture, and the target audience. The ethics and aesthetics of the target culture induce the translator to censor certain facets of the text, often subconsciously. Translators reject what they do not like, downplay what is distasteful to them, and help hide what is not likely to please others. *See also* Foreignizing Translation.

DOWN-TO-EARTHERS I use this term to refer to translators who oppose the ennobling impulse to elevate poems to an ideal of a poetry that lifts us above and transcends the mundane everyday world of waking reality. Down-to-earthers obviously consider themselves closer to the world around us, and they often show a great sensitivity to the texture and hues of the world of sensorial experience. This is because they do not seek to be otherworldly. They do, however, often show a perverse taste for all that is ugly, crass, and disappointing, as if the return to reality must entail facing up to what we are tempted to turn away from. Down-to-earthers invariably revel in precisely what ennoblers show distaste for. They usually side with foreignizing translating while ennoblers often tend to be domesticators, but this is not necessarily always the case. *See also* Mixed Strategies.

ELISION   Pronunciation in which syllables are dropped (for instance, "th'other" or "I'm"). Since syllable count is more important for French verse, the manipulation of individual syllables is often more marked in it than in English verse. Multiple unstressed syllables in the offbeat position in English verse, however, will often bring about or encourage elision. *See also* Diaeresis.

ENJAMBMENT   Also known as run-on lines, enjambment means that a phrase overspills the line end and resists slowing down at that point. Enjambments are used in traditional metrics to focus attention on the movement of the line and on the line ending itself, which arrests the onward movement of the syntax. Enjambments are actually commonplace and in no way contradict the meter in English verse. The tendency in traditional metrics to focus on the rhythm only when it does not coincide with the line endings proves perverse, obscuring the constant interaction of line and phrasing in subtle, complex, and interesting ways. Together they generate impetus and bring units to a closure at the ends of lines and stanzas and within the lines themselves. A poem may show no striking enjambments and prove perfectly metrical while generating intense tension in the way the phrasing is organized and units are drawn out or brought to a close.

ENNOBLERS   Translators who like to dignify the poems they translate by using elevated language. Ennoblers may show a predilection for archaic language, but they can use any form of elevation. They often show a complementary distaste for anything ordinary or mundane. Ennoblers tend to prefer domesticating translating. They are the antipodes of Larkin and the "kitchen-sink" poetry of the second half of the twentieth century that tried to debunk outdated modes of expression. Ennoblers are countered by down-to-earthers (see above). *See also* Archaizers; Domesticating Translation.

FALLING RHYTHM   A rhythm pattern that moves from strong to weak and is therefore associated with trochaic and dactylic meters in traditional foot scansion. The connection is spurious, as Derek Attridge has demonstrated (1982). The shape of words and, to be more precise, the shape of the clitic group induces us to perceive a rising or falling rhythm. When the witches in Shakespeare's *Macbeth* chant, "Double, double, toil and trouble, / Fire burn, and cauldron bubble"

(4.1, 1987: 1324), we perceive this trochaic rhythm to be falling, but the impression would be rather similar if the line read "I hear the bubble, toil, and trouble," which traditional foot scansion would read as an iambic tetrameter with a feminine ending.

FIDELITY   A key concept for many translators and theories of translation, interpreted in very different forms. A wide variety of distinct and conflicting strategies are frequently defended in the name of fidelity. While the concept is regularly quoted as an aim or an ideal, it often turns out that translators have very different ideas in mind. Some are speaking of fidelity to the spirit, others are thinking about the mood, and yet others have the meaning of the poem in mind. Translators may suggest that we be faithful to the word, to the line, to the meter, or to the poem as a whole. All these stances imply consequences for other facets of the poem's organization. A translator who wishes to remain faithful to the poem may reorganize the phrasing and the lines. A poet who reproduces the text line by line may drop the meter and the rhyme. A prose translator may feel that he or she is preserving the essence of the poem while abandoning rhythm, meter, phrasing, rhyme, and lines.

FOREGROUNDING   A means of highlighting an element of a text and drawing attention to moments of importance. Foregrounding is used in both prose and poetry. Key moments in the narrative can be foregrounded, just as moments in a lyrical poem can. Words and lines are foregrounded by rhyme, alliteration, metaphor, and metonymy. For the specialist in Czech aesthetics Jan Mukařovský, who coined the concept (as *aktualizace*, 1964), the essential point is that foregrounding is contextual: elements are foregrounded within the structural dynamics of the text. Literary works are foregrounded in relation to other speech or writing, that is, within the context of the language system as a whole. All metrical verse is foregrounded in relation to non-metrical speech. Surprise is fundamental in foregrounding. Half-rhymes and breakdowns in rhyming are foregrounded within the context of metrical verse. When T. S. Eliot reverts to prose, this act is foregrounded within the context of the meter-bound verse of the poem. Foregrounding can refer to patterns that emerge within the poem as a whole, such as the highlighted repetition of phrases in Ted Hughes's verse, or the act of countering the meter in run-on lines at strategic moments of rhythmic intensity. Foregrounding is a key concept Foregrounding is a key concept for the Prague School of Linguistics, and for Mukařovský and Levý, but the full extent of the Czech conceptualization of the concept for language, literature and translation never emerged fully in the Western world, although the term "foregrounding" is now widely used. *See also* Rupture.

FOREIGNIZING TRANSLATION   The counterpart to domesticating translating in a dichotomy promoted by Lawrence Venuti (1995). Under the influence of Antoine Berman, who was in turn heavily influenced by his teacher Henri Meschonnic, Venuti suggested distinguishing between translators who adapt the text to the tastes and ethics of the times (domesticators) and those who allow the foreign text to shock, disrupt, or reshape those tastes (foreignizers). While Meschonnic was defending the poem and its capacity to actively transform the language by imposing its mode of signifying, Berman was doing something similar but put the accent on defending the alterity of the text, not its specificity and its value as a text in its own right. Venuti quite logically took this one step further, suggesting that we can use the language and style of foreign texts to disrupt the canon, and though he has moderated his position somewhat since 1995, it remains implicit to his approach to translating. The poem and its otherness, its value, and its specificity are quite simply forgotten as it is used to fight in the arena of postmodernist aesthetics. For reasons very much his own, Venuti sides with Paul Valéry and Walter Benjamin in assuming that the meaning of the poem is not its essence. My own approach to voice and versification constitutes a reasoned critique of this marginalizing of meaning. *See also* Domesticating Translation.

FORM   A term to which so many meanings are attributed that it is worth considering whether it can usefully serve as a concept in versification. Form can refer to the sound of words or to written script. It can also allude to structure: a rule-bound conventional form such as meter. Then again, when we speak of the form or rhythm of free verse, there is a naive pre-theoretical intuition at play. We perceive a foregrounded organization in free verse, but we recognize that it is not subject to rule-bound conventions; we are dealing with movements and configurations that come and go. Rather than use the term "form," it is preferable to refer to the movement and organization of language in metrical poetry and free verse, the structure of meter and rhyming schemes (if present), the overall patterning and the local patterning. *See also* Free Patterning; Local Pattern; Overall Pattern; Structure.

FORMALIST TRANSLATION The formalist translation commits two "crimes": first it accepts the form/meaning opposition and then it proceeds to sacrifice the latter to the former. Formalist translating entails an aesthetics that attributes the poetry of poems to their form. The meaning of poems is implicitly considered to be secondary, if not irrelevant. Such an aesthetics might seem relevant in nonsense poetry, but even nonsense is meaningful in negating meaning. Such an aesthetics is certainly poorly adapted to transposing poems and re-enacting the ways in which they move us with their meaning.

FORMAL RHYME A rhyme that serves no purpose in terms of the meaning of the poem but simply fulfills its structural requirements. Poets, even great poets, often rhyme words arbitrarily, using rhymes such as "day"/"way," "he"/"happily," "I"/"eye," simply to observe the requirements of the rhyming structure. Often the lines are interesting though the rhymes themselves are not of any particular interest. *See also* Clumsy Rhyme; Hackneyed Rhyme; Meaningful Rhyme; Rhyme.

FREE PATTERNING Salient forms of emerging organization that foreground the act of expression without establishing norms that allow us to anticipate the development of the poem's movement. These forms appear in local and overall patterning. Parallelism and sound patterning are forms of free patterning that give a shape and meaningful movement to both free and metrical verse. *See also* Foregrounding; Local Patterning; Overall Patterning.

HACKNEYED RHYME A rhyme in which pairs of words are overused. Unlike formal rhyming, which is pragmatic and opportunistic, hackneyed rhymes presume to provide something striking, something poetical, while simply churning out clichés, the warmed-up leftovers of former poets. "Dove"/"love," "love"/"glove," and "love"/"above" are among the worst, but they were all used by Shakespeare and are used today. Hackneyed rhymes are predictable. Rather than embellishing the poem, they tarnish it. Rather than animating it, they bore the reader with second-hand wares. *See also* Clumsy Rhyme; Formal Rhyme; Meaningful Rhyme; Rhyme.

INTUITION A key element of translating that allows us to see things as a whole and to perceive how the parts work together. While not vaunted in modern translation theories with their concepts and terms, analysis and reasoning, it is stressed by poets. Standing back from the poem proves an essential stage in the translation process. Even though translators must grapple with the details of a work, an overall impression of it proves essential; a capacity for synthesis as well as analysis is required. Only intuition allows us to apprehend the poem as a whole and to encounter the translation as a poem that exists in its own right.

LINE-BY-LINE TRANSLATION A free-verse translation strategy that corresponds to the ideal of a literal, word-for-word translation. It is supposed that by preserving the poet's meaning line by line, the translator is being faithful to his or her rhythms and, by logical extension, the poem. This idea proves misguided for two reasons. First, the rhythms of languages differ from one to another. An obvious example is that adjectives in French generally follow nouns and in English precede them. Grammar will inevitably dictate what can be highlighted at the line ends of a line-by-line translation. Second, in both metrical and non-metrical verse, poets carve their lines to foreground key words, often highlighted with sound patterning, rhyme, word order, or alliteration. Preserving these manoeuvres in unrhymed free-verse translations is not only pointless, it proves painfully maladroit. *See also* Literal Translation.

LITERAL TRANSLATION Literal, word-for-word translation is an ideal, but one that is never fulfilled. It takes the word for the unit of translation, and a long hermeneutic tradition has consolidated this practice. Poetry translators aiming for a literal translation tend to translate the poem line by line, taking the line as the unit of the poem, irrespective of the poet's intentions and choices in organizing the lines in terms of rhyming and phrasing. *See also* Line-by-Line Translation.

LOCAL PATTERN Configurations that emerge in the poem. Alliteration often allows key passages in a poem to be highlighted in both free and metrical verse. Free internal rhyming is also commonly found in non-metrical verse, allowing the poem to move into a heightened expressive mode of signifying. Patterning is therefore not simply formal embellishment but can also be highly meaningful. Local patterning allows configurations to emerge at strategic moments within the poem and then to subside or disappear without that effacement engendering rupture. *See also* Free Patterning; Rupture.

MEANINGFUL MOVEMENT A term I employ to translate Henri Meschonnic's concept of *sémantique sérielle*—part of his conception of rhythm—as the organization of a poem by the lyrical subject. This concept of rhythm takes us beyond accents and syllable counts. Meschonnic includes alliteration, assonance, and rhyme, as well as all forms of repetition and patterning. Most important, he refuses to view these as formal elements. If the poem moves us, it is because it means something to us, and what it means is charged with a force derived from foregrounding semantic elements at strategic points in the line, and because the poem sets in play sound-patterning and parallels and oppositions between words and phrases. The meaningful movement of a poem is that subtle mixture of what would be lost if the poem were translated into prose or reorganized arbitrarily, even though the essential meaning has been preserved. See also *Sémantique Sérielle*.

MEANINGFUL RHYME The meaningful rhyme realizes the full potential of rhyming, because it highlights words significant for the argument of the poem and enacts meaningful clashes and contrasts. The force of the poem is inseparable from the logic of this intuitive process of weaving meanings together: rhyme reinforces, rhyme surprises. Such rhymes include Dickinson's linking of depth and dumbness in the following lines:

> A second more, had dropped too deep
> For Fisherman to **plumb**—
> The very profile of the Thought
> Puts Recollection **numb**—

> ("Poem 286," 1989: 58; emphasis added)

MECHANICAL FORM   Part of the dichotomy with organic form that emerged in romantic aesthetics. Mechanical form offsets the ideal of organic form, in which the form emerges from within the literary work as the oak emerges from the acorn. Mechanical form is on the side of industry and is therefore considered (at least by romantic and modernist aesthetics) to be forced, alienated and alienating, clumsy and false. As I use the term, examples of mechanical form can include words cut or added to make up the number of syllables or stresses, or trivial, banal, or forced rhymes. It is important to stress that rule-bound metrics are subject to a certain mechanics, but there is nothing mechanical about the way poets create within metrical constraints. The contrary view—that all constraints hinder creativity and limit the poet—belongs to a romantic poetics that nonetheless sustained much metrical verse. While the prejudice persists, all good rule-bound verse demonstrates the implicit absurdity of the romantic dichotomy. Indeed, all poetry that smacks of clumsy forced organization has always been denigrated. *See also* Organic Form.

METER   "Meter" and "rhythm" are not synonyms. Rhythm is a widely used concept that covers all forms of movement and organization in the speech of any language, and one that usually entails a perceived heightened regularity. In this sense we can speak of the undulating pace of Barack Obama's speech as rhythmical, or we can speak of the rhythm of French intonation as it rises and falls. In this work, meter is restricted to a conventional perceived regularity that sets up rules of expectancy and invites the reader to manipulate the line so as to realize the underlying organized structure that is being built. The English sonnet invites us to realize the emergence of a weak-strong undulating meter that is strictly binary and in which the syllable count is preserved. Strong-stress meters are both freer and stricter: they are freer in the number of unstressed syllables that can intervene between accents, and they are stricter in that they force the pace of the meter in order to maintain the perceived regularity of metrical beating. *See also* Rhythm.

METRICAL BEATING   The perceived regularity of metrical accents—beats—returning in an undulating movement.

METRICAL COMPETENCE   A term that Derek Attridge owes to generative metrics, referring to the capacity of the reader to realize a poem's potential to correspond to clearly defined constraints put into play by the opening lines of the poem. Metrical competence is on the wane. Since free verse became the norm rather than the exception, many readers have difficulty responding to metrical constraints (one reason they find declamation to be ridiculous and absurd). Metrical competence continues to be passed on and assimilated in the reading and reciting of nursery rhymes, which inculcate four-beat metrical rules. Iambic pentameter, which must be assimilated through reading and listening to poems from the literary tradition, has now, technically speaking, become something of a mystery for many students of literature.

MIXED STRATEGIES   Our Baudelaire case study revealed the inefficiency of oppositions and categories in defining strategies of translating. Ultimately a single translator may translate one poem in one way and another entirely differently. Many of the oppositions that serve some purpose must be modified to account for the way the translator is combining strategies. In the Baudelaire case study we found no less than sixteen strategies designating the different modes of apprehension and recuperation at work in the translating process. We found metrical archaizers, who combine archaic diction with the use of meter. We found metrical ennoblers, who use elevated but not necessarily archaic terms in conjunction with meter. Another strategy involves using meter while toning down Baudelaire's vulgarity and crassness, which can be called "metrical sweetening." In contrast to this strategy, the metrical down-to-earthers use meter but refuse to abandon Baudelaire's feel for the real. The down-to-earthers often downplay his neoclassical lyricism and the elevation of his verse. Some translators, the "lexical prosers," concentrate on the word and prefer prose to meter. Rhythmic phrasers, on the other hand, privilege the movement of the phrase over word-for-word transposition and opt for a metrical refashioning in English verse. Some translators opt for prose, but of a distinctly "poetic" kind. The free-verse/free-content translators feel free to innovate with both meaning and form, unbound by formal constraints or by the poet's intentions. This account certainly does not resemble a clear set of categories, but it does bear witness to the complexity of strategies being adopted in translation, and to the ways in which translators are combining strategies and skipping from one to another as they respond to different poems. This simply goes to prove that classifications are useful only inasmuch as they allow us to logically and meaningfully arrange, compose, and contrast different strategies.

MOVEMENT   A term in the present work that refers to a free organization of syntax and phrasing, untouched by the constraints of meter or the expressive impact of line endings.

OFFBEAT   The weak point in the undulating rhythm of a stress-based or strong-stress-based meter. While the beat is formed of only one syllable, the offbeat can be formed of one or more syllables. In the iambic pentameter, syllable count is strict, and only one syllable is commonly found in the offbeat position, as in this line from King Harry in Shakespeare's *Henry V* (1.1, 1987: 336): "My learnèd lord, we pray you to proceed." "My," "we," "you," and "pro-" are all offbeats, and the meter requires "learnèd" to be pronounced as a trisyllabic word to maintain the meter. The offbeat can, however, fall on a stressable syllable. Demoting stressed syllables is common throughout English verse when three consecutive stresses are encountered. In these lines from Coleridge's *Rime of the Ancient Mariner*, the first "all" is demoted in order to preserve the undulating movement of the meter (weak-strong-weak): "Alone, alone, all, all alone / Alone on a wide wide sea" read so expressively by Richard Burton in a 1954 recording available at https://www.youtube.com/watch?v=1Aa1Fj9pPYI. Notice also that the stress on the first "wide" is not the same as that on the second, because of the expected inverse movement (strong-weak-strong). The second "wide" is demoted to preserve the movement of metrical beats and offbeats. How many syllables are found in the offbeat position in the phrase "Alone on the wide"? A weak syllable is followed by a strong syllable in "Alone" and the first "wide" is stressed. That leaves two unstressed syllables: "on the," between "Alone" and "wide." This is commonplace. In strong-stress meters such as the folk ballad there can be three unstressed syllables in an offbeat position. How many beats are found in these two lines? Seemingly paradoxically, there are four, but the first line is clearly seen to have four metrical stresses and the second to have only three. Conventionally, an "implied offbeat" is found at the end of three-stress lines in the ballad. Emily Dickinson often uses a 3-3-4-3 structure with implied offbeats sounding at the end of each three-stressed line. Invariably the syntax supports this procedure and a pause intervenes naturally at the end of three-stressed lines in a four-beat meter. *See also* Beat.

ORGANIC FORM Originally part of the romantic dichotomy of organic form versus mechanical form and considered to be the ideal of romantic aesthetics. In this ideal, the form emerges from the creative process of writing a poem or novel, making the work's realization seem necessary, inevitable, and perfect—part of its nature. The romantics inevitably used such a concept to resist mechanization, industry, progress, and what they considered to be the instrumentalization, the marginalization, and the humiliation of the human being in history. The free-verse movement took the concept and ran with it. Organic form was also used against the romantics, in that it was used to denigrate the rule-bound structures they had been happy to use flexibly. I have used "organic form" to designate a translated poem that emerges as a coherent balanced meaningful whole: organic form displays none of the clumsy props or incoherence of mechanical form with its hollow conventional rhymes, and forced meter. Organic form refuses to add or cut syllables to make up the number of syllables or stresses. *See also* Mechanical Form; Organic Translation.

ORGANIC TRANSLATION A translation that grows out of the meaningful shaping of rhythmic elements that enunciate and highlight the experience of poetic meaning, and in which the versification and the mode of signifying appear to be necessary and inevitable. A poem cannot be reduced to its meaning or its form, and an organic translation does not enact a clumsy juxtaposition of the two. The form grows out of the work and enfolds it, as a shell grows around the animal that it protects and sustains. Baudelaires exist in English and Shakespeares exist in French, German, and Czech because of organic translations that remoulded them into meaningful signifying wholes that hold together. Translated poems in which rhymes appear forced, or in which syllables are cut or added to maintain the meter, are inevitably censured, just as poems that show the same defects have always been rejected as "rat rhyme." *See also* Organic Form.

OVERALL PATTERN An organizing principle that can structure the free poem as a whole. *See also* Form; Free Patterning; Local Pattern.

POETICO-ACADEMIC TRANSLATION A translation made for students, in which the meaning is held to be the main concern but which might display a certain poetic sensibility. Academics often opt for literal prose translations because of the sheer labour involved in successfully translating each poem as a poem. Despite the obvious drawbacks in the poetico-academic approach, many such translators prove sensitive in the handling of images, phrasing, and the details of the poem (rather than the poem as a whole).

PROMOTION The process of elevating an unstressed syllable to the status of a metrical beat, a concept explicated by Derek Attridge (1982). As he explains, in a series of three unstressed syllables, the internal syllable can be promoted if the meter leads us to expect a beat. In the opening of Shakespeare's "Sonnet 82," the word "to" is promoted, although its semantic weight remains slight: "I grant thou were not married to my muse" (1987: 384). Traditional theories of metrics had long recognized that certain syllables are stressed in verse; Attridge's theory of meter demonstrates how the process is integrated into a larger, more complex series of relationships in which the stress contour interacts with the metrical beating and in which demotion is integral to that interaction. *See also* Demotion; Meter; Stress Contour.

PROSE POEM A poem in prose, invariably written without line endings, as prose is. The prose poem, however, demonstrates heightened organization of rhythm and patterning, and it is often lyrical in nature. Baudelaire's *Petits poèmes en prose* remain models for this kind of poetry. The prose poem is only one of a number of forms that chip away at the prose/poetry opposition that free verse did so much to undermine. Paradoxically, by insisting that this kind of prose is poetic, the prose poem reaffirms by their rapprochement the essentials of both prose and poetry that it had set out to undermine.

RHYME The repetition of sounds, usually at the line end, that must involve at least one stressed syllable. "Wing" and "sing" rhyme, but "walking" and "singing" do not. Comparative versification proves revealing when it comes to studying definitions of rhyme, because different languages have different levels of demands. French requires a stressed vowel plus a consonant: *amour* rhymes with *toujours*, but *touché* does not rhyme with *salé*, while *bouché* does. In English "go" rhymes with "'know," but that would be considered simple assonance in French. What counts in rhyme is the degree to which the repetition is highlighted within the context of the language. Languages that show a high propensity for rhyming (such as French, Italian, and Czech) tend to be more demanding in their requirements; in order to stand out, the repetition must appear novel. In English the variety of vowels and stress patterning in the words themselves makes rhyming so difficult that relatively weak rhymes can be perceived as striking. In this work I have stressed that a formal definition of rhyming is insufficient. *See also* Clumsy Rhyme; Formal Rhyme; Hackneyed Rhyme; Meaningful Rhyme.

RHYTHM   In the present work, the term "rhythm" is restricted to the interaction of line and syntactic movement. We can speak of the rhythm of free verse, thereby designating the way phrases are shaped and organized, cut up and held together by lines. But it is in the study of the interaction of meter and line that rhythm becomes a key concept, because it introduces the ideas of tension and complexity. For this reason I often choose to speak of the movement of free verse. Meter is a simple framework, an expressive space. Rhythm must animate it and make it dynamically eventful if the poem is to attract and sustain our interest. *See also* Rhythmic Phrasing; Rising Rhythm; *Rythme*.

RHYTHMIC PHRASING   A complex concept of rhythm and a mode of analysis developed by Richard D. Cureton (1992). Cureton's fundamental assumption is that it is phrasing that is expressive, not meter, which merely harnesses it and channels it. His theory opens up great perspectives for the study of what makes free verse eventful. More than anyone else in recent decades, Cureton has stressed the importance of phrasing in poetry and denounced the way in which traditional metrics has marginalized all but the most strictly metrical movements of the poem, contenting itself with highlighting only moments of tension when speech rhythms resist meter and line endings.

RISING RHYTHM   An undulation that moves from weak to strong, usually associated with iambic meters. As Derek Attridge demonstrates (1982), rising rhythms depend more on word stress than on meter. In the mixture of rhythms in the opening line of Shakespeare's first sonnet, the first words introduce a falling rhythm. The line then moves into a rising rhythm with "desire" and "increase": "From fairest creatures we desire increase" (1987: 371). Free verse can also display a mixture of rising and falling rhythms. The following lines from Ted Hughes's "Wolfwatching" privilege a falling rhythm, but the last two clitic groups impose a rising rhythm at the end of the second line: "The Asiatic eyes, the gunsights / Aligned effortless in the beam of his power" (2003: 755).

RUPTURE   A transgression of rules or a radical shift in organization in a poem. A rupture is brought about, for example, when T. S. Eliot shifts from a four-beat meter to a pentameter. Eliot invariably sets up a clearly defined context in his verse and then breaks the rules he has set up. Free verse, such as the poems of Ezra Pound, on the other hand, moves freely in and out of metrical lines without stabilizing them sufficiently to make change seem like transgression. Moving from meter to meter in a clearly established manner, as Shakespeare does—for example, in *A Midsummer Night's Dream* the nobles speak in iambic pentameters, the sprites speak in four-beat ballad meter, and the menial workers of Bottom's play speak in prose—does not provoke a rupture. If a poet or a translator breaks off rhyming, on the other hand, that is perceived as a rupture.

RYTHME   The French term that corresponds more or less to the commonly accepted meanings attributed to rhythm in English. As such it partakes in the same confusion as its English counterpart, and it must therefore be excluded from use as a technical term unless its meaning is clearly discerned and defined. In Henri Meschonnic's poetics, *rythme* refers to all those processes, both semantic and formal, that emerge in the patterned configurations of a poem: alliteration, rhyming and repetition, and freely organized forms of discernible accentual patterning. This redefined concept of *rythme* was fundamental for his concept of poetry as a form of speech that transforms and invigorates language as an expressive medium.

Meschonnic was taking a stand against Plato, who had reduced "rhythm" to regularity. Prior to Plato, as Benveniste has demonstrated, rhythms were considered to be varied and not reducible to the weak-strong-weak-strong movement that became associated with the term after Plato. And even in the works of Plato's student Aristotle, the rhythms are various and diverse; "prose rhythms" in

Greek were recognizable forms that were learned and passed on and considered appropriate to certain styles of public speaking. Inevitably, given Meschonnic's own mother tongue, French, and given that he was writing after three generations of free verse, extolling a non-regular form of rhythm was a defence of French contemporary free verse. French poets and translators had long lamented the weak accent in French. French metrical verse is based on syllable count, and French free verse explores alternative forms of patterning without foregrounding undulating accentual rhythms. Meschonnic's redefinition of *rythme* allowed him to sidestep the reductive reflex of seeing all rhythms in terms of stress-based meters, and his concept enabled him to explore what was going on in the verse of his time. Inevitably, however, in swimming against the tide, Meschonnic tended to downplay the importance of regularity and metrical beating, preferring to stress the ways in which individual poets countered it. *See also* Voice.

SCISSORS OF METRICS The interaction of meter and lines in Donald Wesling's poetics (1996). While traditional metrics tends to assume that line ends will coincide with syntactic pauses and considers their non-coincidence only in run-on lines, Wesling stresses paying close attention to what meaningful words are foregrounded at line ends, and to what degree the line end coincides with a significant pause. Major pauses at the ends of long sentences can be found within the line, and often only slight pauses are marked at the line ends. This shift happens less in Pope and more often in Milton and Wordsworth. Nevertheless, all conventional metrical verse shows a great variety of pauses that are not metrically marked. This variation highlights something very fundamental in the movement and organization of verse, something that helps explain the vast varieties of rhythms explored by individual poets. The scissors of metrics and Wesling's grammetrics distinguish between the different ways in which phrasing, rhythm, and meter emerge in the versification of individual poets.

SEMANTIC TRANSLATION A translation that contents itself with transposition of the meaning of the poem. Semantic translations stick closely to the sentence structure and grammatical units of the source text, tending to translate nouns as nouns, verbs as verbs, adverbs as adverbs, and so on. The semantic translator will reorganize the poem, its lines, its syntax, and its grammar, considering all formal elements as merely vehicles for transmitting meaning. *See also* Line-by-Line Translation; Literal Translation; Poetico-academic Translation.

SEMANTICO-FORMAL TRANSLATION   A translation that, in contrast to organic translation, accepts the division of form and content, extracts the meaning, and then tries to remould it in a conventional form, without showing any concern for how formal elements contribute to highlighting and charging the poem with meaning. Semantico-formal translating often results in a stilted translation with a mechanical form that seems to hang on the poem like hand-me-down clothes. *See also* Mechanical Form; Organic Translation.

SÉMANTIQUE SÉRIELLE   The term used by Henri Meschonnic to refer to chains of foregrounded elements in speech. Contrary to traditional formalistic stylistics, which tends to divide form and content and to reduce such effects to formal embellishments, Meschonnic intended this term to remind us that chains of foregrounded elements are elements of meaningful speech, and that it is the meaning that is highlighted in such chains. In the following lines from Ted Hughes's "Wolfwatching," the texture of the animal's fur is foregrounded by the repetition of *w*, which weaves powerful patterns of repetition that link wolf with bear and whiteness:

> Woolly-bear white, the old wolf
> Is listening to London. His eyes, withered in
> Under the white wool [...]

> (2003: 754; emphasis added)

SIGNIFYING   A term used in the present work to translate Henri Meschonnic's concept *signifiance,* the act of making meaning. This action involves the use of formal elements to highlight meaningful moments in the poem. It concerns the way in which sounds link together meanings in powerfully evocative configurations. Rhyming and alliteration not only stress key words but harness words together in meaningful chains of meaning—for example, "foul" and "fair" in Shakespeare's *Macbeth* (1.1, 1987: 1309) and "tomb" and "womb" in his "Sonnet 86" (1987: 385). "Signifying" and "making meaning" are terms used to designate forms of patterning that cannot be reduced to formal flourishes, because they partake in the impact the poem has on us as charged, meaningful speech. Traditional approaches to stylistics, poetics, and metrics tend to downplay the meaning of formal configurations because they consider poetry in general, without paying attention to the way poems make sense, penetrating our world and drawing us into theirs.

STRESS CONTOUR The accentual structure of the phrase. In poetry this becomes a question of diction and reader response. The stress contour is ultimately the way a phrase or passage would be read if it were not subject to a poetic reading. Readers of poems realize the underlying metrical potential of the stress contour. Compare the following two examples, the first invented and the second from the opening lines of Emily Dickinson's "Poem 348":

> I wondered where Bob's daughter was. But she was coming home.

> I dreaded that first Robin so,
> But He is mastered, now.
>
> (Dickinson 1989: 90)

The second example clearly invites a four-beat metrical reading with an implied offbeat at the end of the three-stressed second line. The first example appears totally arbitrary as far as accentuation is concerned. In fact, both examples share exactly the same stress contour. The rhythm we perceive in the second example comes from our response to the meter in what we clearly perceive to be a poem with metrically organized lines. The stress contour is manipulated in our interpretation of the lines from Dickinson, but it is not subjugated. The lines of any one poem move very differently, and this is to be attributed to the stress contour, which bolsters the metrical beating and tugs against it in varied movements that only ever realize the full ideal of alternating stress of strong and weak syllables to an approximate degree. Rather than being considered a weakness, the fact that stress contour and meter only partially coincide must be considered a strength. If they did coincide fully, the verse would rapidly become painfully monotonous.

STRUCTURE   In the present work, the organization involving rule-bound constraints. This definition allows me to distinguish between the free patterning of alliteration, for example, and a codified rhyming scheme. In my own terminology, only the latter involves a structure. The widely used terms "structure" and "form" are often considered to be synonyms. My distinction should enable us to escape those tiresome paradoxes that have become fashionable in modernist poetics, such as "formless structure," "structureless form," and "form without form."

SYNAERESIS   A term (*synérèse* in French) that comes from Greek, meaning "seizing together." It takes place when two normally separate vowels are combined into one syllable. This is a fundamental process in English pronunciation: "I'm" and "you're" are conventional examples. "'Tis" appears to be an archaic or poetical contraction, but the essential process of synaeresis is commonplace and comes with the accelerated flow of familiar speech. It is particularly common in dialects, though the forms vary from one dialect to another. "T'other" has nothing archaic about it in the contemporary Yorkshire dialect, and "going" invariably becomes "goan," a monosyllabic diphthong, in most Scots dialects.

TRANSLATION THEORY   A theory that academics would like to see but that translators are often dubious about. Existing theories are often at odds because they suppose different hierarchies of objectives, obligations, and priorities. It is certainly unclear as to whether a theory of translating poems is possible. As a creative act, translating poems can have no rigidly applied practice. *See also* Versification.

TRANSCREATORS   Translators whose translations breaks free from the original poem. The original is no longer seen as anything but a starting point, a sensibility into which the translator enters to awaken his or her own creative élan. The transcreator will cut stanzas, abandon metaphors, update references to details, and address very different implied readers than the original poems'. Philip Larkin moves into transcreation when he translates a Baudelaire poem by introducing the *Guardian* newspaper (Baudelaire 1997: 210). And when, in my translation of Baudelaire's "Muse vénale," I transform the lamplights into car headlights, I am following the same track (Baudelaire 2015). Transcreators are neither foreignizers nor domesticators; they simply allow the translating experience to take them where it will. Transcreation is closely related to appropriation, but in appropriation the attempt of one poetic persona to speak through the voice of another remains. The transcreator, in contrast, sees the original poem more as an invitation to adventure than as an objective. *See also* Appropriators; Domesticating Translation; Foreignizing Translation.

UNCONSCIOUS AESTHETICS   The underlying aesthetics and attitude to language and poetry expressed in the choices a translator makes to privilege and preserve certain facets of the poem. Each translation strategy entails a hierarchy of priorities. Academics who offer a literal translation seek to preserve the meaning of the poem without always concerning themselves with how the poem's mode of signifying acts upon readers. In privileging the transposition of one form into another, free formalist translators reorganize the whole and often sacrifice images and details in the meaning. Other translators abandon certain images or details because their raison d'être is now null and void. Sacrificing elements belongs to a strategy that is target-oriented and seeks to ensure that the translation functions as a poem. The unconscious aesthetics in any translator's activity demonstrates whether he or she is responding to the source language, the target language, a theory of interpretation or hermeneutics, an ideal of poetry, the poem, the line, the stanza, or the word. The concept of the unit of translation is fundamental for the unconscious aesthetics of the translator. Jean-René Ladmiral (1994) focuses on the word and the sentence. Henri Meschonnic focuses on the poem. Lawrence Venuti (1995, 2004) focuses on the context into which the poem will be brought and that it can be used to disrupt.

VERSIFICATION   In this work, the dynamic interaction of rhythmic elements in the meaningful process of the poem's mode of signifying. Versification is frequently reduced to a concept of meter and rhyming, but that definition gives a very misleading impression of the way rhymes, alliteration, and meters move and of the way they move us. Ultimately it is the meaning and phrasing of poems that move us; meter and other formal elements simply organize and foreground that meaningful movement in powerful and striking ways. Form does not mean anything in verse; poems mean something. Form simply patterns and organizes meaning. In this work I have stressed the importance of obvious forms of organization such as phrasing and repetition, because they are so often forgotten or marginalized in stylistics and theory. A theory of versification and voice that clearly defines the elements at play in the organization of any given poem's mode of signifying is possible. It would involve clearly defining syllables, stress, promotion, demotion, and meters and their constraints, but it should also demonstrate how and why these elements are important to the poem's mode of signifying, and why they should be transposed, directly or by alternative forms of organization and patterning, in the translated poem. *See also* Form; Signifying; Voice.

VERS SIMPLE   In traditional French versification, *vers simple* is used to refer to any verse line of less than eight syllables in length and that has no metrical caesura. *Vers simple* is used in opposition to *vers composé*, a verse line composed of two parts divided by a metrical caesura, as in the decasyllable (usually 4:6) and the alexandrine (usually 6:6).

VOICE   The persona of the poem that emerges in the meaning of the words and the way those words are organized into rule-bound metrical and rhyming structures, or into free patterning with alliteration, free rhyming, repetition, and the like. I have insisted on the relationship between voice and versification to stress that formal patterning invariably creates part of the poem's mode of signifying. Doggerel, rat rhyme, nursery rhymes, and limericks may use sound patterning arbitrarily, but most good poetry uses sound patterning in meaningful ways to heighten the impact of the poem. Because of the inherent difficulty of transposing linguistic terms from one language to another, I prefer not to adopt Henri Meschonnic's use of the term *rythme*. What he understands by *rythme* is very close to what I define as the voice of the poem. This is not a denial of the debt I owe to Meschonnic's poetics, but a way to avoid having to introduce a paragraph of explanation every time the term is used. *See also* Rythme.

Bibliography

Aquien, Michèle. 1990. *La versification*. Paris: PUF.
Aristotle. 1954. *The Rhetoric and the Poetics*. Trans. Ingram Bywater. New York: Random House.
Arrojo, Rosemary. 1994. "Fidelity and the Gendered Translation." *TTR: Traduction, terminologie, rédaction* 7.2: 147–63. http://id.erudit.org/iderudit/037184ar.
Astésano, Corine. 2001. *Rythme et accentuation en français: Invariance et variabilité stylistique*. Paris: L'Harmattan.
Attridge, Derek. 1982. *The Rhythms of English Poetry*. London: Longman.
———. 1995. *Poetic Rhythm: An Introduction*. Cambridge: Cambridge University Press.
———. 1996. "Beyond Metrics: Richard Cureton's *Rhythmic Phrasing in English Verse*." In Christoph Küper, ed., "Metrics 2." Spec. issue of *Poetics Today* 17.1 (Spring): 9–27.
Auden, W. H. 1991. *Poems*. New York: Everyman's Library.
Augustine [of Hippo]. 1964a. *Les confessions*. Paris: Garnier Frères Flammarion.
———. "De Musica." 1964b. In *Philosophies of Art and Beauty: Selected Readings in Aesthetics from Plato to Heidegger*. Ed. Albert Hofstadter and Richard Kuhns. Chicago: University of Chicago Press, 185–202.
———. "De Ordine." 1964c. In *Philosophies of Art and Beauty: Selected Readings in Aesthetics from Plato to Heidegger*. Ed. Albert Hofstadter and Richard Kuhns. Chicago: University of Chicago Press, 173–85.

Baker, Mona, and Carol Maier, eds. 2011. *The Interpreter and Translator Trainer: Ethics and the Curriculum*. Manchester: St. Jerome.

Ballard, Michel. 1992. *De Cicéron à Benjamin: Traducteurs, traductions, réflexions*. Lille: Presses Universitaires de Lille.

Barron, Denis. 1986. *Grammar and Gender*. New York: Yale University Press.

Baudelaire, Charles. 1972. *Baudelaire*. Ed. and trans. Francis Scarfe. Harmondsworth, UK: Penguin.

———. 1975. *Œuvres complètes*. Vol. 1. Paris: Gallimard.

———. 1997. *Baudelaire in English*. Ed. Carol Clark and Robert Sykes. London: Penguin.

———. 1998. *The Flowers of Evil*. Trans. James McGowan. Oxford: Oxford University Press.

———. 2001. *Frae the Flouers o Evil: Baudelaire in Scots*. Trans. James Robertson. Glenrothes: Dolphin Press.

———. 2010. "Five Poems by Baudelaire." Trans. James McColley Eilers. InTranslation. http://intranslation.brooklynrail.org/french/five-poems-by-baudelaire.

———. 2015. Charles Baudelaire's Fleurs du mal/Flowers of Evil. www.fleursdumal.org.

Belloc, Hilaire. 1958. *Selected Cautionary Verses*. Harmondsworth, UK: Penguin.

Benjamin, Walter. (1923) 1963. "Die Aufgabe des Übersetzers." In *Das Problem des Übersetzens*. Ed. Hans Joachim Störig. Wege der Forschung 8. Darmstadt: Wissenschaftliche, 156–69.

———. (1968) 1992. "The Task of the Translator." In *Illuminations*. Trans. Harry Zohn. London: Fontana, 69–82.

Benveniste, Émile. 1966. *Problèmes de linguistiques générales*. Vol 1. Paris: Gallimard.

———. 1974. *Problèmes de linguistiques générales*. Vol. 2. Paris: Gallimard.

Bergonzi, Bernard. 1978. *T. S. Eliot*. London: Faber & Faber.

Berman, Antoine. 1984. *L'épreuve de l'étranger*. Paris: Gallimard.

———. 1985. "La traduction et la lettre ou l'auberge du lointain." In *Les tours de Babel: Essais sur la traduction*. Ed. Antoine Berman. Mauvezin: Trans-Europ-Repress. 33–150.

———. (1985) 2004. "Translation and the Trials of the Foreign." Trans. Lawrence Venuti. In L. Venuti, ed., *The Translation Studies Reader*. 2nd ed. London: Routledge, 276–89.

Brisset, Annie. 2004. "The Search for a Native Language: Translation and Cultural Identity." In Lawrence Venuti, ed., *The Translation Studies Reader*. 2nd ed. London: Routledge, 337–68.

Brooke-Rose, Christine. (1958) 1965. *A Grammar of Metaphor*. London: D. R. Hilman and Sons.

Burns, Robert. 1981. *The Poems and Songs of Robert Burns*. Ed. James Barke. Glasgow: Collins.

Chamberlain, Lori. (1988) 2004. "Gender and the Metaphorics of Translation." In Lawrence Venuti, ed., *The Translation Studies Reader*. 2nd ed. London: Routledge, 306–21.
Chuquet, Hélène, and Michel Paillard. 1989. *Approche linguistique des problèmes de traduction: Anglais–Français*. Rev. ed. Paris: Ophrys.
Coleridge, Samuel Taylor. 2001. *Collected Works*. Ed. J. C. C. Mays. Princeton, NJ: Princeton University Press.
Corneille, Pierre. 1862. *Poésies diverses*. Vol. 10. Paris: Hachette, 87–91. https://fr.wikisource.org/wiki/Sur_la_mort_du_roi_Louis_XIII.
Cornulier, Benoît de. 1980. *Théorie du vers: Rimbaud, Verlaine, Mallarmé*. Paris: Seuil.
Cotnam, Jacques, ed. 1992. *Poètes du Québec*. Cap-Saint-Ignace: Bibliothèque québécoise.
Couper-Kuhlen, Elizabeth. 1993. *English Speech Rhythm: Form and Function in Everyday Verbal Interaction*. Amsterdam: Benjamin.
Crystal, David. 1997. *The Cambridge Encyclopaedia of Language*. 2nd ed. Cambridge: Cambridge University Press.
Cuddon, J. A. 1991. *Dictionary of Literary Terms and Literary Theory*. 3rd ed. London: Penguin.
Cureton, Richard D. 1992. *Rhythmic Phrasing in English Verse*. New York: Longman.
———. 1996. "A Response to Derek Attridge." In Christoph Küper, ed., "Metrics 2." Spec. issue of *Poetics Today* 17.1 (Spring): 29–50.
Cuthbertson, Guy. 2014. *Wilfred Owen*. London: Yale University Press.
Delattre, P. 1966. "A Comparison of Syllable Length Conditioning among Languages." *International Review of Applied Linguistics* 4: 183–98.
Derrida, Jacques. 1985. "Des tours de Babel." In *L'art des confins: Mélanges offerts à Maurice de Gandillac*. Ed. Annie Cazenave and Jean-François Lyotard. Paris: PUF, 209–37.
———. 2004. "What Is a 'Relevant' Translation?" Trans. Lawrence Venuti. In L. Venuti, ed., *The Translation Studies Reader*. 2nd ed. London: Routledge, 423–46.
Dickinson, Emily. 1956. *Poèmes choisis*. Trans. P. Messiaen. Paris: Aubier-Montaigne.
———. 1957. *Emily Dickinson*. Trans. and ed. Alain Bosquet. Poètes d'aujourd'hui 55. Paris: Pierre Seghers.
———. 1963. *The Poems of Emily Dickinson*. 3 vols. Ed. Thomas H. Johnson. Cambridge, MA: Harvard University Press.
———. 1970a. *Gedichte*. Trans. Gertrud Liepe. Stuttgart: Philipp Reclam jun.
———. 1970b. *Poèmes*. Trans. Guy Jean Forgue. [Paris]: Aubier-Flammarion.
———. 1989. *Poèmes d'Emily Dickinson*. Bilingual ed. Trans. Claire Malroux. Paris: Belin.

———. 1997. *Renchérir sur minuit: Vingt-six poèmes*. Trans. Odile des Fontenelles. Évian-les-Bains: Aliades.

———. (1986) 2003. *Emily Dickinson: Quarante-sept poèmes*. Trans. Philippe Denis. Geneva: Dogana.

———. 2004. *The Collected Poems of Emily Dickinson*. New York: Barnes and Noble.

———. 2007a. *Car l'adieu, c'est la nuit*. Bilingual ed. Trans. Claire Malroux. Paris: Gallimard.

———. 2007b. *Lieu-dit l'éternité: Poèmes choisis*. Bilingual ed. Trans. Patrick Reumaux. Paris: Points.

———. 2009. *Poésies complètes*. Bilingual ed. Trans. Françoise Delphy. Paris: Flammarion.

———. 2016. *Emily Dickinson's Poems as She Preserved Them*. Ed. Cristianne Miller. Cambridge, MA: Harvard University Press.

Donne, John. 1990. *John Donne: Selected Poems*. Ed. John Carey. Oxford: Oxford University Press.

Dubois, Jean, et al. 1994. *Dictionnaire de linguistique et des sciences du langage*. Paris: Larousse.

Ducrot, Oswald, and Jean-Marie Schaeffer. 1995. *Nouveau dictionnaire encyclopédique des sciences du langage*. Paris: Seuil.

Ducrot, Oswald, and Tzvetan Todorov. 1972. *Dictionnaire encyclopédique des sciences du langage*. Paris: Seuil.

Duffy, Carol Anne. 1985. *Standing Female Nude*. London: Anvil.

Dupriez, Bernard. 1984. *Gradus: Les procédés littéraires; Dictionnaire*. Paris: Union générale d'éditions.

Eichendorff, Joseph Freiherr von. (1835) 1987. "Auf meines Kindes Tod." In *Gedichte, Vesperen*. Ed. Hartwig Schultz. Vol. 1 of *Joseph von Eichendorff*. 6 vols. Ed. Wolfgang Frühwald, Brigitte Schillbach, and Hartwig Schultz. Frankfurt: Deutscher Klassiker-Verlag, 288–89. http://freiburger-anthologie.ub.uni-freiburg.de.

Eliot, T. S. 1949. Preface. In *Anabasis*. New York: Harcourt & Brace.

———. 1953. *Selected Prose*. London: Penguin.

———. 1969a. *The Complete Poems and Plays of T. S. Eliot*. London: Redwood Burn.

———. 1969b. *Poésie*. Bilingual ed. Trans. Pierre Leyris. Paris: Seuil.

Éluard, Paul. 2001. *Twenty-Four Poems in Translation*. Trans. A. S. [Tony] Kline. Poets of Modernity. http://poetsofmodernity.xyz/POMBR/French/Eluard.htm#anchor_Toc8375613.

———. 2015. "L'amoureuse." Read by Gilles-Claude Thériault. Poetica. www.poetica.fr/poeme-858/paul-eluard-amoureuse/.

Etkind, Efim. 1982. *Un art en crise: Essai de poétique de la traduction poétique*. Trans. Wladimir Troubetzkoy. Lausanne: L'Âge d'Homme.

Fawcett, Peter. 1997. *Translation and Language: Linguistic Theories Explained.* Manchester: St. Jerome.
Ferguson, Rosalind. 1985. *The Penguin Rhyming Dictionary.* Harmondsworth, UK: Penguin.
Folkart, Barbara. 2007. *The Second Finding: A Poetics of Translation.* Ottawa: University of Ottawa Press.
Fontaine, Jacqueline. 1974. *Le cercle linguistique de Prague.* Tours: Mame.
Fontanier, Pierre. (1830) 1977. *Les figures du discours.* Paris: Flammarion.
Frug, Stephen Saperstein. 2011. "Three Translations of Baudelaire's 'L'Albatros' (Accidental Poetry Month 19)." *Attempts* (blog). 28 March. http://stephenfrug.blogspot.fr/2011/03/three-translations-of-baudelaires.html.
Gasparov, M. L. 1996. *A History of European Versification.* Trans. G. S. Smith and Marina Tarlinskaja. Ed. G. S. Smith and Leofranc Holford-Strevens. Oxford: Clarendon Press.
Gelpi, Albert J. 1966. *Emily Dickinson: The Mind of the Poet.* Cambridge, MA: Harvard University Press.
Glen, Duncan, and Tom Hubbard. 2008. *Fringe of Gold: The Fife Anthology.* Edinburgh: Antony Rowe.
Goedemans, R. W. N. 1996. "Syllable Weight and Prominence." In *Stress Patterns of the World.* Vol. 1, *Background.* Ed. R. W. N. Goedemans, H. G. van der Hulst, and E. A. M. Visch. The Hague: Holland Academic Graphics, 115–64.
Goedemans, Rob, and Harry van der Hulst. 2013a. "Chapter 15: Weight-Sensitive Stress." In *The World Atlas of Language Structures Online.* Ed. Matthew S. Dryer and Martin Haspelmath. Leipzig: Max Planck Institute for Evolutionary Anthropology. http://wals.info/chapter/15.
———. 2013b. "Chapter 17: Rhythm Types." In *The World Atlas of Language Structures Online.* Ed. Matthew S. Dryer and Martin Haspelmath. Leipzig: Max Planck Institute for Evolutionary Anthropology. http://wals.info/chapter/17.
———. 2013c. "Chapter 16: Weight Factors in Weight-Sensitive Stress Systems." In *The World Atlas of Language Structures Online.* Ed. Matthew S. Dryer and Martin Haspelmath. Leipzig: Max Planck Institute for Evolutionary Anthropology. http://wals.info/chapter/16.
Goethe, Johann Wolfgang von. 1973. "Drei Stücke zum Thema Übersetzen." In *Das Problem des Übersetzens.* Ed. Hans Joachim Störig. Darmstadt: Wissenschafliche Buchgesellschaft, 34–37.
———. (1962) 1985. *Faust.* Part 1. Trans. Peter Salm. New York: Bantam Books.
Gouvard, Jean-Michel. 1996. "Le vers français: De la syllabe à l'accent." *Poétique* 106 (avril) : 223–47.
Grammont, Maurice. (1906) 1989. *Petit traité de versification française.* Paris: Colin.

Guaïtella, I. 1996–97. "Parole spontanée et lecture oralisée: Activités cognitives différentes, organisations rythmiques différentes." *Travaux de l'Institut de phonétique d'Aix* 17: 9–30.

Guillemin-Flescher, Jacqueline. 1981. *Syntaxe comparée du français et de l'anglais: Problèmes de traduction*. Paris: Ophrys.

Guyaux, André. 2007. *Baudelaire: Mémoire de la critique. Un demi-siècle de lectures des Fleurs du mal: 1855–1905*. Paris: Presses universitaires de Paris-Sorbonne.

Hardy, Thomas. 1995. *Collected Poems*. New York: Everyman's Library.

Harvey, Keith. 2004. "Translating Camp Talk: Gay Identities and Cultural Transfer." In Lawrence Venuti, ed., *The Translation Studies Reader*. 2nd ed. London: Routledge, 402–22.

Hassen, Rim. 2011. "Feminist Translation Strategies and the Quran: A Study of Laleh Bakhtiar's Translation." *MonTI* 3: 211–30

Holmes, James S. 2004. "The Name and Nature of Translation Studies." In Lawrence Venuti, ed., *The Translation Studies Reader*. 2nd ed. London: Routledge, 180–92.

Hooker, Joan Fillmore. 1983. *T. S. Eliot's Poems in French Translation: Pierre Leyris and Others*. Ann Arbor, MI: UMI Research Press.

Hubbard, Tom, ed. 1991. *The New Makars: The Mercat Anthology of Contemporary Poetry in Scots*. Edinburgh: Mercat Press.

———. 2011. *The Chagall Winnocks: Wi Ither Scots Poems and Ballants o Europe*. Ochtertyre: Grace Note.

Hubbard, Tom, and James W. Underhill, eds. 2015. *Scottish Spleen*. Tarland: Tapsalteerie.

Hughes, Ted. 2003. *Collected Poems*. New York: Farrar, Straus & Giroux.

Hugo, Victor. 1967. *Œuvres poétiques*. Vol. 2, *Les Châtiments, les contemplations*. Ed. Pierre Albouy. Paris: Gallimard.

———. 2005. *Poems*. Project Gutenberg. http://www.gutenberg.org/files/8775/8775-h/8775-h.htm#link2H_4_0125.

Hulse, Michael, David Kennedy, and David Morley. 1993. *The New Poetry*. Glasgow: Bloodaxe.

Humbley, John, and Oscar Torres Vera. 2011. *La traduction trilingue: Traduire du français vers l'anglais et l'espagnol*. Paris: Ophrys.

Humboldt, Wilhelm von. 1995. *Schriften zur Sprache*. Stuttgart: Philipp Reclam jun.

———. (1836) 1999. *On Language: On the Diversity of Human Language Construction and Its Influence on the Mental Development of the Human Species*. Trans. Peter Health. Ed. Michael Losonsky. Cambridge: Cambridge University Press.

———. 2000. *Sur le caractère national des langues et autres écrits sur le langage*. Trans. Denis Thouard. Paris: Seuil.

——. 2003. *Über die Verschiedenheit des menschlichen Sprachbaues: Über die Sprache*. Weisbaden: Fourier.
Irigaray, Luce, ed. 1990. *Sexes et genres à travers les langues*. Paris: Bernard Grasset.
Jakobson, Roman. 1971. *Phonological Studies*. Vol. 1 of *Selected Writings*. 2nd ed. Ed. Stephen Rudy. The Hague: Mouton.
——. 1979. *On Verse, Its Masters and Its Explorers*. Vol. 5 of *Selected Writings*. 2nd ed. Ed. Stephen Rudy and Martha Taylor. The Hague: Mouton.
——. 1981. *Poetry of Grammar and Grammar of Poetry*. Vol. 3 of *Selected Writings*. Ed. Stephen Rudy. The Hague: Mouton.
Jones, Ann Rosalind. 2008. "Writing the Body: Toward an Understanding of *l'Écriture feminine*." http://webs.wofford.edu/hitchmoughsa/Writing.html.
Küper, Christoph. 1988. *Sprache und Metrum: Semiotik und Linguistik des Verses*. Tübingen: Niemeyer.
Ladmiral, Jean-René. 1994. *Traduire: Théorèmes pour la traduction*. Paris: Gallimard.
La Fontaine, Jean de. 2007. *Twelve Fables of La Fontaine Made owre intil Scots*. Trans. Walter Perrie. Blair Atholl: Fras.
Larkin, Philip. 1988. *Collected Poems*. London: Faber.
Leech, Geoffrey. 1990. *Semantics: The Study of Meaning*. 2nd ed. London: Penguin.
Léon, Pierre, R. 1996. *Phonétisme, et prononciation du français: Avec des travaux pratiques d'application et leurs corrigés*. 2nd ed. Paris: Fernand Nathan.
Lévy, E. 1926. "Métrique et rythmique." In *Compte rendu du 1e Congrès du rythme: Tenu à Genève du 16 au 18 août 1926*. Ed. Albert Pfrimmer. Geneva: Institut Jaques-Dalcroze, 76–81.
Levý, Jiří. 1963. *Umění překladu* [Art of translation]. Prague: State Publishing House.
——. 1969. *Die literarische Übersetzung: Theorie einer Kunstgattung*. Frankfurt am Main: Athenäum.
——. 2011. *The Art of Translation*. Trans. Patrick Corness. Ed. Zuzana Jettmarová. Amsterdam: John Benjamins.
Littré, Emile. 1962. *Dictionnaire de la langue française*. Paris: Gallimard.
Mailhot, Laurent, and Pierre Nepveu, eds. 1990. *La poésie québécoise: Des origines à nos jours*. Montreal: Typo.
Malblanc, Alfred. 1968. *Stylistique comparée du français et de l'allemand: Essai de représentation linguistique comparée et étude de traduction*. 4th ed. Paris: Didier.
Malmkjær, Kirsten. 1991. *The Linguistics Encyclopedia*. London: Routledge.
Marcotte, Gilles. 1969. *Le temps des poètes: Description critique de la poésie actuelle au Canada français*. Montreal: HMH.
Mazaleyrat, Jan. (1965) 1990. *Éléments de la métrique française*. Paris: Colin.

McArthur, Tom. 1998. *The English Languages*. Cambridge: Cambridge University Press.
McCully, C. B. 1994. *The Poet's Voice and Craft*. London: Carcanet Press.
McGuckian, Medbh. 1997. *Selected Poems*. Winston-Salem, NC: Wake Forest University Press.
Ménélik [Albert Tjamag]. 1999. "Bye Bye." http://paroles.zouker.com/menelik-myas/tu-es-la-seule-qui-m-aille,66883.htm.
Meschonnic, Henri. 1970. *Les Cinq Rouleaux*. Paris: Gallimard.
———. 1972. *Épistémologie de l'écriture: Poétique de la traduction*. Vol. 2 of *Pour la poétique*. Paris: Gallimard.
———. 1978. *Poésie sans réponse*. Vol. 5 of *Pour la poétique*. Paris: Gallimard.
———. 1981. *Jona et le signifiant errant*. Paris: Gallimard.
———. 1982. *Critique du rythme: Anthropologie historique du langage*. 2nd ed. Paris: Verdier.
———. 1985. *Les états de la poétique*. Paris: PUF.
———. 1990. *La rime et la vie*. Paris: Verdier.
———, ed. 1995a. *La pensée dans la langue: Humboldt et après*. Paris: Presses universitaires de Vincennes.
———. 1995b. *Politique du rythme: Politique du sujet*. Paris: Verdier.
———. 1997. *De la langue française: Essai sur une clarté obscure*. Paris: Hachette.
———. 1999. *Poétique du traduire*. Paris: Verdier.
———. 2001a. *Gloires: Traduction des psaumes*. Paris: Desclée de Brouwer.
———. 2001b. *L'utopie du juif*. Paris: Desclée de Brouwer.
———. 2002. *Au commencement: Traduction de la Genèse*. Paris: Desclée de Brouwer.
———. 2003. *Les noms: Traduction de l'Exode*. Paris: Desclée de Brouwer.
———. 2007a. *Ethics and Politics of Translating*. Trans. Pier-Pascale Boulanger. Amsterdam: John Benjamins.
———. 2007b. *Éthique et politique du traduire*. Paris: Verdier.
———. 2007c. *Heidegger ou le national-essentialisme*. Paris: Laurence Teper.
Milton, John. 1997. *Selected Poetry*. Oxford: Oxford University Press.
———. 2008. *The Major Works*. Ed. Stephen Orgel and Jonathan Goldberg. Oxford: Oxford University Press.
Morier, Henri. 1961. *Dictionnaire de poétique et de rhétorique*. Paris: PUF.
Morini, Massimiliano. 2005. "Translating Scottish Poetry." *Babel AFIAL (Aspectos de filoloxía inglese e alemá)* 14: 5–21.
Mounin, Georges. 1974. *Dictionnaire de la linguistique*. Paris: PUF.
Mukařovský, Jan. 1948. *Kapitoly z české poetiky*. Vols. 1 and 2. Prague: Státní pedagogické nakladatelsví.
———. 1964. "Standard Language and Poetic Language." In *A Prague School Reader on Esthetics, Literary Structure and Style*. Trans. and ed. Paul L. Garvin. Washington, DC: Georgetown University Press, 17–30.

Neruda, Pablo. (1977) 1995. *La Centaine d'amour*. Bilingual ed. Trans. André Bonhomme and Jean Marcenac. Paris: Gallimard.
———. 2003. *The Poetry of Pablo Neruda*. Partially bilingual ed. Ed. Ilan Stavans. New York: Farrar, Straus & Giroux.
———. 2006. *The heichts o Macchu Picchu: Set owre frae Pablo Neruda's 'Alturas de Macchu Picchu.'* Trans. John Law. Edinburgh: Chapman.
Nida, Eugene. (1969) 1982. *The Theory and Practice of Translation*. Helps for Translators 7. Leiden: Brill.
———. (1964) 2004. "Principles of Correspondence." In Lawrence Venuti, ed., *The Translation Studies Reader*. 2nd ed. London: Routledge, 153–67.
Obolensky, Dimitri. 1965. *The Heritage of Russian Verse*. Bloomington: Indiana University Press.
Oster, Pierre. 1990. *Dictionnaire de citations françaises*. Vol. 1, *De Villon à Beaumarchais*. Paris: Robert.
———. 1993. *Dictionnaire de citations françaises*. Vol. 2, *De Chateaubriand à J. M. G. Le Clézio*. Paris: Robert.
Perse, Saint-John. 1930. *Anabasis*. Trans. T. S. Eliot. London: Faber & Faber.
———. 1938. *Anabasis*. Trans. T. S. Eliot. New York: Harcourt, Brace.
———. 1949. *Anabasis*. Trans. T. S. Eliot. New York: Harcourt, Brace.
———. 1959. *Anabasis*. Trans. T. S. Eliot. London: Faber & Faber.
———. 1960. *Éloges*. Paris: Gallimard.
Peter, Brigitte, Gerhard Rühm, and Martin Walser. 1995. "Unsinn Poesie: Three Songs for Medium Voice and Piano." Music and Texts of Gary Bachlund. http://www.bachlund.org/Unsinn_Poesie.htm.
Picoche, Jacqueline. 1994. *Dictionnaire étymologique du français*. Paris: Robert.
Pike, K. L. 1945. *The Intonation of American English*. Linguistics 1. Ann Arbor: University of Michigan Press.
Plato. 1961. *The Collected Dialogues*. Trans. Lane Cooper. Ed. Edith Hamilton and Huntington Cairns. Princeton, NJ: Princeton University Press.
———. 1968. *The Republic*. Trans. Allan Bloom. New York: Basic Books.
Poldauf, Ivan. 1986. *Česko-anglický slovník*. 2nd ed. Prague: Státní pedagogické nakladatelství.
Pope, Alexander. 1963. *Selected Poetry and Prose*. New York: Holt, Rinehart & Winston.
———. (1709) 2005. *An Essay on Criticism*. E-book 7407. Project Gutenberg. www.gutenberg.org.
Pound, Ezra. 1954. *Literary Essays of Ezra Pound*. Ed. T. S. Eliot. London: Faber.
———. 1970. *Selected Poems, 1908–1969*. London: Faber & Faber.
———. 1986. "Onze cantos nouveaux." Trans. Philippe Mikriammos. In *Les Cantos d'Ezra Pound*. Trans. Jacques Darras et al. Paris: Flammarion, 31–41.
———. (1934) 1991. *ABC of Reading*. London: Routledge.
———. (1967) 1995. *The Cantos of Ezra Pound*. London: Faber & Faber.

Preminger, Alex, and T. V. F. Brogan, eds. 1993. *The New Princeton Encyclopedia of Poetry and Poetics*. Princeton, NJ: Princeton University Press.

Radice, William, and Barbara Reynolds, eds. 1987. *The Translator's Art: Essays in Honour of Betty Radice*. Harmondsworth, UK: Penguin.

Rancourt, Jacques, ed. 2010. *La traductière: Revue franco-anglaise de la poésie et art visuel* 28 (June).

Rees, William, ed. and trans. 1990. *The Penguin Book of French Poetry, 1820–1950*. London: Penguin.

Rey, Alain. 1998. *Dictionnaire historique de la langue française*. 2nd ed. Paris: Robert.

Rey-Debove, Josette. 2004. *Le Robert Brio: Analyse des mots et régularités du lexique*. Paris: Robert.

Rey-Debove, Josette, and Alain Rey. 1993. *Le nouveau petit Robert: Dictionnaire alphabétique et analogique de la langue française*. Paris: Robert.

Rose, Gillian. (1981) 1995. *Hegel contra Sociology*. London: Athlone.

Royer, Jean, ed. 1989. *Introduction à la poésie québécoise: Poètes et les oeuvres des origines à nos jours*. Cap-Saint-Ignace: Bibliothèque québécoise.

Sardin, Pascale, ed. 2009. "Traduire le genre: Femmes en traduction." Spec. issue of *Palimpsestes: Revue de traduction* 22.

Scholze-Stubenrecht, W., and J. B. Sykes. 1999. *The Oxford-Duden German Dictionary*. Oxford: Clarendon Press.

Scott, Clive. 1990. *Vers Libre: The Emergence of Free Verse in France, 1886–1914*. Oxford: Clarendon Press.

———. 1993. *Reading the Rhythm: The Poetics of French. Free Verse, 1910–1930*. Oxford: Clarendon Press.

———. 1998. *The Poetics of French Verse: Studies in Reading*. Oxford: Oxford University Press.

———. 2000. *Translating Baudelaire*. Exeter, UK: University of Exeter Press.

Seleskovitch, Danica, and Marianne Lederer. 1984. *Interpréter pour traduire*. Paris: Didier.

Shakespeare, William. 1975. *Sonnets*. Trans. Pierre Jean Jouve. Paris: Gallimard.

———. 1987. *The Complete Oxford Shakespeare, in Three Volumes (Histories, Comedies and Tragedies)*. Ed. Stanley Wells and Gary Taylor. London: Guild.

———. 1988. *The Sonnets*. Ed. M. R. Ridley. London: Everyman's Library.

———. 1995. "Macbeth." In *Tragédies*. Vol. 2 of *Œuvres completes*. French–English bilingual ed. Trans. J.-C. Sallé. Ed. Michel Grivelet and Gilles Monsarrat. Paris: Robert Lafont.

———. 2005a. *Hamlet*. Trans. Jean-Michel Déprats. Paris: Folio.

———. 2005b. *The Shakespeare Collection: All 37 Productions from the BBC Television Shakespeare Series*. 38 DVDs. BBC Worldwide Ltd.

———. (1997) 2007a. *Sonety/The Sonnets*. Trans. Martin Hilský. Brno: Atlantis.

———. (1993) 2007b. *Les Sonnets*. Trans. Yves Bonnefoy. Paris: Gallimard.

———. 2011. *Romeo et Juliet.* Trans. Jean-Michel Déprats. Paris: Gallimard.
Shelley, Percy Bysshe. 1917. *The Complete Poetical Works.* Ed. Thomas Hutchinson. London: Oxford University Press.
———. (1840) 2004. *A Defense of Poetry and Other Essays.* E-book 5428. Project Gutenberg. www.gutenberg.org.
Sidney, Philip. 1994. *Astrophil et Stella.* Bilingual ed. Trans. Gérard Gâcon. Paris: Différence.
Silcock, Arnold. 1958. *Verse and Worse.* London: Faber & Faber.
Spivak, Gayatri Chakravorty. (1992) 2004. "The Politics of Translation." In Lawrence Venuti, ed., *The Translation Studies Reader.* 2nd ed. London: Routledge, 369–88.
Steiner, George. 1992. *After Babel: Aspects of Language and Translation.* 2nd ed. Oxford: Oxford University Press.
Tarlinskaja, Marina. 1976. *English Verse: Theory and History.* The Hague: Mouton.
Underhill, James W. 1999. "Voix, Versification et Traduction." PhD diss., Université de Paris.
———. 2000. "Il ritmo nella traduzione poetica: Studio su una traduzione di 'Ione, dead the long year' di Ezra Pound." [Rhythm in poetry translation: An analysis of 'Ione, dead the long year' by Ezra Pound]. In Henri Meschonnic, ed., "Ritmo." *Studi di estetica* ser. III, 21.1: 109–24.
———. 2005. "Form and Meaning in the Translation of Poetry." *Languages, Translations and Communication* (Autumn): 119–41.
———. 2006a. "Does the Translator Exist?: A Critique of the Status of the Translator throughout History with Reference to Lawrence Venuti's *The Translator's Invisibility.*" *Représentations: La revue électronique du CEMRA* [Centre d'études sur les modes de la représentation anglophone], Travaux du Centre 2 (décembre): 101–17. http://www.u-grenoble3.fr/representations.
———. 2006b. "The Forms of Negation: Meter and Metaphysics in the Versification of T. S. Eliot." In *La négation: Formes, figures, conceptualisation. Actes du colloque de littérature et de linguistique, Université François Rabelais de Tours, les 8 et 9 octobre 2004.* Ed. Stéphanie Bonnefille and Sébastien Salbayre. GRAAT 35. Tours: Presses universitaires François Rabelais, 115–37.
———. 2009a. "À quoi ça rime de traduire?": 'Rhyme' et 'rime,' question formelle ou question sémantique?" In *La forme comme paradigme du traduire: Actes du colloque, Mons, 29–31 octobre 2008.* Ed. Nadia D'Amelio. Mons, Belgium: Presses de l'Université de Mons.
———. 2009b. "Métamorphose et la trans-form-ation de poèmes." *La métamorphose: Définitions, formes, thèmes.* Ed. Denis Bonnecase and Anne-Marie Tatham. Paris: Gérard Monfort, 249–76.

———. 2009c. *Humboldt, Worldview and Language*. Edinburgh: Edinburgh University Press.

———. 2009d. "Radikálny preklad: Vzbura proti jazyku alebo vstup subjektu? [Traduction radicale: Une rébellion contre la langue ou l'entrée du sujet?]." Trans. from Slovak by Libuša Vajdová. *World Literature Studies* 1 [18].3: 68–81.

———. 2010a. "Une Emily Dickinson française et eine deutsche Emily Dickinson: Souffle, esprit et poésie du monde." *Plume: Revue d'AILLF* 8: 112–38.

———. 2010b. "Structure and Reconstruction: Jiří Levý and the Translation of Poems." In *The Prague School and Theories of Structure*. Ed. Martin Procházka, Markéta Malá, and Pavlína Šaldová. Göttingen: Vandenhoeck and Ruprecht, 313–39.

———. 2011. "Echoes of Emily Dickinson: Male and Female French Translators Listening to the Poet." Trans. Luise von Flotow. In *Translating Women*. Ed. Luise von Flotow. Ottawa: University of Ottawa Press, 203–38.

———. 2012a. "Poems and Translations from French and German." *The Review* 2 (Autumn/Winter): 26–30.

———. 2012b. "Twenty-Seven Quatrains for La Rochefoucault." *Fras* 17: 4–10.

Untermeyer, Louis, ed. 1963. *The Letters of Robert Frost to Louis Untermeyer*. New York: Holt, Rinehart & Winston.

Valéry, Paul. 1941. *Tel quel*. Vol. 1. Paris: Gallimard.

———. 1943. *Tel quel*. Vol. 2. Paris: Gallimard.

Venuti, Lawrence. 1995. *The Translator's Invisibility: A History of Translation*. London: Routledge.

———, ed. 2004. *The Translation Studies Reader*. 2nd ed. London: Routledge.

Villon, François. 2004. *Œuvres complètes de François Villon: Suivies d'un choix des poésies de ses disciples*. E-book 12246. Project Gutenberg. http://www.gutenberg.org/files/12246/12246-h/12246-h.htm.

Vinay, J.-P., and J. Darbelnet. (1958) 1977. *Stylistique comparée du français et de l'anglais: Méthode de traduction*. Paris: Didier.

von Flotow, Luise. 1997. *Translation and Gender: Translating in the "Era of Feminism."* Ottawa: University of Ottawa Press.

———, ed. 2011. *Translating Women*. Ottawa: University of Ottawa Press.

Ward, Theodora. 1961. *The Capsule of the Mind: Chapters in the Life of Emily Dickinson*. Cambridge, MA: Harvard University Press.

Warnant, Léon. 1998. *Dictionnaire des rimes orales et écrites*. Paris: Larousse.

Wesling, Donald. 1996. *The Scissors of Meter: Grammetrics and Reading*. Ann Arbor: University of Michigan Press.

Whitman, Walt. (1855) 1959. *Leaves of Grass*. New York: Viking Penguin.

———. 1989. *Feuilles d'herbe*. Trans. Jacques Darras. Paris: Bernard Grasset.

———. 2008. *Feuilles d'herbe.*. Trans. Éric Athenot. Paris: José Corti.

Wilhelm, Fabrice. 1999. *Baudelaire: L'écriture du narcissisme*. Paris: Harmattan.

Williams, William Carlos. 1976. *Selected Poems*. Ed. Charles Tomlinson. London: Penguin.

Wylder, Edith. 1971. *The Last Face: Emily Dickinson's Manuscripts*. Albuquerque: University of New Mexico Press.

Yeats, W. B. 1997. *The Collected Poems of W. B. Yeats*. Ed. Richard J. Finneran. New York: Macmillan.

Perspectives on Translation

Series editor: Luise von Flotow

The *Perspectives on Translation* series publishes books that explore translation from a theoretical or practical point of view. In addition to the history, methodology and theory of translation, the series covers lexicology, terminology and interpretation.

Previous titles in this collection

Valerie Henitiuk, *Worlding Sei Shônagon*, 2012

Luise von Flotow (ed.), *Translating Women*, 2011

Kayoka Takeda, *Interpreting the Tokyo War Crimes Tribunal*, 2010

Luise von Flotow, Reingard M. Nischik (eds.), *Translating Canada*, 2007

Barbara Folkart, *Second Findings: A Poetics of Translation*, 2007

For a complete list of our titles in this series, see:
www.press.uottawa.ca/series/french-and-canadian-studies/perspectives-on-translation

www.ingramcontent.com/pod-product-compliance
Lightning Source LLC
Chambersburg PA
CBHW070749230426
43665CB00017B/2307